opta index

Football Yearbook 2002–2003

Acknowledgements

Written by: Duncan Alexander, Rob Bateman, Paul Fowling, Chris Green, Ian Hislam, Matt Pomroy, William Rickson, Benji Romaner, Ed Shirbon, Dominic Sutton, Rupert Webster, Tim Wheal and Mark Willis

Thanks are due to: Simon Fisher, Matt Ralphs, Raffaella Valentino, Stefan Braun, César Jimenez, Paul Townley, Mel Beckett, James Dennis, Russell Clarke, Stuart Burchett, Paul Childs, Iain Turner, James Root, Kris Bromley, Robin Hassan, Richard Ewing, Spencer Field and Mark Pearman; Zoe Ward, Sarah Collins and Philip Don at the FA Premier League; the clubs for their assistance in verifying information; the League Managers Association; and the team at Carlton Books for their hard work and patience.

First published in 2002 by Carlton Books

10 9 8 7 6 5 4 3 2 1

A CIP catalogue record for this book is available from the British Library.

ISBN: 1 84222 542 1

Executive Editor: Vanessa Daubney
Project Art Director: Jim Lockwood
Jacket Design: Steve Lynn
Design: Publish On Demand
Editorial: Martin Richardson
Picture Research: Marc Glanville
Production: Sarah Corteel

Printed and bound in Italy

Carlton Books Limited
20 Mortimer Street
London W1T 3JW

opta
Football
Yearbook
2002–2003

CONTENTS

1

2

3 COMPARATIVE TABLES *236*

INTRODUCTION

This book is the definitive review of the 2001–02 Premiership campaign. In it you will discover how Arsenal won the title after three successive second-place finishes, what factors consigned Ipswich Town, Derby County and Leicester City to relegation and who were the top-rated players in the division.

Every touch of the ball has been recorded, every foul registered and each goal analysed to provide a compelling insight into the performances of all 20 Premiership teams and every player who appeared during the nine months of passion and commitment that characterise the most exciting league in the world.

The first section covers the teams. You will find everything you need to know about each club that featured in the 2001–02 Premiership, plus the three teams that were promoted from the Nationwide League Division One, aiming to pit their wits against the élite in the 2002–03 season.

Following this, the section that is sure to cause debate among football fans everywhere – the Comparative Tables. Here you will see how each team fared in relation to their adversaries, there are some new tables showing how the Premiership compares to Europe's major leagues and you can assess how the top players compare with each other across various categories. There are also the teams of the season and, finally, you will be able to see how the men in black performed in 2001–02 in our unique and exclusive insight into referees.

WHO ARE OPTA?

Opta Index Ltd are the official player and team performance index of the Premier League. The company is six years old and has had a major impact on the way that clubs monitor player performance and how the media offer their customers a revealing and unique insight into the game.

The idea was hatched prior to the 1996–97 season with support from the Premier League and the 20 clubs in the Premiership, who agreed Opta could have access to video footage of all Premiership matches to analyse.

The original system of analysis was developed in conjunction with former Arsenal and England coach Don Howe. He helped Opta create a ranking system to compare players' performances known as the Opta Index.

He worked with a software developer to create a unique database system that would fulfil all of his specifications. The Opta Index was first seen on Sky Sports' *Monday Night Football* with Andy Gray in August 1996.

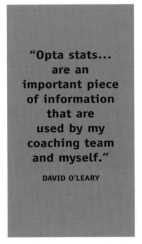

"Opta stats... are an important piece of information that are used by my coaching team and myself."

DAVID O'LEARY

Shortly after this debut media appearance, the statistics appeared in *The Observer* newspaper and interest among the national media and other parties snowballed.

At the end of the first year, the company – Opta Index Ltd – was given the title of official player performance statisticians to the Premier League and a sponsorship deal with the Premier League sponsors Carling was brokered.

At the end of the first season, Opta recruited its first journalist as the media began to demand an element of interpretation as well as the raw data. That demand has increased dramatically as the media seek to satisfy their customers' need for information and Opta's team of journalists continue to supply a wide variety of statistics, stories and copy to a range of media. This meant Opta was able to offer the worldwide media a 24-hour press service during Euro 2000 and the World Cups in 1998 and 2002.

In 2000, Opta Index was acquired by British Sky Broadcasting and Opta expanded into Europe and Asia, becoming the official player performance statisticians to the KPN-Eredivisie in Holland, La Liga in Spain and the Japanese "J" League. The company also covered the Italian Serie "A", the German Bundesliga and the Champions League from its central London headquarters.

Prior to the start of the 2000–01 season, Opta launched its new data collection tool OSCA (Opta Statistical Collection and Analysis), developed with assistance from the FA's technical director Howard Wilkinson, Charlton Athletic boss Alan Curbishley and referees officer Philip Don. This increased the number of categories monitored from 92 to more than 300 without increasing the time taken to analyse the game and has made for even more detailed comparisons of player and team performance for use by the clubs and the media alike.

During the 2001–02 season Opta launched their unique live statistics collection tool, which offers the production of real-time statistics for television as well as traditional and new media clients. The system meant that Opta were able to deliver live statistics on all 64 World Cup 2002 matches dynamically to broadcast media, as well as catering for more traditional media requirements. The software has also been designed to adapt to such sports as Rugby League and Rugby Union.

Six years on from conception, Opta's values remain clearly defined in producing a service that, with time, is becoming a more accepted part of sport, not just by the media, but by the professionals themselves.

The Times
17 November 2001

The Guardian
3 October 2001

Since they began analysing Premiership football in 1996, Opta have developed a reputation as the most trusted and authoritative voice in football statistics. When a big football story breaks, Opta can offer statistical back-up or insight to the topics that drive media debate and increasingly they are creating stories of their own.

The 2001–02 season saw Opta cover more football than ever before. And the company offered detailed statistics on the Italian, Spanish, German, Dutch and Champions Leagues as well as the Premiership and international football scene.

Opta were often asked to provide feature support statistics. For example when Manchester United's goalkeeper Fabien Barthez suffered a loss of form early in the 2001–02 season, Opta were asked by many of their clients to provide the statistics to prove that the French 'keeper was going through a slump in form.

The stats proved that Barthez was saving a lower percentage of opposition shots than any other regular Premiership goalkeeper. Several daily newspapers ran that statistic with the *Daily Express* giving it particular prominence under the headline: "Just stop the shots, Fabien".

United's early season stutter wasn't down to Barthez alone though. There was plenty of talk about United's new 4–5–1 formation and the impact of Juan Veron's arrival at Old Trafford.

Opta compared United's results when playing 4–4–2 to those when playing 4–5–1 and the outcome was striking, proving that United were far more effective when utilising their tried and trusted system of two up front. The story was given considerable coverage both in newspapers and on television.

Sticking with United's strikers, Opta were on hand to help try and settle the first of several arguments between Sir Alex Ferguson and Arsène Wenger during the 2001–02 season.

Following some terrific performances from Ruud van Nistelrooy, Ferguson claimed his hitman was the best in Europe. Wenger disagreed saying: "I don't agree with Ferguson. I think we have the best striker in Europe." Referring of course to Thierry Henry.

Opta compared the two target men with another of the Premiership's leading men, Michael Owen and found that the three were in fact very evenly matched, although Owen had a better chance conversion rate than either Henry or van Nistelrooy. Again several newspapers carried the story.

But Opta also create stories of interest to media and fans alike. In November Barcelona visited Liverpool for a Champions League clash which produced plenty of talking points. The Catalan giants went a goal down, but came back to win 3–1 with a fantastic exhibition of passing football.

Daily Express
19 October 2001

Daily Mirror
22 November 2001

Opta were so impressed by Barca's third goal that they thought it was worth breaking down pass by pass. The *Daily Mirror* agreed. They turned Opta's break-down of the 3-minute move into a graphic which illustrated the brilliance of Barca's play.

On the international front, Opta's increased coverage of England saw them produce some features on the nation's biggest stars. A comparison of David Beckham's statistics since being made England captain with his figures from before his promotion revealed a marked improvement in every area of his game. *The Daily Mirror* was one of several papers to use the statistics.

Match previews have always been a big part of Opta's output. But while they produce plenty of player and team head-to-heads, Opta also provide their clients with other ideas ahead of the big games.

For example, before Arsenal travelled to Spurs in November, Opta decided to take a look at Sol Campbell. The Arsenal defender had come in for a lot of criticism after moving to Highbury from White Hart Lane. But the statistics proved that he had actually improved in several key areas since his move across north London.

Opta were also the first people to draw attention to the fact that Arsenal were on course to set several Premiership records in the 2001–02 season. The statisticians provided Arsenal's website and matchday programme with the information which included the fact that the Gunners' star man Robert Pires had matched the record for Premiership goal assists and also drew attention to the fact that the Gunners were in line to break the record for scoring in consecutive games.

Several newspapers and television stations picked up on these stories, but it was Opta who uncovered the information initially and when Arsenal were producing their end-of-season matchday programme, they turned to Opta to provide a detailed breakdown of the Gunners' record-breaking season.

They were not alone in turning to Opta for the facts. Radio stations were regular callers in 2001–02 asking Opta to comment on the burning football issues of the day.

Opta spokespeople featured on Radio Five Live and talkSPORT a number of times during 2001–02, providing statistics on issues ranging from John Gregory's claim that "big teams" get more penalties than smaller teams, to listeners' views on Tottenham's run of defeats against Chelsea.

Opta's statistics are now such an important part of the game that they can be seen in newspapers or on television every day of the week. And increasingly Opta's statistics are an integral part of television sports programming and newspaper sports pages.

HOW IS PLAYER PERFORMANCE MEASURED?

Opta originally developed the system of analysis in conjunction with former England coach Don Howe. The manual system has since been replaced by a custom-built, PC-based video analysis system called OSCA, which has cut the time required to analyse a game and dramatically increased the amount and type of data that is collected.

There are more than 300 distinct actions and outcomes for players which range from different kinds of shots and passes, to tackles and blocks and from different kinds of fouls and yellow cards to saves made by the goalkeeper. Every close season, the list of actions is discussed to determine the value of each element and then new categories may be added.

OSCA allows a specially-trained person to watch a match on video through a PC and using the unique software, to click on icons to record each action performed by every single player on the ball, their fouls and discipline and also key decisions made by the officials. The new system was launched prior to the start of the 2000–01 Premiership season.

Opta receive footage of a game after the match and then begin the analysis. An analyst takes several hours to complete a full match, depending on the flow of the game and the number of contentious decisions. Once the game is analysed, the data is downloaded into a database from which Opta are able to provide information in many diverse ways.

Managers' reports are created for each match and sent to a number of key personnel at the Premiership clubs involved, including managers, directors and coaching staff. In addition, some clubs request further details on player positions at set-pieces, moves leading to goalscoring opportunities, or where free-kicks are conceded or won, for both their own teams and forthcoming opposition.

Referees' reports are produced identifying key decisions (including commendable and controversial) made in each match, details of goals and disciplinary issues. These are sent to referees officer Philip Don.

The data that is collected is then downloaded from the database into a spreadsheet, from which all of the media requirements for player profiles, match reports and key data about the Premiership can be provided.

The analysis is checked by the operations manager and key information such as cards issued is checked with the official referees' reports.

Opta also produce a video tape highlighting disputed goals and the FA Premier League's goal committee rules on them within 48 hours. This system replaces the previous controversial goal committee, which only convened every six months and attracted a measure of controversy. Any discrepancies or differences are checked and the database is updated if necessary.

The system of analysis is under constant review at Opta's central London head-quarters. The 2001–02 season saw the implementation of the live tool service developed to give the ultimate live statistical service to clients across the globe.

Opta has worked with the League Managers Association to enhance the analysis and modify the data output from OSCA still further so that coaches are getting the information they want. That, coupled with the company's detailed analysis of other leagues across Europe, also means that the media are supplied with even more information with which to inform, provoke and entertain its football-hungry audience.

Opta is a relatively young company but it has grown rapidly year on year since its inception and has stayed at the forefront of sports analysis across Europe by constantly refining and expanding its analysis and output. That process will continue in the 2002–03 season as the company continues to develop and diversify.

> "I am always interested to read the Opta statistics after each game and I find them both informative and useful. Congratulations to Opta for providing an excellent service."
>
> **GERARD HOULLIER**
> Manager, Liverpool FC

THE OPTA INDEX

The Opta Index is basically a form guide. When a match is analysed, each player's actions are recorded. For each of these actions, a player earns or loses points.

Over the course of a game, a player will accumulate a total number of points to give him a Game Score. This can be used to compare his performance with other players and the player with the most points is nominated as Opta's man-of-the-match.

The Index, which has featured in many newspapers and on television, uses these Game Scores to provide a form guide which is calculated over a period encompassing the previous six Premiership matches. You can see an example in the table below.

Each player's points from the last six games are added to give him a total, which is then divided by the number of minutes played and then multiplied by 90 (minutes), to give him an average score

per game played. This is his Index Score.

These Index Scores can then be used to compare players' performances over those six games, with the player who has the highest average being the most in-form player.

The players are then divided by the position in which they play – goalkeepers, defenders, midfielders, attacking midfielders and attackers – to create a series of tables providing an at-a-glance guide to current Premiership player form.

The following week, when Arsenal play again, Bergkamp's score will change as the Manchester United match drops out of the last six games recorded and is replaced with his score against the Gunners' next opponents.

Opta also produce a Season Index. This shows each player's average score across every game they have played during the 2001–02 season and this is the figure which is featured in tables throughout this book.

DENNIS BERGKAMP

OPPOSITION	MINS PLAYED	OPTA GAME SCORE
v Manchester United	90	1,112
v Everton	90	1,258
v Leeds United	90	1,473
v Southampton	0	0
v Sunderland	90	1,515
v West Ham United	71	1,611
Total	431	6,969

Opta Index Score	6,969/431 x 90(mins) = 1,455

LEAGUE COMPARISON – NATIONALITIES

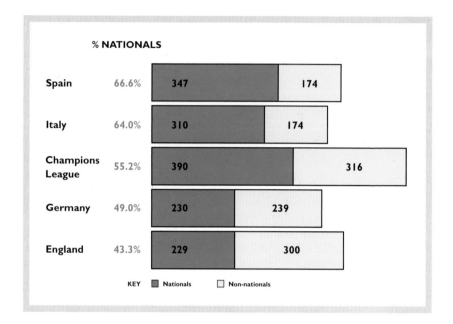

% NATIONALS

		Nationals	Non-nationals
Spain	66.6%	347	174
Italy	64.0%	310	174
Champions League	55.2%	390	316
Germany	49.0%	230	239
England	43.3%	229	300

KEY ■ Nationals ☐ Non-nationals

It's official: the English Premiership was the most cosmopolitan of all Europe's top leagues in 2001–02 – good news for the fans who wanted to see stylish continental stars on their doorstep, but bad news for England coach Sven-Göran Eriksson.

Just 43.3% of the 529 players to appear in the Premiership were eligible for inclusion in Eriksson's national side – a percentage far lower than in Spain or Italy where well over half of the top-flight personnel were homegrown.

Of the 300 non-nationals plying their trade in England – a number that includes those from Scotland, Wales and Ireland – the highest amount were from France, some 40 in total. Among those to shine were Arsenal pair Thierry Henry and Patrick Vieira – the division's top goalscorer and tackler respectively – and Newcastle United's Laurent Robert who scored the most free kicks.

Employing Frenchmen by the dozen was a practice mainly carried out by English clubs. In the other top European competitions, South Americans were the order of the season, particularly in Spain where a massive 53 Argentines plied their trade along with 22 Brazilians.

Yet overall, 67.4% of the players in the Primera Liga were Spanish natives – the highest percentage of homegrown talent in any of Europe's top leagues.

Serie A's clubs were not far behind in saving their jobs for the boys, with 64.0% of the division's stars coming from Italy. Of the 174 imports, 28 came from Brazil with internationals like Inter's Ronaldo and the Roma trio Cafu, Emerson and Aldair helping to make up that figure.

Like the Premiership, more than half of the German Bundesliga's 469-strong workforce hailed from abroad. And as in Italy, Brazilians were the most popular recruits and included in their number Borussia Dortmund's Marcio Amoroso – the league's joint-leading goalscorer. Croatian players were also widespread in the Bundesliga where as many as 20 earned their crust – more than in England, Italy and Spain combined, where there were just four, seven and four respectively.

In addition, the Bundesliga was the most multinational league, representing, as it did, 56 different countries.

FANTASY FOOTBALL

Come on, admit it – you know that you could do a better job than half the managers that get appointed to football league clubs. All you need is the chance to showcase your talents, but having not been a professional player it seems unlikely that the chance will come.

So to prove your skills you turn to the world of fantasy football. Easy, you think, I can pick the best team from the Premiership roster using my limited budget – I know the ins and outs of football better than anyone else.

But more often than not a costly injury will ruin a fantasy team, or that bargain buy that was about to explode onto the scene will fail to deliver. Before you know it your team has plummeted faster than a Big Ron pun.

Oh for a way to improve the chances of managing a fantasy team that might actually win something.

That's where Opta comes in. Using Opta's statistics during the campaign can significantly improve a fantasy manager's prospects, as the overrated players in the roster are shown to be exactly that, while the hidden gems are unearthed.

From players who deliver an unexpected number of assists (e.g. Mark Venus), defenders who fancy their chances in attack (e.g. Christian Ziege, Ian Harte), to strikers with an eye for Row Z (examples removed for fear of litigation), Opta can provide the budding gaffer with the inside knowledge required to make their side a respectable one.

The *Opta Football Yearbook* is the perfect place to start, as a fantasy team can often fall at the first hurdle with a poorly selected original line-up. With a comprehensive guide to 2001–02's best and worst performers in your possession you will have the ultimate tool for beating the legions of chancers that take to the fantasy football world.

Opta also provide the data for a string of online fantasy football games. From the ever-popular Yahoo online game to the Sporting News Global Soccer Challenge, based around World Cup 2002, Opta are proving as useful to games providers as they are the players themselves.

With so many hazards and pitfalls ready to foul up your fantasy season, can you afford to be without us?

THE OPTA PORTFOLIO

The Sun
19 March 2002

Southern Daily Echo
9 January 2002

Opta's back catalogue of statistics is growing all the time and because of the inherent versatility of the database used to store and compile the statistics, the raw data can be presented in a variety of media-friendly ways.

Whether it is on an individual match, season-long or season-on-season basis, Opta's system of analysis allows statistics to be tailored depending on their clients' different needs.

The full range of Opta's statistics can now be found in their comprehensive website. You can access the site by typing www.optaindex.com into your web browser to access a whole range of player performance statistics on the Premiership, the Scottish Premier League, Italy's Serie "A", Spain's Primera Liga and Germany's Bundesliga, as well as Champions League, Danish and Japanese leagues and internationals.

There are team tables comparing key areas of performance such as shooting, discipline and tackling, match previews and features, highlighting trends that may prove useful to those people interested in betting or fantasy football.

One of the most popular statistical services is Opta's Team of the Week. Opta's system of analysis makes their Team of the Week the most objective around. Opta now compile similar teams for each league they cover in Europe.

The Team of the Week is used in a host of regional newspapers. It can also be seen in the nationals such as the *Daily Express* and the *Sunday Mirror*, while various "teams" can be seen in magazines and *The Times Monthly Handbook*.

As well as the Team of the Week, Opta produce a weekly Index of player form showing their top 50 players. The Index is an objective guide to form, but has certainly sparked many a debate and can be seen in a variety of regional newspapers as well as in the *News of the World* and the *Sunday Mirror*.

Discipline, or the lack of it, is always a hot issue. While data on bookings and dismissals is freely available, only Opta provide accurate data on fouls. Their discipline tables take a number of forms including team, player and referee tables. All these rankings are based on Opta's own disciplinary points system and are a popular feature in several national newspapers including *The Sun* and the *News of The World*.

Of course, many of Opta's clients require a more in-depth service. Opta cover every match played in the Premiership and also monitor European and international matches. Opta's statistical match reports are a popular feature of many regional newspapers and for big games they can also be seen in many national and international newspapers.

THE OPTA PORTFOLIO

News of the World
14 April 2002

The Times Football Handbook
September 2001

West Ham programme
2 February 2002

A host of top clubs including Chelsea, Liverpool and Manchester United also use Opta's comprehensive match statistics in their own match report sections in their official club magazines.

For those clients who do not have room for a full statistical match report, Opta provide a "Quick Stats" service. Featuring analysis of shots on and off target, fouls, offsides and cards, quick stats are used by a wide variety of clients including the *Daily Mirror, The Sun,* Skytext and Teletext.

Season 2000–01 saw the launch of Opta's new live service. Opta now has access to every match live and is therefore able to produce performance statistics on every team and every player. This has proved immensely popular with clients such as *The Observer,* the *News of the World* and *Sky Sports,* for whom the data was previously not available in time to meet their deadlines.

Season 2001–02 saw the introduction of an electronic version, which allows dynamic update of data. So, instead of having to wait until after games for statistics, websites and TV companies are able to show and update the data on screen, during the match as it happens.

Opta's statistical expertise is not limited to post-match analysis, though. One of the most popular services they provide is their pre-match head-to-head material. Comparing rival players' statistics

has proved a big hit and Opta's head-to-head profiles were featured in regional newspapers, match day programmes and on websites during 2001–02.

Opta also provide clients such as Skytext and Teletext with comprehensive previews of the forthcoming weekend's fixtures.

Also popular are Opta's "splat stats". These are used by a variety of clients to highlight intriguing aspects of player and team performance. You can see a selection of these statistics running along the bottom of many of the pages in this book.

The regional and national press often picks up Opta's own statistical features from the website.

While their regular features are popular, Opta are often called on to provide statistics to accompany breaking news. If a big transfer story breaks, Opta will invariably be asked to provide the statistics to prove the player's worth. If one player claims to be better than another, Opta will be asked to prove or disprove their claims and if a manager is appointed or sacked, Opta will usually be asked to provide statistics on his past achievements.

In fact, such is Opta's reputation that many clients now approach them for football-related information that they might be able to find elsewhere. They come to Opta because of the company's growing reputation as THE authoritative voice of football statistics.

COMPLETE
YOUR COLLECTION

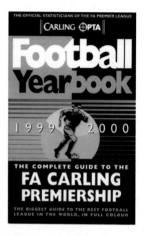
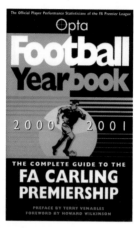
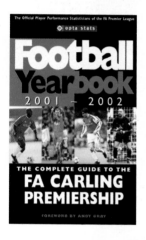

Now that you own the *Opta Football Yearbook 2002–03*, you may wish to complete the set by acquiring previous editions.

To order all three editions, send a cheque payable to "Opta Index Ltd" for just £27 (plus £9.00 postage and packing).

To order two editions send a cheque payable to "Opta Index Ltd" for just £20 (plus £6.00 postage and packing), specifying which Yearbooks you require.

To order one edition send a cheque payable to "Opta Index Ltd" for £11.99 (plus £3.00 postage and packing), specifying which Yearbook you require.

Opta Index Ltd,
Welby House,
96–97 Wilton Road,
London SW1 1DW

email: enquiries@optaindex.com

(Offer available while stocks last. Postage applies to UK only,
for overseas orders please use the email address above)

THE TEMS

Each club that participated in the 2001–02 Premiership season has its own section within this part of the book. The sections are in alphabetical order with Arsenal at the beginning and West Ham at the end.

You will find:

- important details about each club, highlighting key personnel and contact details;
- a review of the season;
- a full breakdown of appearances, goalscorers and disciplinary issues;
- a profile of the manager;
- a graph charting the league position across the course of the season;
- charts that show how, when and where each team scored and conceded their goals as well as who netted for and against each side;
- a full breakdown of each player's performance;
- Index scores for the top players at each club and Opta's nomination for their player of the season;
- the top performers at each club across a series of key categories.

After this, you can find key details on the three sides who were promoted to the Premiership from Nationwide League Division One and who will feature in the forthcoming 2002–03 season.

For Birmingham City, Manchester City and West Bromwich Albion

You will find:

- important details about each club, highlighting key personnel and contact details;
- a review of the season;
- a full breakdown of appearances and goalscorers;
- a profile of the manager;
- a graph charting the league position across the course of the season;
- charts that show how, when and where each team scored and conceded their goals as well as who netted for and against each side.

ARSENAL

Arsenal Stadium, Avenell Rd,
Highbury, London N5 1BU

CONTACT NUMBERS

Telephone: 020 7704 4000
Fax: 020 7704 4001
Ticket Office: 020 7704 4040
Ticket Information: 020 7704 4242
GunnersLine: 0906 474 4000
(calls cost 60p per minute)
The Gunners Shop: 020 7704 4120
e-mail: info@arsenal.co.uk
Website: www.arsenal.com

KEY PERSONNEL

Life President: Sir Robert Bellinger, GBE,
D.Sc.
Life Vice President: C E B L Carr
Directors: P D Hill-Wood (Chairman)
D B Dein (Vice Chairman)
Sir Roger Gibbs
R C L Carr
D D Fiszman
K J Friar OBE
K G Edelman (Managing Director)
Club Secretary: D Miles
Manager: Arsène Wenger

SPONSORS

2001–02 SEGA, 2002–03 O₂

FANZINES

Up The Arse, The Gooner,
Highbury High

COLOURS

Home: Red shirts with white sleeves,
white shorts and white stockings
Away: Gold shirts, navy shorts
and navy stockings

NICKNAME

The Gunners

HONOURS

League Champions:
1930–31, 1932–33, 1933–34,
1934–35, 1937–38, 1947–48,
1952–53, 1970–71, 1988–89,
1990–91, 1997–98, 2001–02
FA Cup Winners: 1930, 1936, 1950, 1971,
1979, 1993, 1998, 2002
League Cup Winners: 1987, 1993
European Cup Winners' Cup Winners:
1994
Fairs Cup Winners: 1970

RECORD GOALSCORER

Cliff Bastin – 150 league goals 1930–47

BIGGEST WIN

12–0 v Loughborough Town –
Division Two, 12 March 1900

BIGGEST DEFEAT

0–8 v Loughborough Town –
Division Two, 12 December 1896

SEASON REVIEW

After three seasons as the perennial bridesmaids of English football, Arsenal finally got to walk down the aisle in 2001–02. The Gunners' record-breaking campaign, which ended with a second double in four years, saw Arsène Wenger's side hailed as the best ever to emerge from Highbury's Marble Halls.

Arsenal's determination to win something was clear before the season had even started. The club drafted in Francis Jeffers, Junichi Inamoto, Giovanni van Bronckhorst, Richard Wright and, to the consternation of Tottenham, Sol Campbell.

Despite a summer of continued speculation, Patrick Vieira also started the season in an Arsenal shirt. And while he still hadn't put pen to paper on a new deal, Wenger was adamant that he too would be staying.

A 4–0 away win at Middlesbrough on the opening day underlined Arsenal's potential, but while they continued to sparkle away from north London with their incisive brand of

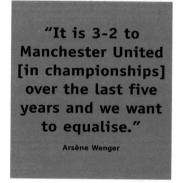

"It is 3-2 to Manchester United [in championships] over the last five years and we want to equalise."

Arsène Wenger

counter-attacking football, the Gunners laboured to break down the packed defences which teams fielded at Highbury.

Already beaten by Leeds and Charlton and held to frustrating draws by Blackburn and Bolton at Highbury, Arsenal's poor home form plunged to a new low when they were beaten 3–1 by Newcastle in one of the most talked about games of the season.

The match was a controversial one which saw the Magpies leapfrog Arsenal to go top of the Premiership and, not for the first time under Arsène Wenger, put Arsenal's disciplinary record under the microscope.

Ray Parlour became the 39th player to be dismissed under Wenger and, after Graham Poll enraged Arsenal further by awarding Newcastle a dubious penalty, Thierry Henry created further unwanted headlines with a verbal assault on the referee after the final whistle.

Ironically, the Newcastle defeat was to be Arsenal's last of the season in the Premiership. Their next game saw them overcome the dismissal of yet another player to beat Liverpool at Anfield and after that they never looked back.

With Arsène Wenger signing a new contract and the team well placed in the second group stage of the Champions League – a competition they were eventually eliminated from before the knockout stages – Arsenal kicked off the New Year in high spirits.

By the time they faced Everton on 10 February, Arsenal were going well in the FA Cup and handily placed in the Premiership, four points behind Liverpool, but with two games in hand.

The Gunners won a forgettable encounter against Everton 1–0, but it will go down in Highbury history as the first victory in a record-breaking run of 13 consecutive wins which famously included the Gunners taking the title with a 1–0 triumph at Old Trafford in their penultimate match of the season.

On the way to the championship, the Gunners became the first team to go an entire season unbeaten away from home since 1889 and they scored in every single game.

A 2–0 victory over Chelsea secured the FA Cup and there were further awards for inspirational midfielder Robert Pires, who missed the last month of the season through injury, but still took the Football Writers' Footballer of the Year award and Thierry Henry, who scored 24 goals to win the Golden Boot.

The eventual seven-point margin between Arsenal and second-placed Liverpool disguised the fact that the title race had been a close one, but surely no one can argue with the fact that the Gunners deserved their triumph.

ARSENAL

DATE	OPPONENT	SCORE	ATT.	ADAMS	ALIADIERE	BERGKAMP	CAMPBELL	COLE	DIXON	EDU	GRIMANDI	HENRY	JEFFERS	LAUREN
18.08.01	Middlesbro A	4–0	31,557	90□	–	s17²	90	90	–	–	s25□	73¹	–	90
21.08.01	Leeds Utd H	1–2	38,062	90	–	s24	90	90□	–	–	–	90□	s13□	90
25.08.01	Leicester H	4–0	37,909	90	–	75	90	90	–	–	s27	s23¹	–	90
08.09.01	Chelsea A	1–1	40,855	78	–	69	s12	90□	–	–	90□	90¹	–	90
15.09.01	Fulham A	3–1	20,805	–	s15¹	90	90	–	–	s6	84¹	75	90□	
22.09.01	Bolton W H	1–1	38,014	90	–	90	–	90	–	–	31	90	s21¹	–
29.09.01	Derby Co A	2–0	29,200	–	–	–	–	90	–	–	s12	78²	48	90
13.10.01	Southampton A	2–0	29,759	–	–	s13	90	90□	–	–	s6	90¹	–	90
20.10.01	Blackburn H	3–3	38,108	–	–	90¹	–	–	–	–	90	90¹	–	90
27.10.01	Sunderland A	1–1	48,029	–	–	s5	90	–	–	–	–	s13	–	90□
04.11.01	Charlton H	2–4	38,010	–	–	90	–	68□	–	–	90	90²	–	90□
17.11.01	Tottenham A	1–1	36,049	–	–	70	90	90	–	–	90	–	–	90
25.11.01	Man Utd H	3–1	38,174	–	–	s26	90	90	–	–	s7	90²	–	90
01.12.01	Ipswich A	2–0	24,666	–	–	s22	90	90	–	s4	–	90¹	–	90
09.12.01	Aston Villa H	3–2	38,074	–	–	68□	90	90	–	–	–	90²□	–	90□
15.12.01	West Ham A	1–1	34,523	–	–	90	90	90¹	–	s19	90	90	–	90□
18.12.01	Newcastle H	1–3	38,012	–	–	s22	90□	90	–	–	–	90	–	90
23.12.01	Liverpool A	2–1	44,297	–	–	–	90	90	–	–	–	89¹	–	90□
26.12.01	Chelsea H	2–1	38,079	–	–	s17	90¹	90	–	–	–	90	–	90
29.12.01	Middlesbro H	2–1	37,948	–	–	s20	90	90¹□	–	–	s7	83	–	–
13.01.02	Liverpool H	1–1	38,132	–	–	s34	90	–	s5	–	90	90	–	–
20.01.02	Leeds Utd A	1–1	40,143	–	–	70	90	90□	s9	–	–	90	–	–
23.01.02	Leicester A	3–1	21,344	–	–	79	90	90	–	–	s11	90¹	–	–
30.01.02	Blackburn A	3–2	25,893	–	–	90²	90	90	–	–	s10	90¹	–	–
02.02.02	Southampton H	1–1	38,024	–	–	71	90	52	–	s19□	s38	90□	–	–
10.02.02	Everton A	1–0	30,859	–	–	–	90□	–	s59	–	90	90□	–	–
23.02.02	Fulham H	4–1	38,029	–	s8	–	90	–	s47	–	s16	82²	–	90¹
02.03.02	Newcastle A	2–0	52,067	–	–	70¹	90¹	–	90	s3	90	–	–	90
05.03.02	Derby Co H	1–0	37,878	–	–	90	90	–	s45	s10	–	90	–	90
17.03.02	Aston Villa A	2–1	41,520	–	–	77	90	–	s45	90¹	s19	–	–	90
30.03.02	Sunderland H	3–0	38,047	90	–	77¹	90	90	–	90	s22	90	s13	–
01.04.02	Charlton A	3–0	26,339	–	–	82	90	28	90	s8	90	90²	–	–
06.04.02	Tottenham H	2–1	38,186	90	–	73□	90	–	s2	83	–	90	–	90¹
21.04.02	Ipswich H	2–0	38,058	90	–	76	–	90	–	57	s14	90	–	90□
24.04.02	West Ham H	2–0	38,038	90	–	82	–	90	s1	64□	s8	90	–	90
29.04.02	Bolton W A	2–0	27,351	90	–	70	s1	90	s23	67	–	–	–	90
08.05.02	Man Utd A	1–0	67,580	–	–	–	90	90	s1	90□	–	–	–	90□
11.05.02	Everton H	4–3	38,254	–	–	90¹	–	90	90	90	90	90²	s26¹	–

□ Yellow card, ■ Red card, s Substitute, 90² Goals scored

For more information visit our website:

2001–02 PREMIERSHIP APPEARANCES

LJUNGBERG	LUZHNY	KANU	KEOWN	PARLOUR	PIRES	SEAMAN	STEPANOVS	TAYLOR	UPSON	VAN BRONCKHORST	VIEIRA	WILTORD	WRIGHT	TOTAL
65	–	–	51□	90[1]	90	90	–	–	–	s7	90	83	–	951
77	–	–	66	90□	90	90	–	–	–	s13	90	77[1]	–	990
63[1]	–	s15[1]	–	–	90	90	–	–	–	90	61□	67[1]	–	961
s3	–	s21	90□	–	90□	90	–	–	–	90□	–	87	–	990
90[1]	–	–	90□	90□	81	90	–	–	–	–	90□	s9	–	990
–	90	–	–	72	s18	90	–	–	s59	69□	90	90	–	990
61	s29	s42	58□	–	90	–	–	–	90□	90	90□	–	90	958
85	–	–	–	s5	90[1]	–	–	–	90	84	90	77	90	990
–	–	s20	90	70	76[1]	–	–	–	90	90□	90	s14	90	990
90	–	85[1]	90	90□	–	–	–	–	90	90	90□	77	90	990
90	–	–	90	–	90	–	–	–	–	90	90□	s22	90	990
–	–	s20	90□	90	90[1]	–	–	–	–	–	90	90	90	990
90[1]□	–	64	–	90	83	–	–	90	90□	–	90	–	–	990
86[1]□	–	68	–	90□	80	–	–	90	90	s10	90	–	–	990
45	–	s22	s45	90	90	–	–	90	45	–	90□	s45[1]	–	990
–	–	s12	90	–	78□	–	–	90	–	–	90□	71	–	990
–	–	45	90	42□	90[1]	–	–	90	–	s45	90□	68	–	942
90[1]□	s1	89	90	90	85	–	–	90□	s5	37□	–	s1	–	937
67	–	73□	90□	45	90	–	–	90	–	s45	90	s23[1]	–	990
70	90	70□	90	–	90[1]□	–	–	90	–	90	90	s20	–	990
90[1]	85	56	90	–	78	–	–	90	90	–	90□	s12	–	990
66	81	–	90	90	90[1]□	–	–	–	–	s24	90	s20	90	990
–	90	–	90	79	90	–	–	–	s1	89[1]	90	s11[1]	90	990
–	57□	–	68	90	80	–	–	–	s22	s28□	90	62	90	957
–	90	–	–	90	90	–	–	–	90	s63	27	90[1]	90	990
–	90□	–	–	90□	–	–	90□	–	31	90	90	90[1]	90	990
–	90	–	–	90	74	90	90	–	–	43	90[1]	90	–	990
–	90	s20	–	–	90□	90	90	–	–	–	90	87	–	990
–	45	–	–	90□	90[1]	90	90	–	–	–	90	80	–	990
71□	90□	s13	–	–	90[1]	90	45	–	–	–	90	90	–	990
77	90	s13	–	–	–	90	–	–	–	–	90[1]	68[1]	–	990
90[1]	s62□	–	90	–	–	90	–	–	–	–	90□	90	–	990
90[1]	90	s7	–	s17	–	90	–	–	–	–	90	88	–	990
90[2]	–	s33	90	90	–	90	–	–	–	–	90	–	–	990
89[1]	–	s26[1]	90	90	–	90	–	–	–	–	90□	–	–	990
90[1]	–	s20	90	90	–	90	–	–	–	–	90	89[1]	–	990
90	–	89	90	90	–	90	–	–	–	–	90	90[1]	–	990
–	90	–	–	64	–	90	s6	–	–	s25	65	84	–	990

THE MANAGER

ARSENE WENGER

Appointed as Arsenal manager in 1996, Arsène Wenger started the 2001–02 season with question marks hanging over his future at Highbury.

After considerable success in north London, the former Nancy Lorraine, Monaco and Grampus Eight manager had been courted by several of the world's leading clubs and there were many who believed that 2001–02 would be his last season at Highbury.

In December though, Wenger committed himself to a new deal that tied him to Arsenal until 2005 and his team responded to their manager's decision to stay by winning the domestic double.

The feat matched that achieved during Wenger's first full season in charge at Highbury and underlined Arsenal's status as the main challengers to Manchester United's domination of the Premiership.

In his five and a half seasons in charge at Highbury, Wenger has guided Arsenal to two Championships, two FA Cup victories, three runners-up places, a UEFA Cup Final and a further FA Cup final.

The club have also qualified for the Champions League for five seasons in a row and, under Wenger's guidance, the Gunners have become a magnet for some of the world's most exciting and talented players.

LEAGUE POSITION

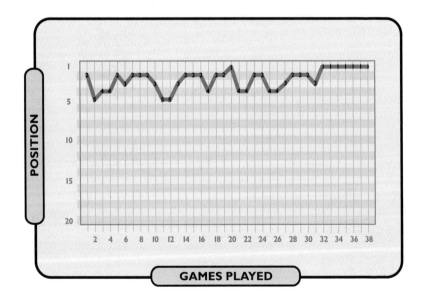

POSITION

GAMES PLAYED

13 Arsenal set a new Premiership

THE GOALS

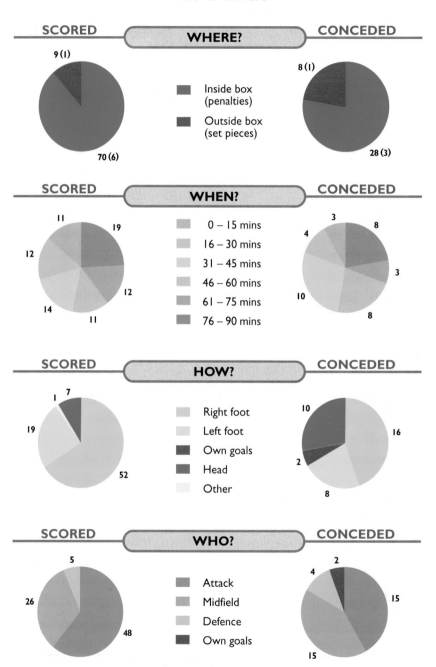

SCORED · **WHERE?** · **CONCEDED**

- Inside box (penalties)
- Outside box (set pieces)

Scored: 9 (1), 70 (6)
Conceded: 8 (1), 28 (3)

SCORED · **WHEN?** · **CONCEDED**

- 0 – 15 mins
- 16 – 30 mins
- 31 – 45 mins
- 46 – 60 mins
- 61 – 75 mins
- 76 – 90 mins

Scored: 11, 19, 12, 12, 14, 11
Conceded: 3, 8, 4, 3, 10, 8

SCORED · **HOW?** · **CONCEDED**

- Right foot
- Left foot
- Own goals
- Head
- Other

Scored: 1, 7, 19, 52
Conceded: 10, 16, 2, 8

SCORED · **WHO?** · **CONCEDED**

- Attack
- Midfield
- Defence
- Own goals

Scored: 5, 26, 48
Conceded: 2, 4, 15, 15

record for consecutive wins

ARSENAL

	ADAMS	ALIADIERE	BERGKAMP	CAMPBELL	COLE	DIXON	EDU	GRIMANDI	HENRY
APPEARANCES									
Start	10	0	22	29	29	3	8	11	31
Sub	0	1	11	2	0	10	6	15	2
Minutes on pitch	888	8	1954	2623	2488	507	694	1159	2775
GOAL ATTEMPTS									
Goals	0	0	9	2	2	0	1	0	24
Shots on target	2	0	32	6	9	0	2	2	68
Shots off target	4	0	29	5	10	1	7	2	66
Shooting accuracy %	33%	0%	52%	55%	47%	0%	22%	50%	51%
Goals/shots %	0%	0%	15%	18%	11%	0%	11%	0%	18%
PASSING									
Goal assists	0	0	12	1	3	0	1	0	5
Long passes	163	0	197	304	272	83	128	166	153
Short passes	291	4	710	564	992	182	313	485	792
PASS COMPLETION									
Own half %	91%	100%	82%	88%	85%	77%	82%	87%	79%
Opposition half %	80%	0%	69%	57%	80%	74%	69%	79%	62%
CROSSING									
Total crosses	0	0	54	4	42	9	34	6	195
Cross completion %	0%	0%	26%	50%	21%	22%	18%	33%	23%
DRIBBLING									
Dribbles & runs	11	0	70	24	77	6	22	10	236
Dribble completion %	100%	0%	63%	88%	65%	100%	86%	100%	61%
DEFENDING									
Tackles made	24	1	32	51	102	13	38	51	24
Tackles won %	83%	100%	66%	76%	69%	69%	84%	73%	92%
Blocks	4	0	2	19	28	6	2	5	2
Clearances	78	0	4	339	117	16	12	33	7
Interceptions	8	0	0	11	6	1	6	6	2
DISCIPLINE									
Fouls conceded	11	0	49	41	25	9	17	21	36
Fouls won	4	0	25	14	52	4	22	15	37
Offside	0	0	24	0	5	0	0	0	51
Yellow cards	1	0	2	2	6	0	3	2	4
Red cards	0	0	0	0	0	0	0	0	0

GOALKEEPER NAME	START/ (SUB)	TIME ON PITCH	GOALS CONCEDED	MINS/GOALS CONCEDED	SAVES MADE	SAVES/ SHOTS
SEAMAN	17 (0)	1530	8	191	38	83%
TAYLOR	9 (1)	816	12	68	10	45%
WRIGHT	12 (0)	1074	16	67	26	62%

For more information visit our website:

PLAYERS' STATISTICS

	JEFFERS	KANU	KEOWN	LAUREN	LJUNGBERG	LUZHNY	PARLOUR	PIRES	STEPANOVS	UPSON	VAN BRONCKHORST	VIEIRA	WILTORD	TOTAL	RANK
	2	9	21	27	24	15	25	27	6	10	13	35	23		
	4	14	1	0	1	3	2	1	0	4	8	1	10		
	196	923	1881	2430	1915	1350	2041	2353	495	883	1277	3083	2043		
	2	3	0	2	12	0	0	9	0	0	1	2	10	79	2nd
	5	8	3	5	26	2	8	25	0	1	12	7	32	255	2nd
	2	23	2	2	20	1	14	18	0	2	9	22	19	258	4th
	71%	26%	60%	71%	57%	67%	36%	58%	0%	33%	57%	24%	63%	50%	1st
	29%	10%	0%	29%	26%	0%	0%	21%	0%	0%	5%	7%	20%	15%	3rd
	0	1	1	0	4	1	0	15	0	0	0	2	7	53	2nd
	7	62	226	312	106	199	298	383	47	124	175	632	136	4516	3rd
	41	346	528	1000	575	530	706	1057	126	268	417	1499	833	12363	3rd
	91%	85%	88%	88%	82%	87%	86%	88%	85%	87%	88%	85%	86%	86%	4th
	68%	72%	66%	81%	69%	75%	79%	80%	50%	67%	71%	79%	74%	73%	2nd
	3	11	1	66	48	33	49	145	0	4	97	10	60	871	14th
	33%	9%	0%	20%	21%	24%	22%	27%	0%	25%	29%	40%	20%	24%	14th
	4	83	17	109	95	25	65	252	3	8	23	115	120	1377	2nd
	100%	70%	100%	79%	62%	96%	69%	80%	100%	88%	83%	83%	67%	73%	2nd
	0	14	33	83	79	55	101	75	12	21	57	202	36	1104	4th
	0%	64%	79%	76%	78%	82%	73%	80%	50%	86%	61%	80%	81%	76%	1st
	0	4	9	19	5	5	6	8	4	9	6	10	1	154	20th
	0	4	180	88	8	61	13	15	35	91	8	84	5	1257	19th
	0	6	9	20	5	13	10	10	4	2	2	22	5	148	12th
	4	32	23	47	30	27	50	32	8	10	36	87	19	615	4th
	1	28	24	46	46	10	50	69	5	7	13	93	34	604	3rd
	3	5	0	2	7	0	4	4	0	0	1	3	27	140	8th
	1	2	4	8	4	3	5	6	1	4	2	4	10	71	3rd
	0	0	1	0	0	1	2	0	0	0	1	1	0	6	3rd

CROSSES CAUGHT	CROSSES PUNCHED	CROSSES DROPPED	CATCH SUCCESS	THROWS/ SHORT KICKS	% COMPLETION	LONG KICKS	% COMPLETION
24	3	2	92%	47	100%	240	56%
7	6	4	64%	17	100%	146	42%
17	8	5	77%	31	97%	171	60%

PLAYER OF THE SEASON

PLAYER	INDEX SCORE
THIERRY HENRY	1,262
Robert Pires	1,229
Sylvain Wiltord	989
Fredrik Ljungberg	983
Dennis Bergkamp	916
Ashley Cole	839
David Seaman	821
Patrick Vieira	815
Lauren	769
Sol Campbell	735

Thierry Henry added the Golden Boot to his Premiership and FA Cup winners medals in 2001–02, pipping Jimmy Floyd Hasselbaink, Ruud van Nistelrooy and Alan Shearer to the award on the final day of the campaign.

In a season where Henry also became Arsenal's all-time leading scorer in European competition, Opta ranked the French striker as not only Arsenal's player of the season, but also the top player in the Premiership as well.

Henry's 24 Premiership goals came from a total of 134 shots, the second-highest tally in the top flight. No one else managed more shots on target than Henry though and the France international also laid on five goals for his team-mates.

The Football Writers' Footballer of the Year, Robert Pires, was just behind Henry in Opta's ratings. Since Opta began monitoring the Premiership in 1996–97, no other player has ever set up more than the 15 goals which Pires laid on in 2001–02. He also scored nine league goals before

succumbing to a knee ligament injury, which kept him out of the World Cup in Japan and South Korea.

Barclaycard's Player of the Year was Fredrik Ljungberg and Opta also rated the Swedish midfielder highly. Ljungberg finished just behind Sylvain Wiltord in Opta's list of the Gunners' top performers.

Like Pires, Ljungberg missed a large chunk of the 2001–02 season with injury, but he returned as the title race reached its climax to score some vital goals taking his total for the season to 12 – more than any other midfielder in the Premiership.

Dennis Bergkamp set up a large number of Ljungberg's goals in the run-in to Arsenal's season and his fine form was recognised with fifth place in Opta's top 10 Gunners.

Patrick Vieira only made eighth place after a season where he did not always rise to the high standards he had set in previous campaigns. There were also places in the list for Ashley Cole, David Seaman and Sol Campbell.

FIVE OF THE BEST

The records tumbled as Arsenal swept all before them in the race for the 2001–02 Premiership. The Gunners scored plenty of goals and were among the best passers and tacklers in the Premiership. Disciplinary problems continued to haunt the Highbury men, but they were able to overcome the handicaps placed on their squad by suspension to claim their second double under Arsène Wenger.

TOP GOALSCORERS

	GOALS	GOALS/SHOTS
THIERRY HENRY	24	18%
Fredrik Ljungberg	12	26%
Sylvain Wiltord	10	20%
Robert Pires	9	21%
Dennis Bergkamp	9	15%

Thierry Henry was the Gunners' top scorer. The France international also grabbed the Premiership Golden Boot with a brace against Everton on the final day of the season. But he was not the only Gunner in the goals. Fredrik Ljungberg finished with 12 goals making him the highest-scoring midfielder in the Premiership and there were also important contributions from Robert Pires, Sylvain Wiltord and Dennis Bergkamp.

Patrick Vieira continued to be the lynchpin in the Gunners' midfield and made more passes than any of his team-mates. The influence of Robert Pires was also highlighted by his high total of successful passes. He still finished the season as Arsenal's second-most prolific passer despite missing the run-in. Lauren boasted the highest pass completion rate in the top five, while Ray Parlour proved his ability by completing a high number of passes.

TOP PASSERS

	SUCC PASSES	COMPLETION
PATRICK VIEIRA	1,730	81%
Robert Pires	1,187	82%
Lauren	1,097	84%
Ashley Cole	1,040	82%
Ray Parlour	820	82%

TOP TACKLERS

	WON	SUCCESS
PATRICK VIEIRA	161	80%
Ray Parlour	74	73%
Ashley Cole	70	69%
Lauren	63	76%
Fredrik Ljungberg	62	78%

Arsenal have built a reputation as one of the most competitive teams in the Premiership and the Gunners were once again among the best tacklers in England during 2001–02. Leading the way was Patrick Vieira who made more tackles than any other player in the top flight. Ray Parlour and Arsenal's two full-backs, Ashley Cole and Lauren, also made plenty of important challenges, but no one could match Vieira's tackle success rate of 80%.

Arsenal were often in trouble with referees during 2001–02 and, although he only received one red card, Patrick Vieira was once again the Gunner most frequently picking up cautions. Vieira earned more Opta disciplinary points than any other Premiership player and was one of six Arsenal players to see red during the 2001–02 Premiership campaign. Ray Parlour was dismissed twice and also received his marching orders once in Europe.

DISCIPLINE

	POINTS	FOULS & CARDS
PATRICK VIEIRA	123	87F, 10Y, 1R
Ray Parlour	77	50F, 5Y, 2R
Lauren	71	47F, 8Y, 0R
Dennis Bergkamp	55	49F, 2Y, 0R
Giovanni van Bronckhorst	54	36F, 4Y, 1R

number of assists in a season since Opta records began

ASTON VILLA

ADDRESS

Villa Park, Trinity Road,
Birmingham B6 6HE

CONTACT NUMBERS

Telephone: 0121 327 2299
Fax: 0121 322 2107
Commercial: 0121 327 5399
Ticket Office: 0121 327 5353
ClubCall: 09068 12 11 48
Villa Village Superstore:
0121 327 2800
e-mail: postmaster@astonvilla-fc.co.uk
Website: www.avfc.co.uk

KEY PERSONNEL

Chairman: H D Ellis
President: J A Alderson
Executive Directors:
M J Ansell (Deputy Chief Executive)
S M Stride (Operations Director)
Non-Executive Directors: D M Owen,
A J Hales, P D Ellis
Manager: Graham Taylor

SPONSORS

2001–02 NTL
2002–03 MG Rover Group

FANZINES

Heroes and Villains,
The Holy Trinity

COLOURS

Home: Claret shirts, white shorts
and sky blue stockings
Away: Platinum shirts, navy shorts
and navy stockings

NICKNAME

The Villans

HONOURS

League Champions: 1893–94,
1895–96, 1896–97, 1898–99,
1899–00, 1909–10, 1980–81
Division Two Champions:
1937–38, 1959–60
Division Three Champions: 1971–72
FA Cup Winners: 1887, 1895,
1897, 1905, 1913, 1920, 1957
League Cup Winners: 1961,
1975, 1977, 1994, 1996
European Cup Winners: 1982
European Super Cup Winners: 1983

RECORD GOALSCORER

Harry Hampton – 215 league goals,
1904–15

BIGGEST WIN

13–0 v Wednesbury Old Ath – FA Cup 1st
round, 30 October 1886

BIGGEST DEFEAT

1–8 v Blackburn Rovers – FA Cup 3rd
round, 16 February 1889

37% No team drew a higher percentage of

SEASON REVIEW

Qualification for the Intertoto Cup at the end of the 2000–01 season meant that 2001–02 was always going to be a long campaign for Villa. Their season started on 14 July with a trip to Croatian side Slaven Belupo.

They headed into the fixture without two of their star players though, as England internationals David James and Gareth Southgate had moved on from Villa Park to West Ham United and Middlesbrough respectively.

The summer transfers were certainly not all one way though, with several new faces arriving in the West Midlands. Moroccans Hassan Kachloul and Moustapha Hadji were already familiar faces in the Premiership while John Gregory also brought in Swedish defender Olof Mellberg and Croatian forward Bosko Balaban. One of the biggest surprises over the close season was Villa's capture of Peter Schmeichel from Sporting Lisbon, who returned to England two years after winning the treble at Manchester United.

> "I want to go one better than I did in 1990 when we finished runners-up. If I didn't think it was possible, I would not be having a go."
>
> **Graham Taylor**

The Intertoto Cup served as a healthy pre-season warm up for Villa with victories against Slaven Belupo, Rennes and FC Basel earning the Villans a place in the first round of the UEFA Cup. They also appeared better prepared than most for the new season and got off to an impressive start. They were unlucky to only draw with Manchester United, but won away at Liverpool and beat Premiership new boys Fulham and Blackburn in a seven-game unbeaten run from the start of the campaign.

A defeat at Everton – despite a Peter Schmeichel goal – brought an end to this run, but two wins in their next two games had Villa sitting proudly on top of the Premiership by the end of October.

They did not have it all their own way though, losing to Croatians FC Varteks in the first round of the UEFA Cup. However, with Schmeichel playing like he'd never been away, Mellberg and Alpay looking a formidable partnership in defence and Juan Pablo Angel and Darius Vassell firing on all cylinders up front, the immediate future looked bright.

After they reached the Premiership summit however, things began to take a turn for the worse. Defeats to strugglers Leicester and Derby in the run-up to Christmas and a two-goal lead thrown away at Arsenal saw Villa sliding down to mid-table by the turn of the year. Added to this, a Worthington Cup exit at the hands of Sheffield Wednesday and an injury to defensive lynchpin Alpay, meant the early season optimism all but disappeared.

A two-goal lead was overturned in the last 15 minutes by Manchester United to put Villa out of the FA Cup at the first hurdle and, with rumours rife of friction between boss John Gregory and chairman Doug Ellis, things came to a head in late January with Gregory resigning as manager, before taking over at Derby shortly afterwards.

After being linked with several big names both at home and abroad, Villa invited former boss Graham Taylor to take over at the helm and provided him with £5 million to sign England under-21 striker Peter Crouch from Portsmouth.

Taylor's first win in his second spell at Villa came at home to West Ham, but this was the only success in his first nine games in charge. He turned it around at the season's climax though and victories over Southampton and Chelsea in their last two games meant that season 2002–03 would get off to another early start with the Intertoto Cup looming in July.

ASTON VILLA

DATE	OPPONENT	SCORE	ATT.	ALPAY	ANGEL	BALABAN	BARRY	BOATENG	CROUCH	DELANEY	DUBLIN	ENCKELMAN	GINOLA
18.08.01	Tottenham A	0–0	36,059	90	63	–	–	90□	–	90□	–	–	s27
26.08.01	Man Utd H	1–1	42,632	90	79	s11	–	90	–	90	–	–	–
08.09.01	Liverpool A	3–1	44,102	90□	–	–	–	90	–	90	90¹	–	–
16.09.01	Sunderland H	0–0	31,668	90	–	s22	–	90	–	90	68	–	s35
24.09.01	Southampton A	3–1	26,794	90	74¹	s16	–	90¹	–	90	57■+	–	–
30.09.01	Blackburn H	2–0	28,623	90	85¹	–	–	90	–	90	s5	–	–
14.10.01	Fulham H	2–0	28,579	90	62	s28	–	90	–	–	–	–	–
20.10.01	Everton A	2–3	33,352	63	63	–	–	90	–	90	s27□	–	s13
24.10.01	Charlton H	1–0	27,701	90	–	–	–	90	–	90	90	–	–
27.10.01	Bolton W H	3–2	33,599	90□	73¹	–	–	90	–	90	s17	–	–
03.11.01	Newcastle A	0–3	51,057	90□	60	–	–	90	–	90□	s30	–	–
17.11.01	Middlesbro H	0–0	35,424	90	90	–	–	90	–	13	–	–	s19
25.11.01	Leeds Utd A	1–1	40,159	90	62	–	–	90	–	–	s28	–	–
01.12.01	Leicester H	0–2	30,711	60	90	–	–	90	–	90	s18	–	s23■
05.12.01	West Ham A	1–1	28,377	–	–	–	90	90	–	45	90¹	90	–
09.12.01	Arsenal A	2–3	38,074	–	–	–	78	90	–	–	90	90	–
17.12.01	Ipswich H	2–1	29,320	–	85²	–	90	90	–	–	s23	–	–
22.12.01	Derby Co A	1–3	28,001	–	90¹	s10	45	80	–	–	90	–	–
26.12.01	Liverpool H	1–2	42,602	–	90	–	–	90□	–	–	–	–	–
29.12.01	Tottenham H	1–1	41,134	–	90¹	–	–	89	–	–	–	–	–
01.01.02	Sunderland A	1–1	45,324	–	–	–	s22	–	–	–	90	–	–
12.01.02	Derby Co H	2–1	28,881	–	90¹	–	s1	90	–	90	–	–	–
21.01.02	Charlton A	2–1	25,681	–	90¹□	–	s2	90	–	90	–	–	–
30.01.02	Everton H	0–0	32,460	–	90□	–	–	90	–	90	s45	90	–
02.02.02	Fulham A	0–0	20,041	–	77	–	–	90□	–	90	–	90	–
09.02.02	Chelsea H	1–1	41,137	–	90	–	s45	90	–	90	s3	90	–
23.02.02	Man Utd A	0–1	67,592	–	90	–	90	90	–	90	s11	–	–
02.03.02	West Ham H	2–1	37,341	–	90¹	–	90	90	–	90	–	–	–
05.03.02	Blackburn A	0–3	21,988	–	72	s18	90	90□	–	90□	–	–	–
17.03.02	Arsenal H	1–2	41,520	–	–	–	90	90□	–	90	s45¹	–	–
23.03.02	Ipswich A	0–0	25,247	–	–	–	90	90	–	90□	90□	–	–
30.03.02	Bolton W A	2–3*	24,600	–	s19	–	90	90	90	71	–	–	–
01.04.02	Newcastle H	1–1	36,597	–	90	s14	90	89	76¹	90	–	–	–
06.04.02	Middlesbro A	1–2	26,003	–	90¹	–	90	90	90	90	–	–	–
13.04.02	Leeds Utd H	0–1	40,039	–	65□	–	90	65	90	90□	–	90	–
20.04.02	Leicester A	2–2	18,125	–	–	s10	90	90	90	90	–	90	–
27.04.02	Southampton H	2–1	35,255	–	s24	–	66	90	66	90	–	90	–
11.05.02	Chelsea A	3–1	40,709	–	s5	–	90	90	85¹	90	s5¹	90	–

□ Yellow card, ■ Red card, s Substitute, 90² Goals scored
*including own goal, +card rescinded

For more information visit our website:

2001–02 PREMIERSHIP APPEARANCES

HADJI	HENDRIE	HITZLSPERGER	KACHLOUL	MELLBERG	MERSON	SAMUEL	SCHMEICHEL	STAUNTON	STONE	TAYLOR	VASSELL	WRIGHT	TOTAL
s16	90	–	81	90	90	–	90	–	s9	–	74	90	990
s26	90	–	90	90	64	–	90	–	–	–	90[1]	90	990
s19	89[1]	–	90	90□	71	–	90	s1	–	–	90[1]	90	990
–	90	–	90	90	55	–	90	–	–	–	90	90	990
90[1]	87□	–	69□	90	–	–	90	s21	s3	–	–	90	957
90□	90	–	85	–	–	s5	90	90	–	–	90[1]□	90	990
90□	90	–	16	–	–	–	90	90	90	s74[1]	90[1]	90	990
90[1]	77	–	–	–	–	s27	90[1]	90	–	90	90	90	990
90	70	–	90[1]	–	–	–	90	90	–	s20	90	90	990
90	86	–	90□	–	s17	–	90	90	–	s4	73[1]	90	990
90	60	–	90□	–	–	–	90	90	–	s30	90	90	990
–	90	–	71	90	–	–	90	–	90	s77	90□	90	990
–	51□	–	90[1]	90	90	–	90	–	90	s39	90	90□	990
–	61	–	–	90	90	–	90	s30	90	–	72	90	984
–	90	–	–	90	68	s45	–	90	90□	–	s22	90	990
–	90	–	–	90	90[1]	90	–	90	90[1]	–	s12	90	990
–	67	–	–	90	90	90	90	90	90	–	s5	90	990
–	s45□	–	s45	90	90	45	90	90	90	–	–	90	990
–	47[1]	–	90	90	90	82	90	90	s8	s43	90	90	990
–	90	–	90	90	90	90	90	90	s18	s1	90	72	990
–	90	–	68	90	–	90	90	90	90□	90[1]□	90□	90	990
s10	80	–	s33	90□	89	90□	90	90	–	57	90[1]	–	990
90	88	–	–	90	90	90	90	90	–	–	90[1]	–	990
90	75	–	s15	90	90	90	–	90	–	–	45	–	990
90□	86	–	s13	90	90	90	–	90	s4	–	90	–	990
90	58	–	–	45	90[1]	90□	–	90	s32	–	87	–	990
64	–	s26	–	90	–	79	90	90	90	–	90	–	990
78	–	90	–	90	s12	90	90	90	–	–	90[1]	–	990
45	s45	45	–	90	s45	90	90	90	–	–	90	–	990
s45	s11	90	45	90	79	90	90	90	–	–	45	–	990
–	–	90	–	90	–	80	90	90	90	s10	90	–	990
90	–	90	–	90	–	s19	90□	90□	–	90[1]	71	–	990
76	–	90	–	90	–	–	90	90	s1	90	s14	–	990
74	–	90	–	90	–	–	90	90	–	90	s16	–	990
–	–	90	45	90	–	s45	–	90	s25	90□	s25	–	990
–	–	90	90[1]	s10	90	–	80	–	90	90	–	80[1]	990
s24	–	90	–	90□	–	s24	–	90□	66	–	90[2]	90	990
–	s36	54□	–	90	–	–	–	90	90	–	85[1]	90	990

THE MANAGER

GRAHAM TAYLOR

Graham Taylor returned to the managerial hotseat at Villa Park in February 2002 following the resignation of John Gregory.

It is Taylor's second spell in charge of the club following a successful period in the late 1980's. Back then, Taylor won promotion to the top flight and took Villa up to second place in the old first division.

In the summer of 1990 he left Villa in order to take over from Bobby Robson as England manager. But a disappointing exit from Euro '92 and failure to qualify for the 1994 World Cup seriously damaged Taylor's reputation and he eventually resigned from his position.

He returned to club management with a period at Wolves before he enjoyed more success in a second spell at Watford, where the club won successive promotions to get to the Premiership.

Taylor announced his retirement from football management in the summer of 2001 and took up a role as a non-executive director at Aston Villa. After the departure of John Gregory and a little persuasion from Doug Ellis, Taylor returned to management once more and helped steer Villa towards a place in the Intertoto Cup in 2002–03.

LEAGUE POSITION

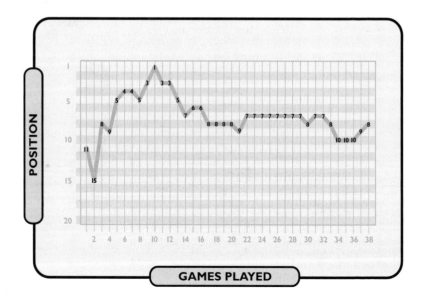

GAMES PLAYED

15 No team scored more headed goals

THE GOALS

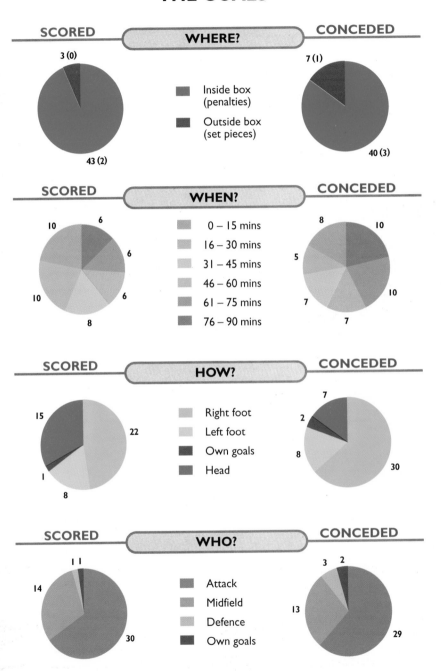

SCORED **WHERE?** CONCEDED

3 (0)
43 (2)

7 (1)
40 (3)

- Inside box (penalties)
- Outside box (set pieces)

SCORED **WHEN?** CONCEDED

6
6
6
8
10
10

8
10
10
7
7
5

- 0 – 15 mins
- 16 – 30 mins
- 31 – 45 mins
- 46 – 60 mins
- 61 – 75 mins
- 76 – 90 mins

SCORED **HOW?** CONCEDED

22
15
1
8

7
2
8
30

- Right foot
- Left foot
- Own goals
- Head

SCORED **WHO?** CONCEDED

1 1
14
30

3 2
13
29

- Attack
- Midfield
- Defence
- Own goals

in the Premiership than Aston Villa

ASTON VILLA

	ALPAY	ANGEL	BALABAN	BARRY	BOATENG	CROUCH	DELANEY	DUBLIN	GINOLA	HADJI
APPEARANCES										
Start	14	26	0	16	37	7	30	9	0	17
Sub	0	3	8	4	0	0	0	12	5	6
Minutes on pitch	1203	2138	129	1429	3293	587	2559	1012	117	1557
GOAL ATTEMPTS										
Goals	0	12	0	0	1	2	0	4	0	2
Shots on target	3	30	1	5	5	12	1	10	1	13
Shots off target	3	36	0	3	14	11	3	22	4	18
Shooting accuracy %	50%	45%	100%	63%	26%	52%	25%	31%	20%	42%
Goals/shots %	0%	18%	0%	0%	5%	9%	0%	13%	0%	6%
PASSING										
Goal assists	0	3	0	3	1	2	0	4	0	2
Long passes	134	110	3	128	493	22	254	38	9	117
Short passes	261	667	31	446	1273	183	751	274	41	401
PASS COMPLETION										
Own half %	86%	83%	71%	75%	83%	79%	79%	87%	89%	77%
Opposition half %	61%	70%	63%	69%	77%	63%	72%	54%	85%	56%
CROSSING										
Total crosses	3	10	4	74	46	0	62	1	30	122
Cross completion %	67%	20%	0%	28%	17%	0%	27%	0%	27%	28%
DRIBBLING										
Dribbles & runs	9	52	8	53	104	16	70	11	32	129
Dribble completion %	67%	58%	50%	62%	72%	50%	77%	45%	53%	45%
DEFENDING										
Tackles made	47	29	4	17	180	5	120	13	2	48
Tackles won %	81%	83%	50%	88%	77%	80%	78%	69%	100%	79%
Blocks	15	0	0	6	17	1	37	0	0	5
Clearances	146	3	0	35	57	0	114	16	0	36
Interceptions	18	2	1	1	18	0	14	1	0	4
DISCIPLINE										
Fouls conceded	21	41	6	22	93	16	19	29	1	24
Fouls won	19	18	1	28	61	14	52	21	7	25
Offside	0	51	2	5	2	8	1	7	2	2
Yellow cards	3	3	0	0	5	0	5	2	0	3
Red cards	0	0	0	0	0	0	0	1+	1	0

+ one card rescinded

GOALKEEPER NAME	START/ (SUB)	TIME ON PITCH	GOALS CONCEDED	MINS/GOALS CONCEDED	SAVES MADE	SAVES/ SHOTS
ENCKELMAN	9 (0)	810	10	81	29	74%
SCHMEICHEL	29 (0)	2610	37	71	85	70%

For more information visit our website:

PLAYERS' STATISTICS

	HENDRIE	HITZLSPERGER	KACHLOUL	MELLBERG	MERSON	SAMUEL	STAUNTON	STONE	TAYLOR	VASSELL	WRIGHT	TOTAL	RANK
	25	11	17	32	18	17	30	14	7	30	23		
	4	1	5	0	3	6	3	8	9	6	0		
	2119	935	1406	2835	1580	1611	2752	1336	895	2616	2052		
	2	1	2	0	2	0	0	1	3	12	0	46	=10th
	13	16	11	0	10	2	5	6	3	40	1	189	7th
	22	12	13	3	14	3	8	8	9	32	4	242	=7th
	37%	57%	46%	0%	42%	40%	38%	43%	25%	56%	20%	44%	11th
	6%	4%	8%	0%	8%	0%	0%	7%	25%	17%	0%	10%	15th
	3	2	1	1	2	3	3	4	1	2	1	38	8th
	213	66	89	340	181	210	577	132	62	72	298	4057	12th
	859	273	458	664	678	453	672	467	291	704	785	10686	12th
	86%	80%	83%	83%	89%	73%	82%	79%	84%	81%	82%	82%	13th
	82%	71%	72%	55%	71%	66%	61%	75%	77%	70%	76%	69%	5th
	28	59	80	6	107	78	135	91	9	71	50	1066	4th
	21%	31%	23%	33%	35%	28%	27%	25%	56%	17%	16%	26%	7th
	52	19	81	10	58	61	41	64	12	224	23	1133	9th
	79%	63%	33%	100%	66%	70%	88%	66%	83%	50%	87%	61%	20th
	49	19	36	77	17	39	68	50	40	71	50	986	13th
	59%	79%	69%	73%	76%	85%	71%	88%	78%	66%	68%	75%	3rd
	5	1	4	27	1	16	24	3	2	1	24	189	17th
	18	6	13	308	16	88	264	15	12	0	96	1318	=15th
	9	3	8	26	2	10	22	6	7	4	11	167	7th
	23	16	34	26	14	12	25	37	19	67	10	556	12th
	28	12	33	33	21	16	31	25	5	69	16	544	10th
	6	0	9	0	9	2	0	3	0	43	0	152	=2nd
	3	1	3	3	0	2	2	2	2	3	1	44	=17th
	0	0	0	0	0	0	0	0	0	0	0	2	=15th

CROSSES CAUGHT	CROSSES PUNCHED	CROSSES DROPPED	CATCH SUCCESS	THROWS/ SHORT KICKS	% COMPLETION	LONG KICKS	% COMPLETION
15	10	1	94%	12	92%	186	45%
56	10	5	92%	49	88%	585	49%

PLAYER OF THE SEASON

PLAYER	INDEX SCORE
DARIUS VASSELL	815
Juan Pablo Angel	782
Mark Delaney	727
Steve Staunton	702
Peter Schmeichel	662
Alan Wright	657
Olof Mellberg	629
George Boateng	602
Lee Hendrie	599
Jlloyd Samuel	597

Few Premiership players progressed as much as Darius Vassell during the 2001–02 season. Opta's Aston Villa player of the year began the campaign hoping to nail down a first-team slot at Villa Park and ended it by being named in the England World Cup squad.

The young striker was Villa's joint top scorer in the Premiership with 12 goals – his best ever return for the first team – and this helped him to become the highest-ranked Villa player in the Opta Index.

His run of good form, combined with some strong showings for David Platt's England under-21 side, led to his first call-up to the full England squad in February, when he marked his debut by scoring with a spectacular volley against Holland in Amsterdam.

That international debut earned him some rave reviews and few have spoken more highly of him than Graham Taylor: "We're all proud of him," said the Villa boss. "He's come through as a 10-year-old at Villa to the first team and now to a World Cup. He's not boastful, he's not a Jack-the-lad. In fact, he finds it difficult to handle all the attention."

Attention of the wrong kind was heaped on Colombian Juan Pablo Angel when he arrived at Villa in 2000–01, as the £9.5 million signing struggled to make an impact. He proved his doubters wrong though and the Villa faithful got to see the real Juan Pablo Angel. His strike rate of 18% was the best of any Villa striker and he formed a promising partnership alongside Vassell for much of the season.

Villa's third-highest ranked player was Mark Delaney. The 1999-2000 player of the season, finished just ahead of World Cup-bound defender Steve Staunton who is in his second spell at the club.

Surprise summer capture Peter Schmeichel became the first goalkeeper ever to score in the Premiership when he fired home a consolation goal at Everton and he finished the season as Villa's fifth-highest ranked player.

I Peter Schmeichel became the first goalkeeper

FIVE OF THE BEST

2001–02 was a season of mixed fortunes at Villa. Riding high at the top of the table in the early part of the campaign, a mid-season slump saw them assume a familiar mid-table position. John Gregory's exit from Villa Park in January opened the door for Graham Taylor to come in and try to improve on this position with the Villans.

TOP GOALSCORERS

	GOALS	GOALS/SHOTS
JUAN PABLO ANGEL	12	18%
Darius Vassell	12	17%
Dion Dublin	4	13%
Ian Taylor	3	25%
Peter Crouch	2	9%

Juan Pablo Angel bore the brunt of a great deal of criticism in 2000–01 as he struggled to settle into English football, but this time around he looked a different player. The Colombian hit 12 goals in the Premiership to make him Villa's joint-leading scorer alongside Darius Vassell who enjoyed his most prolific season in the first team.

George Boateng celebrated his first international call up during 2001–02 and showed why it was so deserved by bossing the Villans' midfield throughout the season. The Dutchman made 1,406 successful passes during the campaign – over 500 more than any other Villa player. Lee Hendrie was the only other Villa midfielder to manage more than 700 successful passes over the season.

TOP PASSERS

	SUCC PASSES	COMPLETION
GEORGE BOATENG	1,406	80%
Lee Hendrie	889	83%
Steve Staunton	886	71%
Alan Wright	844	78%
Mark Delaney	752	75%

TOP TACKLERS

	WON	SUCCESS
GEORGE BOATENG	139	77%
Mark Delaney	93	78%
Olof Mellberg	56	73%
Steve Staunton	48	71%
Darius Vassell	47	66%

George Boateng has always been known as a keen competitor in the middle of the field so it was no surprise to see that he won more tackles than any of his colleagues. 77% of his 180 attempted challenges were won and only Patrick Vieira managed a higher number of successful tackles in the Premiership during the course of the season.

While George Boateng can always be relied upon to "get stuck in" for Villa, this inevitably led to him running into trouble with referees. The former Coventry man was Villa's most penalised player during 2001–02, committing a total of 93 fouls during the season – more than any other player in the Premiership – and this also saw him cautioned on five occasions.

DISCIPLINE

	POINTS	FOULS & CARDS
GEORGE BOATENG	108	93F, 5Y, 0R
Darius Vassell	76	67F, 3Y, 0R
Juan Pablo Angel	50	41F, 3Y, 0R
Hassan Kachloul	43	34F, 3Y, 0R
Steve Stone	43	37F, 2Y, 0R

ever to score in the Premiership

BLACKBURN ROVERS

ADDRESS

Ewood Park, Blackburn,
Lancashire BB2 4JF

CONTACT NUMBERS

Telephone: 01254 698 888
Fax: 01254 671 042
Ticket Office: 01254 671 666
ClubCall: 09068 121 179
The Roverstore: 01254 665 606
e-mail: enquiries@rovers.co.uk
Website: www.rovers.co.uk

KEY PERSONNEL

Club President: W H Bancroft
Chairman: R D Coar BSc
Vice-Chairman: R L Matthewman
Chief Executive: J O Williams BSc
Directors: D M Brown, K C Lee,
G R Root FCMA, I R Stanners
Club Secretary: T M Finn
Manager: Graeme Souness

SPONSORS

Time Computers

FANZINES

Loadsamoney

COLOURS

Home: Blue and white halved shirts,
white shorts and white stockings
Away: Navy shirts, navy shorts
and navy stockings

NICKNAME

Rovers

HONOURS

League Champions 1911–12,
1913–14, 1994–95
Division Two Champions 1938–39
Division Three Champions 1974–75
FA Cup Winners: 1884, 1885, 1886,
1890, 1891, 1928
League Cup Winners: 2002

RECORD GOALSCORER

Simon Garner 168 league goals,
1978–1992

BIGGEST WIN

11–0 v Rossendale – FA Cup 1st Round,
13 October 1884

BIGGEST DEFEAT

0–8 v Arsenal – Division 1,
25 February 1933

8 Matt Jansen netted eight left-footed goals

SEASON REVIEW

Rovers fans can look back on an immensely satisfying return to the big-time in 2001–02. An enthralling campaign in the Worthington Cup led to Millennium Stadium glory for Graeme Souness's men, while a 10th-placed finish in the Premiership was better than many expected at the start of the season.

Still, there were times when Rovers fans were shifting uncomfortably in their seats, particularly from January through to March – "our sticky months" as Souness called them – but the players ultimately emerged triumphant after battling through this challenging period.

The Rovers boss plunged into the transfer market in the summer months following Blackburn's promotion from Division One, shrewdly attaining the services of his former charge Tugay from Glasgow Rangers for £1.3 million along with Alan Mahon from Sporting Lisbon and Ternana's free-scoring Corrado Grabbi.

A patchy start to their Premiership campaign saw Blackburn pick up two wins and three draws in their opening eight league encounters, but it was a 7–1 thrashing of West Ham United in October – in £2.5 million FC Nurnberg recruit Nils-Eric Johansson's debut – that kick-started their season.

That victory was preceded by an extra-time win over Middlesbrough in the third round of the Worthington Cup, with Craig Short's late strike acting as the catalyst in Rovers' unbroken League Cup run.

Manchester City were Blackburn's next victims in the fourth round, before an under-strength Arsenal were soundly beaten 4–0 at Ewood Park.

But while they were cruising in the cups, Blackburn's league form suffered. A run of six defeats in seven matches from the start

> **"We've underachieved this season. We've young players and you have to think that they can continue to get better next season."**
>
> **Graeme Souness**

of December to New Year's Day left Rovers near the drop-zone and prompted Souness to take swift action.

Reinforcement arrived in the form of Andy Cole, while the disappointing Grabbi was loaned out to Serie B side Messina. Souness prised Cole away from Manchester United for £7.5 million, with the ex-Magpie desperate for first-team football to impress Sven-Göran Eriksson. Cole's World Cup hopes were eventually dashed, but the move was a statement of intent by Souness and brought almost instant success.

Cole netted once in each leg of the Worthington Cup semi-final against Sheffield Wednesday to help ensure a trip to Cardiff for his new team.

Blackburn's new strike sensation quickly forged a very impressive partnership with fellow England hopeful Matt Jansen and the two clinched Rovers' first victory in a cup final for 74 years when they both netted in the 2–1 win over Tottenham. Blackburn had UEFA Cup football in 2002–03 to look forward to.

They were also facing the prospect of a swift return to the Nationwide League though, but the victory at the Millennium Stadium seemed to inspire the players.

Having relied on David Dunn's purposeful displays earlier in the campaign, Blackburn's latter-season hero was Damien Duff. The World Cup-bound Republic of Ireland winger sparked Rovers to six wins and three draws in their last dozen matches, with Souness's men picking up 21 points in those 12 games after their League Cup triumph, having amassed just 25 in their first 26 Premiership outings.

An emphatic 3–0 victory over Fulham provided a satisfying end to the season – the three points lifting Blackburn into the top half of the table on their return.

BLACKBURN ROVERS

DATE	OPPONENT	SCORE	ATT.	BENT	BERG	BLAKE	BJORNEBYE	COLE	CURTIS	DUFF	DUNN	FLITCROFT	FRIEDEL	GILLESPIE
18.08.01	Derby Co A	1–2	28,236	s26	90	s26¹	64	–	90	90	45	90	90	90
22.08.01	Man Utd H	2–2*	29,836	–	90	s15	90	–	90	90	–	90□	90	89¹
25.08.01	Tottenham H	2–1	24,992	s21	90	s71	–	–	90	90¹	–	90	90	69□
08.09.01	Sunderland A	0–1	45,103	60	90□	–	90	–	–	90	–	90	90	72□
16.09.01	Ipswich A	1–1	22,126	s6	90	–	–	–	–	90	–	90	90	90
19.09.01	Bolton W H	1–1	25,949	s16	90	–	90	–	–	90	–	90	90	–
22.09.01	Everton H	1–0	27,732	–	90	–	90	–	–	44	–	90	90	–
30.09.01	Aston Villa A	0–2	28,623	–	90	–	90□	–	–	–	81	90□	90	–
14.10.01	West Ham H	7–1*	22,712	–	72	–	90	–	–	–	90¹	90¹	90	–
20.10.01	Arsenal A	3–3*	38,108	s20□	90	–	90	–	–	–	90²	90	90	70
29.10.01	Leicester H	0–0	21,873	s51	90	–	69□	–	–	–	90	90□	90	s26
03.11.01	Southampton A	2–1	30,523	s26	90	–	–	–	–	–	90□	45	90	90
17.11.01	Liverpool H	1–1	28,859	s12□	90	–	90	–	90	78	90	65□	90	90
24.11.01	Chelsea A	0–0	37,976	–	83	–	90	–	90	90□	90	–	90	90
01.12.01	Middlesbro H	0–1	23,849	–	90	–	–	–	–	–	72	90	90	90□
09.12.01	Leeds Utd H	1–2	28,309	–	90¹	–	–	–	61	90	90	–	90	90
15.12.01	Newcastle A	1–2	50,064	–	90	–	–	–	–	78	90	90¹□	90	90
22.12.01	Charlton A	2–0	25,857	–	90	–	90	–	–	90¹	s25¹	90□	90	90
26.12.01	Sunderland H	0–3	29,869	–	45	–	–	–	–	90	90□	90	90	90
29.12.01	Derby Co H	0–1	23,529	–	90	–	90	–	–	90□	s19	71	90	90
01.01.02	Tottenham A	0–1	35,131	–	90	–	61	90	–	90	s29	90	90	71
12.01.02	Charlton H	4–1	23,365	–	90	–	90	90¹	90	90	90	–	90	–
19.01.02	Man Utd A	1–2	67,552	–	–	–	84	90	–	90	65	s25	90	–
30.01.02	Arsenal H	2–3	25,893	–	–	–	80	90	–	90	–	90	90	s28
02.02.02	West Ham A	0–2	35,307	–	–	–	66□	90	–	90	–	80	90	s24
09.02.02	Fulham A	0–2	19,580	–	90	–	–	90	68	89	90	–	90	s21
02.03.02	Bolton W A	1–1	27,203	–	90	–	45	19□	–	s28	90	90	90	s28
05.03.02	Aston Villa H	3–0	21,988	–	90	–	–	90¹	–	90¹	90¹	90	90	s24
13.03.02	Ipswich H	2–1	23,305	–	90	–	–	90¹	–	90¹	72	90□	90	s18
17.03.02	Leeds Utd A	1–3	39,857	–	90	–	–	–	–	90	34	90	90	s50
30.03.02	Leicester A	1–2	16,236	–	–	–	34	–	–	–	–	90	90	s57□
01.04.02	Southampton H	2–0	28,851	–	90	–	90	–	–	90¹	53	s37	90	80
10.04.02	Chelsea H	0–0	25,441	–	90	–	90	90	–	90	90	–	90	90
20.04.02	Middlesbro A	3–1	26,932	–	90□	–	90	90¹□	–	90	90¹	s34□	90	56
23.04.02	Newcastle H	2–2	26,712	–	90	–	–	90¹	–	90	90	–	90	90¹
28.04.02	Everton A	2–1	34,976	–	90	–	–	90¹□	–	90	90	90	90	s26
08.05.02	Liverpool A	3–4	40,663	–	89	–	–	90¹	60	90¹□	90	–	–	s30
11.05.02	Fulham H	3–0	30,487	–	90	–	–	90²	–	90¹	90□	–	–	90

□ Yellow card, ■ Red card, s Substitute, 90² Goals scored
*including own goal

For more information visit our website:

2001–02 PREMIERSHIP APPEARANCES

	GRABBI	HAKAN ÜNSAL	HIGNETT	HUGHES	JANSEN	JOHANSSON	JOHNSON	KELLY	MAHON	McATEER	NEILL	OSTENSTAD	SHORT	TAYLOR	TUGAY	YORDI	TOTAL
	64	–	s45	–	90	–	–	–	–	–	–	–	90	–	–	–	990
	75	–	s1	–	79	–	–	–	90	–	–	–	77▫	s11	–	–	977
	19	–	s30	–	90	–	–	–	60¹	–	–	–	90	90	–	–	990
	–	–	–	s30▫	90	–	–	–	60	s18	90	–	–	90	s30	–	990
	84	–	–	–	90¹	–	–	–	90	–	90	–	–	90	90▫	–	990
	74	–	–	s13	90	–	77	–	56	s34	90¹	–	–	–	90	–	990
	63¹	–	s13	s27	90	–	90	–	s46	77	90▫	–	–	–	90	–	990
	–	–	s9	60	90	–	63	–	90	s27	90	s30	–	–	90	–	990
	76▫	–	s14¹	s14	90¹	90	76¹	–	–	–	90	–	s18	–	90¹	–	990
	–	–	s31	s6	84	–	59	–	–	–	90	–	90▫	–	90	–	990
	39	–	s21¹	–	90	90	64▫	–	–	–	90▫	–	–	–	90▫	–	990
	–	–	s45¹	64	90	90	s10	–	–	–	80	–	–	90	90¹	–	990
	–	–	s25	–	90¹	–	–	–	–	–	–	–	90	–	90	–	990
	–	–	–	s30	90	s7	–	–	60	–	90	–	–	–	90▫	–	990
	s28	–	–	–	90	s22	–	–	s18	–	90	62	68	90	90	–	990
	s29	–	–	–	90	s29	–	–	90	–	90	–	61▫	–	90▫	–	990
	s12	–	–	s45▫	26	–	–	–	–	–	90▫	–	90	s19	90	–	990
	65	–	–	s25	–	–	–	–	90	–	90▫	–	90▫	–	65	–	990
	45	–	–	s45	s45	90	–	–	90	–	66	–	69▫	s24	–	–	969
	–	–	s10	–	90	–	–	–	–	–	90▫	59	80	s31	90	–	990
	–	–	s19	–	80	–	–	–	–	–	90▫	s10	90	–	90▫	–	990
	–	–	90¹	–	90¹	–	–	–	–	–	–	–	–	90	90¹	–	990
	s6	–	90¹	s17	73	90	–	–	–	–	90	–	–	90	90	–	990
	–	–	62	s10	90²▫	90	–	–	–	–	90	–	–	90	90▫	–	990
	–	–	90▫	–	90	90	–	–	s10	–	90	–	–	90	90▫	–	990
	–	–	s22	–	90	s1	–	–	–	–	69▫	–	89▫	90	90▫	–	989
	–	62	–	62	90¹	90	–	–	–	–	90	–	–	–	–	s45	919
	–	57▫	–	–	60	90	–	–	–	–	90	–	–	s33	66	s30	990
	–	82▫	–	s26	–	90	–	–	–	–	90▫	–	–	s8	90	64	990
	–	90	s6	s45▫	90¹	90	–	–	–	–	90	–	–	–	45	90	990
	–	90	s56	74¹	90	90	–	–	–	–	90	–	90	s16	90	33	990
	–	–	s10	s19	90	–	–	–	–	–	90	–	90	–	90	71¹	990
	–	–	–	–	90	–	–	–	–	–	90	–	90	–	90	–	990
	–	–	s22	–	–	–	–	–	–	–	90	–	90	–	90	68¹	990
	–	90	–	–	90	s28	–	–	–	–	62	–	90	–	90	–	990
	–	64	–	–	90¹	s26	–	–	–	–	–	–	90	90	64	–	990
	–	–	–	s1	90¹	90	–	90	–	–	90	–	90	–	90	–	990
	–	s15	–	s15	75	75	–	90	–	–	90▫	–	–	90	83▫	s7	990

THE MANAGER

GRAEME SOUNESS

Graeme Souness is no stranger to success. After a distinguished and trophy-laden career as a midfield enforcer at Middlesbrough, Liverpool, Sampdoria and Glasgow Rangers, the plain-speaking Scot has transferred his trademark tenacity to his various managerial roles to great effect.

The latest in a long line of trophies came in February 2002 when Souness guided Rovers to Worthington Cup final glory, ensuring a run in the 2002–03 UEFA Cup. But perhaps the most significant achievement of the 2001–02 season was that Blackburn finished a highly-respectable 10th under his guidance.

Souness cut his managerial teeth in a hugely productive five-year spell at Rangers, initially as player-manager, where he picked up three league titles and four league cups and set Rangers on their way to their historic nine-in-a-row sequence of league titles. A spell at Liverpool followed, but produced just one FA Cup triumph in 1992, while Southampton were the other English side he has managed

Souness is vastly experienced on the continent and his charges will benefit from this on their European adventure in the 2002–03 campaign. Having managed Galatasaray, Torino and Benfica, Souness is well equipped to lead the side in Europe.

LEAGUE POSITION

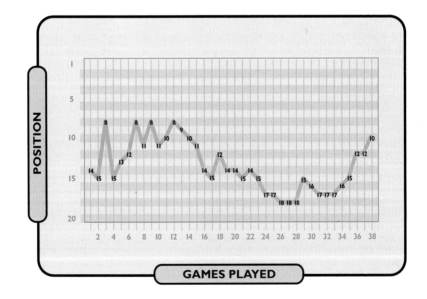

7 Blackburn scored more goals in a single game

THE GOALS

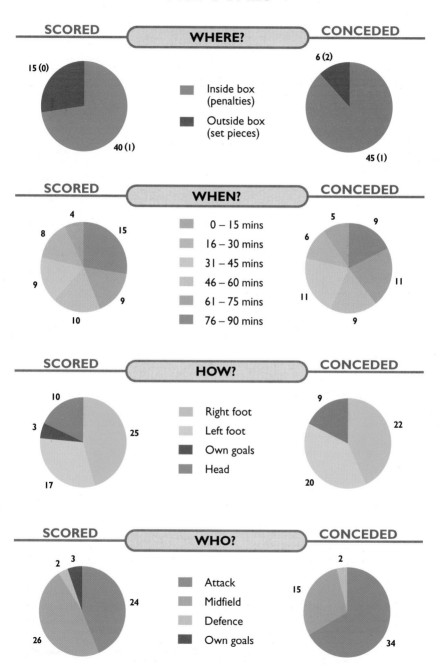

WHERE?

SCORED — CONCEDED

- Inside box (penalties)
- Outside box (set pieces)

SCORED: 15 (0), 40 (1)
CONCEDED: 6 (2), 45 (1)

WHEN?

SCORED — CONCEDED

- 0 – 15 mins
- 16 – 30 mins
- 31 – 45 mins
- 46 – 60 mins
- 61 – 75 mins
- 76 – 90 mins

SCORED: 4, 15, 8, 9, 9, 10
CONCEDED: 5, 9, 6, 11, 11, 9

HOW?

SCORED — CONCEDED

- Right foot
- Left foot
- Own goals
- Head

SCORED: 10, 3, 25, 17
CONCEDED: 9, 22, 20

WHO?

SCORED — CONCEDED

- Attack
- Midfield
- Defence
- Own goals

SCORED: 2, 3, 24, 26
CONCEDED: 2, 15, 34

than any other team – all by different players

BLACKBURN ROVERS

	BENT	BERG	BJORNEBYE	BLAKE	COLE	CURTIS	DUFF	DUNN	FLITCROFT	GILLESPIE	GRABBI	HAKAN ÜNSAL
APPEARANCES												
Start	1	34	23	0	15	10	31	26	26	21	10	7
Sub	8	0	0	3	0	0	1	3	3	11	4	1
Minutes on pitch	238	2989	1853	112	1279	807	2741	2223	2337	2099	679	550
GOAL ATTEMPTS												
Goals	0	1	0	1	9	0	7	7	1	2	1	0
Shots on target	0	3	0	2	20	0	23	28	8	18	4	3
Shots off target	8	10	1	0	21	0	10	29	22	13	11	1
Shooting accuracy %	0%	23%	0%	100%	49%	0%	70%	49%	27%	58%	27%	75%
Goals/shots %	0%	8%	0%	50%	22%	0%	21%	12%	3%	6%	7%	0%
PASSING												
Goal assists	1	2	1	0	2	0	6	5	2	4	3	3
Long passes	12	429	399	4	70	106	139	298	291	174	27	81
Short passes	68	762	619	21	356	242	834	857	804	587	200	138
PASS COMPLETION												
Own half %	64%	85%	87%	86%	79%	82%	85%	84%	86%	82%	83%	71%
Opposition half %	55%	62%	65%	67%	66%	73%	75%	67%	77%	67%	63%	58%
CROSSING												
Total crosses	8	11	46	2	11	7	255	88	15	178	16	17
Cross completion %	38%	55%	17%	0%	27%	43%	27%	31%	40%	26%	31%	24%
DRIBBLING												
Dribbles & runs	20	9	24	5	38	18	287	154	9	229	23	16
Dribble completion %	30%	78%	79%	60%	74%	94%	76%	64%	100%	75%	30%	94%
DEFENDING												
Tackles made	2	89	68	1	15	11	57	76	92	38	10	17
Tackles won %	50%	69%	75%	100%	60%	91%	70%	78%	75%	74%	90%	71%
Blocks	0	27	6	0	0	6	12	9	6	13	1	7
Clearances	2	322	117	2	2	31	22	32	41	36	6	33
Interceptions	2	21	10	0	1	0	6	11	8	8	1	2
DISCIPLINE												
Fouls conceded	7	28	34	3	21	6	30	37	81	17	10	10
Fouls won	3	35	19	3	9	4	88	44	24	32	23	10
Offside	9	1	0	2	16	0	14	3	10	3	12	0
Yellow cards	2	2	3	0	2	0	3	4	7	4	1	2
Red cards	0	0	0	0	1	0	0	0	0	0	0	0

GOALKEEPER NAME	START/ (SUB)	TIME ON PITCH	GOALS CONCEDED	MINS/GOALS CONCEDED	SAVES MADE	SAVES/ SHOTS
FRIEDEL	36 (0)	3240	47	69	126	73%
KELLY	2 (0)	180	4	45	5	56%

For more information visit our website:

PLAYERS' STATISTICS

	HIGNETT	HUGHES	JANSEN	JOHANSSON	JOHNSON	MAHON	McATEER	NEILL	OSTENSTAD	SHORT	TAYLOR	TUGAY	YORDI	TOTAL	RANK
	4	4	34	14	6	10	1	31	2	21	12	32	5		
	16	17	1	6	1	3	3	0	2	1	7	1	3		
	689	650	2952	1358	439	850	156	2707	161	1812	1222	2783	408		
	4	1	10	0	1	1	0	1	0	0	0	3	2	55*	6th
	10	4	34	1	1	3	2	5	0	0	2	8	5	184	=9th
	8	10	37	0	0	10	1	3	2	4	10	20	5	236	10th
	56%	29%	48%	100%	100%	23%	67%	63%	0%	0%	17%	29%	50%	44%	12th
	22%	7%	14%	0%	100%	8%	0%	13%	0%	0%	0%	11%	20%	12%	6th
	3	0	5	0	0	0	0	1	0	0	0	3	0	41	=5th
	88	65	133	189	20	88	23	395	2	159	134	545	17	4293	9th
	292	166	813	451	129	257	56	944	47	466	399	1333	104	11030	11th
	88%	82%	73%	81%	78%	80%	80%	79%	85%	80%	81%	89%	59%	83%	7th
	78%	73%	68%	65%	83%	64%	80%	66%	56%	65%	60%	80%	62%	68%	8th
	60	7	43	16	34	65	16	82	0	0	4	38	1	1020	5th
	27%	29%	14%	38%	18%	22%	25%	20%	0%	0%	25%	21%	0%	25%	9th
	18	10	133	25	30	47	3	90	1	25	26	68	4	1318	5th
	78%	80%	57%	92%	83%	62%	67%	74%	100%	68%	92%	74%	75%	72%	4th
	12	21	69	72	18	39	10	103	1	50	35	129	3	1039	11th
	83%	86%	74%	81%	72%	72%	80%	83%	100%	70%	63%	72%	33%	75%	6th
	1	1	1	19	5	6	0	27	0	26	14	9	1	197	16th
	9	3	14	117	11	14	4	150	0	247	109	15	3	1411	10th
	1	2	3	9	0	2	0	19	0	11	6	13	0	137	18th
	10	38	38	31	3	23	1	63	5	40	13	49	9	608	6th
	6	24	63	27	7	10	1	40	3	23	10	42	8	565	6th
	1	14	50	0	2	1	2	2	5	0	0	0	5	152	=2nd
	2	3	2	0	1	0	0	9	0	3	0	9	0	59	=9th
	0	0	0	0	0	0	0	0	0	3	0	0	0	4	8th

*Including three own goals

CROSSES CAUGHT	CROSSES PUNCHED	CROSSES DROPPED	CATCH SUCCESS	THROWS/ SHORT KICKS	% COMPLETION	LONG KICKS	% COMPLETION
64	23	4	94%	74	96%	677	56%
4	0	1	80%	6	100%	36	67%

PLAYER OF THE SEASON

PLAYER	INDEX SCORE
DAMIEN DUFF	866
David Dunn	864
Matt Jansen	755
Keith Gillespie	726
Brad Friedel	723
Henning Berg	710
Lucas Neill	694
Tugay	693
Craig Short	654
Stig-Inge Bjornebye	611

There were several Rovers heroes in the 2001–02 campaign. Singling one out as player of the year thus proved difficult, as Opta's scientifically calculated rankings illustrated.

Damien Duff pipped David Dunn to the title of Blackburn player of the season by just two points, although Andy Cole recorded an Index rating of 868 and would have scraped above Duff had he racked up more time on the pitch for Blackburn.

Duff's sparkling performances in the latter part of the campaign spurred Rovers not only to safety, but also into the top half of the table.

The Republic of Ireland winger's devilish forays took him past defenders on 81 occasions – more than any other 2001–02 Premiership player. Duff also supplied a club-high six assists and there were some goal-of-the-season contenders among his seven strikes.

Dunn cracked a few spectacular goals himself and, like Duff, four of his seven strikes were from outside the area. Indeed only two midfielders – David Beckham and Laurent Robert – attempted more than Dunn's total of 48 long-range strikes.

Dunn was one of three players disappointed to miss out on a place in England's World Cup squad, Cole being another and Matt Jansen the third. Jansen made the top three of the Index of Blackburn players thanks to his unmatched 10 league goals, his Premiership-high eight goals with the left boot marking him out as a potential future solution to England's left-sided problems.

Keith Gillespie came in at fourth, the ex-Newcastle wide man sending 142 crosses over at an impressive rate of six per game on average, with Brad Friedel's 126 saves – the second-most in the league – earning him fifth spot.

Newcomer and Blackburn's top tackler Tugay made the top 10 just below veteran Henning Berg and fellow new-boy Lucas Neill. The Turk wrested possession from 93 opponents over the course of the league campaign.

3 Craig Short was the only player to be sent

FIVE OF THE BEST

In their first season back in the top flight Graeme Souness's team left it until late to mathematically avoid relegation, but at the same time they played some of the most exciting football in the division. David Dunn, Damien Duff and Matt Jansen thrilled crowds across the land, while Tugay proved to be one of the most complete midfielders in the top flight.

TOP GOALSCORERS

	GOALS	GOALS/SHOTS
MATT JANSEN	10	14%
Andrew Cole	9	22%
Damien Duff	7	21%
David Dunn	7	12%
Craig Hignett	4	22%

Matt Jansen was in the frame for a World Cup call-up until the final week of the season, which was testament to his performances over the campaign. His 10 goals made him Rovers' top scorer, although Andy Cole was close behind with nine – considering he only joined Blackburn at the end of December, it proved that a quality striker can score in any team, especially with a decent 22% goals-to-shots ratio.

Tugay recorded over 600 more successful passes than any of his Blackburn Rovers team-mates and much of the side's play went though the dependable midfielder. His 84% passing accuracy was further proof that he was a player of the highest standard. The second most prolific in terms of distribution was Lucas Neill followed by centre-back Henning Berg, both of whom reached the 900 mark for accurate passes as Rovers built from the back.

TOP PASSERS

	SUCC PASSES	COMPLETION
TUGAY	1,573	84%
Lucas Neill	947	71%
Henning Berg	900	76%
Garry Flitcroft	882	81%
David Dunn	831	72%

TOP TACKLERS

	WON	SUCCESS
TUGAY	93	72%
Lucas Neill	86	83%
Garry Flitcroft	69	75%
Henning Berg	61	69%
David Dunn	59	78%

As well as being the most prolific passer at Ewood Park, Tugay also won more tackles than any other player at the club. With just under a century of successful challenges, the Turkish international provided the bite in midfield while in defence, Lucas Neill won an excellent 83% of his challenges and, having taken the ball 86 times, he was the top-tackling Rover at the back for Souness's team.

Although he was not sent off during 2001–02, Garry Flitcroft racked up the highest number of disciplinary points at Blackburn, largely due to the 81 fouls he committed – the fifth most of any player in the Premiership. The second and third-worst disciplinary records go to Lucas Neill and Tugay who were also the top two tacklers, illustrating that there can be a price to pay for getting stuck in.

DISCIPLINE

	POINTS	FOULS & CARDS
GARRY FLITCROFT	102	81F, 7Y, 0R
Lucas Neill	90	63F, 9Y, 0R
Tugay	76	49F, 9Y, 0R
Craig Short	67	40F, 3Y, 3R
David Dunn	49	37F, 4Y, 0R

off three times in the 2001–02 Premiership

BOLTON WANDERERS

ADDRESS

Reebok Stadium, Burnden Way,
Lostock, Bolton BL6 6JW

CONTACT NUMBERS

Telephone: 01204 673 673
Fax: 01204 673 773
Ticket Office: 0871 871 2932
ClubCall: 09068 121 164
Super Store: 01204 673 650
Website: www.bwfc.co.uk

KEY PERSONNEL

President/Honorary Director:
Nat Lofthouse OBE
Chairman: PA Gartside
Vice Chairman: WB Warburton
Directors: G Seymour
G Warburton, E Davies OBE
I Currie, D McBain
Club Secretary: S Marland
Manager: Sam Allardyce

SPONSORS

Reebok

FANZINES

White Love

COLOURS

Home: White shirts, navy shorts
and white stockings.
Away: Navy shirts, navy
shorts and navy stockings.

NICKNAME

The Trotters

HONOURS

Division One Champions: 1996–97
Division Two Champions:
1908–09, 1977–78
Division Three Champions: 1972–73
FA Cup Winners: 1923, 1926,
1929, 1958
Sherpa Van Trophy Winners: 1989

RECORD GOALSCORER

Nat Lofthouse – 255 league goals,
1946–61

BIGGEST WIN

13–0 v Sheffield United –
FA Cup 2nd round, 1 February 1890

BIGGEST DEFEAT

1–9 v Preston – FA Cup 2nd round,
10 December 1887

36 Fredi Bobic took 36 minutes to score the

SEASON REVIEW

As winners of the 2000–01 Division One play-offs, Bolton Wanderers had less time to prepare for the Premiership season than any other side.

They also had the least amount of money to spend on new signings and Sam Allardyce – more than any other top-flight manager – was forced to spend the summer months sifting through the players available on Bosmans in the quest to strengthen his side.

So while Manchester United were splashing out almost £50 million on a couple of world-class stars just 12 miles down the road, Allardyce was completing the signings of Nicky Southall and Rod Wallace on frees, with Japanese striker Akinori Nishizawa and Djibril Diawara joining on loan. The only cash signing of the close season was Henrik Pedersen, the Danish league's top scorer in 2000–01.

> "One pundit said that we were a First Division club with a couple of Premiership players. Needless to say, we've pinned the article up in the dressing-room."
>
> **Sam Allardyce**

With the odds stacked heavily against them, pundits and punters alike expected Bolton to go straight back down without offering much resistance. But those doom-mongers were in for a shock on the opening day of the season.

The Trotters travelled to Filbert Street and thrashed Leicester 5–0 in a stunning performance, with Per Frandsen scoring two free kicks – an art at which Bolton were to prove very adept, getting six over the course of the season; more than any other side in the Premiership.

They followed the Leicester win with another over Middlesbrough at the Reebok Stadium and then registered their second shock result in three games by beating Liverpool on August Bank Holiday Monday. Dean Holdsworth came off the bench – as he did on 22 occasions in total, making him the Premiership's most-used substitute – to score the late winner in that match, putting Wanderers top of the table.

The excellent form continued, with draws at Leeds, Blackburn and Arsenal vindicating Allardyce's backs-to-the-wall policy away from home. But by far their best result in the opening encounters came at Old Trafford when they came from a goal behind to inflict Manchester United's first home defeat of the term.

Striker Michael Ricketts – who netted the winner that afternoon – was beginning to attract attention in the national press following some impressive goalscoring exploits and his reward eventually came in February when he was capped by England in the friendly against Holland.

But in the meantime, the goals around him were drying up and after a 2–1 victory at Ipswich in November, the Trotters embarked upon a run of 12 winless games and consequently slipped from the comfort of mid-table into the relegation zone.

It was time for Allardyce to act again in the transfer market. This time around, he skipped the bargain bin and went for proven quality, bringing in German striker Fredi Bobic and Denmark's Stig Tøfting – both players of vast experience. However, his real coup was attracting midfielder Youri Djorkaeff to Lancashire on a free transfer from Kaiserslautern.

The French World Cup winner scored both goals in a 2–1 win over Charlton and was also influential in the 3–2 victory over Aston Villa a week later. However, Bobic was the hero in the most important win of Bolton's season when he scored a hat-trick in the 4–1 rout of Ipswich.

If the points had gone the other way that afternoon, Allardyce's team would have finished 18th in place of Ipswich. But despite concluding the campaign with three defeats on the bounce, 2001–02 had a happy ending for all at the Reebok Stadium.

fastest hat-trick of the season against Ipswich

BOLTON WANDERERS

DATE	OPPONENT	SCORE	ATT.	BANKS	BARNESS	BERGSSON	BOBIC	CHARLTON	DIAWARA	DJORKAEFF	ESPARTERO	FARRELLY	FRANDSEN	GARDNER	HANSEN	HENDRY
18.08.01	Leicester A	5–0	21,455	–	90□	76	–	90	–	–	–	–	90²	67	90	–
21.08.01	Middlesbro H	1–0	20,747	–	90	90	–	90	–	–	–	–	90	90	90	–
27.08.01	Liverpool H	2–1	27,205	–	90	90	–	90□	s8	–	–	s21	69	90	90	–
08.09.01	Leeds Utd A	0–0	40,153	–	90	90	–	90	–	–	–	90	90	–	83	–
15.09.01	Southampton H	0–1	24,378	–	90	90	–	90	–	–	–	–	51	s11	90	–
19.09.01	Blackburn A	1–1	25,949	–	90	90	–	90	–	–	–	–	–	90	45□	–
22.09.01	Arsenal A	1–1	38,014	–	90	90	–	90	s10	–	–	–	–	30■	–	–
29.09.01	Sunderland H	0–2	24,520	–	90	90	–	90	–	–	–	–	s45□	90	s7	–
13.10.01	Newcastle H	0–4	25,631	–	66	90	–	69	s21	–	–	–	–	90	90	–
20.10.01	Man Utd A	2–1	67,559	–	s7	90	–	90	–	–	–	–	90	90	83	–
27.10.01	Aston Villa A	2–3	33,599	90	s1	90	–	90□	90□	–	–	73	90	90	45	–
03.11.01	Everton H	2–2	27,343	–	–	90□	–	56	s31■	–	–	s23	90¹	90□	–	–
18.11.01	Ipswich A	2–1	22,335	–	–	90¹	–	90	–	–	–	s23	90	90	–	–
24.11.01	Fulham H	0–0	23,848	–	–	90	–	90	–	–	–	s5	85	77	–	–
03.12.01	Tottenham A	2–3	32,971	–	–	90	–	90	–	–	–	88	90	88	s2	–
08.12.01	Derby Co A	0–1	25,712	–	90	90	–	90	–	–	–	s32	58□	90□	–	–
15.12.01	Charlton H	0–0	20,834	–	–	90	–	90	–	–	–	–	90□	90	–	–
23.12.01	Chelsea A	1–5	34,063	–	–	–	–	90	–	–	–	s32	58	90	s13	90
26.12.01	Leeds Utd H	0–3	27,060	–	85	–	–	90	90	–	–	61	90	90	–	–
29.12.01	Leicester H	2–2	23,037	–	53	–	–	90	s37	–	–	62	90	–	–	84□
01.01.02	Liverpool A	1–1	43,710	–	–	–	–	90	90	–	–	s58	90□	–	–	32□
12.01.02	Chelsea H	2–2	23,891	–	s12	90	s33	90	90	–	–	90	71	s19	–	–
19.01.02	Middlesbro A	1–1	26,104	–	s69	90	84□	59	–	–	–	90	21	90	s31¹	–
29.01.02	Man Utd H	0–4	27,350	–	90	90	75	s45	–	–	–	90	–	90	59	–
02.02.02	Newcastle A	2–3	52,094	–	90	90	85	90	–	–	–	90	–	90¹	s2	–
09.02.02	West Ham H	1–0	24,342	–	–	90	86	90	–	–	–	–	–	90¹	s4	–
23.02.02	Southampton A	0–0	31,380	–	–	90	79□	40	–	59	s11	–	–	90	s50	–
02.03.02	Blackburn H	1–1	27,203	–	s11	90	54	–	–	90	–	–	–	90	–	–
05.03.02	Sunderland A	0–1	43,011	–	s45	90	–	–	–	90	s22	–	–	90	–	–
16.03.02	Derby Co H	1–3	25,893	–	–	54	s19	90	–	90	–	–	s27	90¹	–	–
23.03.02	Charlton A	2–1	26,358	–	90	–	77	90	–	90²	–	–	90	90□	–	–
30.03.02	Aston Villa H	3–2*	24,600	–	–	–	90¹	90	–	66	–	–	32	90□	–	–
01.04.02	Everton A	1–3	39,784	–	–	–	45	90	–	59	–	–	s52	90	–	–
06.04.02	Ipswich H	4–1	25,817	–	90	–	82³	90	–	90¹	–	–	s67	44	–	–
20.04.02	Tottenham H	1–1	25,817	–	–	90	57	90	–	90	–	–	90	–	–	–
23.04.02	Fulham A	0–3	18,107	–	90	90	74	90	–	90	s23	–	90	–	–	–
29.04.02	Arsenal H	0–2	27,351	–	90	90	56	90	–	90	–	90	90	–	–	–
11.05.02	West Ham A	1–2	35,546	–	90	90	90	90	–	90¹	–	90□	90	–	–	–

□ Yellow card, ■ Red card, s Substitute, 90² Goals scored
*including own goal

For more information visit our website:

2001–02 PREMIERSHIP APPEARANCES

HOLDSWORTH	JAASKELAINEN	JOHNSON	KONSTANDINIDIS	MARSHALL	N'GOTTY	NOLAN	PEDERSEN	POOLE	RICHARDSON	RICKETTS	SMITH	SOUTHALL	TØFTING	WALLACE	WARHURST	WHITLOW	TOTAL
–	90	–	–	s14	–	90²	s23	–	–	90¹	–	s19	–	–	71□	90□	990
s14	90	–	–	s1	–	89	–	–	–	76¹	–	s18	–	–	72	90□	990
s34¹□	90	–	–	–	–	82	–	–	–	56¹	–	–	–	–	90	90	990
s6	90	–	–	–	–	90	90	–	s7	84	–	–	–	–	–	90□	990
s23	90	–	–	–	–	79	90	–	–	67	–	s39	–	–	90□	90□	990
s45	90□	–	–	–	s7	90	83	–	–	63	–	–	–	s27¹□	90□	90	990
62	90	90□	–	–	–	90	81	–	–	s28¹	–	–	–	s9	80	90	930
90	90	83	–	–	–	45	–	–	–	s29	–	–	–	61	90	90	990
90□	60□	90	–	–	s24	–	–	–	–	s24	66	–	–	–	90□	90□	960
–	90	s35	–	–	90	90¹	–	–	–	90¹	–	–	–	–	55	90	990
s17	–	–	–	–	89	90	–	–	–	90²□	–	–	–	s45	–	–	990
s14	–	–	–	–	90	90□	–	90	–	90¹	–	–	–	76	67	90	987
s21	90	–	–	–	90	90	–	–	–	90¹	–	–	–	69□	67□	90	990
s13□	90	–	–	–	90	90	–	–	–	90	–	–	–	90	90	90	990
s16	90	s2	–	–	90	90□	–	–	–	74¹□	–	–	–	90¹	–	90	990
s20	90	s12	–	–	–	90	–	–	–	90	–	–	–	70	78□	90□	990
s6	90	–	–	–	90	90	–	–	–	90	–	–	–	84	90	90	990
s32	90	58□	–	–	90	90¹	–	–	–	90	–	–	–	–	77	90□	990
90	90	s20	–	–	–	90	s29	–	–	–	–	s5	–	–	70□	90	990
23■	90	–	–	–	90	90¹	s6	–	–	90¹□	–	s28	–	–	19■	–	852
73	90	–	–	–	90	90¹□	s17	–	–	90	–	90□	–	–	90	–	990
–	90	–	–	–	78	90¹	57	–	–	90¹	–	90	–	–	–	–	990
–	90	–	–	–	90	90□	s6	–	–	90	–	90	–	–	–	–	990
s15	90	s31	–	–	–	90	–	–	–	90	–	45	–	–	–	90	990
s5	90□	–	–	–	–	81	s9	–	–	88	–	90¹	–	–	–	90	990
s7	90	–	–	–	90	90	–	–	–	83	–	s45	90	–	45□	90	990
–	90	–	–	–	90	90□	–	–	–	90	–	–	90□	s31	–	90	990
s5	90	–	–	–	90	90	–	–	–	s36	–	79	90	85¹	–	90□	990
s32	90	–	–	–	90	–	–	–	–	58□	–	90	90	90	68	45	990
–	86■	–	–	–	90	–	–	–	–	90	–	s36	71	90	90	63	986
72	90	–	–	–	90	90□	–	–	–	s13	–	s18	–	–	90	–	990
90□	–	–	90□	–	90	90¹	–	90	–	s24	–	–	–	–	90	s58	990
38	–	–	31■	–	90¹	90	–	90	–	s45	–	–	–	s31	90	90	931
s8	90	–	–	–	90	90	–	–	–	s46	–	–	–	90	23	90	990
s33¹	90	–	–	–	90	90	–	–	–	s33	–	90	–	57	–	90□	990
s16	90	–	–	–	90	90	–	–	–	s16	–	67	–	74	–	–	990
–	90	s28	–	–	90	90	–	–	–	s34	–	–	–	62	–	–	990
s45	90	–	60	–	s45	–	–	–	–	45	s30	–	45	–	–	–	990

THE MANAGER

SAM ALLARDYCE

With virtually no money available to spend on players, keeping Bolton Wanderers in the Premiership for more than a year looked like being an almost impossible task.

But Trotters boss Sam Allardyce worked long hours, pulled off one or two clever coups in the transfer market and made sure his side scrapped for every single point to ensure top-flight survival, which they did with some time to spare.

Allardyce served his managerial apprenticeship in the lower divisions with Preston North End, Blackpool and Notts County before being appointed at Bolton – where he spent most of his playing career – in October 1999.

Since then he has transformed the fortunes of the cash-strapped club, taking them from mid-table in Division One to the semi-finals of both domestic cup competitions, the play offs on two occasions and, of course, eventual promotion to the Premiership in 2001. He was rewarded by the board with a 10-year contract with the club.

Those achievements seem even more remarkable when you consider that Allardyce has managed to replace big-money departees like Eidur Gudjohnsen, Mark Fish and Claus Jensen with bargain-basement signings like Michael Ricketts and Bruno N'Gotty, without sacrificing anything in the way of success.

LEAGUE POSITION

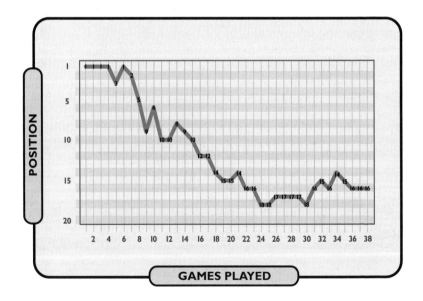

6 Bolton scored more goals from direct free

THE GOALS

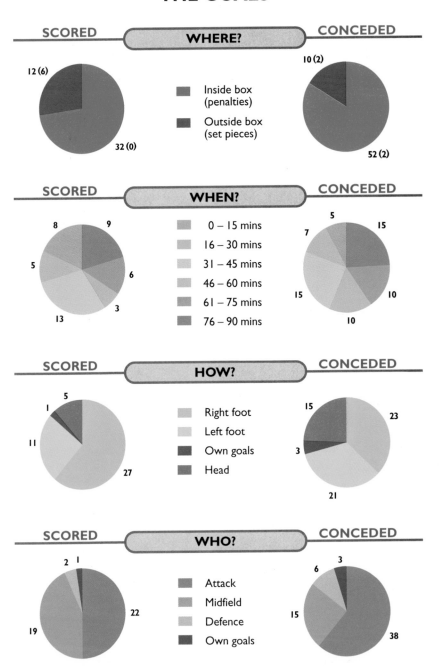

SCORED | **WHERE?** | **CONCEDED**

12 (6)
32 (0)

10 (2)
52 (2)

- Inside box (penalties)
- Outside box (set pieces)

SCORED | **WHEN?** | **CONCEDED**

8 | 9
5
6
3
13

5
7
15
15
10
10

- 0 – 15 mins
- 16 – 30 mins
- 31 – 45 mins
- 46 – 60 mins
- 61 – 75 mins
- 76 – 90 mins

SCORED | **HOW?** | **CONCEDED**

5
1
11
27

15
23
3
21

- Right foot
- Left foot
- Own goals
- Head

SCORED | **WHO?** | **CONCEDED**

2 | 1
22
19

3
6
15
38

- Attack
- Midfield
- Defence
- Own goals

kicks than any other Premiership team

BOLTON WANDERERS

	BARNESS	BERGSSON	BOBIC	CHARLTON	DIAWARA	DJORKAEFF	ESPARTERO	FARRELLY	FRANDSEN	GARDNER	HANSEN	HENDRY	HOLDSWORTH
APPEARANCES													
Start	19	30	14	35	4	12	0	11	25	29	10	3	9
Sub	6	0	2	1	5	0	3	7	4	2	7	0	22
Minutes on pitch	1789	2650	1086	3059	467	994	56	1108	2166	2496	874	206	1055
GOAL ATTEMPTS													
Goals	0	1	4	0	0	4	0	0	3	3	1	0	2
Shots on target	2	9	11	4	0	8	0	1	18	11	5	0	8
Shots off target	4	11	10	2	1	11	0	8	18	23	7	1	20
Shooting accuracy %	33%	45%	52%	67%	0%	42%	0%	11%	50%	32%	42%	0%	29%
Goals/shots %	0%	5%	19%	0%	0%	21%	0%	0%	8%	9%	8%	0%	7%
PASSING													
Goal assists	0	3	2	1	0	1	0	0	5	4	1	1	0
Long passes	214	222	37	500	37	79	5	155	208	163	66	23	26
Short passes	336	480	278	811	115	308	13	400	635	721	175	23	236
PASS COMPLETION													
Own half %	76%	83%	74%	73%	75%	71%	75%	81%	82%	77%	87%	79%	75%
Opposition half %	49%	50%	52%	59%	58%	67%	71%	70%	61%	64%	60%	33%	57%
CROSSING													
Total crosses	32	5	19	117	1	74	1	65	88	138	53	0	17
Cross completion %	25%	40%	21%	28%	0%	36%	0%	18%	30%	22%	23%	0%	29%
DRIBBLING													
Dribbles & runs	21	15	14	84	6	62	3	39	50	143	29	0	32
Dribble completion %	81%	93%	86%	81%	50%	77%	67%	72%	70%	62%	69%	0%	44%
DEFENDING													
Tackles made	44	77	16	86	13	18	5	34	113	76	12	7	11
Tackles won %	73%	88%	88%	62%	69%	67%	60%	68%	68%	67%	67%	86%	55%
Blocks	18	40	0	42	4	1	0	4	7	9	1	4	7
Clearances	104	249	15	139	33	0	0	22	35	23	7	14	20
Interceptions	8	17	0	22	7	0	0	7	11	11	5	2	0
DISCIPLINE													
Fouls conceded	12	41	41	35	6	16	4	5	44	29	4	5	40
Fouls won	18	21	27	38	10	22	0	7	42	31	9	6	38
Offside	0	1	12	1	0	4	0	0	3	7	2	0	20
Yellow cards	1	1	2	2	1	0	0	1	4	4	1	2	4
Red cards	0	0	0	0	1	0	0	0	0	1	0	0	1

GOALKEEPER NAME	START/ (SUB)	TIME ON PITCH	GOALS CONCEDED	MINS/GOALS CONCEDED	SAVES MADE	SAVES/ SHOTS
BANKS	1 (0)	90	3	30	4	57%
HANSEN+	–	–	3	10	2	40%
JAASKELAINEN	34 (0)	3026	48	63	111	70%
POOLE	3 (0)	270	7	39	11	61%
SOUTHALL++	–	–	1	4	1	50%

+ Bo Hansen replaced Jussi Jaaskelainen in goal after the Finn was dismissed against Newcastle (H)
++Nicky Southall replaced Jussi Jaaskelainen in goal after the Finn was dismissed against Derby (H)

For more information visit our website:

PLAYERS' STATISTICS

	JOHNSON	KONSTANDINIDIS	MARSHALL	N'GOTTY	NOLAN	PEDERSEN	RICHARDSON	RICKETTS	SMITH	SOUTHALL	TØFTING	WALLACE	WARHURST	WHITLOW	TOTAL	RANK
	4	3	0	24	34	5	0	26	0	10	6	14	25	28		
	6	0	2	2	1	6	1	11	1	8	0	5	0	1		
	449	181	15	2178	3031	491	7	2462	30	1005	476	1231	1872	2506		
	0	0	0	1	8	0	0	12	0	1	0	3	0	0	44*	13th
	3	0	0	2	22	3	0	35	0	4	1	12	5	2	166	=13th
	11	0	0	1	26	4	0	37	0	4	4	8	4	1	216	15th
	21%	0%	0%	67%	46%	43%	0%	49%	0%	50%	20%	60%	56%	67%	43%	13th
	0%	0%	0%	33%	17%	0%	0%	17%	0%	13%	0%	15%	0%	0%	11%	9th
	0	0	0	0	1	1	0	2	0	1	0	2	1	2	28	14th
	30	8	1	268	259	11	1	69	7	134	55	40	288	197	3558	20th
	112	24	4	544	721	99	2	477	3	234	159	298	684	457	8407	20th
	79%	68%	75%	74%	76%	85%	0%	74%	50%	78%	77%	85%	82%	78%	78%	20th
	65%	31%	0%	56%	64%	70%	67%	57%	38%	51%	58%	68%	65%	59%	58%	20th
	21	0	0	39	54	13	0	55	0	49	12	15	19	7	894	12th
	19%	0%	0%	33%	9%	38%	0%	9%	0%	29%	25%	7%	11%	43%	24%	11th
	45	1	1	19	104	17	0	100	1	26	8	25	25	20	896	18th
	71%	100%	100%	89%	56%	71%	0%	47%	100%	69%	50%	60%	84%	100%	67%	16th
	25	5	0	46	105	3	1	23	0	36	17	16	63	54	908	20th
	76%	80%	0%	80%	74%	100%	100%	61%	0%	69%	59%	69%	76%	83%	73%	19th
	0	3	0	14	15	0	0	6	2	8	3	0	16	27	231	6th
	3	19	2	131	36	4	0	19	1	29	3	1	62	240	1290	18th
	6	0	0	22	14	0	0	3	0	4	2	2	18	7	169	6th
	10	8	0	25	47	5	0	52	0	18	13	18	61	46	588	8th
	12	1	0	22	38	14	2	28	1	11	3	27	28	21	488	18th
	0	0	0	0	3	2	0	63	0	0	0	17	0	1	137	11th
	2	1	0	0	5	0	0	4	0	1	1	2	8	9	58	11th
	0	1	0	0	0	0	0	0	0	0	0	0	1	0	7	=1st

*Including one own goal

CROSSES CAUGHT	CROSSES PUNCHED	CROSSES DROPPED	CATCH SUCCESS	THROWS/ SHORT KICKS	% COMPLETION	LONG KICKS	% COMPLETION
1	2	0	100%	0	0%	26	27%
0	1	0	0%	0	0%	8	50%
69	16	10	87%	44	98%	776	42%
6	3	0	100%	4	100%	70	44%
0	0	0	0%	0	0%	0	0%

PLAYER OF THE SEASON

PLAYER	INDEX SCORE
GUDNI BERGSSON	696
Jussi Jaaskelainen	673
Michael Ricketts	663
Per Frandsen	656
Kevin Nolan	547
Mike Whitlow	495
Simon Charlton	494
Ricardo Gardner	472
Bruno N`Gotty	465
Anthony Barness	441

Bolton's Icelandic defender Gudni Bergsson was all set to hang up his boots to embark on a career as a lawyer in his homeland. But Sam Allardyce, his manager, talked Bergsson into giving the English big time one more crack – and it was just as well that he did.

Bergsson – who spent a successful spell with Tottenham Hotspur in the early nineties – enjoyed a fantastic campaign in the heart of the Trotters' backline, making 249 clearances, the most in the squad.

And as captain, the veteran set a shining example and won possession with 88% of the tackles he attempted. In addition, he scored a vital goal in the 2–1 win over Ipswich in November and was an important presence in both penalty areas.

According to the stats, Bergsson's nearest challenger in Bolton's player of the year chart was goalkeeper Jussi Jaaskelainen, who attracted attention from several of Europe's top clubs following some remarkable displays – not least the one he produced in the 2–1 victory at Manchester United.

In fact, United were one of the sides vying for his signature if reports were to be believed and it's easy to see why – Jaaskelainen pulled off 111 saves in the season, only five other Premiership 'keepers managed more.

His Index score may even have been higher but for the two red cards he received in the matches against Newcastle United and Derby County at the Reebok Stadium.

At the other end of the pitch, Michael Ricketts was also a star, netting 12 goals from 72 shots and earning an England cap in the process. Danish midfielder Per Frandsen helped out on the scoring front too, providing the most goal assists at the club – five in total.

Other notable protagonists in the list were eight-goal midfielder Kevin Nolan, who hit a brace on his Premiership debut in the 5–0 romp at Leicester, and the club's player of the year Simon Charlton, who featured in all but two of the Trotters' matches in 2001–02.

FIVE OF THE BEST

Many of the players that helped Bolton win promotion to the Premiership via the play-offs kept their first-team places in 2001–02 and played vital parts in the Trotters' season. The new arrivals also did their fair share of work, particularly on the goalscoring front, but one man was always going to top the club's scoring chart following his blistering start to the campaign.

TOP GOALSCORERS

	GOALS	GOALS/SHOTS
MICHAEL RICKETTS	12	17%
Kevin Nolan	8	17%
Youri Djorkaeff	4	21%
Fredi Bobic	4	19%
Rod Wallace	3	15%

Michael Ricketts' place as Bolton's top marksman was never really in doubt after he scored 10 times in the first 15 games of the Premiership season. And even though he netted just twice in the next 23 matches, Ricketts still finished the season four goals ahead of midfielder Kevin Nolan, his nearest challenger. Star imports Youri Djorkaeff and Fredi Bobic both hit four following their late arrivals at the Reebok.

Left back Simon Charlton, Bolton's most-used player in the 2001–02 Premiership, was also the team's top passer. The former Birmingham City man completed 830 deliveries and was rewarded for his consistency when he won the club's player of the year award in May. Paul Warhurst was his nearest challenger in the squad, finding a team-mate with 73% of his passes. His midfield colleagues Kevin Nolan and Per Frandsen also saw plenty of the ball.

TOP PASSERS

	SUCC PASSES	COMPLETION
SIMON CHARLTON	830	63%
Paul Warhurst	712	73%
Kevin Nolan	671	68%
Ricardo Gardner	604	68%
Per Frandsen	578	69%

TOP TACKLERS

	WON	SUCCESS
KEVIN NOLAN	78	74%
Per Frandsen	77	68%
Gudni Bergsson	68	88%
Simon Charlton	53	62%
Ricardo Gardner	51	67%

The emergence of Kevin Nolan as a goalscoring midfielder of Premiership class was a major boost to Bolton's season. But the homegrown talent also put in plenty of hard graft and ended the campaign with more successful tackles to his name than any other Trotter, some 78 in all. It was a close run thing as Danish star Per Frandsen managed 77 and skipper Gudni Bergsson wasn't too far behind either, with 68.

Although they were by no means a dirty side, Bolton players finished the season having been shown seven red cards in total – the joint-highest tally. Two of those came in controversial circumstances against Leicester when Paul Warhurst and Dean Holdsworth were dismissed. Both of those players were in Opta's bad boy top five and they were joined by gritty defender Mike Whitlow who was booked nine times.

DISCIPLINE

	POINTS	FOULS & CARDS
PAUL WARHURST	91	61F, 8Y, 1R
Mike Whitlow	73	46F, 9Y, 0R
Michael Ricketts	64	52F, 4Y, 0R
Kevin Nolan	62	47F, 5Y, 0R
Dean Holdsworth	58	40F, 4Y, 1R

CHARLTON ATHLETIC

ADDRESS

The Valley, Floyd Road,
Charlton, London SE7 8BL

CONTACT NUMBERS

Telephone: 020 8333 4000
Fax: 020 8333 4001
Box Office: 020 8333 4010
Club Shop: 020 8333 4035
e-mail: info@cafc.co.uk
Website: www.cafc.co.uk

KEY PERSONNEL

Chairman: M Simons
Deputy Chairman: R Murray
Chief Executive: P Varney
Directors: R Alwen, D G Bone,
N Capelin, R Collins, G Franklin
D Hughes, M Stevens
D Sumners, D Ufton
D White, R Whitehand
Club Secretary: C Parkes
Manager: Alan Curbishley

SPONSORS

Redbus

FANZINES

Goodbye Horse

COLOURS

Home: Red shirts, white
shorts and red stockings
Away: White shirts, red shorts
and white stockings

NICKNAME

The Addicks

HONOURS

Division One Champions: 1999–2000
Division Three (South) Champions:
1928–29, 1934–35
FA Cup Winners: 1947

RECORD GOALSCORER

Stuart Leary – 153 league goals,
1953–62

BIGGEST WIN

8–1 v Middlesbrough – Division One,
12 September 1953

BIGGEST DEFEAT

1–11 v Aston Villa – Division Two,
14 November 1959

8 Charlton had more shots cleared off

SEASON REVIEW

Following their relatively successful 2000–01 Premiership campaign, Charlton were under pressure to prove that they were no flash in the pan during the 2001–02 season.

Alan Curbishley had a respectable kitty to delve into during the close season, although £2m was immediately set aside to make permanent the transfer of on-loan striker Shaun Bartlett from FC Zurich. Another addition to the front line was Wimbledon's Jason Euell, who made the short journey east for a club record fee of £4.75m, while at the back Curbishley snapped up Spurs' Luke Young – a snip at just £3m.

The Charlton fans' optimistic bubble was immediately burst by an opening day defeat to Everton, as their team succumbed to a 2–1 loss despite taking the lead through Finnish striker Jonatan Johansson.

Thankfully, the first win of the campaign was just around the corner. A visit to Portman Road provided the travelling support with a 1–0 success, although they had to wait until Kevin Lisbie netted on 85 minutes to earn it.

Unfortunately, all thoughts of the previous season's triumphant return to the top flight were soon banished by a poor run of results leading into November. An eight-game period containing just one victory – 2–0 at home to Leicester – left the Addicks just two places outside the bottom three.

So if ever a result was needed to boost morale in the camp it was on 4 November. A trip to Highbury may not seem like the most appealing of prospects on a chilly Sunday afternoon, but Charlton produced their performance of the season to make light work of the out-of-sorts Gunners and come away with a fine 4–2 win.

The entertainment continued into the next Charlton match, even if the result was not quite as pleasing for Curbishley and his men. West Ham were the visitors to the Valley and in one of the Premiership's most enjoyable games of the season, the lead changed hands three times, before Johansson's second strike of the match in the 90th minute earned the Addicks a point in a thrilling 4–4 draw.

Performances against London teams were one of Charlton's strong suits during 2001–02. Of the 10 games played by each capital club, the Addicks won the second-highest number behind Arsenal, securing 18 points from a possible total of 30.

Indeed, without such an impressive record against their neighbours, Charlton may have found themselves in severe trouble, given the ordinary nature of their post-Christmas form. The team seemed incapable of stringing a run of wins together – victories against Everton and Ipswich either side of the New Year were the only successive triumphs the team enjoyed for the remainder of the campaign.

To make matters worse, January also saw the Addicks' second cup defeat of the season to lower-league opposition. Walsall put paid to Charlton's FA Cup hopes with a 2–1 win at the Valley after Watford had dumped Curbishley's side out of the Worthington Cup two months earlier.

Holes began to appear in the previously respectable defence as the season wore on, with the loan capture of Portuguese international Jorge Costa unable to prevent a disappointing record of 15 goals conceded in the club's final eight matches.

The season ended on a respectable note, with a goalless draw at Old Trafford. The point was enough to see the Addicks finish in 14th – not the result they would have hoped for, but on such limited resources certainly no disgrace.

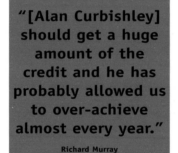

> "[Alan Curbishley] should get a huge amount of the credit and he has probably allowed us to over-achieve almost every year."
>
> **Richard Murray**

CHARLTON ATHLETIC

DATE	OPPONENT	SCORE	ATT.	BARTLETT	BART-WILLIAMS	BROWN	COSTA	EUELL	FISH	FORTUNE	JENSEN	JOHANSSON	KIELY	KISHISHEV
18.08.01	Everton H	1-2	20,451	72	–	90	–	90	90	s45	–	90¹	90	–
25.08.01	Ipswich A	1-0	22,804	–	–	s55	–	90□	90	–	–	78	90	–
09.09.01	Fulham H	1-1*	20,451	81□	–	90□	–	90	90	–	–	–	90	–
16.09.01	Leeds Utd H	0-2	20,451	90□	–	90	–	66	90	–	–	–	90	–
22.09.01	Sunderland A	2-2*	46,825	90	–	90¹	–	s14	90□	–	–	76□	90	–
29.09.01	Leicester H	2-0	20,451	67¹	–	24■	–	s23	90	–	–	90¹	90	–
13.10.01	Middlesbro H	0-0	20,451	79	–	–	–	s11	90	–	s30	90	90	–
20.10.01	Derby A	1-1	30,221	70	–	–	–	s20¹	90	–	86	90	90	–
24.10.01	Aston Villa A	0-1	27,701	45	–	90	–	s45	90	–	70	90	90	–
27.10.01	Liverpool H	0-2	22,887	s29	–	90	–	90	90	–	85	90	90	–
04.11.01	Arsenal A	4-2*	38,010	s9	–	90¹	–	90¹	90	–	81¹	79	90	–
19.11.01	West Ham H	4-4	23,198	s5	–	90	–	90²□	90	–	90	90²	90	–
24.11.01	Southampton A	0-1	31,198	90	–	90□	–	–	–	–	90	90	90	–
01.12.01	Newcastle H	1-1	24,151	39	–	26	–	–	90	s64	90	90	90	–
05.12.01	Chelsea A	1-0	33,504	–	–	–	s9	90	81□	90	90	65	90	–
08.12.01	Tottenham H	3-1	25,125	–	s8	–	90	82	90	90	88	s8	90□	–
15.12.01	Bolton W A	0-0	20,834	–	–	–	90	90	90	90□	90	s22	90	–
22.12.01	Blackburn H	0-2	25,857	–	s8	–	90	90	90□	65	90	s25	90	–
26.12.01	Fulham A	0-0	17,900	–	s11	–	s45	90	45	90	90	–	90	–
29.12.01	Everton A	3-0	31,131	–	s4	–	90□	90¹	90	–	86	–	90	–
01.01.02	Ipswich H	3-2	25,893	s4	s8	–	90	90¹	90	–	89	s1	90	–
12.01.02	Blackburn A	1-4	23,365	–	s14	–	90□	90¹	90	76	90	s14	90	–
21.01.02	Aston Villa H	1-2	25,681	–	–	–	90□	90	90	s1	69	90	90	–
29.01.02	Derby Co H	1-0	25,387	–	90¹	–	90	84	–	90	–	76	90	s6
03.02.02	Middlesbro A	0-0	24,189	–	90	–	90□	83	35	90	–	74	90	–
10.02.02	Man Utd H	0-2	26,475	–	90	–	90	82	90	–	–	s8	90	–
24.02.02	Leeds Utd A	0-0	39,374	–	90□	–	90	90	–	90	–	–	90	s5
02.03.02	Chelsea H	2-1	26,354	–	90	s1	90	90²	–	90	–	–	90	s1
09.03.02	Leicester A	1-1	18,562	–	90	s9□	90□	90¹	–	90	–	–	90	–
18.03.02	Tottenham A	1-0	29,602	–	90	–	90	90	–	90	–	–	90	–
23.03.02	Bolton W H	1-2	26,358	–	45	–	90	90□	–	s2	–	s45¹	90	–
30.03.02	Liverpool A	0-2	44,094	–	90□	–	90	90	–	–	–	s14	90	–
01.04.02	Arsenal H	0-3	26,339	–	–	–	90□	90	–	–	–	90	90	–
06.04.02	West Ham A	0-2	32,389	–	–	–	90□	90	–	90□	–	90	90□	–
13.04.02	Southampton H	1-1	26,557	–	–	–	90	90	–	90	–	90	90	–
20.04.02	Newcastle A	0-3	51,360	–	–	–	90□	89	–	s1	–	90	90	–
27.04.02	Sunderland H	2-2	26,614	–	–	–	90□	90¹	–	–	–	90	90	–
11.05.02	Man Utd A	0-0	67,571	–	90	–	90	90	–	–	s14	s8	90	–

□ Yellow card, ■ Red card, s Substitute, 90² Goals scored

*including own goal

2001–02 PREMIERSHIP APPEARANCES

KINSELLA	KONCHESKY	LISBIE	MACDONALD	PARKER	PEACOCK	POWELL	ROBINSON	RUFUS	SALAKO	STUART	SVENSSON	TODD	YOUNG	TOTAL
–	–	s18	–	45	s45	90	–	–	45	90	–	–	90	990
–	s12	s29¹	–	90□	90	90□	–	35□	61	90□	–	–	90□	990
–	s19	45	–	71	–	90	s45	–	s9	90	–	90	90	990
s24	90	s12	–	90	–	90	90	–	–	37■	–	–	78■	937
90	90y	–	–	84	–	90	s44	–	–	46	–	s6	90	990
89	90	–	–	90	–	45	s1	–	–	90	–	s45□	90	924
90	90	–	–	90□	–	90	60	–	–	–	–	90□	90	990
90	90	–	–	90	s4	90	s31	–	–	–	–	90	59	990
90	90	–	–	90	s5	85	s20	–	–	–	–	–	90	990
90	61	–	–	s5	–	90	90	–	–	–	–	–	90	990
90	90□	–	–	68□	s22	90	s11	–	–	–	–	–	90	990
90	90	–	–	85	–	90	s5	–	–	–	–	–	85	990
71	65	–	s7	s19	–	90	s25	–	–	83	–	–	90	990
–	–	s51	s9¹	90□	–	90	90	–	–	81	–	–	90	990
–	s87	s25¹	–	90	–	90	3	–	–	90	–	–	90	990
–	s2	90²□	–	90	–	90	–	–	–	82¹	–	–	90□	990
–	s1	90	–	68	–	89	–	–	–	90□	–	–	90	990
–	s8	90	–	82□	–	82	–	–	–	90	–	–	90	990
–	75	90	–	79□	–	90	s15	–	–	90	–	–	90	990
–	s14¹	90□	–	90	–	90	90	–	–	76¹	–	–	90□	990
–	90	86	–	82¹	–	90	90¹□	–	–	–	–	–	90□	990
–	–	76	–	64■	–	90	90	–	–	82	s8	–	–	964
–	s61	s21	–	89	–	90	90	–	–	90¹	–	–	29	990
–	90	s14	–	77	–	90	90	–	–	90□	s13	–	–	990
–	s55	s16	–	90	–	90	90□	–	–	90	s7	–	–	990
–	s8	82	–	90	–	90	90	–	–	73	s17	–	90	990
s10	90□	–	–	80	–	90	–	–	–	90	85□	–	90	990
–	89□	–	–	90	–	90□	–	–	–	90	89	–	90	990
–	81	–	–	90	–	90□	–	–	–	90	90	–	90	990
–	s7	–	–	83	–	89¹	s1	90	–	90	90	–	90	990
–	90	–	–	90	–	88	s45	90	–	90	90	–	45	990
s32	70	–	–	58□	–	90	s20	90	–	90	76	–	90	990
90	–	s24	–	90	–	90	66□	90	–	90	–	–	90	990
90□	90	–	–	90	–	–	–	90	–	90	–	–	90	990
84	s6	s23	–	67□	–	90	90□	90¹	–	90	–	–	–	990
90	90	s17	–	73□	–	–	90	90	–	90	–	–	90	990
67□	45	s23¹	–	90	–	s45	74	90	–	90	s16	–	90	990
–	82	89	–	90	–	90	–	90	–	76	s1	–	90	990

THE MANAGER

ALAN CURBISHLEY

After taking over from Lennie Lawrence alongside Steve Gritt in 1991, Alan Curbishley has become Charlton's longest-serving manager since the end of Jimmy Seed's tenure in 1956. With the management merry-go-round more active than ever these days, it is testament to the loyalty, ability and the character of the native Londoner that he has retained his post for so long.

Curbishley is invariably linked with other posts when a high-profile job becomes available, such as West Ham in the summer of 2001 and the Aston Villa vacancy upon the departure of John Gregory. But as yet he has remained faithful to the only club he has ever managed.

Curbishley's association with Charlton began as a player – he had two spells at the club, scoring six times from midfield in 84 appearances. He also turned out for Aston Villa, Brighton, Birmingham City and West Ham, which is why he is continually linked with a return to Upton Park.

He will need to use his considerable managerial skills to keep Charlton in the top flight for another season with limited transfer funds, although his capture of Gary Rowett from relegated Leicester suggests Curbishley understands which areas of the side need shoring up.

LEAGUE POSITION

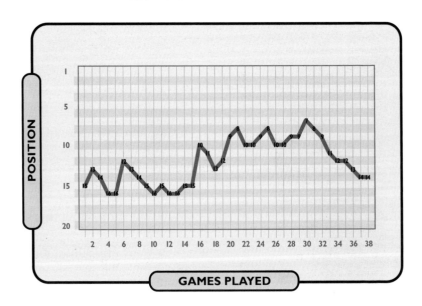

POSITION

GAMES PLAYED

76% Charlton fired 76% of their free kicks

THE GOALS

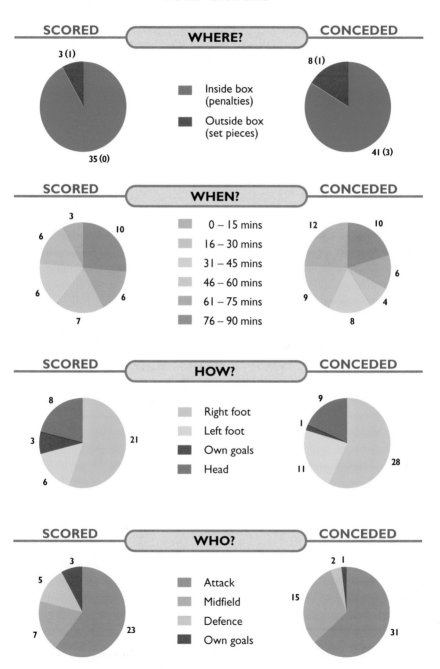

SCORED | WHERE? | CONCEDED

3 (1)

35 (0)

8 (1)

41 (3)

Inside box (penalties)

Outside box (set pieces)

SCORED | WHEN? | CONCEDED

3

6

6

7

10

6

0 – 15 mins

16 – 30 mins

31 – 45 mins

46 – 60 mins

61 – 75 mins

76 – 90 mins

12

9

8

10

4

6

SCORED | HOW? | CONCEDED

8

3

6

21

Right foot

Left foot

Own goals

Head

9

1

11

28

SCORED | WHO? | CONCEDED

3

5

7

23

Attack

Midfield

Defence

Own goals

2 1

15

31

on target – the Premiership's best ratio

CHARLTON ATHLETIC

	BARTLETT	BART-WILLIAMS	BROWN	COSTA	EUELL	FISH	FORTUNE	JENSEN	JOHANSSON	KINSELLA	KISHISHEV
APPEARANCES											
Start	10	10	11	22	31	25	14	16	21	14	0
Sub	4	6	3	2	5	0	5	2	9	3	3
Minutes on pitch	770	908	925	2034	2849	2141	1334	1418	1943	1277	12
GOAL ATTEMPTS											
Goals	1	1	2	0	11	0	0	1	5	0	0
Shots on target	4	4	3	3	30	5	1	12	21	5	0
Shots off target	8	8	3	4	33	5	3	11	19	8	1
Shooting accuracy %	33%	33%	50%	43%	48%	50%	25%	52%	53%	38%	0%
Goals/shots %	8%	8%	33%	0%	17%	0%	0%	4%	13%	0%	0%
PASSING											
Goal assists	0	2	0	0	3	2	0	1	3	0	0
Long passes	24	127	94	154	144	194	115	115	43	271	3
Short passes	203	315	189	412	742	488	225	589	398	519	6
PASS COMPLETION											
Own half %	76%	81%	84%	80%	76%	83%	72%	88%	85%	88%	100%
Opposition half %	60%	75%	55%	51%	60%	60%	46%	82%	66%	74%	40%
CROSSING											
Total crosses	11	73	3	2	48	3	6	101	63	60	0
Cross completion %	27%	19%	0%	0%	13%	0%	17%	32%	21%	28%	0%
DRIBBLING											
Dribbles & runs	9	5	2	7	92	16	1	48	48	7	0
Dribble completion %	89%	60%	100%	100%	49%	100%	100%	73%	50%	86%	0%
DEFENDING											
Tackles made	15	32	33	87	89	68	40	21	35	43	1
Tackles won %	73%	75%	73%	68%	76%	72%	85%	71%	86%	70%	100%
Blocks	7	5	9	21	9	39	12	3	2	8	0
Clearances	22	34	140	190	36	268	124	12	8	21	0
Interceptions	2	6	5	11	6	12	9	2	1	6	0
DISCIPLINE											
Fouls conceded	25	12	21	49	64	30	26	8	41	9	0
Fouls won	5	12	22	32	57	25	17	21	24	12	1
Offside	3	0	0	1	54	0	2	5	34	0	0
Yellow cards	2	2	3	9	3	3	2	0	1	2	0
Red cards	0	0	1	0	0	0	0	0	0	0	0

GOALKEEPER NAME	START/ (SUB)	TIME ON PITCH	GOALS CONCEDED	MINS/GOALS CONCEDED	SAVES MADE	SAVES/ SHOTS
KIELY	38 (0)	3420	49	70	140	74%

For more information visit our website:

PLAYERS' STATISTICS

	KONCHESKY	LISBIE	MACDONALD	PARKER	PEACOCK	POWELL	ROBINSON	RUFUS	SALAKO	STUART	SVENSSON	TODD	YOUNG	TOTAL	RANK
	22	10	0	36	1	35	16	10	2	31	6	3	34		
	12	12	2	2	4	1	12	0	1	0	6	2	0		
	2108	1101	16	2989	166	3133	1546	845	115	2616	582	321	2906		
	1	5	1	1	0	1	1	1	0	3	0	0	0	38*	15th
	5	16	1	16	0	2	5	2	2	16	5	0	3	161	=15th
	12	13	0	28	0	2	10	5	1	17	4	0	10	205	16th
	29%	55%	100%	36%	0%	50%	33%	29%	67%	48%	56%	0%	23%	44%	10th
	6%	17%	100%	2%	0%	25%	7%	14%	0%	9%	0%	0%	0%	10%	16th
	2	1	0	2	0	1	1	0	0	1	1	0	1	22	=16th
	282	37	0	295	10	348	102	68	12	269	37	32	315	3566	19th
	678	309	2	1085	56	835	471	179	38	964	213	83	749	9795	16th
	74%	79%	0%	79%	76%	80%	72%	80%	81%	84%	85%	82%	74%	80%	17th
	64%	66%	100%	68%	76%	65%	67%	49%	59%	74%	56%	71%	58%	65%	16th
	157	27	2	31	4	111	58	3	6	75	9	1	92	946	10th
	20%	15%	0%	39%	25%	32%	16%	33%	33%	13%	11%	0%	17%	22%	18th
	91	79	1	111	3	107	58	6	4	95	3	2	120	919	15th
	77%	65%	0%	80%	67%	71%	66%	100%	75%	76%	67%	100%	49%	68%	13th
	60	23	0	180	4	54	40	30	5	90	19	11	116	1098	5th
	77%	61%	0%	74%	25%	78%	80%	73%	80%	63%	58%	82%	73%	73%	16th
	12	1	0	31	1	21	3	10	0	2	1	6	23	227	=7th
	84	6	0	36	4	125	18	89	2	45	4	25	135	1482	8th
	9	5	0	19	0	10	6	6	0	6	0	4	10	135	19th
	27	23	1	59	5	26	29	16	1	29	22	8	26	559	10th
	17	28	0	68	3	32	25	15	1	33	10	3	22	492	17th
	1	19	0	2	0	2	12	0	0	0	7	0	0	142	6th
	4	2	0	9	0	3	4	1	0	3	1	2	5	63	8th
	0	0	0	1	0	0	0	0	0	1	0	0	0	3	=9th

*Including three own goals

CROSSES CAUGHT	CROSSES PUNCHED	CROSSES DROPPED	CATCH SUCCESS	THROWS/ SHORT KICKS	% COMPLETION	LONG KICKS	% COMPLETION
57	28	4	93%	46	93%	787	46%

PLAYER OF THE SEASON

PLAYER	INDEX SCORE
MARK FISH	795
Dean Kiely	785
Jason Euell	711
Jonatan Johansson	612
Graham Stuart	586
Scott Parker	580
Jorge Costa	575
Luke Young	532
Paul Konchesky	503
Chris Powell	489

South African defender Mark Fish came out on top for Charlton in the overall Opta Index for 2001–02. His main contribution to the team was his excellent tally of 268 clearances during the season to get the danger away from the Charlton box.

Frequently he could be found up in attack looking to capitalise from a set-piece and twice Fish provided a colleague with a goal assist, proving his usefulness in all areas of the pitch.

He also made 12 vital interceptions during the campaign and with 39 blocks to his name, he put himself in the way of more opponents than any of his colleagues. It was surely no coincidence that when injury forced Fish to miss the final 12 games of the season Charlton's form dipped considerably and the team dropped from ninth to 14th position.

The situation would have been far worse were it not for the impressive goalkeeping of Dean Kiely, whose notable outings between the sticks earned him a call-up to the Ireland squad for the World Cup,

despite conceding 15 goals in the final eight Premiership matches of the season. His 74% saves-to-shots ratio during the campaign was one of the best among the league's regular starting 'keepers.

Jason Euell had a fine debut season for the Addicks, racking up an average of 711 Opta Index points. His 11 goals made him easily the club's top scorer – Jonatan Johansson and Kevin Lisbie were tied far behind on five apiece.

The former Wimbledon man also turned provider with three goal assists – the joint-highest tally at the club along with Johansson, who was the next player in Charlton's top 10. The Finn may not have emulated his success of 2000–01, but he kept opposing 'keepers busy nonetheless, with 40 shots attempted.

Scott Parker finally nailed down a first-team place at Charlton and was rewarded by finishing as Opta's sixth-highest ranked Addick. The midfielder made more passes and tackles than any team-mate, forcing his way into the England under-21 squad.

FIVE OF THE BEST

Following their fine showing in 2000–01, Charlton suffered something of a comedown with a disappointing follow-up campaign in comparison. Alan Curbishley had a number of injuries to contend with, such as the continuing lack of fitness of the previous season's player of the year Mark Kinsella, but he will know that the Addicks could have done better.

TOP GOALSCORERS

	GOALS	GOALS/SHOTS
JASON EUELL	11	17%
Kevin Lisbie	5	17%
Jonatan Johansson	5	13%
Graham Stuart	3	9%
Steve Brown	2	33%

For the most part Charlton disappointed in attack, but Jason Euell helped himself to 11 of the team's 38 goals in his first season at the Valley. The former Wimbledon man put away 17% of his attempts on goal – youngster Kevin Lisbie showed great promise by converting the same proportion of his chances. Last season's hero, Jonatan Johansson, was also above the Premiership average with a 13% ratio.

Scott Parker will be hoping to make the step up from the England under-21 side to the full squad during the Euro 2004 qualifiers and a fine haul of 997 successful passes suggested the leap cannot come too soon for the youngster. His completion rate was eclipsed by that of team-mate Graham Stuart, however, who was the most clinical passer of the ball among the Addicks' regular starters.

TOP PASSERS

	SUCC PASSES	COMPLETION
SCOTT PARKER	997	72%
Graham Stuart	948	77%
Chris Powell	827	70%
Luke Young	677	64%
Paul Konchesky	648	68%

TOP TACKLERS

	WON	SUCCESS
SCOTT PARKER	133	74%
Luke Young	85	73%
Jason Euell	68	76%
Jorge Costa	59	68%
Graham Stuart	57	63%

The key to making the most passes is having the most time on the ball and Scott Parker did his utmost to enjoy as much possession as possible. Only two Premiership players won more tackles than Parker during 2001–02 as he once again showed his promise at the tender age of 21. New recruit Luke Young was a full 48 challenges behind, but acquitted himself well nonetheless.

Throwing himself into challenges earned Scott Parker a little more attention from match officials than he would have liked. His nine bookings and a red card against Blackburn hinted at a level of aggression within him that he would do well to curb, although summer-signing Jason Euell in fact committed more fouls overall. Nine yellow cards for Jorge Costa in just 24 appearances suggested some difficulty adapting to the English game.

DISCIPLINE

	POINTS	FOULS & CARDS
SCOTT PARKER	92	59F, 9Y, 1R
Jorge Costa	76	49F, 9Y, 0R
Jason Euell	73	64F, 3Y, 0R
Graham Stuart	44	29F, 3Y, 1R
Jonatan Johansson	44	41F, 1Y, 0R

any other Premiership goalkeeper

CHELSEA

ADDRESS

Stamford Bridge, Fulham Road,
London SW6 1HS

CONTACT NUMBERS

Telephone: 020 7385 5545
Fax: 020 7381 4831
Ticket Office: 020 7915 2951
Credit Card Booking Service:
020 7386 7799
ClubCall: 09068 121 159
Chelsea Megastore: 020 7565 1490
Website: www.chelseafc.com

KEY PERSONNEL

Chairman: K W Bates
Managing Director: T Birch
Directors: Ms Y S Todd, M Russell
Assistant Club Secretary: C Lait
Head Coach: Claudio Ranieri

SPONSORS

Emirates Airlines

FANZINES

The Chelsea Independent,
Cockney Rebel,
Curious Blue,
Matthew Harding's Blue & White Army

COLOURS

Home: Royal blue shirts with
white trim, royal blue shorts
with white trim and white stockings
Away: White shirts with royal blue trim,
white shorts with royal blue trim and
royal blue stockings with white trim

NICKNAME

The Blues

HONOURS

League Champions: 1954–55
Division Two Champions:
1983–84, 1988–89
FA Cup Winners: 1970, 1997, 2000
League Cup Winners: 1965, 1998
European Cup Winners' Cup Winners:
1971, 1998
UEFA Super Cup Winners: 1998

RECORD GOALSCORER

Bobby Tambling –
164 league goals, 1958–70

BIGGEST WIN

13–0 v Jeunesse Hautcharage – European
Cup Winners' Cup, 1st round 2nd leg, 29
September 1971

BIGGEST DEFEAT

1–8 v Wolverhampton Wanderers –
Division One, 26 September 1953

0 Chelsea were the only side not to win

SEASON REVIEW

After collecting five trophies in two-and-a-half years under Gianluca Vialli, Chelsea found silverware more elusive in the first 18 months of his replacement Claudio Ranieri's reign.

In his first full campaign as manager, Ranieri set about rebuilding the squad, offloading terrace heroes Gustavo Poyet and Dennis Wise to Tottenham and Leicester respectively, while Frank Leboeuf returned to France with Marseille. Ranieri replaced experience with youth, recruiting William Gallas, Boudewijn Zenden and Frank Lampard among others.

As the outcome suggests, 2001–02 was a season of transition for the west London club. A sixth-placed finish in the Premiership was perhaps worse than anticipated, while defeat in the FA Cup final and the Worthington Cup semi-final dashed Chelsea hopes of adding to the trophy cabinet.

Hapoel Tel Aviv surprisingly dumped the Londoners out of the UEFA Cup, after a handful of high-profile Blues had dropped out of the trip due to the ongoing crisis in the Middle East. Two very late goals for the Israeli side in October left Ranieri's men with a deficit they could not overturn at Stamford Bridge.

Chelsea's Premiership campaign stuttered under the weight of inconsistency – their results from mid-November to mid-December perhaps best illustrated this point. The Blues comprehensively outplayed Manchester United in a 3–0 victory at Old Trafford on 1 December and then convincingly beat Liverpool 4–0. But in four matches either side of those encounters Chelsea could not beat Everton, Blackburn, Charlton or Sunderland.

The focus switched to cup competition in January, with the Blues playing host to former boss Glenn Hoddle's Tottenham in

> **"We have not reached the objectives I set. I think we have improved, but we will have to do better next season."**
>
> **Claudio Ranieri**

the Worthington Cup semi final. A 2–1 home victory for the Pensioners set up an exciting second leg, but it was Spurs' fans who were toasting their heroes, the north London outfit remarkably gaining their first win in 12 years against Chelsea - and 5–1 at that. But Chelsea avenged that defeat with a 4–0 demolition of Spurs in the FA Cup quarter final six weeks on and then beat them by the same scoreline in the league three days later.

Coming into late March, a last-gasp winner from Vladimir Smicer at Anfield realistically ended the Blues' slim chances of winning the league.

Three weeks later though, John Terry's solitary strike was enough to see off next-door neighbours Fulham in the FA Cup semi final and set up a meeting with Arsenal in Cardiff.

Back in the league, Manchester United then emulated Liverpool by gaining revenge over Chelsea and effectively cost Ranieri's men a Champions League qualification spot, with United running out comfortable 3–0 winners in west London.

With Newcastle having clinched fourth position in the league, Chelsea's attentions turned to the FA Cup final. Unfortunately the curse of the unlucky south dressing room at the Millennium Stadium struck the Blues. Wonder goals from Ray Parlour and Freddie Ljungberg made Chelsea the 10th consecutive side to lose a major final after changing in the aforementioned quarters.

The season ended in further disappointment, with a 3–1 defeat at home to Aston Villa, allowing Leeds to leapfrog Chelsea into fifth place.

There were encouraging signs though. Ranieri committed himself to the club by signing a new five-year deal and the Italian's fledgling vision of a successful, youthful side slowly began to take shape.

CHELSEA

DATE	OPPONENT	SCORE	ATT.	BABAYARO	BOSNICH	COLE	CUDICINI	DALLA BONA	DE GOEY	DESAILLY	FERRER	FORSSELL	GALLAS	GUDJOHNSEN
19.08.01	Newcastle H	1–1	40,124	–	–	–	–	–	90	90□	–	–	s64□	–
25.08.01	Southampton A	2–0	31,107	–	–	–	–	–	90	90	–	–	–	–
08.09.01	Arsenal H	1–1	40,855	–	–	–	–	–	90	90	–	–	90	–
16.09.01	Tottenham A	3–2	36,037	–	–	–	–	–	90	90¹□	–	–	s46	s2
23.09.01	Middlesbro H	2–2	36,767	78	–	–	–	–	90	90□	–	–	90	90
30.09.01	Fulham A	1–1	20,197	90	–	–	–	s5	90	90□	s10	–	90□	s19
13.10.01	Leicester H	2–0	40,370	90	–	–	90	–	–	90	–	s21	90	69¹
21.10.01	Leeds Utd A	0–0	40,171	62	90	–	–	90□	–	–	–	s3	90	87
24.10.01	West Ham A	1–2	26,520	–	90	–	–	s28	–	–	–	s9	90	72
28.10.01	Derby Co A	1–1	28,910	–	90	–	–	–	–	90□	–	s45	90□	–
04.11.01	Ipswich H	2–1	40,497	90	90	–	–	90¹	–	90	–	72	s44	s6
18.11.01	Everton A	0–0	30,555	90□	80	–	s10	45	–	–	–	–	90	–
24.11.01	Blackburn H	0–0	37,978	–	–	–	90	s45	–	–	–	–	90	s45
01.12.01	Man Utd A	3–0	67,544	90□	–	–	90	90	–	–	–	s8	90	88¹
05.12.01	Charlton H	0–1	33,504	90	–	–	90	90□	–	–	–	s11	90	79
09.12.01	Sunderland A	0–0	48,017	90	–	–	90	90□	–	–	–	s1	90	89
16.12.01	Liverpool H	4–0	41,174	90	–	–	90	90¹	–	–	–	–	90	90¹□
23.12.01	Bolton W H	5–1*	34,063	–	–	–	90	90	–	–	s8	–	90	80¹□
26.12.01	Arsenal A	1–2	38,079	90□	–	–	90□	s17	–	–	–	s7	90	83
29.12.01	Newcastle A	2–1	52,123	90□	–	–	90	90	–	–	–	s20	90	70²
01.01.02	Southampton H	2–4	35,156	67	–	–	90	84	–	–	–	s6	90	90¹
12.01.02	Bolton W A	2–2	23,891	–	–	–	90	90	–	90	–	s25¹	–	90¹
20.01.02	West Ham H	5–1	40,035	–	–	–	90	–	–	90	–	s11¹	90	90²
30.01.02	Leeds Utd H	2–0	40,614	–	–	–	90	90¹	–	90	–	s6	–	84¹
02.02.02	Leicester A	3–2	19,950	–	–	–	90	90	–	90	–	s45□	–	45
09.02.02	Aston Villa A	1–1	41,137	–	–	–	90	90□	–	90	63	s26	–	64
02.03.02	Charlton A	1–2	26,354	76	–	–	90	–	–	–	–	s6	90	90
06.03.02	Fulham H	3–2	39,744	90	–	–	90	s30□	–	90	–	s16¹	90	74¹
13.03.02	Tottenham H	4–0	39,652	90	–	–	90	–	–	90	–	s7	90	73
16.03.02	Sunderland H	4–0	40,218	90□	–	–	90	90¹□	–	90	–	s8¹	90¹	82¹
24.03.02	Liverpool A	0–1	44,203	90□	–	–	90	–	–	90	–	–	90	82
30.03.02	Derby Co H	2–1	37,849	–	–	–	90	–	–	90	–	s19	45	71
01.04.02	Ipswich H	0–0	28,053	–	–	–	90	66	–	90	–	66	–	s24
06.04.02	Everton H	3–0	40,545	–	–	s13	90	–	–	90	–	–	–	90
10.04.02	Blackburn A	0–0	25,441	–	–	–	90	–	–	90	90	–	–	76
20.04.02	Man Utd H	0–3	41,725	–	–	–	90	s11□	–	90	–	–	90□	45
27.04.02	Middlesbro A	2–0	28,686	–	–	76¹	90	s11	–	90	–	–	90	–
11.05.02	Aston Villa H	1–3	40,709	–	–	90	90	s45	–	–	–	–	90	s45¹

□ Yellow card, ■ Red card, s Substitute, 90² Goals scored

*including own goal, Δ no suspension served, card remained on record, + card rescinded

For more information visit our website:

2001–02 PREMIERSHIP APPEARANCES

GRONKJAER	HASSELBAINK	HUTH	JOKANOVIC	KEENAN	LAMPARD	LE SAUX	MELCHIOT	MORRIS	PETIT	STANIC	TERRY	ZENDEN	ZOLA	TOTAL
90	90	–	s25	–	90	90	90□	–	90	–	26	65¹	90	990
73□	90¹	–	90	–	90	90	90	s40	50	s17¹	90	73	s17	990
84□	72¹■Δ	–	–	–	90	90	s1	–	90	s6	90	89	90	972
90□	90²	–	s8	–	89■	90□	90	–	90	–	44	82	88	989
–	90²□	–	90□	–	68	s12	90□	s22	–	–	90	89	s1	990
–	90¹	–	83■	–	–	–	80	–	90	–	90□	85	71	983
–	74¹	–	90	–	s16	–	s45	–	90	–	90	45	90	990
–	90	–	–	–	90	90□	90	–	90□	–	90	s28	–	990
–	90¹	–	90	–	81	90	90	–	62	–	90	s18	90	990
–	90¹□	–	45	–	s45	90	45	–	90□	s45	90	90	45	990
–	90	–	46	–	90	–	84	–	–	s18	90	–	90¹	990
–	90	–	45□	–	90	–	90□	–	90	s45	90	s45	90	990
–	90	–	–	–	90	90	90	–	90	90	90	45	45	990
–	82¹	–	90□	–	90	84□	90¹	–	–	s6	90	–	s2	990
–	90□	–	90	–	90	–	90	–	–	–	90	46	s44	990
–	90	–	90□	–	90	–	90	–	–	90□	90	–	–	990
–	87¹	–	s22	–	90	89¹	90	–	–	68□	90	s1	s3	990
–	90¹	–	–	–	90¹	82	90	–	s23	90	90□	67¹	s10	990
–	90	–	–	–	90¹	83□	90	–	90	73□	90	–	s7	990
–	89	–	s5	–	90	90	90	–	–	85□	90□	–	s1	990
–	90¹	–	s45	–	90	90□+	90	–	–	45	90□	–	s23	990
–	–	–	s14	–	90	90	90	76	–	90□	90	–	65	990
–	79²	–	–	–	90	–	90	s28□	62	90□	90	s15	75□	990
–	90	–	–	–	90	90	90	–	90	90□	90	–	–	990
–	90²	–	–	–	90	90	90	–	90□	45□	90	–	s45¹	990
–	90	–	–	s13	90¹	90	–	–	90	90	77	–	s27	990
s14	90	–	–	–	90¹	90	90□	76	90	84	–	–	s14	990
s25	90	–	–	–	90	90	90¹	–	60	–	–	–	65	990
78□	83³	–	–	–	90¹	90	90	–	90	s12	–	–	s17	990
80	90	–	–	–	90	85	90	–	–	s10	–	–	s5	990
90	90	–	–	–	90	–	90	–	90	90	–	–	s8	990
76	90□	–	–	–	90□	90□	90	–	90¹	71	s45¹	–	s19	976
–	90	–	90	–	s24	90	90	–	–	60	90	s30	–	990
–	77²	–	s19	–	90	90	90	–	71	90	15	s75	90¹	990
–	90	–	–	–	90	–	90	–	90	90	90	s14	90	990
90□	90□	–	–	–	90	–	90	–	79	–	90	s45	90	990
79	–	–	s18	–	90	–	90	–	72	s14	90	90¹□	90	990
45	–	s45	–	–	90	45	90	–	90	–	90	45	90	990

THE MANAGER

CLAUDIO RANIERI

The jury was out on Chelsea boss Claudio Ranieri in 2001–02. With the Blues failing to keep pace in the title race and subsequently missing out on a Champions League spot, many followers of the west London club regarded the campaign as a poor one – especially after their defeat in the FA Cup final to capital rivals Arsenal.

Barcelona were reportedly interested in recruiting the former Cagliari, Napoli, Fiorentina, Valencia and Atletico Madrid boss, as his position at the club remained unclear. But amid speculation regarding his future, Ranieri quashed the rumours by signing a five-year deal with the Stamford Bridge club in April.

"The important thing is that Claudio has a long-term view. He wants to bring in the youth, improve the youth policy and scouting and to do that he needs time to develop," Chelsea supremo Ken Bates said after Ranieri had committed himself to the club until 2007.

Ranieri's track record is good. He won successive promotions with Cagliari before leading Fiorentina to Italian Cup and Super Cup triumphs and launched Valencia into Spain's elite after guiding them to a fourth-placed finish in La Liga in 1998–99.

LEAGUE POSITION

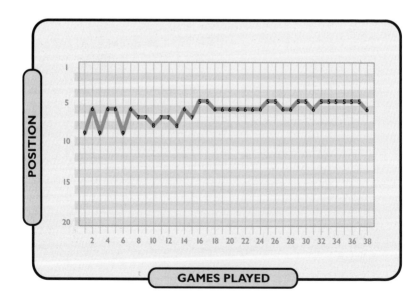

POSITION

GAMES PLAYED

16 Chelsea scored more goals from

THE GOALS

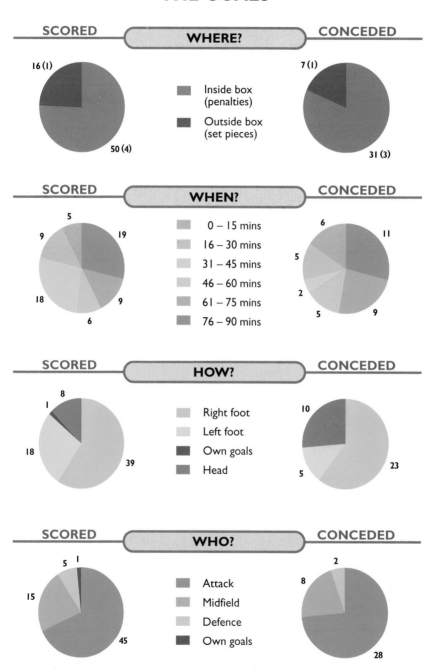

SCORED | **WHERE?** | **CONCEDED**

16 (1)
50 (4)

7 (1)
31 (3)

- Inside box (penalties)
- Outside box (set pieces)

SCORED | **WHEN?** | **CONCEDED**

5
9
19
18
9
6

6
11
5
2
5
9

- 0 – 15 mins
- 16 – 30 mins
- 31 – 45 mins
- 46 – 60 mins
- 61 – 75 mins
- 76 – 90 mins

SCORED | **HOW?** | **CONCEDED**

8
1
18
39

10
5
23

- Right foot
- Left foot
- Own goals
- Head

SCORED | **WHO?** | **CONCEDED**

5
1
15
45

2
8
28

- Attack
- Midfield
- Defence
- Own goals

outside the area than anyone else

CHELSEA

	BABAYARO	COLE	DALLA BONA	DESAILLY	FERRER	FORSSELL	GALLAS	GRONKJAER	GUDJOHNSEN
APPEARANCES									
Start	18	2	16	24	2	2	27	11	26
Sub	0	1	8	0	2	20	3	2	6
Minutes on pitch	1543	179	1557	2160	171	438	2539	914	2184
GOAL ATTEMPTS									
Goals	0	1	4	1	0	4	1	0	14
Shots on target	0	4	6	3	0	10	1	1	34
Shots off target	3	3	11	5	0	10	4	4	33
Shooting accuracy %	0%	57%	35%	38%	0%	50%	20%	20%	51%
Goals/shots %	0%	14%	24%	13%	0%	20%	20%	0%	21%
PASSING									
Goal assists	1	0	0	1	0	2	0	3	6
Long passes	172	8	207	341	17	17	243	50	105
Short passes	618	42	595	605	74	152	766	222	678
PASS COMPLETION									
Own half %	81%	86%	80%	88%	75%	57%	87%	85%	86%
Opposition half %	77%	67%	69%	72%	69%	58%	79%	67%	63%
CROSSING									
Total crosses	40	5	21	0	3	7	10	82	24
Cross completion %	10%	20%	14%	0%	33%	0%	30%	23%	21%
DRIBBLING									
Dribbles & runs	42	12	23	26	4	31	48	117	127
Dribble completion %	74%	42%	78%	85%	75%	71%	75%	57%	51%
DEFENDING									
Tackles made	57	3	67	77	12	5	92	18	16
Tackles won %	81%	100%	72%	71%	67%	80%	80%	83%	81%
Blocks	6	0	8	25	1	0	26	1	4
Clearances	105	1	38	243	10	2	214	8	10
Interceptions	8	0	6	25	3	0	21	0	3
DISCIPLINE									
Fouls conceded	27	9	37	29	8	16	27	23	29
Fouls won	14	1	31	22	0	13	17	16	37
Offside	1	2	1	0	0	4	2	7	28
Yellow cards	6	0	7	5	0	1	4	5	2
Red cards	0	0	0	0	0	0	0	0	0

+ one card rescinded

GOALKEEPER NAME	START/ (SUB)	TIME ON PITCH	GOALS CONCEDED	MINS/GOALS CONCEDED	SAVES MADE	SAVES/ SHOTS
BOSNICH	5 (0)	440	4	110	22	85%
CUDICINI	27 (1)	2440	27	90	75	74%
DE GOEY	6 (0)	540	7	77	17	71%

For more information visit our website:

PLAYERS' STATISTICS

	HASSELBAINK	HUTH	JOKANOVIC	KEENAN	LAMPARD	LE SAUX	MELCHIOT	MORRIS	PETIT	STANIC	TERRY	ZENDEN	ZOLA	TOTAL	RANK
	35	0	12	0	34	26	35	2	26	18	32	13	19		
	0	1	8	1	3	1	2	3	1	9	1	9	16		
	3073	45	1095	13	3113	2280	3135	242	2189	1604	2727	1182	1777		
	23	0	0	0	5	1	2	0	1	1	1	3	3	66*	5th
	62	0	2	0	23	7	5	0	6	8	8	8	20	208	=5th
	61	0	1	0	26	7	3	1	10	22	8	15	20	247	6th
	50%	0%	67%	0%	47%	50%	63%	0%	38%	27%	50%	35%	50%	46%	8th
	19%	0%	0%	0%	10%	7%	25%	0%	6%	3%	6%	13%	8%	14%	5th
	6	0	0	0	3	7	0	0	3	2	1	2	4	41	=5th
	187	1	196	2	462	278	330	24	353	92	422	105	193	4240	10th
	985	8	506	3	1130	818	1114	91	1020	461	908	367	694	11979	5th
	83%	86%	84%	0%	86%	78%	85%	80%	86%	78%	88%	83%	88%	85%	5th
	66%	100%	69%	25%	72%	67%	75%	74%	71%	61%	64%	71%	79%	69%	7th
	111	0	5	1	37	147	38	3	85	49	7	91	97	863	15th
	23%	0%	20%	0%	14%	31%	21%	33%	26%	14%	29%	18%	19%	22%	19th
	155	2	19	0	86	117	106	3	35	114	31	78	118	1301	6th
	57%	100%	74%	0%	64%	54%	71%	67%	80%	51%	87%	60%	69%	63%	19th
	28	1	57	0	108	92	105	10	107	83	83	13	25	1061	9th
	79%	0%	68%	0%	75%	62%	73%	90%	64%	81%	72%	77%	88%	74%	10th
	1	0	5	0	8	26	34	3	7	6	35	1	3	200	15th
	10	5	25	0	44	72	134	3	52	41	284	10	2	1371	12th
	3	0	5	0	14	13	13	0	24	13	22	4	3	180	5th
	41	0	27	0	33	40	34	2	36	55	48	17	8	546	16th
	57	1	16	0	53	49	50	6	31	33	34	19	29	534	14th
	23	0	0	0	1	1	0	0	1	3	2	7	5	88	19th
	5	0	4	0	1	6+	4	1	3	8	4	1	1	69	=4th
	1	0	1	0	1	0	0	0	0	0	0	0	0	3	=9th

*Including one own goal

CROSSES CAUGHT	CROSSES PUNCHED	CROSSES DROPPED	CATCH SUCCESS	THROWS/ SHORT KICKS	% COMPLETION	LONG KICKS	% COMPLETION
17	2	0	100%	15	93%	97	46%
41	22	2	95%	49	98%	419	47%
15	17	0	100%	22	100%	110	49%

PLAYER OF THE SEASON

PLAYER	INDEX SCORE
JIMMY HASSELBAINK	1,018
Eidur Gudjohnsen	861
Marcel Desailly	836
John Terry	810
Mario Melchiot	713
William Gallas	708
Carlo Cudicini	707
Celestine Babayaro	699
Frank Lampard	697
Graeme Le Saux	661

Given the success they had spearheading Chelsea's attack so effectively in tandem, it was not surprising to see Jimmy Floyd Hasselbaink and Eidur Gudjohnsen heading the Opta Index ratings for Chelsea.

The pair raced to 52 goals between them in all competitions and 37 in the 2001–02 Premiership, making them one of the country's most prolific partnerships.

Dutch powerhouse Hasselbaink matched his 2000–01 tally of 23 league goals, hammering 123 shots at goal in 2001–02. But his unselfish link-up play was just as impressive; Hasselbaink supplied six assists and 49 other passes leading to scoring chances for his colleagues – both tallies the second-best at the club.

Gudjohnsen benefited from this supply line and was actually slightly more clinical than his ebullient partner, netting with 21% of all efforts compared to Hasselbaink's 19%. He also returned the favours he received regularly, directly creating half-a-dozen Blues goals.

Marcel Desailly edged into the top three just ahead of the man he forged such an outstanding partnership with – John Terry. Chelsea lost just one of the 20 Premiership matches the pair appeared in together and the duo provided a formidable barrier to opposition strikers.

Desailly recorded club-high tallies of 165 and 25 for headed clearances and interceptions respectively, while Terry made the most defensive clearances and blocks of any Stamford Bridge star.

Mario Melchiot and William Gallas made it a good campaign for defenders at the Bridge on Opta's Index – the latter settling superbly in his first full campaign. Carlo Cudicini, whose 68% saves-to-shots ratio from close-range efforts was the third best in the Premiership, provided excellent cover behind the back four.

New boy Frank Lampard was steady and made the top 10, while Gianfranco Zola might have graced the top three, but did not feature regularly enough to qualify for the Index.

FIVE OF THE BEST

In what was another season of underachievement for the Blues, there were still plenty of plus points to be taken from the campaign. The partnership of Jimmy Floyd Hasselbaink and Eidur Gudjohnsen was awesome and summer signing Frank Lampard fared well in his first term at Stamford Bridge.

TOP GOALSCORERS

	GOALS	GOALS/SHOTS
JIMMY HASSELBAINK	23	19%
Eidur Gudjohnsen	14	21%
Frank Lampard	5	10%
Sam Dalla Bona	4	24%
Mikael Forssell	4	20%

Dutchman Jimmy Floyd Hasselbaink proved yet again that he can score in any league and for any team. He may not have topped the league's goalscoring charts, but arguably no player in the Premiership scored as many spectacular strikes this season. Second in the table was Eidur Gudjohnsen who came away with 14 goals to his name, having taken a greater proportion of his chances than his strike partner.

In his first season at Stamford Bridge, Frank Lampard made more accurate passes than any other player at the club, as the former West Ham star found a team-mate with 78% of his distribution. Dutchman Mario Melchiot was just behind him and did a sterling job on the right side of the pitch, while Emmanuel Petit showed he can still have a big impact on games with more than 1,000 passes successfully delivered.

TOP PASSERS

	SUCC PASSES	COMPLETION
FRANK LAMPARD	1,234	78%
Mario Melchiot	1,154	80%
Emmanuel Petit	1,066	78%
John Terry	1,065	80%
William Gallas	848	84%

TOP TACKLERS

	WON	SUCCESS
FRANK LAMPARD	81	75%
Mario Melchiot	77	73%
William Gallas	74	80%
Emmanuel Petit	69	64%
Mario Stanic	67	81%

Frank Lampard won the ball for Chelsea more often than any other player and came away with possession in three out of every four attempted challenges on average. Second was defender Mario Melchiot with 77 successful tackles to his name and in his first full season for the Blues, Frenchman William Gallas was third. Of the three, Gallas demonstrated the more clinical tackling with four-fifths of his attempts winning possession for the Blues.

Mario Stanic sat out a great many Chelsea matches, making just 18 starts, yet with more fouls and bookings than any of his colleagues, he still managed to build up the poorest disciplinary record at the club. Close behind was Jimmy Floyd Hasselbaink as again he showed that with his ice-cool striking ability comes a fiery temperament. England defender John Terry came third in the Index, with seven more fouls conceded than the Dutchman.

DISCIPLINE

	POINTS	FOULS & CARDS
MARIO STANIC	79	55F, 8Y, 0R
Jimmy Hasselbaink	62	41F, 5Y, 1R
John Terry	60	48F, 4Y, 0R
Sam Dalla Bona	58	37F, 7Y, 0R
Graeme Le Saux	58	40F, 6Y, 0R

goals from open play than any other player

DERBY COUNTY

ADDRESS

Pride Park Stadium, Pride Park,
Derby DE24 8XL

CONTACT NUMBERS

Telephone: 01332 202 202
Fax: 01332 667 540
Ticket Office: 01332 209 209
Ticket Line: 09068 332 213
ClubCall: 09068 12 11 87
Superstore: 01332 209 000
e-mail:press.office@dcfc.co.uk
Website: www.dcfc.co.uk

KEY PERSONNEL

Chairman: L Pickering
Director: F Vinton
Chief Executive: K Loring
Club Secretary: K Pearson ACIS
Manager: John Gregory

SPONSORS

Marston's Pedigree Bitter

COLOURS

Home: White shirts, black shorts
and white stockings
Away: Dark navy shirts, dark navy
shorts and dark navy stockings

NICKNAME

The Rams

HONOURS

League Champions:
1971–72, 1974–75
Division Two Champions:
1911–12, 1914–15, 1968–69,
1986–87
Divsion Three (North) Champions:
1956–57
FA Cup Winners: 1946

RECORD GOALSCORER

Steve Bloomer –
292 league goals, 1892–1906,
1910–14

BIGGEST WIN

12–0 v Finn Harps – UEFA Cup, 1st
round 1st leg, 15 September 1976

BIGGEST DEFEAT

2-11 v Everton – FA Cup 1st Round,
1889–90

3 The Rams had more penalties

SEASON REVIEW

Derby's stay in the top flight came to an end, as did their association with manager Jim Smith, as 2001–02 turned out to be a season of turmoil and transition for the Rams.

Before the season started, Derby signed striker Fabrizio Ravanelli amid raised eyebrows over his wage demands, but the Italian was on the scoresheet as they got off to a winning start on the opening day with a 2–1 victory against Blackburn.

That promising result was soon forgotten though, as the Rams then went 10 league games without a win, although Ravanelli seemed to lead a one-man charge, scoring six more goals in that time. Derby's reliance on the Italian was eventually one of the reasons they got into trouble and only Middlesbrough hit the target with fewer shots all season.

In October, manager Smith – who had planned to stay until the end of the season – made an early exit and Colin Todd took over the first-team affairs. Derby's fortunes changed very little though, as they were knocked out of the Worthington Cup by Fulham and won only two of their next 10 games. They slipped down into the relegation zone in the middle of November and never re-emerged from the bottom three.

A humiliating FA Cup Third Round exit at home to Bristol Rovers was probably the final straw for the board. Derby sacked Todd at the end of January, just over three months after promoting him to the manager's position at Pride Park and appointed John Gregory, who had resigned from Aston Villa less than a week earlier.

Todd's departure, just 17 games after he replaced Smith, left Gregory with 14 matches in which to avoid relegation. He said: "There are no excuses, you're in the position you're in because we've not been

> **"Fans will always support 100 per cent triers and I don't think we've had enough people playing for us this year."**
>
> **John Gregory**

playing well enough, but we can improve and we will get better."

It all started well for the new boss with a 1–0 victory over Tottenham thanks to a Lee Morris goal and then Derby made it two wins out of three when they overcame Leicester 3–0 in a relegation six-pointer, but the good fortune was not to last.

A 4–3 defeat against fellow-strugglers Everton was a major blow in itself, but it also began a run of seven consecutive defeats, including a heartbreaking 3–2 reverse at home to Newcastle after being two goals to the good.

The Rams were relegated long before drawing 1–1 with Sunderland on the final day of the season, but at least that prevented them equalling a Premiership record of eight consecutive losses.

A lack of goals was a problem all season and the fact that Derby put in the lowest number of successful crosses and corners illustrated how starved of chances their forwards were.

There was a youthful quality to the side and Chris Riggott and Danny Higginbotham made 822 clearances between them throughout the season, but the Rams were still only able to keep seven clean sheets from 38 games during the campaign.

Throughout the season 14 of Derby's defeats were by a one-goal margin which was more than any other side in the division.

While there will inevitably be departures, the squad does have some quality players like Morris, Riggott, Higginbotham and Malcolm Christie. With Gregory promising to scour the lower leagues for English players who are prepared to roll up their sleeves and get stuck in and vowing to clear out the players who are not prepared to fight for the club, Derby will be hopeful of returning to the top flight before too long.

DERBY COUNTY

DATE	OPPONENT	SCORE	ATT.	BARTON	BOERTIEN	BOLDER	BURTON	BURLEY	CARBONARI	CARBONE	CHRISTIE	DAINO	DUCROCQ	ELLIOTT	EVATT	FEUER	FOLETTI	GRENET
18.08.01	Blackburn H	2-1	28,236	–	90	–	–	90	–	–	90^1	90	–	–	–	–	–	–
21.08.01	Ipswich A	1-3	21,097	–	90	–	s35	90▫	–	–	90	77	–	–	–	–	–	–
25.08.01	Fulham A	0-0	15,641	–	90	–	90	90▫	–	–	38	–	–	–	–	–	–	–
08.09.01	West Ham A	0-0	27,802	–	90	–	80▫	90▫	–	–	–	–	–	–	–	–	–	–
15.09.01	Leicester H	2-3	26,863	–	90▫	–	90^1	90▫	–	–	s14	–	–	–	–	–	–	–
23.09.01	Leeds Utd A	0-3	39,155	–	90▫	–	s9	–	–	–	90	–	–	–	–	–	–	–
29.09.01	Arsenal H	0-2	29,200	–	90	–	s24	–	–	–	90	–	–	–	–	–	–	–
15.10.01	Tottenham A	1-3	30,148	–	–	–	71	90	–	–	s19	–	–	–	90	–	–	–
20.10.01	Charlton H	1-1	30,221	–	–	–	s27	90	–	90	63▫	–	85	–	90	–	–	–
28.10.01	Chelsea H	1-1	28,910	–	–	–	80	90	–	90	s10	–	90	–	–	–	–	–
03.11.01	Middlesbro A	1-5	28,117	–	–	–	90	90	–	90	s23	–	67	–	–	–	–	–
17.11.01	Southampton H	1-0	32,063	–	s22	–	–	90	–	90	s7	–	90	–	–	–	–	83
24.11.01	Newcastle A	0-1	50,070	–	s3	–	–	90	–	90	s15	–	90	–	–	–	–	90
01.12.01	Liverpool H	0-1	33,289	–	–	–	–	–	–	90	90	–	90	–	–	–	–	90
08.12.01	Bolton W H	1-0	25,712	–	–	s5	s2	–	–	85	88^1	–	90	–	–	–	–	90
12.12.01	Man Utd A	0-5	67,577	–	s20	90	s26	–	–	90	70	–	74▫	–	–	–	–	90
15.12.01	Everton A	0-1	30,615	–	s1	s25	90	–	–	90	90	–	90	90	–	–	–	89
22.12.01	Aston Villa H	3-1	28,001	–	90	s25	s15	–	–	70^1	s20^1	–	90	–	–	–	–	65
26.12.01	West Ham A	0-4	31,379	–	90	s29	–	–	–	54▪	–	–	45	–	–	–	–	90▪
29.12.01	Blackburn A	1-0	23,529	–	s20	s4	–	90▫	–	86	90^1	–	90▫	–	–	–	–	70▫
02.01.02	Fulham H	0-1	28,165	–	s2	s26	s6	–	88▫	84	90	–	64	–	–	–	–	90
12.01.02	Aston Villa A	1-2	28,881	–	90▫	s22	–	–	–	–	90	–	90	22	–	–	–	24▪
19.01.02	Ipswich H	1-3	29,658	–	s21	–	90	–	69	–	90^1	–	–	–	–	–	–	–
29.01.02	Charlton A	0-1	25,387	–	90	–	–	–	–	–	90	–	85	–	–	–	–	–
02.02.02	Tottenham H	1-0	27,721	90	s16	–	–	–	–	–	90▫	–	90	–	–	–	–	–
09.02.02	Sunderland H	0-1	31,771	90	s36	–	s13	–	–	–	90	–	90	–	–	–	–	–
23.02.02	Leicester A	3-0	21,620	90	90	–	–	–	–	–	90	–	90	–	–	–	s58	90
03.03.02	Man Utd H	2-2	33,041	90	90	–	–	–	–	–	90^2	–	63▫	s7	–	–	–	–
05.03.02	Arsenal A	0-1	37,878	90	90	–	–	–	–	–	90	–	–	–	–	–	–	s36
16.03.02	Bolton W A	3-1	25,893	90	90	–	–	–	–	–	77^1	–	–	–	–	–	–	s8
23.03.02	Everton H	3-4	33,297	90	90	–	–	–	–	–	44	–	–	–	–	90	–	–
30.03.02	Chelsea A	1-2	37,849	90	90	–	–	–	–	–	–	–	–	s1	–	–	–	–
01.04.02	Middlesbro H	0-1	30,822	90▫	90	–	–	–	–	–	s45	–	–	s7	–	–	–	–
06.04.02	Southampton A	0-2	29,263	90	90	s45	–	–	–	–	90	–	–	–	–	–	–	s16
13.04.02	Newcastle H	2-3	31,031	90	90▫	–	–	–	–	–	65^1	–	–	s1	s9	–	–	–
20.04.02	Liverpool A	0-2	43,510	90	90▫	–	–	–	–	–	90	–	–	–	–	–	–	–
27.04.02	Leeds Utd H	0-1	30,705	90	90▫	s45	–	–	–	–	90	–	–	–	s69▫	–	–	–
11.05.02	Sunderland A	1-1	47,989	90▫	66	90	–	–	–	–	90	–	–	–	90	–	–	–

▫ Yellow card, ▪ Red card, s Substitute, 90^2 Goals scored

For more information visit our website:

2001–02 PREMIERSHIP APPEARANCES

HIGGINBOTHAM	JACKSON	JOHNSON	KINKLADZE	LEE	MAWENE	MORRIS	MURRAY	OAKES	O'NEIL	POOM	POWELL	RAVANELLI	RIGGOTT	ROBINSON	STRUPAR	TWIGG	VALAKARI	ZAVAGNO	TOTAL
90	–	–	s26	–	–	64	–	–	90	90	90□	90[1]	90	–	–	–	–	–	990
90□	–	90	–	–	–	–	s13	–	32□	90	55□	90[1]	90	–	–	–	–	–	932
90□	–	90	s52□	–	84	–	s6	90	90	–	90	–	90	–	–	–	–	–	990
90	–	90□	90	–	90	s10	–	90	–	–	90	90□	90□	–	–	–	–	–	990
90	–	90□	90	–	76	–	–	90	90	–	–	90[1]	90□	–	–	–	–	–	990
90	–	90□	s9	–	90	–	81	90	90	–	90	81	90	–	–	–	–	–	990
90□	66	90	s45	–	–	–	45	90□	90□	–	90	90	90	–	–	–	–	–	990
90	–	90	s28	–	90□	–	62	–	–	–	90	90[1]□	90	–	–	–	90	–	990
90□	–	–	–	–	90	–	–	–	–	–	90□	90[1]	90	–	–	–	s5	90	990
90	–	–	–	–	90	–	–	–	–	90	90	90[1]□	90	–	–	–	–	90	990
90	–	–	–	–	90□	–	–	–	–	90	90	90[1]	90	–	–	–	–	90	990
90	–	–	–	–	90[1]	–	–	–	–	90	90	90	90	–	–	–	–	68	990
90	–	–	–	–	90□	–	–	–	–	90	75	90□	90	–	–	–	–	87	990
90□	–	–	–	–	90	–	–	–	–	90	90	90	90	–	–	–	–	90	990
90	–	–	–	–	90	–	–	–	–	90	90	90	90	–	–	–	–	90	990
90□	–	–	–	–	64	–	s16	90	–	–	–	90	90	–	–	–	–	90	990
–	–	–	s11	–	79	–	–	90	–	–	65	–	90□	–	–	–	–	90□	990
90	–	–	75	–	90	–	–	–	–	90	–	90[1]	90	–	–	–	–	90	990
90	–	–	s45	–	90	–	–	90	90	90	61	–	–	–	–	90□	–	–	954
90	–	–	–	–	–	–	–	–	–	90	90	90	90	–	–	–	–	90□	990
90	–	–	–	–	–	–	–	–	–	90	90	90	90	–	–	–	–	90	990
90	–	–	s68□	–	–	–	–	–	–	90	90[1]	90	90	–	–	–	–	68□	924
90	90	–	s30	–	–	–	–	90	–	–	90	90	90	–	–	–	90	60	990
90	90	–	s5	–	90□	–	–	90	–	–	90	90	90□	–	–	–	90	–	990
90	–	–	–	–	74[1]	–	90	s7	–	90□	90□	90	–	–	–	–	83	90	990
90	–	–	–	90	77	–	90	–	–	54	90	90	–	–	–	–	90		990
90	–	–	83[1]	90□	–	s7[1]	32	–	–	–	–	–	70[1]	–	s20	90□	–		990
90	–	–	83	90	–	s27	90	–	–	–	75	90	s15	–	–	90□			990
90	–	–	54	55□	–	90	90	s35□	–	–	–	90	69	–	s21	90			990
90[1]	–	–	82	90	–	s13	90	90	–	–	89[1]	90	s1	–	–	90			990
90	–	–	90	90	–	s46[1]	–	90□	–	–	90	90	s35[2]	–	–	55□			990
90	–	–	90	90□	–	s3	90	–	–	–	90	90□	87[1]	–	90□	89□			990
90	–	–	s45	90	–	90	90	–	–	–	45	90	45	–	90	83			990
90	–	–	74	90	–	90	90	–	–	–	55	90	s35	–	–	45			990
90□	90	–	90	81	–	89[1]	90	–	–	–	s25	90□	90	–	–	–			990
90	90	–	90□	90	–	90□	90	–	–	–	–	90	90	–	–	–			990
90	90	–	45	90	–	21	–	–	90	–	–	90	s14	76	–	–			990
90	s17	–	–	90	–	–	–	–	90	–	–	90	s32[1]	58	s24	–	73		990

THE MANAGER

JOHN GREGORY

John Gregory was appointed Derby boss on 30 January 2002, less than a week after resigning for "personal reasons" from the managerial post at Aston Villa. Following the departures of Jim Smith and Colin Todd, he became the third Derby manager of the season.

Gregory ended his playing career at Derby in the mid-80s where his tough, uncompromising style made him a terrace favourite with the fans. Through managerial spells at Portsmouth, Plymouth, then in a coaching capacity at Leicester City and Villa, he always remained as ambitious as he was passionate.

He departed Villa to become manager of Wycombe Wanderers in October 1996 and delivered the Chairboys from relegation in the 1996–97 season. He returned to Villa as the manager in 1998 and during his time there the club never finished outside the top eight, despite his fractious relationship with chairman Doug Ellis.

Gregory promised to get rid of those who "don't give a monkey's about the club" at Derby and said it was not so much about cost cutting as cutting out the fat. As a coach with supporter-like passion, there are few managers more suited to the task ahead of him.

LEAGUE POSITION

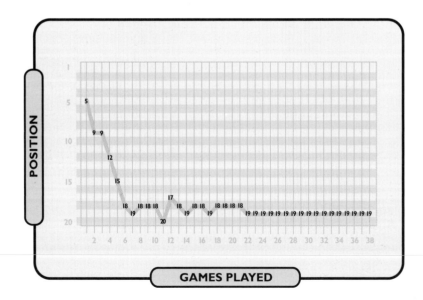

POSITION

GAMES PLAYED

11 Derby conceded more goals from shots

THE GOALS

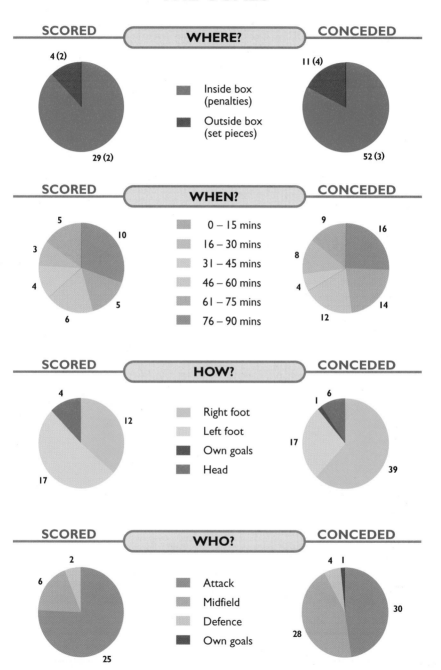

SCORED — **WHERE?** — **CONCEDED**

Inside box (penalties)

Outside box (set pieces)

4 (2)   29 (2)   11 (4)   52 (3)

SCORED — **WHEN?** — **CONCEDED**

0 – 15 mins
16 – 30 mins
31 – 45 mins
46 – 60 mins
61 – 75 mins
76 – 90 mins

5, 10, 3, 4, 6, 5   9, 16, 8, 4, 12, 14

SCORED — **HOW?** — **CONCEDED**

Right foot
Left foot
Own goals
Head

4, 12, 17   6, 1, 17, 39

SCORED — **WHO?** — **CONCEDED**

Attack
Midfield
Defence
Own goals

2, 6, 25   4, 1, 30, 28

outside the area than anyone else

DERBY COUNTY

	BARTON	BOERTIEN	BOLDER	BURLEY	BURTON	CARBONARI	CARBONE	CHRISTIE	DAINO	DUCROCQ	ELLIOTT	EVATT	GRENET	HIGGINBOT
APPEARANCES														
Start	14	23	2	11	8	3	13	27	2	19	2	1	12	37
Sub	0	9	9	0	9	0	0	8	0	0	4	2	3	0
Minutes on pitch	1260	2187	406	990	838	247	1099	2398	167	1563	128	168	1021	3330
GOAL ATTEMPTS														
Goals	0	0	0	0	1	0	1	9	0	0	0	0	0	1
Shots on target	0	6	1	3	12	0	10	28	0	11	0	1	0	2
Shots off target	2	3	0	8	7	1	16	19	0	8	0	2	8	4
Shooting accuracy %	0%	67%	100%	27%	63%	0%	38%	60%	0%	58%	0%	33%	0%	33%
Goals/shots %	0%	0%	0%	0%	5%	0%	4%	19%	0%	0%	0%	0%	0%	17%
PASSING														
Goal assists	1	1	0	2	3	0	3	1	0	0	0	0	0	0
Long passes	234	201	39	150	34	29	116	80	21	215	13	20	111	509
Short passes	419	667	152	308	239	55	415	585	26	476	22	53	321	652
PASS COMPLETION														
Own half %	79%	80%	76%	87%	87%	81%	78%	84%	71%	76%	79%	68%	72%	74%
Opposition half %	61%	66%	73%	76%	67%	65%	71%	69%	55%	61%	38%	57%	67%	47%
CROSSING														
Total crosses	66	85	8	72	11	0	82	34	4	32	0	3	38	13
Cross completion %	23%	26%	25%	28%	9%	0%	26%	6%	0%	28%	0%	0%	11%	31%
DRIBBLING														
Dribbles & runs	21	64	16	35	14	3	76	99	3	37	1	6	15	46
Dribble completion %	76%	64%	38%	71%	50%	100%	58%	59%	33%	70%	100%	33%	60%	87%
DEFENDING														
Tackles made	63	103	11	30	12	11	27	22	6	69	2	5	30	89
Tackles won %	75%	79%	82%	70%	92%	73%	78%	59%	83%	72%	100%	60%	57%	67%
Blocks	17	25	2	1	5	4	1	3	3	5	1	0	8	58
Clearances	54	66	8	16	4	25	0	5	5	22	20	2	45	402
Interceptions	9	17	0	6	0	1	4	0	1	10	0	0	6	15
DISCIPLINE														
Fouls conceded	19	22	7	14	25	11	22	30	3	27	4	1	12	12
Fouls won	10	49	5	9	15	2	30	56	3	17	2	2	11	55
Offside	0	8	0	3	19	0	22	36	0	0	0	0	2	0
Yellow cards	2	6	0	4	1	2	0	2	0	3	0	1	2	7
Red cards	0	0	0	0	0	0	1	0	0	0	0	0	1	0

GOALKEEPER NAME	START/ (SUB)	TIME ON PITCH	GOALS CONCEDED	MINS/GOALS CONCEDED	SAVES MADE	SAVES/ SHOTS
FEUER	2 (0)	180	4	45	10	71%
FOLETTI	1 (1)	148	4	37	7	64%
OAKES	20 (0)	1742	33	53	73	69%
POOM	15 (0)	1350	22	61	72	77%

For more information visit our website:

PLAYERS' STATISTICS

	JACKSON	JOHNSON	KINKLADZE	LEE	MAWENE	MORRIS	MURRAY	O'NEIL	POWELL	RAVANELLI	RIGGOTT	ROBINSON	STRUPAR	TWIGG	VALAKARI	ZAVAGNO	TOTAL	RANK
	6	7	13	13	17	9	3	8	23	30	37	0	8	0	6	26		
	1	0	11	0	0	6	3	2	0	1	0	2	4	1	3	0		
	533	630	1400	1126	1473	791	223	704	1959	2620	3301	46	671	24	579	2158		
	0	0	1	0	1	4	0	0	1	9	0	1	4	0	0	0	33	18th
	1	2	4	3	1	7	0	0	9	26	4	1	6	0	2	3	143	=18th
	1	3	9	6	2	4	0	3	7	36	5	0	10	0	2	3	169	19th
	50%	40%	31%	33%	33%	64%	0%	0%	56%	42%	44%	100%	38%	0%	50%	50%	46%	7th
	0%	0%	8%	0%	33%	36%	0%	0%	6%	15%	0%	100%	25%	0%	0%	0%	11%	13th
	0	0	0	1	0	1	0	0	0	3	2	0	0	1	0	1	20	=18th
	46	107	107	177	151	21	30	116	159	170	354	1	49	2	66	216	3865	16th
	131	187	548	490	478	200	90	242	625	874	664	11	216	8	193	576	9985	15th
	68%	87%	87%	84%	78%	73%	74%	83%	81%	80%	80%	100%	85%	100%	75%	67%	79%	19th
	63%	68%	82%	75%	69%	60%	63%	79%	70%	66%	54%	73%	61%	75%	64%	61%	65%	15th
	17	21	27	15	24	37	3	11	23	22	1	0	5	0	12	103	769	18th
	12%	24%	19%	20%	25%	16%	0%	0%	9%	18%	0%	0%	20%	0%	8%	18%	20%	20th
	3	10	124	21	30	67	8	22	46	61	12	1	7	1	6	42	903	17th
	100%	90%	73%	76%	97%	52%	88%	77%	74%	62%	92%	0%	86%	100%	67%	79%	69%	8th
	12	20	35	47	63	11	6	27	58	40	92	0	4	1	24	110	1030	12th
	75%	80%	77%	81%	78%	91%	83%	59%	72%	78%	77%	0%	50%	100%	58%	71%	73%	11th
	5	6	2	8	19	0	1	10	19	7	54	0	1	1	2	18	286	1st
	21	13	3	20	102	2	3	31	25	29	420	0	5	2	3	113	1501	7th
	1	5	2	7	17	0	1	3	7	3	25	0	1	0	5	17	163	8th
	3	6	23	32	25	18	5	21	49	54	37	1	13	1	11	42	551	14th
	0	10	26	7	20	18	2	11	58	49	15	2	13	0	6	27	542	11th
	0	0	3	0	0	0	0	0	1	63	1	1	6	0	1	5	171	1st
	0	3	3	3	4	1	0	3	4	5	7	0	0	0	1	8	73	2nd
	0	0	0	0	0	0	0	1	0	0	0	0	0	0	0	0	3	=9th

CROSSES CAUGHT	CROSSES PUNCHED	CROSSES DROPPED	CATCH SUCCESS	THROWS/ SHORT KICKS	% COMPLETION	LONG KICKS	% COMPLETION
9	3	3	75%	4	75%	42	43%
3	0	1	75%	1	0%	26	42%
31	16	5	86%	22	95%	426	40%
52	16	2	96%	20	95%	310	43%

PLAYER OF THE SEASON

PLAYER	INDEX SCORE
CHRIS RIGGOTT	686
Danny Higginbotham	673
Fabrizio Ravanelli	631
Andy Oakes	628
Paul Boertien	626
Warren Barton	609*
Malcolm Christie	599
Luciano Zavagno	527
Darryl Powell	428
Pierre Ducrocq	355*

All players played 75 minutes in at least 15 matches except those marked * who played that amount in 14.

In a season when Derby were relegated there was still much to admire at Pride Park – the performances of Chris Riggott being one of the major plus-points for the Rams. Described as the most talented defender at the club since Mark Wright, he won Derby's player of the year award for the 2000–01 season and spent most of 2001–02 showing us why.

The England under-21 international was one of the hardest-working players at Derby throughout the 2001–02 season and racked up 420 defensive clearances – the fourth-highest total by any player in the entire top flight.

Of the 92 tackles that he got stuck into, the young defender won 77% of them and with 37 shots blocked, six saving tackles as the last defender and a clearance off the line, it was clear how influential he was for the team throughout the campaign.

Elegant and assured, he made more than 700 successful passes for the side and even got forward to set up two goals. As a product of the youth system and a Derby

fan himself, he never gave less than 100% and will be a key player if the Rams are to return to the top flight at the first attempt.

Alongside Riggott at the heart of the defence was fellow youngster Danny Higginbotham, who amassed the second-highest Opta Index score for the Rams. With 402 clearances to his name, the former Manchester United player put in performances beyond his tender years and, along with Riggott at the back, the Derby defence should only get better if they stay at the club.

Third was a player at the other end of his career. Italian striker Fabrizio Ravanelli averaged 631 points and was responsible for eight of Derby's first 14 goals of the season, threatening defences whenever he played, despite limited service.

Injury problems for first-choice 'keeper Mart Poom allowed his understudy Andy Oakes the opportunity to shine between the sticks, while former Carlisle youngster Paul Boertien impressed in the first team following the appointment of John Gregory.

FIVE OF THE BEST

Although the 2001–02 season ended in disappointment for Derby County, there were some huge plusses that came out of the ashes of relegation. Despite the upheaval of having three different managers throughout the campaign, young defenders Chris Riggott and Danny Higginbotham showed some fine form, while pacy striker Malcolm Christie confirmed that he had the ability to score against the best.

TOP GOALSCORERS

	GOALS	GOALS/SHOTS
MALCOLM CHRISTIE	9	19%
Fabrizio Ravanelli	9	15%
Lee Morris	4	36%
Branko Strupar	4	25%
Marvin Robinson	1	100%

Derby's strikeforce scored nine goals apiece as experienced Italian Fabrizio Ravanelli teamed up with exciting England under-21 striker Malcolm Christie. It was, in fact, the youngster who was the deadlier of the two, scoring with 19% of his shots – four percentage points better than the White Feather. After largely being ignored by Jim Smith and Colin Todd, Lee Morris weighed in with four strikes.

Player of the season Chris Riggott saw more of the ball than any other Derby player, but despite the often constant pressure that the Rams' defence was put under, the highly-rated youngster found a team-mate with 71% of his passes. Fellow centre-back Danny Higginbotham was the second-most prolific passer as he formed a successful partnership in defence with Riggott.

TOP PASSERS

	SUCC PASSES	COMPLETION
CHRIS RIGGOTT	725	71%
Danny Higginbotham	721	62%
Fabrizio Ravanelli	720	69%
Paul Boertien	624	72%
Darryl Powell	583	74%

TOP TACKLERS

	WON	SUCCESS
PAUL BOERTIEN	81	79%
Luciano Zavagno	78	71%
Chris Riggott	71	77%
Danny Higginbotham	60	67%
Pierre Ducrocq	50	72%

Paul Boertien was one of the most underrated ball-winners in the top flight – amassing a total of 81 successful tackles. The fact that he won 79% of the challenges that he went in for speaks volumes for his ability to time his tackles. Fiery defender Luciano Zavagno was the second-most prolific. The Argentine was Colin Todd's first signing and one of the few successes of 2001–02.

Passionate striker Fabrizio Ravanelli posted the worst disciplinary record for the Rams during the 2001–02 season after committing 54 fouls as he battled hard up front. Luciano Zavagno was tough in the tackle, but paid the price for an occasional lack of timing and amassed a significant total of eight yellow cards – no player at Derby saw more, but he managed to avoid a red card throughout 2001–02.

DISCIPLINE

	POINTS	FOULS & CARDS
FABRIZIO RAVANELLI	69	54F, 5Y, 0R
Luciano Zavagno	66	42F, 8Y, 0Y
Darryl Powell	61	49F, 4Y, 0R
Chris Riggott	58	37F, 7Y, 0R
Robert Lee	41	32F, 3Y, 0R

more often than any other side

EVERTON

ADDRESS

Goodison Park, Liverpool L4 4EL

CONTACT NUMBERS

Telephone: 0151 330 2200
Fax: 0151 286 9112
Ticket Office: 0151 330 2300
Ticket Line: 09068 121599
ClubCall: 09068 121199
Everton FC Megastore: 0151 330 2030
e-mail: everton@evertonfc.com
Website: www.evertonfc.tv

KEY PERSONNEL

Chairman: Sir Phillip Carter CBE
Deputy Chairman: Bill Kenwright CBE
Directors: Keith Tamlin,
Arthur Abercromby,
Paul Gregg, Jon Woods
Chief Executive: Michael Dunford
Manager: David Moyes

SPONSORS

2001–02 One2One

FANZINES

When Skies Are Grey,
Speke From The Harbour,
Satis?

COLOURS

Home: Blue shirts, white
shorts and blue stockings
Away: Silver shirts, black shorts
and silver stockings

NICKNAME

The Toffees

HONOURS

League Champions:
1890–91, 1914–15 1927–28, 1931–32,
1938–39, 1962–63, 1969–70, 1984–85,
1986–87
Division Two Champions: 1930–31
FA Cup Winners: 1906, 1933,
1966, 1984, 1995
European Cup Winners' Cup Winners:
1985

RECORD GOALSCORER

William Ralph 'Dixie' Dean –
349 league goals, 1925–37

BIGGEST WIN

11–2 v Derby County – FA Cup 1st round,
18 January 1890

BIGGEST DEFEAT

4–10 v Tottenham Hotspur – Division One,
11 October 1958

SEASON REVIEW

The battle-weary supporters of Everton could only have expected another season of hard graft in the 2001–02 Premiership, given five bottom-half finishes in as many seasons. It would turn out to be just that – but the manner of the campaign's finale gave their long-suffering fans some cause for optimism.

The close-season changes in personnel were limited by financial constraints on manager Walter Smith. Alan Stubbs arrived from Celtic on a free transfer while Smith spent £4.5m of the £8m raised from the sale of Francis Jeffers to Arsenal on Anderlecht's Canadian striker Tomasz Radzinski. However, the deals did not end there as Michael Ball joined Rangers for £6.5m.

A fine start to the season brought seven points from a possible nine, as the Toffees secured victories away at Charlton and at home to Middlesbrough.

The club even found themselves briefly on top of the Premiership table, but vertigo sufferers were soon relieved to see Everton sliding towards the more familiar surrounds of mid-table after three straight defeats.

But the Blues then produced their most convincing performance of the campaign to restore some hope – a 5–0 thrashing of West Ham including Radzinski's first goal for the club. Sadly, it was to be Everton's only truly emphatic win of the season.

Indeed, following a 3–2 success over Aston Villa in mid-October the Toffeemen failed to net more than twice in any league match for a full five months, with a 2–0 win at home to Southampton in early December their only genuinely worthy success during the period.

Pressure was mounting on manager Smith, although deputy chairman Bill Kenwright continued to stand by him: "I have supported the man rock solid for two years and I always will."

Unfortunately one result in particular convinced Kenwright and his fellow directors that the time for change was upon them.

The excitement of reaching the FA Cup quarter finals soon turned to horror at the Blues' performance – a 3–0 stuffing at the hands of Middlesbrough proved to be the final straw and Smith was shown the door. The club acted swiftly to appoint a replacement and Preston boss David Moyes was seen as the ideal candidate.

The wisdom of the appointment was soon clear for all to see. His first game in charge ended with a hard-fought, but deserved, 2–1 win over fellow strugglers Fulham, which gave the Toffeemen a three-point cushion above the relegation zone – a margin which would only increase as the season reached its climax.

> "When he [David Moyes] was appointed he spoke of "The People's Club" and the fans loved that. I firmly believe Everton needed to hear something different."
>
> **Bill Kenwright**

Three wins in Moyes's opening four games practically assured Everton's survival in the top flight, although that's not to say defeat wasn't tasted by the new man at the helm – the Scot found himself on the losing side four times during his first nine games in charge.

Nonetheless the team appeared to be playing with renewed vigour, as Moyes wrung every last drop of effort from his new charges and got the best out of the likes of Niclas Alexandersson and David Unsworth at the crucial moment. The hope at Goodison Park will therefore be that the turnaround can continue and that a top-half finish at the very least can be achieved in 2002–03.

But one thing seems certain – Moyes will more than likely continue to be restricted by the financial difficulties at the Merseyside club.

Toffees' back line the most prolific in the Premiership

EVERTON

DATE	OPPONENT	SCORE	ATT.	ALEXANDERSSON	BLOMQVIST	CADAMARTERI	CAMPBELL	CARSLEY	CHADWICK	CLARKE	CLELAND	FERGUSON	GASCOIGNE	GEMMILL	GERRARD	GINOLA
18.08.01	Charlton A	2–1	20,451	81	–	–	90	–	–	–	–	90¹□	–	90	90	–
20.08.01	Tottenham H	1–1	29,503	88	–	–	90	–	–	–	–	90¹□	–	90	90	–
25.08.01	Middlesbro H	2–0	32,829	89	–	–	90¹	–	–	–	–	90	–	90¹	–	–
08.09.01	Man Utd A	1–4	67,534	65	–	–	90¹	–	–	–	–	90	–	90	90	–
15.09.01	Liverpool H	1–3	39,554	77	–	–	90¹	–	–	–	–	90	s45	–	90	–
22.09.01	Blackburn A	0–1	27,732	90□	–	–	90	–	–	–	–	90	90	–	90	–
29.09.01	West Ham H	5–0*	32,049	90	–	–	90¹	–	–	–	–	–	9	–	90	–
13.10.01	Ipswich A	0–0	22,820	90	–	–	90	–	–	–	–	85	–	–	90	–
20.10.01	Aston Villa H	3–2	33,352	90	–	–	90	–	–	–	–	s13	s10	s48	90	–
27.10.01	Newcastle H	1–3	37,524	90	–	–	68	–	–	–	–	s22	s8	90□	90	–
03.11.01	Bolton W A	2–2	27,343	90	–	s3	–	–	–	s1	–	89¹	90	–	–	–
18.11.01	Chelsea H	0–0	30,555	74	–	–	–	–	–	–	–	s16	–	–	–	–
24.11.01	Leicester A	0–0	21,539	90	–	–	–	–	–	–	–	–	s29	90	–	–
02.12.01	Southampton H	2–0	28,138	45	–	–	–	–	–	–	–	–	s45	90	–	–
08.12.01	Fulham A	0–2	19,338	s32	–	–	–	–	–	–	–	–	58	90	–	–
15.12.01	Derby Co H	1–0	38,615	90	–	–	–	–	–	–	–	–	s27	90□	–	–
19.12.01	Leeds Utd A	2–3	40,201	75	–	–	–	–	–	–	–	–	s68□	90	–	–
22.12.01	Sunderland A	0–1	48,013	s62	s16	–	–	–	s1	–	–	–	90□	90	–	–
26.12.01	Man Utd H	0–2	39,948	82	73	–	–	–	–	–	–	s17	s8	90	–	–
29.12.01	Charlton H	0–3	31,131	70	79	–	–	–	–	–	–	s79	s20	90□	–	–
01.01.02	Middlesbro A	0–1	27,463	45	s45	37	–	–	–	–	–	90□	–	90	–	–
12.01.02	Sunderland H	1–0	30,736	85	83¹	–	90	–	s7	–	s5	–	90	90	–	–
19.01.02	Tottenham A	1–1	36,056	60	–	–	90	–	–	s30	–	90□	82	90	–	–
30.01.02	Aston Villa A	0–0	32,460	–	–	71	90	–	s19	90□	s64	90□	–	90	–	–
02.02.02	Ipswich H	1–2	33,069	–	90	–	90	–	45	–	–	90	90	90	–	–
10.02.02	Arsenal H	0–1	30,859	–	78	–	90	90	–	86	–	–	s20	–	–	90
23.02.02	Liverpool A	1–1	44,371	–	–	–	90	90	–	90□	–	–	–	90	–	45
03.03.02	Leeds Utd H	0–0	33,226	–	80	–	90	90	–	–	–	–	–	90	–	s10
06.03.02	West Ham A	0–1	29,883	68	90□	–	63	68	–	–	–	–	–	90	–	s27
16.03.02	Fulham H	2–1	34,639	–	s15	–	–	90	–	–	–	90¹	–	90	–	–
23.03.02	Derby Co A	4–3	33,297	s61¹	90	–	s31□	29	–	s7	–	90¹□	–	90	–	–
30.03.02	Newcastle A	2–6	51,921	90¹	s16	–	–	–	s16	–	–	90¹	–	90	–	–
01.04.02	Bolton W H	3–1	39,784	90	70	–	–	–	s20¹	–	–	20■	–	90	–	–
06.04.02	Chelsea A	0–3	40,545	78	55	–	–	–	s12	90	–	90	–	90	–	–
13.04.02	Leicester H	2–2	35,580	90	–	–	–	s7	–	s28¹	–	90¹	–	90	90	–
20.04.02	Southampton A	1–0	31,785	–	–	–	90	90	27	–	–	–	–	90	90	–
28.04.02	Blackburn H	1–2	34,976	74	s8	–	90	–	90¹	–	–	–	–	90	90	–
11.05.02	Arsenal A	3–4	38,254	78	–	–	90	90¹	–	–	–	–	–	–	–	s12

□ Yellow card, ■ Red card, s Substitute, 90² Goals scored
*including own goal

For more information visit our website:

2001–02 PREMIERSHIP APPEARANCES

GRAVESEN	HIBBERT	LINDEROTH	MOORE	NAYSMITH	PEMBRIDGE	PISTONE	RADZINSKI	SIMONSEN	STUBBS	TAL	UNSWORTH	WATSON	WEIR	XAVIER	TOTAL
90□	-	-	-	-	90	90□	-	-	90	-	s9	90	90¹	-	990
43	-	-	s17	-	90	90□	-	-	90	s2	s47	73	90□	-	990
-	-	-	-	s1	28	90□	-	-	90	s62	90□	90	90	-	990
-	-	-	s25	-	90	90	-	-	66	s24	90	90	65□	s25	990
90	s13	-	-	90	-	-	s45	-	90	-	45	90	90	45	990
73	73	-	s17□	90	-	-	-	-	90	-	s17	-	90	90	990
90¹	s7	-	s7	90	s74	90	83¹	-	-	-	-	90¹	90	90	990
-	-	-	-	90	68	90□	90	-	s34	s5	s22	56	90	90□	990
80¹	-	-	-	90□	42	90	77¹	-	-	-	-	90¹	90	90	990
90	-	-	-	90	-	90	90	-	s68	-	82	-	90¹	22	990
90□	-	-	-	90	-	90	87	90	90¹□	-	90	-	90	-	990
90□	-	-	-	90	-	90	90	90	90	-	90	90	90	-	990
61	-	-	-	88	s2	90	90	90	90	-	90	90	90□	-	990
90	-	-	-	90	s45¹	90	90¹	90	90	-	45	90	90	-	990
73	-	-	s17	90	90	90□	90	90□	90□	-	-	90	75■	-	975
63	-	-	s45¹	90	90	45	90	90	15	-	s75	90	90	-	990
-	-	-	s38¹	90	22	52	90	90	-	s15	90	90	90¹	90	990
28□	-	-	90	90□	-	-	89	90	-	74	90	90	-	90	990
8	-	-	s82	90	-	-	90	90	-	-	90	90	90	90	990
-	-	-	90	90	-	-	11	90	-	s11	90	90	90	90	990
-	s41	-	s53	90	-	-	-	90	90□	-	90	49	90	90	990
-	90	-	-	90	-	-	-	90	90	-	90□	-	90	-	990
-	90	-	s8	90	-	-	-	90	90	-	90	-	90¹□	-	990
-	26	-	90	90□	-	-	-	90	90	-	90	-	-	-	990
-	-	s45	s7	90	-	-	-	90	90□	-	83¹	-	90	-	990
-	-	90	s4	90	s12	-	-	90	90	-	70	-	90	-	990
s45□	-	45	-	90	-	90	s45¹	90	90	-	-	-	90	-	990
s10	-	80	-	-	-	90	90□	90	90	-	90	-	90	-	990
s22	-	s22	-	-	-	90□	90	90	90	-	90	-	90	-	990
28■	90	-	s45□	-	-	90	45	90	90	-	75¹□	-	90	-	928
90	90□	-	-	-	-	-	59	90	83¹	-	90¹	-	90	-	990
90	31	-	-	-	-	74□	74	90	90	-	90□	s59□	90	-	990
-	-	s2	-	-	-	90¹	88¹	90	90	-	90□	90	90□	-	920
90□	-	s35	-	-	-	90	90	90	-	-	-	90	90	-	990
90□	-	-	-	-	-	90	62	-	90	-	90	83	90	-	990
90	-	-	-	-	-	90	s63	-	90	-	90	90¹	90	-	990
90	-	-	-	-	-	90	s16	-	90□	-	82□	90	90	-	990
-	-	90	-	-	90	-	90¹	90	90	-	90	90¹	90	-	990

THE MANAGER

DAVID MOYES

The level of optimism was huge when David Moyes was appointed Everton manager in March 2002, following the dismissal of Walter Smith. Moyes was charged with a single task – ensuring the Toffeemen survived in the top flight – and he managed it with two games to spare.

The youngest manager in the Premiership when appointed, Moyes has managed just one other club so far – his former charges Preston North End. The Lilywhites were also Moyes's final club as a player – he previously plied his defensive trade at a number of others including Cambridge United, Bristol City and Celtic.

Moyes's record at Preston was an impressive one as he guided the club to promotion from Division Two in his second full season in charge. His third campaign saw Preston into the Division One play-offs which, despite defeat in the final to Bolton, increased his standing in the eyes of his contemporaries.

Before securing his new post at Goodison Park, Moyes was linked with a coaching job at Manchester United and a role with the Scotland national team – the highly sought-after boss certainly has the weight of expectation on his shoulders.

LEAGUE POSITION

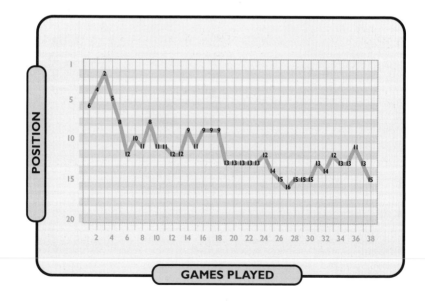

GAMES PLAYED

0 Duncan Ferguson has scored 12 times for Everton

THE GOALS

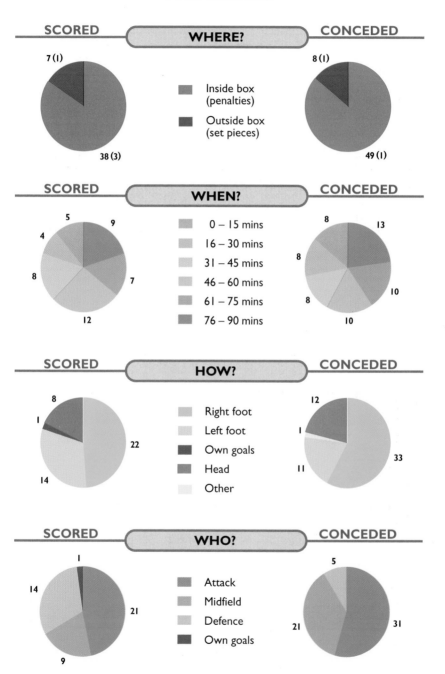

WHERE?

SCORED · CONCEDED

- Inside box (penalties)
- Outside box (set pieces)

Scored: 7 (1), 38 (3)
Conceded: 8 (1), 49 (1)

WHEN?

SCORED · CONCEDED

- 0 – 15 mins
- 16 – 30 mins
- 31 – 45 mins
- 46 – 60 mins
- 61 – 75 mins
- 76 – 90 mins

Scored: 5, 9, 4, 8, 7, 12
Conceded: 8, 13, 8, 8, 10, 10

HOW?

SCORED · CONCEDED

- Right foot
- Left foot
- Own goals
- Head
- Other

Scored: 8, 1, 22, 14
Conceded: 12, 1, 33, 11

WHO?

SCORED · CONCEDED

- Attack
- Midfield
- Defence
- Own goals

Scored: 1, 14, 21, 9
Conceded: 5, 21, 31

since returning to the club, but none were headers

EVERTON

	ALEXANDERSSON	BLOMQVIST	CADAMARTERI	CAMPBELL	CARSLEY	CHADWICK	CLARKE	CLELAND	FERGUSON	GASCOIGNE	GEMMILL	GINOLA	GRAVESEN
APPEARANCES													
Start	28	10	2	21	8	2	5	0	17	8	31	2	22
Sub	3	5	1	2	0	7	2	3	5	10	1	3	3
Minutes on pitch	2379	888	111	1879	637	220	438	70	1602	878	2838	184	1704
GOAL ATTEMPTS													
Goals	2	1	0	4	1	3	0	0	6	1	1	0	2
Shots on target	13	2	0	19	7	8	0	0	22	4	7	1	20
Shots off target	16	5	0	15	4	6	0	0	18	4	11	5	20
Shooting accuracy %	45%	29%	0%	56%	64%	57%	0%	0%	55%	50%	39%	17%	50%
Goals/shots %	7%	14%	0%	12%	9%	21%	0%	0%	15%	13%	6%	0%	5%
PASSING													
Goal assists	4	0	0	1	0	0	0	0	1	0	4	0	5
Long passes	124	68	0	82	63	9	54	5	116	115	354	19	223
Short passes	614	307	21	554	184	61	82	17	548	333	1011	75	550
PASS COMPLETION													
Own half %	75%	82%	80%	82%	79%	71%	59%	60%	87%	81%	81%	87%	82%
Opposition half %	63%	66%	56%	69%	64%	52%	49%	71%	61%	72%	74%	75%	72%
CROSSING													
Total crosses	187	49	2	11	9	3	2	4	6	41	16	12	72
Cross completion %	30%	27%	50%	27%	11%	0%	50%	50%	33%	24%	50%	8%	18%
DRIBBLING													
Dribbles & runs	103	66	2	30	7	5	3	3	26	61	54	21	74
Dribble completion %	60%	55%	100%	73%	71%	20%	100%	67%	65%	69%	81%	52%	61%
DEFENDING													
Tackles made	121	45	2	42	29	9	23	8	15	30	93	3	67
Tackles won %	76%	80%	100%	69%	69%	89%	78%	50%	67%	80%	65%	33%	84%
Blocks	17	1	0	4	5	1	7	1	1	2	33	0	5
Clearances	36	5	0	11	15	1	32	3	39	13	32	0	11
Interceptions	7	3	0	3	5	1	4	0	2	7	36	0	5
DISCIPLINE													
Fouls conceded	29	12	5	48	16	2	8	1	66	25	42	5	49
Fouls won	30	19	1	35	7	7	4	0	51	24	34	9	30
Offside	5	4	4	28	4	3	1	0	8	1	2	2	4
Yellow cards	1	2	0	1	0	0	2	0	6	2	3	0	7
Red cards	0	0	0	0	0	0	0	0	1	0	0	0	1

GOALKEEPER NAME	START/ (SUB)	TIME ON PITCH	GOALS CONCEDED	MINS/GOALS CONCEDED	SAVES MADE	SAVES/ SHOTS
GERRARD	13 (0)	1170	19	62	29	60%
SIMONSEN	25 (0)	2250	38	59	79	68%

For more information visit our website:

PLAYERS' STATISTICS

	HIBBERT	LINDEROTH	MOORE	NAYSMITH	PEMBRIDGE	PISTONE	RADZINSKI	STUBBS	TAL	UNSWORTH	WATSON	WEIR	XAVIER	TOTAL	RANK
	7	4	3	23	10	25	23	29	1	28	24	36	11		
	3	4	13	1	4	0	4	2	6	5	1	0	1		
	551	409	635	2069	833	2151	2014	2606	193	2542	2120	3200	902		
	0	0	2	0	1	1	6	2	0	3	4	4	0	45*	12th
	1	2	8	7	5	3	23	13	0	6	5	8	0	184	=9th
	1	1	5	9	5	4	17	18	1	15	13	9	2	204	17th
	50%	67%	62%	44%	50%	43%	58%	42%	0%	29%	28%	47%	0%	47%	5th
	0%	0%	15%	0%	10%	14%	15%	6%	0%	14%	22%	24%	0%	11%	8th
	0	0	0	4	4	1	3	0	1	1	2	2	0	33	=10th
	45	55	34	143	70	294	74	377	18	430	318	349	57	3872	15th
	117	158	169	606	264	646	539	484	67	753	524	609	198	9535	18th
	62%	76%	81%	82%	71%	81%	74%	82%	67%	81%	75%	77%	83%	80%	18th
	58%	66%	65%	68%	72%	67%	63%	53%	67%	59%	58%	54%	73%	64%	17th
	13	15	12	54	52	49	41	2	10	152	58	5	1	878	13th
	38%	40%	33%	35%	21%	20%	17%	0%	40%	32%	26%	0%	100%	27%	3rd
	13	10	21	62	16	33	85	20	10	42	106	35	2	913	16th
	62%	50%	86%	76%	88%	73%	59%	100%	70%	83%	62%	89%	100%	68%	11th
	36	13	31	105	32	66	28	68	12	71	59	90	30	1129	3rd
	69%	77%	81%	74%	56%	83%	61%	75%	75%	72%	71%	69%	77%	73%	12th
	9	0	3	18	2	19	4	22	0	14	18	29	12	227	=7th
	25	1	4	79	12	139	4	369	3	151	97	440	71	1658	2nd
	4	3	2	13	3	19	2	16	0	19	19	22	8	203	2nd
	5	9	7	31	12	21	28	38	10	47	38	62	20	637	1st
	6	2	13	23	15	25	42	29	3	35	31	52	13	547	9th
	0	0	1	3	1	1	33	0	0	2	3	2	0	112	16th
	1	0	2	3	0	7	1	5	0	6	1	5	1	57	12th
	0	0	0	0	0	0	0	0	0	0	0	1	0	3	=9th

*Including one own goal

CROSSES CAUGHT	CROSSES PUNCHED	CROSSES DROPPED	CATCH SUCCESS	THROWS/ SHORT KICKS	% COMPLETION	LONG KICKS	% COMPLETION
26	9	6	81%	26	96%	251	57%
65	13	9	88%	43	98%	550	50%

PLAYER OF THE SEASON

PLAYER	INDEX SCORE
ALAN STUBBS	806
David Weir	803
Duncan Ferguson	774
Steve Simonsen	705
Steve Watson	665
Niclas Alexandersson	664
Kevin Campbell	663
Alessandro Pistone	653
Gary Naysmith	651
Tomasz Radzinski	647

A free transfer from Celtic in the summer of 2001, Alan Stubbs made an immediate impact at Goodison Park with his high work-rate and committed defending. The Liverpool-born centre-back was also a threat in attack, scoring twice from outside the area – once direct from a free kick – from a total of 29 attempts during the season.

Stubbs also won an above-average 75% of his tackles and whacked 369 clearances during the course of the season, putting him in the Premiership's top 10 of players clearing their lines. However, second only to Liverpool's Sami Hyypia in that list was David Weir, whose 440 clearances and four goals of his own helped him to within three Index points of his Everton team-mate.

Seen by many as one of Everton's best-ever purchases, Weir also provided two goal assists for colleagues as he proved equally useful going forward as at the back, although his 69% tackle success rate saw him pipped to the top spot by Stubbs

who proved more effective on average.

Inspirational striker Duncan Ferguson followed his compatriot with an Index score of 774 points. The giant Scot may have missed chunks of the season through injury and suspension, but nonetheless finished as the club's joint-top goalscorer, with six strikes to his name thanks to a fine shooting accuracy of 55%.

Steve Simonsen also performed well having wrested the goalkeeper's jersey from Paul Gerrard early in the season. The ex-Tranmere stopper has a bright future ahead of him at just 23 years of age, as he showed by saving over two-thirds of the shots that came his way during 2001–02 and with two of England's goalkeepers perhaps nearing the end of their international careers, a spot in one or two Euro 2004 qualifying squads may not be out of the question.

Simonsen was followed in the rankings by more experienced players Steve Watson, Niclas Alexandersson and Kevin Campbell who were separated by just two points.

FIVE OF THE BEST

So often a managerial change instils new belief in a squad and that was certainly the case at Everton. Overall 2001–02 was a season to forget, but while the appointment of David Moyes may not have engendered a massive turnaround in form, the side certainly began to show signs that it can improve in the top flight during 2002–03.

TOP GOALSCORERS	GOALS	GOALS/SHOTS
DUNCAN FERGUSON	6	15%
Tomasz Radzinski	6	15%
David Weir	4	24%
Steve Watson	4	22%
Kevin Campbell	4	12%

Injuries played a large part in Everton's 2000–01 campaign and the trend continued with no striker able to command a regular place in the starting XI. Duncan Ferguson and summer signing Tomasz Radzinski tied for top scorer on six apiece, both converting 15% of their chances. Defenders seemed to pick the best time to shoot – both David Weir and Steve Watson commanded very high goals-to-shots ratios as each netted four times.

Comfortably the best passer of the ball in the squad was Scot Gemmill. Not only did he hit around 250 accurate passes more than runner-up David Unsworth, but his 77% completion rate beat that of each of the club's regular starters. Unsworth himself benefited from Moyes's appointment with a good run in the side, delivering 792 cleanly hit passes in all, despite a disappointing level of overall accuracy.

TOP PASSERS	SUCC PASSES	COMPLETION
SCOT GEMMILL	1,045	77%
David Unsworth	792	67%
Alessandro Pistone	694	74%
David Weir	632	66%
Alan Stubbs	597	69%

TOP TACKLERS	WON	SUCCESS
N ALEXANDERSSON	92	76%
Gary Naysmith	78	74%
David Weir	62	69%
Scot Gemmill	60	65%
Thomas Gravesen	56	84%

Nowhere near the top five during 2000–01, Niclas Alexandersson was the chief ball-winner for the Toffeemen, with 92 challenges won and a fine 76% success rate to boot. The Swede thus out-tackled defenders Gary Naysmith and David Weir as well as top passer Scot Gemmill, although last term's number one Thomas Gravesen demonstrated more clinical challenging with an 84% success rate and may have retained top spot, but for a series of injuries.

With all due respect to the Scotsman, it's not much of a surprise to see Duncan Ferguson at the top of the discipline chart. Sixty-six fouls sealed the top spot for the uncompromising forward, although Thomas Gravesen – top of the table last time around – picked up an extra yellow card. Sandwiched between them was David Weir, whose tally of 62 offences prevented him from becoming Opta's Everton player of the season.

DISCIPLINE	POINTS	FOULS & CARDS
DUNCAN FERGUSON	90	66F, 6Y, 1R
David Weir	83	62F, 5Y, 1R
Thomas Gravesen	76	49F, 7Y, 1R
David Unsworth	65	47F, 6Y, 0R
Alan Stubbs	53	38F, 5Y, 0R

FULHAM

ADDRESS

Correspondence Address: Fulham Football
Club Training Ground,
Motspur Park, New Malden,
Surrey KT3 6PT
Stadium: Loftus Road Stadium, South
Africa Road, London W12 7PA

CONTACT NUMBERS

Telephone: 020 7893 8383
Fax: 020 7384 4715
Ticket Office: 020 7384 4710
ClubCall: 09068 440 044
Club Shop: 020 7384 4807
e-mail: enquiries@ffc.uk.com
Website: www.fulhamfc.com

KEY PERSONNEL

Chairman: M Al Fayed
Vice-Chairman: B Muddyman
Directors: S Benson
T Delaney, A Muddyman
Acting Managing Director: M Collins
Deputy Managing Director: L Hoos
Manager: Jean Tigana

SPONSORS

Pizza Hut

FANZINES

There's Only One F In Fulham

COLOURS

Home: White shirts, black shorts
and white stockings
Away: Red and black striped shirts,
red shorts and red stockings

NICKNAME

The Cottagers

HONOURS

Division One Champions: 2000–01
Division Two Champions:
1948–49, 1998–99
Division Three (South) Champions
1931–32

RECORD GOALSCORER

Gordon Davies – 159 league goals,
1978–84, 1986–91

BIGGEST WIN

10–1 v Ipswich Town, Division 1,
26 December 1963

BIGGEST DEFEAT

0–10 v Liverpool –
League Cup 2nd Round 1st leg,
23 September 1986

SEASON REVIEW

After taking the first division by storm, Fulham were back in the top flight after a 34-year absence. The Cottagers marked their return to the big time with a bang by playing their part in a thrilling game at Manchester United.

Despite leading twice through Louis Saha, a second-half brace from Dutch hot-shot Ruud van Nistelrooy meant Jean Tigana's team returned from Old Trafford empty-handed. In what was to be a regular feature of their campaign, Fulham won many plaudits for the quality of their football, but failed to yield the points their performance deserved.

Nevertheless, Peter Reid's Sunderland were the Cottagers' first victims. The Black Cats were sent packing thanks to goals from Saha and Barry Hayles. But these two players were not scoring enough for manager Tigana's liking and he soon purchased French centre forward Steve Marlet from Lyon for a club record £11.5 million to boost the squad.

However, the new man suffered injury problems in the early stages of his career in the Premiership and spent two months on the sidelines. Marlet returned just before the turn of the year to net against Manchester United, but once again Fulham went down by the odd goal in five to Sir Alex Ferguson's team.

Meanwhile, the club was progressing well in the FA Cup, winning potential banana-skin matches against Wycombe, York and Walsall. But the Cottagers' league form began to slip in early February as the team went on a miserable sequence of six consecutive league defeats.

After stopping the rot with a point at Southampton, the club announced record losses of £24 million in the previous financial year, leading many critics to question Tigana's future, especially as the club sat in danger of suffering relegation back to Division One.

Therefore the manager decided that Fulham's FA Cup semi-final meeting with west London neighbours Chelsea – after a quarter-final win at West Brom – was not the most important match in their run-in. However, they were unfortunate not to reach their first Cup Final in 27 years as they performed well at Villa Park, but again a lack of firepower in front of goal cost them dear.

> **"The main thing all along has been for us to stay in the Premiership. We have come a long way since we were back in the Third Division."**
>
> **Sean Davis**

Nevertheless, their spirits were soon lifted, as they virtually guaranteed their Premiership status a week later with a 1–0 win at Leeds United. Steed Malbranque netted the only goal just after half-time to give the Cottagers their first league win in 10 games.

This victory was also their first on the road in the league since early January and was certainly one of the highlights of the season for the club's travelling supporters.

Republic of Ireland defender Steve Finnan – who was one of only four outfield Premiership players to play in every single minute of their team's 38 matches – said after the win at Elland Road that ensured their safety: "I don't think you can call it an achievement. We were aiming for much higher, maybe to finish mid-table or nick a European place."

However, the team did qualify for Europe via the Intertoto Cup and the Cottagers' 2002–03 season will begin early in July as they aim to make an impact on the continent.

The 2001–02 season was a period of consolidation for Fulham Football Club, but even if they can add a few more quality players to the squad, they still seem some way short of challenging for major honours.

FULHAM

DATE	OPPONENT	SCORE	ATT.	BETSY	BOA MORTE	BREVETT	CLARK	COLLINS	DAVIS	FINNAN	GOLDBAEK	GOMA	HARLEY
19.08.01	Man Utd A	2–3	67,534	s6	–	–	–	90	90	90	80	90□	90
22.08.01	Sunderland H	2–0	20,197	–	–	65	–	90	90	90	90	90	s25
25.08.01	Derby Co H	0–0	15,641	–	–	90	–	66	90	90	66□	15	s24
09.09.01	Charlton A	1–1	20,451	–	90¹	90	62	90	90	90	–	–	–
15.09.01	Arsenal H	1–3	20,805	–	88□	90	–	90	90	90	–	–	–
22.09.01	Leicester A	0–0	18,918	–	46□	90	90	90	90□	90	–	–	–
30.09.01	Chelsea H	1–1	20,197	–	s45	90	66	88	90□	90	45	–	–
14.10.01	Aston Villa A	0–2	28,579	–	s24	90	–	90	66□	90	–	s24	–
21.10.01	Ipswich H	1–1	17,221	–	44□	90□	63	90	s27	90	–	90	–
27.10.01	Southampton H	2–1	18,771	–	90	90	–	90	–	90	–	90	–
03.11.01	West Ham A	2–0	26,217	–	90□	90	–	83	s16	90	s7	90	–
17.11.01	Newcastle H	3–1	21,159	–	–	90	s23	67	90	90	s2	90	–
24.11.01	Bolton W A	0–0	23,848	–	s22	90□	s22	90	90	90	–	90	–
02.12.01	Leeds Utd H	0–0	20,918	–	90	90	–	90	s12	90	–	90	–
08.12.01	Everton H	2–0	19,338	–	75□Δ	90	–	90	s10	90	–	90	–
12.12.01	Liverpool A	0–0	37,163	–	90	90	–	90	59	90	–	90	–
15.12.01	Tottenham A	0–4	36,054	–	90□	90	s17	73	–	90	–	90	–
26.12.01	Charlton H	0–0	17,900	–	s78□	90	12	s26	90	90	–	90	–
30.12.01	Man Utd H	2–3	21,159	–	90	90	–	90	s14	90	–	90	–
02.01.02	Derby Co A	1–0*	28,165	–	–	90	–	90	90□	90	–	90	–
12.01.02	Middlesbro H	2–1	18,975	–	–	90	–	90	90	90	–	90	–
19.01.02	Sunderland A	1–1	45,124	–	s12	90□	–	90	–	90	–	90□	–
30.01.02	Ipswich A	0–1	25,156	–	–	90	–	s45	–	90□	45	90□	–
02.02.02	Aston Villa A	0–0	20,041	–	–	–	–	–	–	90	s26	90	90
09.02.02	Blackburn H	2–0	19,580	–	–	90	–	90	90	90	–	90	–
19.02.02	Middlesbro A	1–2	26,235	–	–	90	–	80	90	90	–	90	–
23.02.02	Arsenal A	1–4	38,029	–	s34	64	–	90	–	90	–	90□	s26
02.03.02	Liverpool H	0–2	21,103	–	66□	90□	s50	s14	26	90	–	90	–
06.03.02	Chelsea A	2–3	39,744	–	71	90	–	90	–	90	–	90	90
16.03.02	Everton A	1–2	34,639	–	45	90□	–	90	–	90□	s11	45	–
24.03.02	Tottenham H	0–2	15,885	–	–	s32	–	–	90	90	–	90□	58
30.03.02	Southampton A	1–1	31,616	–	s18	90□	–	84	71	90	–	90	s6
01.04.02	West Ham H	0–1	19,416	–	s30	90	–	59	79	90□	–	90	s11
08.04.02	Newcastle A	1–1	50,017	–	–	90	–	90	90	90	–	90	–
20.04.02	Leeds Utd A	1–0	39,811	–	9	90	–	–	87	90	s81	90□	–
23.04.02	Bolton W H	3–0	18,107	–	–	90	–	s9	81	90	90¹	90	–
27.04.02	Leicester H	0–0	21,106	–	–	90	–	s27	90	90	63	90□	–
11.05.02	Blackburn A	0–3	30,487	–	–	–	–	–	90	90	90	–	90

□ Yellow card, ■ Red card, s Substitute, 90² Goals scored

*including own goal Δ no suspension served, card remained on record

For more information visit our website:

2001–02 PREMIERSHIP APPEARANCES

HAYLES	KNIGHT	LEGWINSKI	LEWIS	MALBRANQUE	MARLET	MELVILLE	OUADDOU	SAHA	STOLCERS	SYMONS	TAYLOR	WILLOCK	VAN DER SAR	TOTAL
84	–	–	–	88	–	90	s2	90²	s10	–	–	–	90	990
90¹	–	–	–	90	–	90	–	90¹	–	–	–	–	90	990
90	–	s24	–	90	–	90	–	90□	–	s75	–	–	90	990
s13	–	90	–	s28	–	90	–	77	–	90	–	–	90	990
s2	–	72□	–	90¹	s18	90	–	90	–	90□	–	–	90	990
–	64	s23	–	s21	90	90	–	90	–	s26	–	–	90	990
90¹	90	–	–	s24	s2	90	–	90	–	–	–	–	90	990
s24	66	90	–	90	66	90	–	90	–	–	–	–	90	990
68¹	–	90□	–	s27	63	90	–	s22	–	–	–	–	90	944
90	–	90	–	90²	46	90	–	s44	–	–	–	–	90	990
90□	–	90¹	–	89¹	–	90□	–	74	s1	–	–	–	90	990
90¹	–	90¹	–	88	–	90	–	90¹	–	–	–	–	90	990
68	–	90	–	68	–	90	–	90	–	–	–	–	90	990
90	–	78□	–	90	–	90	–	90	–	–	–	–	90	990
90²	–	90□	–	90	–	90□	–	80	–	–	–	–	90	975
90	–	s31	–	90	–	90	–	90	–	–	–	–	90	990
90	–	90	–	90□	–	90	–	90	–	–	–	–	90	990
90□	–	64	–	90	–	90	–	90	–	–	–	–	90	990
66	–	76¹	–	90	s24¹	90	–	90	–	–	–	–	90	990
66□	90	–	–	90	90	90	–	s24	–	–	–	–	90	990
73□	s17	36	–	90	90¹	90	–	s54¹	–	–	–	–	90	990
77	90	90	–	90¹	90	90	–	–	s1	–	–	–	90	990
s45	45	68	–	90	90	90	s22	90	–	–	–	–	90	990
90	64	90	–	90	90	90	–	90□	–	–	–	–	90	990
90¹	–	90	–	90¹□	89□	90□	–	–	–	–	–	s1	90	990
90	–	90□	–	90	90¹	90	–	s10□	–	–	–	–	90	990
61	56	90	–	90	90¹	90	–	s29	–	–	–	–	90	990
s24	–	90□	–	90	90	–	90	90	–	–	–	–	90	990
s19	–	–	–	90	90	–	90	90²	–	–	–	–	90	990
s45□	–	79	–	90¹□	90	90	s45	90	–	–	–	–	90	990
90	–	90	–	90□	90	–	90	90	–	–	–	–	90	990
72	–	90	–	90	90¹	90	–	s19	–	–	–	–	90	990
90	–	90	–	90	s31	90	–	60	–	–	–	–	90	990
–	–	90	–	90	90	90	–	90¹	–	–	–	–	90	990
s13	–	90□	–	90¹	90	90	s3	77	–	–	–	–	90□	990
90¹	–	90	–	85	s32¹	90	–	58	s5	–	–	–	90	990
90□	–	63□	–	90	90	90	–	s27□	–	–	–	–	90	990
–	s45	83	90	–	83	90	45	90	s7	–	90	s7	–	990

THE MANAGER

JEAN TIGANA

Fulham manager Jean Tigana was a French midfield legend, capped 52 times by his country. He was instrumental in Les Bleus reaching the World Cup semi-finals in 1982 and 1986 and sandwiched in-between was a European Championship success on home soil in 1984.

Domestically, he helped Bordeaux win three league titles and three French cups, while more success followed at Marseille.

In 1993 he began his managerial career with Lyon and took them to runners-up spot in his second season before moving to Monaco. Tigana brought the French title to the principality, but resigned in acrimonious circumstances in 1999.

Fulham chairman Mohamed Al Fayed lured him to England in the summer of 2000 where Tigana proved an instant success by leading the club to the first division championship, finishing 10 points clear of runners-up Blackburn.

However Tigana found himself under pressure during Fulham's first campaign back in the top flight as they lost seven out of eight games between mid-February and early April, before clinching safety in the final few matches. The Frenchman did, however, guide the club to the FA Cup semi-finals, their best showing in the competition since 1975.

LEAGUE POSITION

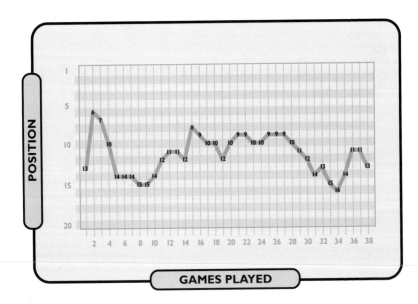

POSITION

GAMES PLAYED

341 Steed Malbranque conceded possession on

THE GOALS

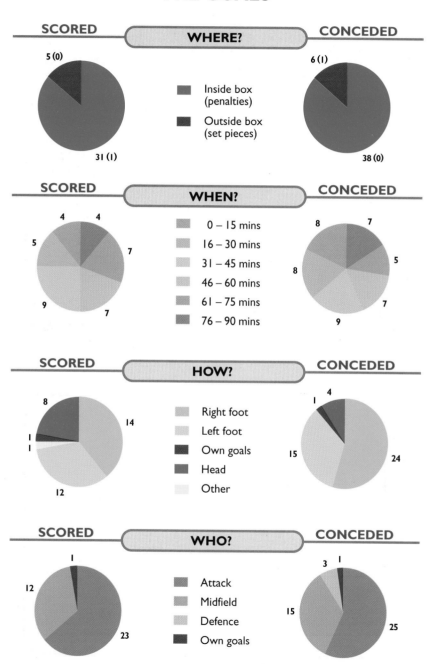

SCORED · **WHERE?** · CONCEDED

5 (0)
31 (1)

Inside box (penalties)
Outside box (set pieces)

6 (1)
38 (0)

SCORED · **WHEN?** · CONCEDED

4   4
5
7
9
7

0 – 15 mins
16 – 30 mins
31 – 45 mins
46 – 60 mins
61 – 75 mins
76 – 90 mins

8   7
5
8
7
9

SCORED · **HOW?** · CONCEDED

8
1
1
14
12

Right foot
Left foot
Own goals
Head
Other

4
1
15
24

SCORED · **WHO?** · CONCEDED

1
12
23

Attack
Midfield
Defence
Own goals

3   1
15
25

more occasions than any other Premiership player

FULHAM

	BETSY	BOA MORTE	BREVETT	CLARK	COLLINS	DAVIS	FINNAN	GOLDBAEK	GOMA
APPEARANCES									
Start	0	15	34	5	29	25	38	8	32
Sub	1	8	1	4	5	5	0	5	1
Minutes on pitch	6	1337	3041	405	2611	2168	3420	696	2784
GOAL ATTEMPTS									
Goals	0	1	0	0	0	0	0	1	0
Shots on target	0	9	1	3	8	4	3	4	4
Shots off target	0	16	3	1	19	22	5	3	10
Shooting accuracy %	0%	36%	25%	75%	30%	15%	38%	57%	29%
Goals/shots %	0%	4%	0%	0%	0%	0%	0%	14%	0%
PASSING									
Goal assists	0	1	3	0	0	1	0	1	1
Long passes	0	57	496	51	388	478	541	74	275
Short passes	4	377	1322	187	1247	973	1604	352	763
PASS COMPLETION									
Own half %	100%	76%	85%	94%	88%	89%	88%	88%	87%
Opposition half %	67%	64%	75%	76%	79%	72%	74%	83%	57%
CROSSING									
Total crosses	0	54	110	17	69	23	171	42	1
Cross completion %	0%	15%	25%	35%	26%	39%	25%	17%	0%
DRIBBLING									
Dribbles & runs	0	142	108	12	72	54	173	31	27
Dribble completion %	0%	51%	87%	67%	78%	83%	80%	65%	93%
DEFENDING									
Tackles made	2	77	86	5	167	95	124	18	107
Tackles won %	50%	77%	77%	100%	71%	55%	75%	67%	75%
Blocks	0	6	23	0	19	8	27	3	27
Clearances	0	13	152	2	33	31	132	3	299
Interceptions	0	8	15	2	8	9	14	0	24
DISCIPLINE									
Fouls conceded	0	43	49	5	26	45	22	8	39
Fouls won	1	57	46	2	41	18	52	11	26
Offside	0	6	0	0	5	0	1	0	0
Yellow cards	0	6	6	0	0	4	3	1	7
Red cards	0	2	0	0	0	0	0	0	0

GOALKEEPER NAME	START/ (SUB)	TIME ON PITCH	GOALS CONCEDED	MINS/GOALS CONCEDED	SAVES MADE	SAVES/ SHOTS
TAYLOR	1 (0)	90	3	30	7	70%
VAN DER SAR	37 (0)	3330	41	81	113	73%

For more information visit our website:

PLAYERS' STATISTICS

	HARLEY	HAYLES	KNIGHT	LEGWINSKI	LEWIS	MALBRANQUE	MARLET	MELVILLE	OUADDOU	SAHA	STOLCERS	SYMONS	WILLOCK	TOTAL	RANK
	5	27	8	30	1	33	21	35	4	28	0	2	0		
	5	8	2	3	0	4	5	0	4	8	5	2	2		
	510	2440	627	2587	90	3038	1894	3150	387	2635	24	281	8		
	0	8	0	3	0	8	6	0	0	8	0	0	0	36*	16th
	2	25	2	13	1	21	27	1	0	31	1	0	0	160	17th
	3	18	3	21	0	29	21	4	2	50	0	1	0	231	12th
	40%	58%	40%	38%	100%	42%	56%	20%	0%	38%	100%	0%	0%	41%	17th
	0%	19%	0%	9%	0%	16%	13%	0%	0%	10%	0%	0%	0%	9%	19th
	0	3	0	1	0	8	3	0	0	1	0	0	0	23	15th
	59	62	120	299	5	255	72	434	49	124	4	36	0	4424	4th
	192	776	169	1096	27	1310	519	821	151	934	20	83	4	13108	2nd
	78%	79%	91%	82%	90%	85%	70%	90%	92%	86%	75%	84%	0%	87%	2nd
	65%	66%	65%	70%	77%	68%	59%	62%	73%	68%	70%	67%	100%	69%	6th
	23	59	2	27	9	280	58	5	1	32	2	0	0	985	7th
	9%	15%	0%	22%	33%	28%	16%	40%	0%	22%	50%	0%	0%	24%	15th
	17	152	11	39	4	220	95	24	8	202	5	2	0	1418	1st
	35%	45%	100%	74%	75%	61%	57%	92%	100%	63%	60%	100%	0%	67%	17th
	13	55	26	145	2	110	26	55	14	40	1	7	0	1176	2nd
	85%	76%	81%	77%	50%	76%	81%	80%	79%	65%	0%	86%	0%	74%	9th
	6	3	5	10	0	2	2	39	5	0	0	2	0	188	18th
	16	18	56	70	1	6	7	327	30	21	1	30	0	1318	=15th
	2	2	4	29	0	6	3	11	0	2	1	0	0	140	16th
	7	84	8	62	2	31	50	22	3	36	0	5	0	547	15th
	2	80	8	37	2	68	33	17	2	97	2	3	0	614	1st
	0	22	0	5	0	6	26	1	0	5	1	0	0	78	20th
	0	6	0	8	0	4	1	3	0	4	0	1	0	55	13th
	0	0	0	0	0	0	0	0	0	0	0	0	0	2	=15th

*Including one own goal

CROSSES CAUGHT	CROSSES PUNCHED	CROSSES DROPPED	CATCH SUCCESS	THROWS/ SHORT KICKS	% COMPLETION	LONG KICKS	% COMPLETION
0	1	0	0%	5	100%	13	62%
82	27	3	96%	82	98%	675	61%

PLAYER OF THE SEASON

PLAYER	INDEX SCORE
EDWIN VAN DER SAR	818
Steed Malbranque	811
Steve Finnan	796
Louis Saha	769
John Collins	741
Alain Goma	730
Rufus Brevett	720
Sylvain Legwinski	667
Barry Hayles	655
Andy Melville	640

Fulham declared their intentions to the rest of the Premiership when they signed Edwin van der Sar from Juventus for £7 million in August 2001. And the big Dutchman did not disappoint as he scooped Opta's Fulham player of the season award.

The goalkeeper turned down a return to his first club Ajax in order to try his luck in the English Premiership and was a solid last line of defence for Jean Tigana's team.

Van der Sar kept 15 clean sheets throughout the course of the 2001–02 season and only Jerzy Dudek and Nigel Martyn boasted more shutouts than the Fulham shot-stopper. Furthermore, he used his 6' 5" height to full advantage by claiming 82 high balls in his penalty area.

Close behind in the Opta Index was Steed Malbranque. The popular midfielder had a fantastic first season in English football scoring eight league goals – including the winner at Leeds in April 2002 that secured the Cottagers' top-flight status.

The former Lyon trainee was also the team's chief provider, setting up eight goals for his team-mates, several of them coming via his accurate deliveries from the flanks. Malbranque's tally of 52 successful corners was the highest tally by any individual in the Premiership.

Defender Steve Finnan – who did not miss a single minute of Premiership football – also featured highly in the Index for his consistent displays on the right in the team's first taste of top-flight football in 34 years.

Meanwhile, striker Louis Saha can consider himself unfortunate not to have added to his eight league goals in 2001–02, as no other Premiership player hit the woodwork more often than the former French under-21 star.

Other Cottagers to feature in the Index for their high level of performance were more senior players such as former Monaco man John Collins, ex-Newcastle defender Alain Goma and Rufus Brevett, who joined the club in 1998 and has been part of their rise from Division Two all the way up to the Premiership.

FIVE OF THE BEST

Fulham, like the other two promoted teams, Blackburn and Bolton, managed to survive their first season back in the Premiership. A dismal run of form between February and April saw the Cottagers pick up just two points, but an improvement in results after Easter guaranteed top-flight football at their temporary home of Loftus Road for 2002–03.

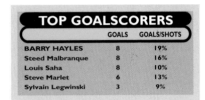

TOP GOALSCORERS

	GOALS	GOALS/SHOTS
BARRY HAYLES	8	19%
Steed Malbranque	8	16%
Louis Saha	8	10%
Steve Marlet	6	13%
Sylvain Legwinski	3	9%

Former electrician Barry Hayles certainly set a few sparks flying in his first season in the Premiership as he found the back of the net with almost a fifth of his attempts on goal. Meanwhile, club record signing Steve Marlet will hope to stay clear of injury and be more productive in 2002–03 after bagging just six league goals following his £11.5m arrival from Lyon last August.

Republic of Ireland international Steve Finnan made the fourth-highest number of successful passes in the Premiership with 1,720 of his intended balls picking out a colleague. The right-back, who played every single minute of the 2001–02 campaign, was supported by fellow defender Rufus Brevett who completed 79% of his distribution. Talented youngster Sean Davis did not look out of place among the elite with some fine individual performances.

TOP PASSERS

	SUCC PASSES	COMPLETION
STEVE FINNAN	1,720	80%
Rufus Brevett	1,440	79%
John Collins	1,347	82%
Sean Davis	1,141	79%
Steed Malbranque	1,135	73%

TOP TACKLERS

	WON	SUCCESS
JOHN COLLINS	119	71%
Sylvain Legwinski	112	77%
Steve Finnan	93	75%
Steed Malbranque	84	76%
Alain Goma	80	75%

In his previous spell in English football's top flight in 1999–2000, John Collins made the highest number of successful tackles in the Premiership. Therefore it was not surprising to learn that the former Scotland international was Fulham's chief ball-winner in 2001–02 with 119 successful challenges. The Cottagers' only other individual to come away with the ball from more than a century of challenges was French midfielder Sylvain Legwinski.

Overall, Fulham were a relatively well-disciplined team in 2001–02, but striker Barry Hayles's robust challenges made him the most indisciplined Englishman in the Premiership with 84 fouls and six yellow cards. Meanwhile, Sylvain Legwinski amassed more cautions than any other Cottager and Luis Boa Morte's two red cards in the first half of the campaign explained why the Portuguese international featured high in Fulham's discipline chart.

DISCIPLINE

	POINTS	FOULS & CARDS
BARRY HAYLES	102	84F, 6Y, 0R
Sylvain Legwinski	86	62F, 8Y, 0R
Luis Boa Morte	73	43F, 6Y, 2R
Rufus Brevett	67	49F, 6Y, 0R
Alain Goma	60	39F, 7Y, 0R

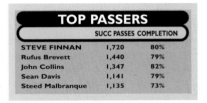

crosses than any other goalkeeper

IPSWICH TOWN

ADDRESS

Portman Road, Ipswich,
Suffolk IP1 2DA

CONTACT NUMBERS

Telephone: 01473 400 500
Fax: 01473 400 040
Ticket Office: 01473 400 555
Club Information Line:
0845 3300 442 (local rate)
Superstore: 01473 400 563
e-mail: enquiries@itfc.co.uk
Website: www.itfc.co.uk

KEY PERSONNEL

Chairman and Chief Executive:
D Sheepshanks
Directors: R Finbow, P Hope-Cobbold,
J Kerr MBE, R Moore,
Rt Hon Lord Ryder OBE
Club Secretary: D Rose
Manager: George Burley

SPONSORS

TXU Energi

FANZINES

Those Were The Days

COLOURS

Home: Royal blue shirts, white shorts and
royal blue stockings
Away: White shirts, black shorts
and white stockings

NICKNAMES

Blues or Town

HONOURS

Division One Champions: 1961–62
Division Two Champions: 1960–61,
1967–68, 1991–92
Division Three (South) Champions:
1953–54, 1956–57
FA Cup Winners: 1978
UEFA Cup Winners: 1981
Texaco Cup Winners: 1973

RECORD GOALSCORER

Ray Crawford – 203 league goals
1958–63, 1966–69

BIGGEST WIN

10–0 v Floriana – European Cup
preliminary round,
25 September 1962

BIGGEST DEFEAT

1–10 v Fulham – Division One,
26 December 1963

SEASON REVIEW

Just as few people would have predicted Ipswich finishing fifth in the Premiership in 2000–01 and qualifying for Europe, very few people would have anticipated that George Burley's men would fall from grace so swiftly, ending the 2001–02 season in the bottom three and heading back down to Division One.

It has been a roller coaster couple of seasons for Town fans and after the top five finish, they were looking forward to seeing European football back at Portman Road for the first time since 1982.

The close season was anything but quiet for George Burley, as Ipswich were at the centre of a great deal of transfer activity. Fans' favourites like James Scowcroft and Richard Wright moved on in multi-million pound moves to Leicester and Arsenal respectively, while there was an influx of new recruits. Pablo Counago, Andy Marshall, Tommy Miller, Thomas Gaardsoe, Matteo Sereni, Sixto Peralta and Finidi George all signed up to bolster the squad as the Tractor Boys attempted to repeat the previous season's heroics.

The signs in Town's first home game of the season against Derby County were that Burley's men were once again a force to be reckoned with. The Rams were swept aside by a rampant Ipswich team and only a fantastic performance from Derby 'keeper Mart Poom kept the score down to single figures. Winger George was a revelation for the hosts and hopes for the season were very high in East Anglia.

Sadly that game was to be a one off. In the following weeks Ipswich then went on a run of 15 games in the Premiership without a win – despite playing some good football – a run that would leave them at the foot of the table by Christmas.

> **"The early days of the season saw our eyes being on Europe and over the whole course of the season we finished where we deserved to finish."**
>
> **David Sheepshanks**

Europe proved to be a welcome distraction with away victories at Torpedo Moscow and Helsingborgs taking Ipswich into the third round. There they were paired with Italian giants Internazionale. Alun Armstrong headed the winner at Portman Road in the first leg, but in the second leg Inter's class told with Ipswich going down 4–1 at the San Siro in front of 8,000 travelling supporters.

Town now had to get back to concentrating on domestic matters, which meant a battle against relegation. Injuries to the likes of Marcus Stewart, Titus Bramble, and French winger Ulrich Le Pen – just 10 minutes into his debut – did not make their task any easier, but Burley was allowed to strengthen his squad further with the £3 million capture of striker Marcus Bent from Blackburn.

With the Tractor Boys propping up the Premiership table on Christmas Day, the signs were not good – no side had ever survived from that position before. But a sequence of good results threatened to rewrite the record books. From late December to early January, Ipswich went on a run of seven wins in eight games – a run which lifted them up to a more respectable 12th place.

They crashed back down to earth though when Liverpool won 6–0 at Portman Road and failed to fully recover from this. A run-in which included games against Arsenal, Manchester United and Liverpool now cast Ipswich as firm relegation favourites and Town could only manage one more win, at home to Middlesbrough.

Relegation was confirmed with a 5–0 drubbing at Anfield, but Town returned to the first division in better shape than they left it and also qualified for the UEFA Cup through the fair play system.

into the box than anyone else

IPSWICH TOWN

DATE	OPPONENT	SCORE	ATT.	AMBROSE	ARMSTRONG	BENT D	BENT M	BRAMBLE	BRANAGAN	CLAPHAM	COUNAGO	GAARDSOE	GEORGE	HREIDARSSON
18.08.01	Sunderland A	0–1	47,370	–	–	–	–	90	–	s18	s35	–	90	90
21.08.01	Derby Co H	3–1	21,197	–	s11	–	–	90	–	62	s24	–	90²	90
25.08.01	Charlton H	0–1	22,804	–	s3	–	–	90□	–	87	s38	–	90	90
08.09.01	Leicester A	1–1	18,774	–	s1	–	–	90	s31	–	–	–	59	90
16.09.01	Blackburn H	1–1	22,126	–	64¹	–	–	90□	–	–	s1	–	79	90□
22.09.01	Man Utd A	0–4	67,551	–	90	–	–	90	–	s31	–	–	59	90
30.09.01	Leeds Utd H	1–2	22,643	–	90	–	–	–	–	s18	s3	–	72	90
13.10.01	Everton H	0–0	22,820	–	90	–	–	–	–	–	–	–	s13	90
21.10.01	Fulham A	1–1	17,221	–	90□	–	–	–	–	90	–	–	13	90
24.10.01	Southampton A	3–3	29,614	–	45	–	–	–	–	90	–	–	–	90
28.10.01	West Ham H	2–3	22,834	–	56	–	–	–	–	46	s34	90□	–	90¹
04.11.01	Chelsea A	1–2	40,497	–	–	–	–	90	–	76	s24	–	–	90
18.11.01	Bolton W H	1–2	22,335	–	–	87	–	90	–	–	90	–	–	90
25.11.01	Middlesbro A	0–2	32,586	–	62	–	68	90	–	90	s28	–	–	90
01.12.01	Arsenal H	0–2	24,666	–	–	–	90	90	–	90	s22	s8	s26	90
09.12.01	Newcastle H	0–1	24,748	–	67	–	90	–	–	90	s23□	–	67	90□
17.12.01	Aston Villa A	1–2	29,320	–	80	–	s10	–	–	s25	–	–	65¹	90
22.12.01	Tottenham A	2–1	36,040	–	s19¹	–	77	s6	–	–	–	–	90¹	90
26.12.01	Leicester H	2–0	24,403	–	75	–	90¹	90	–	–	–	–	62	90
29.12.01	Sunderland H	5–0	24,517	–	72²	–	80□	–	–	s18¹	–	90¹	90¹	90
01.01.02	Charlton A	2–3	25,893	–	90	–	90²	–	–	67	–	90	90	90□
12.01.02	Tottenham H	2–1	25,077	–	58	–	90¹	–	–	s45	–	–	–	90
19.01.02	Derby Co A	3–1	29,658	–	s1	–	89¹	–	–	s2	–	–	–	90□
30.01.02	Fulham H	1–0	25,156	–	70	–	90¹	–	–	90	–	–	–	90
02.02.02	Everton A	2–1	33,069	–	56	–	90	–	–	90	–	–	–	90
09.02.02	Liverpool H	0–6	25,608	–	71	–	90	–	–	90	–	–	–	90
02.03.02	Southampton H	1–3	25,440	–	–	–	90	90	–	s34	s12	–	90¹	90
06.03.02	Leeds Utd A	0–2	39,414	–	79	–	s11	–	–	90	s11	–	85	90
13.03.02	Blackburn A	1–2	23,305	–	57	–	s33	–	–	81	–	–	s9	90
16.03.02	Newcastle A	2–2	51,115	–	s4	–	86²	–	–	90	–	–	–	90
23.03.02	Aston Villa H	0–0	25,247	–	s7	–	90	–	–	90	–	–	83	90
30.03.02	West Ham A	1–3	33,871	–	–	–	90¹□	–	–	90	–	–	s36	90
01.04.02	Chelsea H	0–0	28,053	–	70	s20	90	–	–	s6	–	–	84	90
06.04.02	Bolton W A	1–4	25,817	–	90	–	90	s45	–	s45¹	–	–	45	90
21.04.02	Arsenal A	0–2	38,058	s5	s5	–	85	90	–	90	–	–	51	90
24.04.02	Middlesbro H	1–0	25,979	–	s33	s33¹	57	90	–	90	–	–	–	90
27.04.02	Man Utd H	0–1	28,433	–	s5	s20	85	90□	–	90	–	–	52	90□
11.05.02	Liverpool A	0–5	44,088	–	s8	69	82	90	–	90	–	–	–	90

□ Yellow card, ■ Red card, s Substitute, 90² Goals scored

*including own goal Δ red card reduced to yellow on appeal

For more information visit our website:

2001–02 PREMIERSHIP APPEARANCES

HOLLAND	LE PEN	MAGILTON	MAKIN	MARSHALL	McGREAL	MILLER	NAYLOR	PERALTA	REUSER	SERENI	STEWART	VENUS	WILNIS	WRIGHT	TOTAL
90	–	55	90□	–	72	–	–	–	90	90	90	–	–	90	990
90	–	–	90	–	–	–	79¹	–	90	90	66	–	s28	90	990
90	–	s25	90	–	–	–	52	–	90	90	65	–	–	90□	990
90	–	90□	90□	–	90	–	–	–	90□	58■Δ	89¹	–	–	90	958
90	–	90	90	–	90	–	s26	–	89□	90	90	–	s11	–	990
90	–	90	59	–	90□	–	–	–	s31	90	90	–	75	s15	990
90	–	90	88	–	90	–	–	–	–	90	90¹	90	s2	87	990
90	–	90	45	–	90	–	–	–	90	90	90	90	s45	77	990
90	–	s17	90	–	90	–	–	73□	s45	90	s77	–	45□	90¹	990
90	–	–	45	–	90	–	s45	90□	–	90	90²	90¹	s45	90	990
90¹	–	s2	90	–	–	–	–	s44	90□	90	90	90	–	88	990
90	–	90	90	–	–	–	66□	–	s14	90	90¹	90	–	90□	990
90¹	s10	45	80	–	–	–	s3	90	90	90	–	90	–	s45	990
90	–	–	90	–	–	s15	s22□	75	–	90	–	90	–	90	990
90	–	–	64	–	–	–	68	82	–	90	–	90□	–	90	990
90	–	–	90	–	90□	–	s5	s23	–	90	–	90	–	85	990
90	–	90	90	–	90	–	90□	–	–	90	–	90	–	90	990
90	–	71	90	–	84□	–	s13	–	90□	90	–	90	–	90	990
90	–	s5	90	–	–	–	s15	85¹	90	90	–	90	–	s28	990
90	–	90	90□	–	–	–	s18	–	72	90	–	90	–	s10	990
90	–	67	90	–	–	–	–	s23	s23	90	–	90□	–	–	990
90	–	64	90	90	90¹	–	–	s26	45	–	s32	90	–	90	990
90	–	–	90	90	90	–	s5	90¹	88¹□	–	85	90	–	90	990
90	–	–	90	90	90□	–	–	90	s7	–	s20	90	–	83	990
90¹	–	s45	90	90	90	–	–	90¹	–	–	s34	90	–	45	990
90	–	s19	90	90	90	–	–	90	–	–	s52	90	–	38	990
90	–	90	56	90	–	–	–	–	56	–	78	90	–	s34	990
90	–	90	–	90□	90□	s5	–	–	–	–	79	90	90□	–	990
90	–	57	90□	–	90□	–	–	s33	–	90	90¹	90	–	90	990
90	–	s7	90	–	90	–	–	83	–	90	90	90□	–	90	990
90	–	s80	10	–	90	–	–	–	s7	90	83	90	–	90	990
90	–	–	–	–	90	s45□	–	54	–	90	90	90	90	45	990
90	–	–	–	90	90	90	–	70	–	–	s20	90	90	–	990
90	–	–	–	90	90	90	–	45	–	–	s45	45	90	–	990
90	–	–	–	90	90	90	–	s39	85	–	90	–	–	–	990
90	–	–	–	90	90	–	–	90	90	–	57	83	s7	–	990
90	–	–	–	90	90□	90	–	90	70	–	–	–	s38	–	990
90	–	–	–	90	40	90	–	–	90	–	s21	90	s50	–	990

THE MANAGER

GEORGE BURLEY

A year is a long time in football – something that George Burley will all too readily agree with.

At the end of 2000–01 the Ipswich boss was named Manager of the Year by both Carling and the League Managers' Association after guiding Ipswich into Europe in their first season back in the top flight. But relegation in 2001–02 means he now faces another season in Division One.

Burley is a Portman Road legend having made almost 400 appearances for the club as a player and featured in Bobby Robson's FA Cup-winning side.

The Scot had a brief spell in management at Colchester before taking over the reigns at Ipswich in December 1994.

He could do little to stop the club's relegation from the Premiership that season, but over the next few years he put together a talented young side. They reached the play-offs in three consecutive seasons before finally returning to the top flight by winning at Wembley in 1999–2000.

Fifth place in their first season back was a huge success, but a feat which could not be repeated and now Burley faces the task of getting the Tractor Boys back into the top flight once again.

LEAGUE POSITION

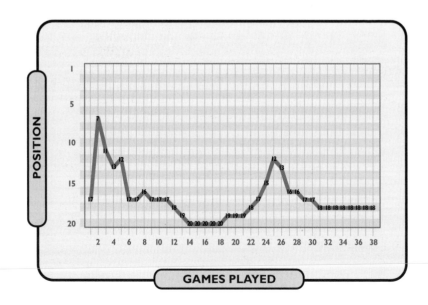

POSITION

GAMES PLAYED

18 Ipswich won the most corners in a game

THE GOALS

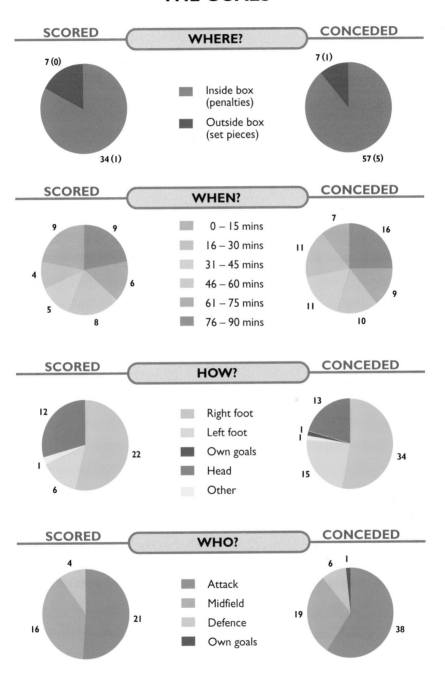

IPSWICH TOWN

	AMBROSE	ARMSTRONG	BENT D	BENT M	BRAMBLE	CLAPHAM	COUNAGO	GAARDSOE	GEORGE	HOLLAND	HREIDARSSON
APPEARANCES											
Start	0	21	2	22	16	22	1	3	21	38	38
Sub	1	11	3	3	2	10	12	1	4	0	0
Minutes on pitch	5	1619	229	1933	1491	2101	345	278	1590	3420	3420
GOAL ATTEMPTS											
Goals	0	4	1	9	0	2	0	1	6	3	1
Shots on target	0	13	2	26	1	8	6	1	20	19	6
Shots off target	0	19	1	22	7	15	10	1	13	33	19
Shooting accuracy %	0%	41%	67%	54%	13%	35%	38%	50%	61%	37%	24%
Goals/shots %	0%	13%	33%	19%	0%	9%	0%	50%	18%	6%	4%
PASSING											
Goal assists	0	0	0	1	0	2	0	0	2	3	1
Long passes	2	65	9	88	247	253	10	31	116	350	437
Short passes	1	501	59	568	422	674	129	64	545	1193	957
PASS COMPLETION											
Own half %	0%	85%	87%	82%	80%	87%	71%	72%	82%	86%	78%
Opposition half %	33%	68%	70%	60%	58%	71%	66%	45%	68%	77%	60%
CROSSING											
Total crosses	0	25	2	42	23	170	3	1	81	19	112
Cross completion %	0%	12%	0%	17%	26%	28%	33%	0%	23%	32%	21%
DRIBBLING											
Dribbles & runs	0	25	9	107	33	61	17	1	72	40	165
Dribble completion %	0%	48%	67%	52%	85%	79%	41%	100%	78%	88%	72%
DEFENDING											
Tackles made	0	16	4	15	78	59	2	11	43	122	89
Tackles won %	0%	75%	75%	87%	76%	73%	100%	73%	60%	75%	81%
Blocks	0	1	0	2	14	13	0	5	3	18	51
Clearances	0	5	1	4	187	38	0	36	9	38	250
Interceptions	0	0	0	0	12	6	1	1	5	20	20
DISCIPLINE											
Fouls conceded	0	26	0	29	31	11	11	2	23	38	63
Fouls won	0	38	2	55	18	29	14	7	36	42	70
Offside	0	19	5	28	0	2	1	0	4	0	1
Yellow cards	0	1	0	2	3	0	1	1	0	0	5
Red cards	0	0	0	0	0	0	0	0	0	0	0

GOALKEEPER NAME	START/ (SUB)	TIME ON PITCH	GOALS CONCEDED	MINS/GOALS CONCEDED	SAVES MADE	SAVES/ SHOTS
BRANAGAN	0 (1)	31	1	31	1	50%
MARSHALL	13 (0)	1170	26	45	52	67%
SERENI	25 (0)	2218	37	60	88	70%

For more information visit our website:

PLAYERS' STATISTICS

	LE PEN	MAGILTON	MAKIN	McGREAL	MILLER	NAYLOR	PERALTA	REUSER	STEWART	VENUS	WILNIS	WRIGHT	TOTAL	RANK
	0	16	30	27	5	5	16	18	20	29	6	24		
	1	8	0	0	3	9	6	6	8	0	8	5		
	10	1459	2427	2356	515	507	1475	1622	1983	2558	706	2120		
	0	0	0	1	0	1	3	1	6	1	0	1	41	14th
	0	5	2	2	1	8	4	14	26	8	2	3	177	11th
	0	10	1	4	3	7	8	34	22	9	1	17	256	5th
	0%	33%	67%	33%	25%	53%	33%	29%	54%	47%	67%	15%	41%	18th
	0%	0%	0%	17%	0%	7%	25%	2%	13%	6%	0%	5%	9%	17th
	0	1	0	0	0	3	3	4	4	8	0	0	32	=12th
	0	266	371	349	47	25	134	105	114	516	104	371	4349	8th
	6	707	829	512	210	158	552	480	709	652	268	843	11050	10th
	0%	88%	80%	83%	87%	84%	81%	84%	90%	84%	88%	83%	83%	8th
	100%	77%	66%	52%	72%	66%	71%	71%	78%	58%	66%	74%	67%	11th
	4	32	92	17	5	10	16	198	31	166	39	101	1189	1st
	25%	41%	25%	29%	60%	10%	38%	23%	23%	25%	23%	33%	25%	8th
	0	20	36	6	7	12	111	72	38	42	23	37	940	14th
	0%	80%	78%	83%	86%	58%	61%	65%	63%	86%	78%	86%	70%	6th
	0	35	97	71	29	7	52	46	29	60	38	48	952	18th
	0%	69%	77%	82%	79%	57%	81%	76%	79%	72%	71%	65%	75%	4th
	0	8	15	29	4	0	2	4	2	25	7	5	208	=11th
	0	19	91	229	5	3	5	10	3	256	30	23	1303	17th
	0	6	8	18	6	0	11	4	3	12	6	5	145	14th
	0	20	30	41	8	20	35	26	33	36	14	19	520	17th
	0	25	32	33	4	11	29	23	35	26	11	12	560	7th
	1	2	0	0	0	4	1	7	35	0	0	1	111	17th
	0	1	4	7	1	3	2	5	0	3	2	2	44	=17th
	0	0	0	0	0	0	0	0	0	0	0	0	1	=18th

CROSSES CAUGHT	CROSSES PUNCHED	CROSSES DROPPED	CATCH SUCCESS	THROWS/SHORT KICKS	% COMPLETION	LONG KICKS	% COMPLETION
2	1	0	100%	0	0%	7	71%
20	12	3	87%	22	95%	253	53%
41	19	2	95%	41	95%	439	47%

PLAYER OF THE SEASON

PLAYER	INDEX SCORE
MARCUS STEWART	787
Mark Venus	782
Marcus Bent	712
Jamie Clapham	665
Matteo Sereni	660
Hermann Hreidarsson	649
Matt Holland	647
John McGreal	609
Chris Makin	539
Jermaine Wright	509

For the second season in succession, Marcus Stewart was ranked as Ipswich's player of the season by the Opta Index, but the campaign was one of bitter disappointment for all at the club compared to 2000–01.

Stewart was a key figure that season as Ipswich claimed fifth spot and qualified for Europe, with the former Huddersfield man hitting 19 goals and narrowly missing out on the Golden Boot.

This time around, Stewart's season was interrupted by injury, but he still managed to hit six Premiership goals and claim four assists. Only Mark Venus in the Ipswich side created more goals while Stewart was also a key figure in the cup competitions, netting a further four goals in the UEFA and FA Cups.

Just as in 2000–01, Stewart was pushed all the way for player of the season by Venus, whose effectiveness from set pieces has been a great weapon for Town over recent campaigns. The veteran defender was the chief creator for the Tractor Boys

with eight assists and he got on the scoresheet himself at Southampton. Venus also stood firm in defence where Ipswich came under great pressure. The former Wolves man made 256 clearances at the back – more than any other Town player during the campaign.

Marcus Bent arrived at Portman Road in late November and contributed nine goals making him Town's top scorer and seeing him ranked the third-highest Ipswich player. His goal tally was boosted by a fantastic run of six goals in six games over the Christmas and New Year period that helped take Ipswich up to 12th in the table, giving them hopes of survival.

Former Tottenham man Jamie Clapham was ranked as the fourth-best player, while Italian 'keeper Matteo Sereni came in fifth. The summer signing from Sampdoria showed some fantastic shot-stopping ability, particularly in Europe and managed to remain the first choice 'keeper in the face of strong competition from another summer capture, Andy Marshall.

0 No team has ever avoided relegation having

FIVE OF THE BEST

Relegation on the final day of the season was a bitter pill for Ipswich to swallow, after they had performed so well to finish in the top five in 2000–01. The Tractor Boys stuck to their principles of neat passing football, which had served them so well, but they were unable to get the results needed to keep them in the top flight.

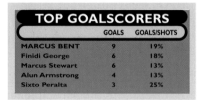

TOP GOALSCORERS	GOALS	GOALS/SHOTS
MARCUS BENT	9	19%
Finidi George	6	18%
Marcus Stewart	6	13%
Alun Armstrong	4	13%
Sixto Peralta	3	25%

Marcus Bent proved to be a sound signing for George Burley after he joined from Blackburn Rovers for £3million in November. The big hitman bagged nine goals during Town's fight to beat the drop, making him the club's top scorer for the season. He was followed by summer capture Finidi George and 2000–01's top scorer Marcus Stewart who both managed six goals in a disappointing campaign.

Slick passing was an important part of Ipswich's game and – while they missed the cultured play of Jim Magilton for much of the season – there were plenty of other fine ball players in the Town ranks. Republic of Ireland international Matt Holland contributed more than most with 1,247 successful passes – far higher than the next highest totals from Jermaine Wright and Hermann Hreidarsson.

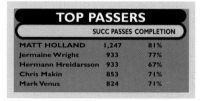

TOP PASSERS	SUCC PASSES	COMPLETION
MATT HOLLAND	1,247	81%
Jermaine Wright	933	77%
Hermann Hreidarsson	933	67%
Chris Makin	853	71%
Mark Venus	824	71%

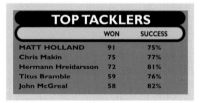

TOP TACKLERS	WON	SUCCESS
MATT HOLLAND	91	75%
Chris Makin	75	77%
Hermann Hreidarsson	72	81%
Titus Bramble	59	76%
John McGreal	58	82%

Not only was he the best passer at the club during the course of the season, but Matt Holland was also the side's top tackler. The Ipswich skipper won three-quarters of all the tackles he attempted, gaining possession on 91 occasions. But he was the only Ipswich midfielder to win in excess of 50 challenges in 2001–02 and only four teams won fewer tackles than Town.

Ipswich's excellent disciplinary record saw them win a place in the 2002–03 UEFA Cup despite relegation from the Premiership. Very few Town players were in trouble on a regular basis – in fact, Hermann Hreidarsson was the biggest sinner for the Tractor Boys and he commited just 63 fouls. He was followed by John McGreal, who picked up seven cautions during the campaign – more than any other Ipswich player.

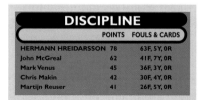

DISCIPLINE	POINTS	FOULS & CARDS
HERMANN HREIDARSSON	78	63F, 5Y, 0R
John McGreal	62	41F, 7Y, 0R
Mark Venus	45	36F, 3Y, 0R
Chris Makin	42	30F, 4Y, 0R
Martijn Reuser	41	26F, 5Y, 0R

LEEDS UNITED

ADDRESS

Elland Road, Leeds,
West Yorkshire LS11 0ES

CONTACT NUMBERS

Telephone: 0113 226 6000
Fax: 0113 226 6050
Ticket Office: 0845 121 1992
ClubCall: 09068 121180
Club shop: 0113 225 1144
e-mail: football@leedsunited.com
Website: www.leedsunited.com

KEY PERSONNEL

President: The Right Honourable
Earl of Harewood KBE LLD
Chairman: R P Ridsdale
Leeds United Directors: R P Ridsdale,
S J Harrison, A Hudson,
D A Spencer, D J Walker
Club Secretary: I Silvester
Manager: David O'Leary

SPONSORS

Strongbow

FANZINES

The Square Ball,
Till the World Stops,
We Are Leeds,
To Ell And Back

COLOURS

Home: White shirts, white
shorts and white stockings
Away: Blue shirts, blue shorts
and blue stockings

NICKNAMES

United
The Whites

HONOURS

League Champions:
1968–69, 1973–74, 1991–92
Division Two Champions:
1923–24, 1963–64, 1989–90
FA Cup Winners: 1972
League Cup Winners: 1968
Fairs Cup Winners: 1968, 1971

RECORD GOALSCORER

Peter Lorimer – 168 league goals
1965–79, 1983–86

BIGGEST WIN

10–0 v Lyn (Oslo), European Cup 1st
round 1st leg, 17 September 1969

BIGGEST DEFEAT

1–8 v Stoke City –
Division One, 27 August 1934

SEASON REVIEW

By the end of the 2001–02 campaign, Leeds United's season had disintegrated into anti-climax and a classic tale of what might have been had emerged. The team who had topped the table on 1 January ended up languishing 21 points adrift of the summit and also missed out on Champions League qualification.

Waves of optimism had swept through Yorkshire ahead of the 2001–02 campaign and with justifiable reason. David O'Leary had assembled a talented squad which had proved itself against the cream of Europe just a few months earlier and Leeds appeared to be in with a realistic chance of wresting the title from the opposite end of the M62.

With a number of key players returning from injury, Leeds did not feel the need to delve into the transfer market over the summer months. Pre-season form backed this policy as the side rifled home 42 goals in 10 outings.

> "I still have great faith in my players. I will tinker a bit with the squad in the summer but not too much."
>
> **David O'Leary**

Southampton were the first visitors to Elland Road and despite a stubborn display, eventually fell victim to strikes from Lee Bowyer and Alan Smith. The ensuing victory at Highbury underlined the seriousness of Leeds' challenge.

Despite two dismissals – United would eventually finish third in the disciplinary table – O'Leary's side clung on to a slender 2–1 advantage against Arsenal to send a warning shot to the rest of the Premiership. The Yorkshire outfit remained undefeated in the league until midway through November, while progressing in both the UEFA and Worthington Cups.

Robbie Keane grabbed a hat-trick at Filbert Street to end Leicester City's league cup ambitions, yet even this decisive contribution did not prevent O'Leary from strengthening his forward line. At the end of November Leeds prised Robbie Fowler from the Anfield substitutes bench for the knockdown price of £11 million.

While the pundits debated the merits of swapping a red shirt for a white one, Fowler duly rammed home a dozen league strikes for his new club and United's goals-to-shots ratio leapt from 9% prior to the striker's arrival to 14% after he had signed.

While an Eidur Gudjohnsen brace put paid to any Worthington Cup aspirations, consecutive away wins over Bolton and Southampton straight after Christmas lifted the club to within a point of leaders Arsenal. Victory over West Ham on New Year's Day sent Leeds to the top of the pile ahead of an FA Cup trip to Ninian Park, which undoubtedly signalled the turning point of the team's season.

Alan Smith was controversially sent off two minutes before the interval as the visitors crashed to a shock 2–1 defeat to Cardiff City, amid a turbulent atmosphere. In the bleak period that followed, Leeds' league form slumped dramatically with the team enduring a run of seven games without a win. O'Leary saw his side take just one point from crucial clashes with high-flying rivals Newcastle, Arsenal, Chelsea and Liverpool. To make matters worse, a solitary strike from PSV Eindhoven striker Jan Vennegoor of Hesselink ended United's UEFA Cup challenge.

An epic 4–3 defeat at the hands of Manchester United at the end of March all but ended the club's title bid and it took a clinical finish from Smith in the final game against Middlesbrough to secure a fifth-placed finish. Lengthy suspensions to Lee Bowyer and Danny Mills, combined with a steady stream of injuries, certainly contributed to Leeds' prolonged New-Year hangover. They underachieved, but nonetheless earned a UEFA Cup berth.

LEEDS UNITED

DATE	OPPONENT	SCORE	ATT.	BAKKE	BATTY	BOWYER	DACOURT	DUBERRY	FERDINAND	FOWLER	HARTE	JOHNSON
18.08.01	Southampton H	2–0	39,715	s30	60	90¹□	90	–	90	–	90	–
21.08.01	Arsenal A	2–1	38,062	89■	s43	78■	90□	–	90	–	90¹	–
25.08.01	West Ham A	0–0	24,517	–	90	90	75	–	90	–	80	–
08.09.01	Bolton W H	0–0	40,153	s31	90	–	90□	–	90	–	90	–
16.09.01	Charlton A	2–0	20,451	–	90	90	66	–	90	–	90	–
23.09.01	Derby Co H	3–0	39,155	90¹	90	90	–	–	90	–	90	–
30.09.01	Ipswich A	2–1*	22,643	90	90	90	–	–	90	–	90	–
13.10.01	Liverpool A	1–1	44,352	90□	s2	90	90	–	90	–	90	–
21.10.01	Chelsea H	0–0	40,171	90□	–	90	90□	–	90	–	90	–
27.10.01	Man Utd A	1–1	67,555	90□	s19	90	90	–	90	–	90	–
04.11.01	Tottenham H	2–1	40,203	90	s9	39	81	–	90	–	90¹	s51
18.11.01	Sunderland A	0–2	48,005	90	90	–	90	–	90	–	90	90
25.11.01	Aston Villa H	1–1	40,159	90	90	–	–	–	90	–	90	90□
02.12.01	Fulham A	0–0	20,918	–	90	–	s20	–	90	90	90	90□
09.12.01	Blackburn A	2–1	28,309	–	90□	–	66	90	90	90□	90□	–
16.12.01	Leicester H	2–2	38,337	s72□	90	–	–	–	90	90	90	18
19.12.01	Everton H	3–2	40,201	s9	81□	–	–	–	90	90²	90	90
22.12.01	Newcastle H	3–4	40,287	s43	90	90¹	–	–	90	90	90¹	90
26.12.01	Bolton W A	3–0	27,060	6	90	90	–	–	90	90³	s46	–
29.12.01	Southampton A	1–0	31,622	–	90	90¹	–	–	90	89	90	–
01.01.02	West Ham H	3–0	39,320	–	90	87□	–	–	90	90¹	90	–
12.01.02	Newcastle A	1–3	52,130	–	90□	90	–	90□	–	–	–	66
20.01.02	Arsenal H	1–1	40,143	–	90	90	–	–	90	90¹	–	90□
30.01.02	Chelsea A	0–2	40,614	–	90	90	–	–	90	64	s45	38
03.02.02	Liverpool H	0–4	40,216	–	90	90	57	–	90	90	90	–
09.02.02	Middlesbro A	2–2	30,221	90¹□	90	–	86	–	90	90¹	90	–
24.02.02	Charlton H	0–0	39,374	90	s45	–	45	–	90	90	90	–
03.03.02	Everton A	0–0	33,226	90	90	–	–	90	–	90	90	–
06.03.02	Ipswich H	2–0	39,414	90	90□	–	–	–	90	90¹	90¹	–
17.03.02	Blackburn H	3–1	39,857	s18	90□	–	72	–	90	90²	90	–
23.03.02	Leicester A	2–0	18,976	–	90□	–	14	–	–	90¹	90	s76
30.03.02	Man Utd H	3–4	40,058	s30	60	s78¹	–	–	–	90	90¹	65
01.04.02	Tottenham A	1–2	35,167	90	66	90	–	–	–	90	90	–
07.04.02	Sunderland H	2–0*	39,195	90	90□	90□	–	–	–	61	90	–
13.04.02	Aston Villa A	1–0	40,039	90	90□	90□	–	–	–	–	90	–
20.04.02	Fulham H	0–1	39,811	90	90	90□	–	–	90	90	90	–
27.04.02	Derby Co A	1–0	30,705	90	s3	90¹	–	–	90	21	90	90
11.05.02	Middlesbro H	1–0	40,218	90	–	90	–	–	90	–	90	90

□ Yellow card, ■ Red card, s Substitute, 90² Goals scored
*including own goal

For more information visit our website:

2001–02 PREMIERSHIP APPEARANCES

KEANE	KELLY	KEWELL	MARTYN	MATTEO	MAYBURY	McPHAIL	MILLS	SMITH	VIDUKA	WILCOX	WOODGATE	TOTAL
65	–	90	90	90	–	–	90	s25¹	90	–	–	990
–	s1	89	90	90	–	–	86□	47	90¹□	–	s1	974
90	–	90	90	90□	s15□	–	90	–	90	–	s10	990
90	90	90	90	90	–	–	–	–	90	59	–	990
90¹□	–	90	90	90	–	s24	90¹	–	90	–	–	990
90	–	90²	90	90□	–	–	90	–	90	–	–	990
90¹	–	90	90	90	–	–	90□	–	90	–	–	990
88	–	90¹	90	90	–	–	90□	–	90	–	–	990
77	–	90	90	90	–	–	90	s13	90	–	–	990
71□	–	89□	90	90	–	–	90	s1	90¹	–	–	990
74	–	90¹	90	90	–	–	90	s16	90	–	–	990
90□	–	–	90	90	–	–	90□	90□	–	–	–	990
90	–	–	90	90	–	–	90□	32¹□	–	90	–	932
–	90	70	90	–	–	–	90	90□	90	–	–	990
–	90□	90²	90	–	–	–	90□	–	90	s24	–	990
–	90	90¹	90	90	–	–	90	–	90¹	–	–	990
s1	90	90	90	90	–	–	90	–	89¹	–	–	990
–	90□	47	90	–	–	–	90	–	90¹□	–	–	990
–	90	–	90	44□	–	–	–	90□	90	s84□	90	990
–	90	–	90	–	–	–	90□	90	90	s1	90	990
–	90	–	90	–	–	–	90□	90□	90²	s3	90	990
–	90	–	90	90	–	–	70□	90¹	90□	s24□	90□	970
–	–	–	90	90	–	–	90	–	90	90	90	990
s52	90	s26	90	90	–	–	–	–	90	90□	45□	990
s15	90	75□	90	90□	–	–	–	–	90	s33	–	990
–	90	90	90	90	–	–	–	–	90	s4	–	990
90	90	90	90	90	–	–	–	–	90	–	–	990
–	90	90	90	39□	–	–	–	90□	90	–	–	939
s10	90	80	90	90	–	–	–	–	90	–	–	990
s26	–	82¹	90	–	–	–	90□	64	90	s8	90	990
–	–	90	90	90□	–	–	90	90	90¹	–	90	990
s25	–	12	90	90	–	–	90□	90	90¹	–	90	990
s24	–	–	90	90	–	–	90	90	90¹	–	90	990
s29¹	–	–	90	90	–	–	90	90	90	–	90	990
90	90	–	90	90	–	–	90□	90	90¹	–	–	990
90	–	–	90	90□	–	–	90	90	–	–	–	990
s69	90	87	90	90	–	–	–	90	–	–	–	990
90	90	89	90□	90□	–	–	–	90¹	–	s1	–	990

THE MANAGER

DAVID O'LEARY

Leeds United may have failed to put any silverware in their trophy cabinet in 2001–02, but for David O'Leary another rigorous nine months of valuable managerial experience was gained.

Having taken charge in October 1998, the Irishman continued to work in tandem with ever-supportive chairman Peter Ridsdale to raise the club's on-field profile during 2001–02. While their title challenge ultimately disappointed, O'Leary guaranteed the Yorkshire outfit European football for the fifth season in succession.

He has a wealth of knowledge at the highest level having plied his trade as a central defender with Arsenal for 20 years. A loyal servant, the Dubliner continues to hold the Gunners' appearance record to this day. He signed for Leeds in 1993 where he featured in just 10 games before injury eventually ended his playing career.

Having served his apprenticeship as George Graham's number two at Elland Road, O'Leary was promoted to manager when his mentor left for Tottenham. Since then he has supplemented the side with some of the best of the nation's homegrown talent.

It is a measure of the former Republic of Ireland international's growing reputation that he has been cited as a potential successor to Sir Alex Ferguson at Old Trafford.

LEAGUE POSITION

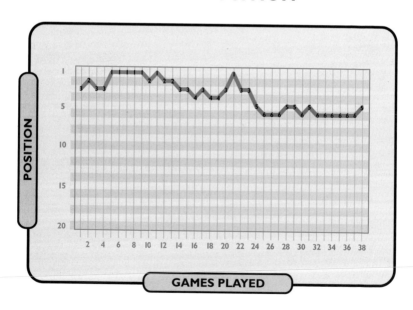

POSITION

GAMES PLAYED

18 Nigel Martyn kept more clean sheets

THE GOALS

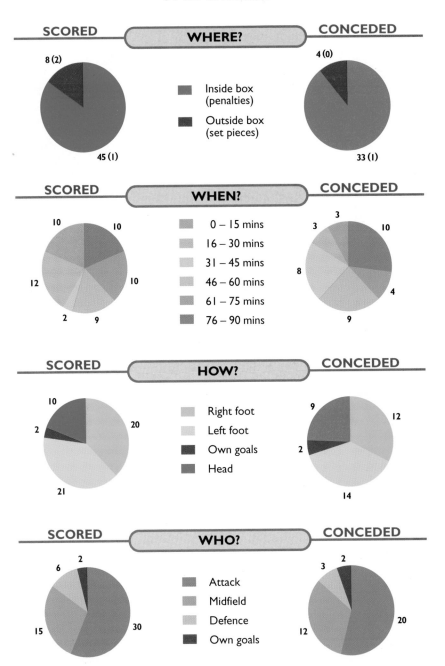

SCORED | **WHERE?** | **CONCEDED**

8 (2)
45 (1)

4 (0)
33 (1)

- Inside box (penalties)
- Outside box (set pieces)

SCORED | **WHEN?** | **CONCEDED**

10, 10, 10, 9, 2, 12

3, 10, 4, 9, 8, 3

- 0 – 15 mins
- 16 – 30 mins
- 31 – 45 mins
- 46 – 60 mins
- 61 – 75 mins
- 76 – 90 mins

SCORED | **HOW?** | **CONCEDED**

10, 20, 2, 21

9, 12, 2, 14

- Right foot
- Left foot
- Own goals
- Head

SCORED | **WHO?** | **CONCEDED**

2, 6, 30, 15

2, 3, 20, 12

- Attack
- Midfield
- Defence
- Own goals

than any other goalkeeper

LEEDS UNITED

	BAKKE	BATTY	BOWYER	DACOURT	DUBERRY	FERDINAND	FOWLER	HARTE	JOHNSON
APPEARANCES									
Start	20	30	24	16	3	31	22	34	12
Sub	7	6	1	1	0	0	0	2	2
Minutes on pitch	1948	2728	2172	1212	270	2790	1855	3141	1034
GOAL ATTEMPTS									
Goals	2	0	5	0	0	0	12	5	0
Shots on target	8	1	24	6	0	3	37	13	2
Shots off target	15	3	32	11	0	6	33	24	3
Shooting accuracy %	35%	25%	43%	35%	0%	33%	53%	35%	40%
Goals/shots %	9%	0%	9%	0%	0%	0%	17%	14%	0%
PASSING									
Goal assists	1	2	5	0	0	1	3	4	1
Long passes	190	528	233	132	10	352	109	679	146
Short passes	690	1634	693	416	45	785	487	1066	321
PASS COMPLETION									
Own half %	83%	89%	76%	83%	77%	82%	78%	81%	89%
Opposition half %	69%	78%	62%	70%	42%	66%	68%	69%	69%
CROSSING									
Total crosses	23	24	76	10	0	8	19	295	9
Cross completion %	17%	29%	29%	30%	0%	13%	11%	25%	33%
DRIBBLING									
Dribbles & runs	69	72	89	45	3	42	63	96	28
Dribble completion %	59%	81%	52%	53%	100%	90%	59%	90%	79%
DEFENDING									
Tackles made	74	132	62	79	6	83	37	83	34
Tackles won %	81%	67%	61%	77%	83%	80%	62%	76%	74%
Blocks	12	15	11	4	3	42	4	36	4
Clearances	32	39	24	4	33	402	3	120	20
Interceptions	15	22	6	7	1	24	3	9	3
DISCIPLINE									
Fouls conceded	45	75	45	33	6	24	23	31	21
Fouls won	35	57	37	47	4	35	28	27	8
Offside	6	2	21	0	0	0	18	5	0
Yellow cards	6	8	5	3	1	0	1	1	4
Red cards	0	0	1	0	0	0	0	0	0

GOALKEEPER NAME	START/ (SUB)	TIME ON PITCH	GOALS CONCEDED	MINS/GOALS CONCEDED	SAVES MADE	SAVES/ SHOTS
MARTYN	38 (0)	3420	37	92	111	75%

For more information visit our website:

PLAYERS' STATISTICS

	KEANE	KELLY	KEWELL	MATTEO	MAYBURY	McPHAIL	MILLS	SMITH	VIDUKA	WILCOX	WOODGATE	TOTAL	RANK
	16	19	26	32	0	0	28	19	33	4	11		
	9	1	1	0	1	1	0	4	0	9	2		
	1616	1711	2186	2783	15	24	2496	1638	2969	511	956		
	3	0	8	0	0	0	1	4	11	0	0	53*	7th
	26	5	20	2	0	0	5	20	43	2	0	217	3rd
	29	2	21	2	0	0	6	6	36	2	1	232	11th
	47%	71%	49%	50%	0%	0%	45%	77%	54%	50%	0%	48%	3rd
	5%	0%	20%	0%	0%	0%	9%	15%	14%	0%	0%	11%	7th
	4	3	3	0	0	0	2	3	7	1	0	40	7th
	58	220	146	336	4	16	357	113	117	60	80	4142	11th
	397	508	818	757	2	15	735	590	903	195	216	11367	7th
	84%	84%	83%	83%	0%	86%	77%	82%	84%	83%	79%	83%	10th
	69%	71%	72%	64%	100%	82%	58%	70%	64%	64%	55%	68%	10th
	32	49	110	4	0	0	81	54	17	24	1	836	16th
	31%	33%	24%	25%	0%	0%	17%	17%	24%	17%	0%	24%	12th
	118	49	250	41	1	1	148	61	145	22	8	1356	3rd
	54%	78%	59%	95%	0%	100%	71%	59%	58%	77%	88%	66%	18th
	18	44	45	79	0	0	116	55	57	29	56	1089	6th
	61%	75%	80%	78%	0%	0%	79%	75%	79%	83%	79%	75%	5th
	1	13	9	38	0	1	25	1	8	2	10	239	5th
	4	73	11	308	0	1	157	21	29	6	148	1502	6th
	0	9	5	13	0	0	13	3	3	2	9	147	13th
	24	19	39	47	1	0	50	51	61	11	19	625	2nd
	30	12	46	20	0	1	57	37	75	3	4	568	5th
	28	0	8	0	0	0	2	13	46	3	0	152	=2nd
	3	2	2	7	1	0	10	6	3	3	2	69	=4th
	0	0	0	1	0	0	2	1	0	0	0	5	=4th

*Including two own goals

CROSSES CAUGHT	CROSSES PUNCHED	CROSSES DROPPED	CATCH SUCCESS	THROWS/ SHORT KICKS	% COMPLETION	LONG KICKS	% COMPLETION
45	26	4	92%	94	98%	683	48%

PLAYER OF THE SEASON

PLAYER	INDEX SCORE
ROBBIE FOWLER	931
Rio Ferdinand	924
Ian Harte	897
Mark Viduka	825
Harry Kewell	800
Nigel Martyn	738
Alan Smith	723
Danny Mills	700
Lee Bowyer	675
Gary Kelly	673

After securing the services of the Toxteth Terror for £11 million, David O'Leary enthused: "I think what we've paid for Robbie Fowler is excellent business." The striker repaid the manager's faith by notching a dozen league goals for the Whites to become the club's leading marksman in 2001–02.

Captured at the end of November, the former Liverpool man endured a frustrating televised debut at Craven Cottage and had to wait three games before opening his Leeds account. Ironically, the crucial strike came against Everton – the team he supported as a boy – and was quickly followed by a second on the night.

With the pressure released, Fowler went on to net a superb hat-trick at Bolton and scored in three consecutive matches during March to help build his tally. By the season's end, an impressive 17% of his shots had beaten the 'keeper.

While the England striker was applying the finishing touch, his international colleague Rio Ferdinand was effectively co-ordinating the United rearguard. The Londoner averaged a headed clearance every 12 minutes and got his body in the way of 30 shots as he led by example while donning the skipper's armband.

Fellow defender Ian Harte made the Yorkshire outfit's top three rankings for the second successive year after a number of influential displays at full-back. As part of his five-goal haul, the Republic of Ireland representative netted two trademark set pieces against Arsenal and Manchester United respectively and also created four strikes for his team-mates with his trusted left peg.

However, Mark Viduka was the club's unlikely chief architect, weighing in with seven goal assists throughout the 2001–02 season. Equally capable of beating the 'keeper himself, the Australian centre forward was second only to Fowler in the scoring stakes, which ensured him a marginally higher Index score than fellow Antipodean Harry Kewell, who finished fifth in the Leeds rankings.

FIVE OF THE BEST

Leeds United finished the 2001–02 season on a high as they pipped Chelsea for fifth place in the Premiership table to earn a UEFA Cup place. Nevertheless, celebrations were muted by the fact that having led the title charge at the turn of the year, David O'Leary's star-studded side fell dramatically off the pace.

TOP GOALSCORERS

	GOALS	GOALS/SHOTS
ROBBIE FOWLER	12	17%
Mark Viduka	11	14%
Harry Kewell	8	20%
Ian Harte	5	14%
Lee Bowyer	5	9%

After arriving from Liverpool in November, Robbie Fowler netted 12 Premiership goals to make him Leeds' top marksman. The England international found the back of the net every 155 minutes on average and is sure to be spearheading United's attack for years to come. Meanwhile, Antipodean front man Mark Viduka will have been disappointed that his 14% goals-to-shots ratio was a decline on his 27% ratio in 2000–01.

David Batty completed more successful passes than any other Englishman in the Premiership, with 1,780 of his intended balls finding their target. However, the midfielder would be the first to admit that his distribution was not as incisive as Ian Harte's, who set up four goals for the team compared to Batty's two assists. Meanwhile, central defenders Rio Ferdinand and Dominic Matteo were more than capable of retaining possession for the side.

TOP PASSERS

	SUCC PASSES	COMPLETION
DAVID BATTY	1,780	82%
Ian Harte	1,284	74%
Rio Ferdinand	876	77%
Dominic Matteo	838	77%
Harry Kewell	728	76%

TOP TACKLERS

	WON	SUCCESS
DANNY MILLS	92	79%
David Batty	88	67%
Rio Ferdinand	66	80%
Ian Harte	63	76%
Dominic Matteo	62	78%

Despite missing large chunks of the campaign through suspension, Leeds' right-back Danny Mills still managed to chalk up 92 successful tackles in the Premiership – more than any other United player. It was also the highest tally by an individual named in England's World Cup squad and the 25-year-old's experience in the Far East could make him an improved defender upon his return to Elland Road.

Leeds United's disciplinary record was nothing to be proud of in 2001–02 as only Everton committed more than the Peacocks' 625 fouls. Midfielder David Batty was the main offender, giving away 75 free kicks. Danny Mills' aggressive approach saw the former Charlton man pick up 10 cautions and two red cards, while Alan Smith let the team down when he was dismissed for an elbow on Aston Villa's Alpay in November 2001.

DISCIPLINE

	POINTS	FOULS & CARDS
DAVID BATTY	99	75F, 8Y, 0R
Danny Mills	92	50F, 10Y, 2R
Alan Smith	75	51F, 6Y, 1R
Dominic Matteo	74	47F, 7Y, 1R
Mark Viduka	70	61F, 3Y, 0R

LEICESTER CITY

ADDRESS

The Walkers Stadium,
Filbert Way, Leicester

CONTACT NUMBERS

Telephone: 0116 291 5000
Fax: 0116 247 0585
Ticket Office: 0116 291 5232
ClubCall: 09068 121185
Fox Leisure: 0116 291 5253
Website: www.lcfc.com

KEY PERSONNEL

PLC Chairman: Greg Clarke
Directors: Greg Clarke, John Elsom, Mark
Fenoughty, Martin George,
Steve Kind, Bill Shooter,
Brigid Simmonds
Company Secretary: Jonathan Waltho
Club Secretary: Andrew Neville
Manager: Micky Adams

SPONSORS

LG Electronics

FANZINES

The Fox

COLOURS

Home: Blue shirts, white shorts
and blue stockings
Away: White shirts, blue shorts
and white stockings

NICKNAME

The Foxes

HONOURS

Division Two Champions:
1924–25, 1936–37, 1953–54,
1956–57, 1970–71, 1979–80
League Cup Winners: 1964, 1997, 2000

RECORD GOALSCORER

Arthur Chandler –
259 league goals, 1923–35

BIGGEST WIN

10–0 v Portsmouth – Division One,
20 October 1928

BIGGEST DEFEAT

0–12 (as Leicester Fosse) v Nottingham
Forest – Division One,
21 April 1909

SEASON REVIEW

Some might say that the writing was on the wall for Leicester City before a ball had even been kicked in 2001–02. The Foxes lost nine of their last 10 league games at the tail end of 2000–01 and despite a three-month period of rehabilitation, they never really looked to have recovered.

Peter Taylor started his second term at the helm and brought in fresh faces to help stabilise his battered ship. Three major signings were added – goalkeeper Ian Walker, striker James Scowcroft and midfielder Dennis Wise – in a bid to strengthen the spine of the team.

Of this trio, only the latter featured in the opening game of the season – the other two are probably thankful that they didn't. An embarrassing 5–0 home defeat to newly promoted Bolton revealed that Leicester's wounds were far from healed. By week two, the Foxes had yet to open their account, while their defensive frailties had been exposed nine times.

A growing list of injuries was largely accountable for the team's lack of resilience. Gary Rowett, who missed just 14 minutes of the previous campaign, was sidelined for a total of 27 games throughout the season, while a knee injury restricted Gerry Taggart to a 13-minute cameo appearance on the final day. "The last 12 months have been a total nightmare, my worst ever in football", he complained.

Taylor's agony was short-lived by comparison. With just one win from eight games the Leicester board terminated his contract and the former England coaching assistant became the first Premiership managerial casualty of 2001–02.

Dave Bassett was installed as saviour and Micky Adams appointed as his assistant with a view to taking over in the future. "I think Micky is the young sexy one and I'm the old codger. I am not going to be going on forever", Bassett stated.

Prior to the decision, managerless Leicester succumbed to their heaviest defeat of the campaign when Leeds hit them for six in the Worthington Cup. Similarly, Bassett's debut ended in defeat at Chelsea, which was not surprising given that the Foxes won fewer away games than any other team in the division.

> **"I have seen appalling finishing... and defending which is non-league standard. Some of the goals we've conceded have been really poor."**
>
> **Dave Bassett**

By the end of October scoring was proving a major problem with the team averaging little more than a goal every other game. Striker Ade Akinbiyi was singled out for ridicule by the press after missing a host of easy chances, but was best remembered for his shirtless celebration after notching the winner against Sunderland. Nevertheless, he netted only twice and was eventually off-loaded to Crystal Palace.

A narrow FA Cup win over Mansfield brought welcome relief from the rigours of the Premiership in January, however, West Bromwich Albion soon put paid to any dreams of Cardiff in round four. By this stage, Wise had been added to the lengthening injury list and would later be joined by Scowcroft in missing the remainder of the season.

A run of 11 games without a win after the turn of the year virtually sealed Leicester's fate, although they were not officially condemned until the visit of Manchester United on 6 April. Adams was unveiled as the new manager ahead of the final four games of the season, with Bassett employed as a director of football.

The Foxes remained unbeaten under their third boss of the season and fittingly won their last ever game at Filbert Street, beating Tottenham 2–1.

cards than any other side

LEICESTER CITY

DATE	OPPONENT	SCORE	ATT.	AKINBIYI	ASHTON	BENJAMIN	DAVIDSON	DEANE	DELANEY	DICKOV	ELLIOTT	FLOWERS	GUNNLAUGSSON	HEATH	IMPEY	IZZET	JONES
18.08.01	Bolton W H	0–5	19,987	45□	–	–	45	–	–	–	90	90	s45	–	90□	90	–
25.08.01	Arsenal A	0–4	37,909	90	–	–	–	–	s59□	–	–	90	–	–	90	31	s23
08.09.01	Ipswich H	1–1	18,774	62□	–	–	90	–	–	–	90	–	–	–	90	90□	–
15.09.01	Derby Co A	3–2	26,863	90	–	s8□	90	–	–	–	90	–	–	–	–	90¹	90
17.09.01	Middlesbro H	1–2	15,412	90	–	s21	90	–	–	–	90	–	–	–	s1	–	45¹
22.09.01	Fulham H	0–0	18,918	–	–	–	90	–	–	–	90	–	–	–	s9	90	–
26.09.01	Newcastle A	0–1	49,185	s45	–	–	–	–	–	–	–	–	–	–	90	90	s21
29.09.01	Charlton A	0–2	20,451	–	–	s51	–	–	–	–	–	–	–	90	s29	90□	90
13.10.01	Chelsea A	0–2	40,370	90	–	–	90	–	–	–	–	–	s26	–	s8	90	60
20.10.01	Liverpool H	1–4	21,886	90	–	90	90	–	–	–	90	–	–	–	s34	–	72
29.10.01	Blackburn A	0–2	21,873	90	–	70	90	–	–	–	90	–	–	–	90	90	–
03.11.01	Sunderland H	1–0	20,573	90¹	–	74	90	–	–	–	90	–	–	–	90	90	–
17.11.01	Man Utd A	0–2	67,651	90	–	57	45	–	–	–	90	–	–	–	90	90	–
24.11.01	Everton H	0–0	21,539	76	–	s14□	90	–	–	–	90	–	–	–	72	90	–
01.12.01	Aston Villa A	2–0	30,711	89¹	–	s1	90	–	–	–	90	–	–	–	90	–	–
08.12.01	Southampton H	0–4	20,321	65	–	–	90	s25	–	–	–	–	–	90	90	s32□	–
16.12.01	Leeds Utd A	2–2	38,237	s18	–	–	90	90¹	–	–	90□	–	–	–	72	90	–
22.12.01	West Ham H	1–1	20,131	s9	–	–	–	81	–	–	71▪	–	–	–	74	90¹	–
26.12.01	Ipswich A	0–2	24,403	s32	–	–	s23	90	–	–	90	–	–	–	s23	90□	–
29.12.01	Bolton W A	2–2*	23,037	73	–	–	90	90¹	–	–	90	–	–	–	s22	s44▪	s17
12.01.02	West Ham A	0–1	34,698	85	–	–	90□	90	–	–	–	–	–	–	90	–	–
19.01.02	Newcastle H	0–0	21,354	90	–	–	90	–	–	–	s65	–	–	–	90□	90	–
23.01.02	Arsenal H	1–3	21,344	s45	–	s45	45	–	–	–	90	90	–	–	90	90¹□	s45
30.01.02	Liverpool A	0–1	42,305	–	–	s4	90	–	–	–	90	–	–	–	90	90	61
02.02.02	Chelsea H	2–3	19,950	–	–	–	90	–	–	–	90	–	–	–	69	90	–
09.02.02	Tottenham A	1–2	35,973	–	–	–	90	–	–	–	90	–	–	–	90□	–	–
23.02.02	Derby Co H	0–3	21,620	–	–	–	90	s32□	–	s21□	90	–	–	–	69	90□	–
02.03.02	Middlesbro A	0–1	25,734	–	–	–	90□	90	–	85	90□	–	–	–	–	90□	–
09.03.02	Charlton H	1–1	18,562	–	–	–	–	90	90	90	–	–	–	–	–	90	–
16.03.02	Southampton A	2–2	30,012	–	–	–	–	77²	90	81□	90□	–	–	–	s13	–	–
23.03.02	Leeds Utd H	0–2	18,976	–	90	–	–	90	–	90□	90	–	–	–	–	90	–
30.03.02	Blackburn H	2–1	16,236	–	65	–	–	90	–	90²	90	–	–	–	–	90	–
01.04.02	Sunderland A	1–2	44,950	–	s60	–	–	90y	–	90¹□	90	–	–	–	30	–	–
06.04.02	Man Utd H	0–1	21,447	–	s7	–	83	90	–	90	90	–	–	–	–	–	–
13.04.02	Everton A	2–2	35,580	–	s21	–	90	69²	–	83	–	–	–	90	–	–	–
20.04.02	Aston Villa H	2–2	18,125	–	s39	–	89	–	–	90	90	–	–	–	s1	90¹□	–
27.04.02	Fulham A	0–0	21,106	–	–	–	20	–	–	77□	90	–	–	–	90□	–	–
11.05.02	Tottenham H	2–1	21,716	–	58	–	90	–	–	77¹	90	–	–	–	90	89	–

□ Yellow card, ▪ Red card, s Substitute, 90² Goals scored

*including own goal, + card rescinded, Δ no suspension served, card remained on record

For more information visit our website:

2001–02 PREMIERSHIP APPEARANCES

LAURSEN	LEWIS	MARSHALL	OAKES	PIPER	REEVES	ROGERS	ROWETT	SAVAGE	SCOWCROFT	SINCLAIR	STEVENSON	STEWART	STURRIDGE	TAGGART	WALKER	WILLIAMSON	WISE	WRIGHT	TOTAL
–	s45	s45	–	–	–	–	90□	90	–	90□	–	–	45	–	–	–	90	–	990
–	90	s49	–	–	–	–	41	90□	67	90□	–	90	–	–	–	–	61□	–	961
–	90	82□△	–	–	–	–	–	90□	90	45	–	s45	s28²	–	90	–	–	–	982
–	–	90	–	–	–	–	–	90□	–	90□	–	90	82²	–	90	–	–	–	990
–	–	90	s45	–	–	–	–	90	–	89	–	90	69	–	90	–	90	–	990
–	–	90	–	–	–	s56	90	90	34□	–	81□	90	–	90	–	90	90	–	990
–	90	90□	–	–	–	–	71□	90	90	s19□	–	–	45	–	90	–	69	–	990
–	41□+	90	–	–	–	–	–	90	10	61□	–	–	90	–	90	–	s29	–	941
–	s30	82	–	–	–	90	90	–	–	–	–	64	–	90	–	90	90	–	990
–	–	90	–	s18	–	–	–	90	–	90□	–	–	56	–	90	–	90¹	–	990
–	–	90	–	–	–	–	–	90□	s20	90	–	–	–	–	90	–	90□	–	990
–	–	90	–	–	–	–	–	90□	s16	90	–	–	–	–	90	–	90	–	990
–	–	90	–	–	–	s45	–	–	s33	90	–	90	–	–	90	–	90□	–	990
–	–	90	–	–	–	s18	–	90	90	90	–	–	–	–	90	–	90□	–	990
–	–	90	–	–	–	76□	–	90□	90¹	90	–	s14	–	–	90	–	90□	–	990
–	–	58	s10	–	–	80	–	90	90	90	–	–	–	–	90	–	90	–	990
–	–	90□	90	–	–	–	–	90□	90¹	90	–	–	–	–	90	–	–	–	990
–	–	90	84	–	–	s16	–	90□	90	90	–	90	–	–	90	–	s6	–	971
–	–	67	90	–	–	58	–	90	90	90□	–	67	–	–	90	–	–	–	990
–	–	90	–	–	–	68	–	25	90□	90	–	–	–	–	90	–	90□	–	969
90	–	s26	–	–	–	64	–	90□	90	90	s5	–	–	–	90	–	90	–	990
90	–	–	88	–	–	90	–	90□	90	90	–	s2	–	–	25	–	–	–	990
90	–	–	45	–	–	90	–	90	45□	62	–	–	–	–	–	–	–	–	962
90	–	s29	86	90	–	s73	–	–	90□	–	–	17□	–	–	90	–	–	–	990
90□	–	s21	90	90	–	–	–	90	90²	90	–	–	–	–	90	–	–	–	990
90	–	–	90¹	90	–	–	–	90	90	90	–	90	–	–	90	–	–	–	990
90	–	s21	58	69	–	–	–	90□	90	90	–	–	–	–	90	–	–	–	990
–	–	90	s5	–	–	–	–	90□	90	90	–	–	–	–	90	–	–	–	990
90	–	90	s37□	90	–	–	–	90	53¹	90	–	–	–	–	90	–	–	–	990
90	–	90	90□	90	s9□	–	–	90	–	–	–	–	–	–	90	–	–	–	990
90	–	53	86	90	–	–	–	90□	–	s37	–	–	–	–	90	–	–	s4	990
–	–	90	90	78	s12	–	s25	90	–	90	–	–	–	–	90	–	–	–	990
–	–	90	61	s29	73	–	90	90	–	90	s17	–	–	–	90	–	–	–	990
–	–	90	80	90	s10	–	90	90	–	90	–	–	–	–	90	–	–	–	990
–	–	90□	90	72	s18	–	90	90	–	90	s7	–	–	–	90	–	–	–	990
–	–	51	51	90	–	–	90	90	–	90	s39¹	–	–	–	90	–	–	–	990
–	–	90	s70	90	–	90	90□	90□	–	90	s13	–	–	–	90	–	–	–	990
–	–	90	–	90¹	–	90	–	–	–	90	s32	–	–	s13	90	s1	–	–	990

THE MANAGER

MICKY ADAMS

For Micky Adams, the managerial merry-go-round began in August 1996 – he has hopped on and off five times since.

His reward for guiding Fulham into the second division was the sack after chairman Mohammed Al Fayed employed Kevin Keegan to spend his millions. Adams then ventured to Swansea, where limited funds saw his tenure last less than a fortnight.

Next stop was a return to the capital with second division Brentford, who Adams led to sixth place in 1997–98. The former Saint then accepted a post as assistant manager at Nottingham Forest in early 1999, but he left a year later after a brief stint as caretaker boss.

Fast forward three months and Adams was appointed head honcho of third division Brighton and Hove Albion. He steered the Sussex outfit to promotion during his first full season and swiftly earned a reputation as one of the country's brightest managerial prospects.

In September 2001, Adams left the flourishing Seagulls for struggling Leicester and eventually became the club's third manager of the season. Peter Taylor was dismissed after six weeks of the campaign, while Dave Bassett moved upstairs after failing to save the Foxes from relegation.

LEAGUE POSITION

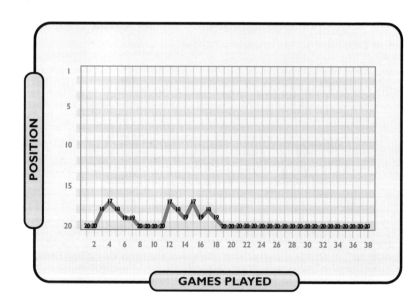

11 Saves made by Ian Walker when Leicester played

THE GOALS

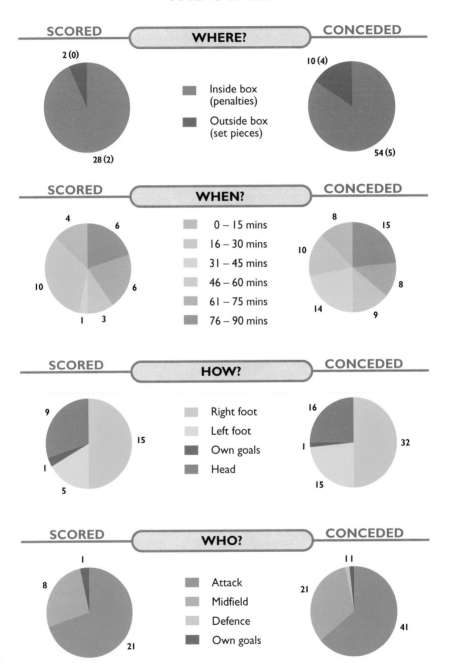

SCORED | **WHERE?** | **CONCEDED**

2 (0)
28 (2)

10 (4)
54 (5)

- Inside box (penalties)
- Outside box (set pieces)

SCORED | **WHEN?** | **CONCEDED**

4 6
10
1 3
6

8 15
10
14 9
8

- 0 – 15 mins
- 16 – 30 mins
- 31 – 45 mins
- 46 – 60 mins
- 61 – 75 mins
- 76 – 90 mins

SCORED | **HOW?** | **CONCEDED**

9
1
5
15

16
1
15
32

- Right foot
- Left foot
- Own goals
- Head

SCORED | **WHO?** | **CONCEDED**

1
8
21

11
21
41

- Attack
- Midfield
- Defence
- Own goals

Aston Villa – the most by a goalkeeper in a single game

LEICESTER CITY

	AKINBIYI	ASHTON	BENJAMIN	DAVIDSON	DEANE	DELANEY	DICKOV	ELLIOTT	GUNNLAUGSSON	HEATH	IMPEY	IZZET	JONES	LAURSEN	LEWIS
APPEARANCES															
Start	16	3	4	29	13	2	11	31	0	3	20	29	6	10	4
Sub	5	4	7	1	2	1	1	0	2	2	7	2	4	0	2
Minutes on pitch	1454	340	435	2420	1184	239	964	2771	71	284	1832	2566	524	900	386
GOAL ATTEMPTS															
Goals	2	0	0	0	6	0	4	0	0	0	0	4	1	0	0
Shots on target	14	0	4	8	17	0	15	5	1	0	4	13	4	1	1
Shots off target	18	2	7	4	13	1	14	6	1	0	4	18	5	0	3
Shooting accuracy %	44%	0%	36%	67%	57%	0%	52%	45%	50%	0%	50%	42%	44%	100%	25%
Goals/shots %	6%	0%	0%	0%	20%	0%	14%	0%	0%	0%	0%	13%	11%	0%	0%
PASSING															
Goal assists	1	0	0	3	1	0	1	2	0	0	1	1	0	0	0
Long passes	45	55	17	306	44	30	37	322	5	26	137	308	100	135	39
Short passes	288	88	86	629	301	39	216	553	15	66	414	971	181	181	117
PASS COMPLETION															
Own half %	83%	69%	72%	75%	77%	80%	83%	84%	67%	78%	81%	85%	88%	83%	85%
Opposition half %	61%	46%	54%	60%	60%	52%	63%	60%	71%	56%	65%	69%	67%	55%	69%
CROSSING															
Total crosses	15	6	7	73	4	1	15	5	1	1	74	93	9	8	3
Cross completion %	13%	17%	14%	34%	25%	0%	27%	40%	100%	0%	22%	31%	11%	38%	33%
DRIBBLING															
Dribbles & runs	31	6	12	53	33	3	23	13	8	3	85	104	12	4	4
Dribble completion %	74%	67%	50%	83%	70%	67%	61%	100%	38%	100%	65%	74%	92%	100%	50%
DEFENDING															
Tackles made	13	7	8	102	13	7	31	39	1	4	49	133	16	9	9
Tackles won %	54%	100%	50%	73%	92%	71%	81%	59%	0%	100%	78%	71%	88%	78%	78%
Blocks	2	6	3	22	2	2	1	42	0	4	16	23	3	11	1
Clearances	7	27	2	143	12	15	0	291	0	21	41	27	10	76	18
Interceptions	0	1	0	11	1	0		13	0	2	9	26	3	3	1
DISCIPLINE															
Fouls conceded	37	9	11	28	31	4	22	37	1	5	18	65	7	6	6
Fouls won	19	4	8	38	20	2	14	26	2	1	21	79	4	7	6
Offside	26	0	7	0	8	1	21	2	0	1	2	5	0	0	0
Yellow cards	3	0	2	3	2	1	5	4	0	0	3	9	0	1	0
Red cards	0	0	0	0	0	0	0	1	0	0	0	1	0	0	1+

+card rescinded

GOALKEEPER NAME	START/ (SUB)	TIME ON PITCH	GOALS CONCEDED	MINS/GOALS CONCEDED	SAVES MADE	SAVES/ SHOTS
FLOWERS	3 (1)	335	12	28	14	54%
WALKER	35 (0)	3085	52	59	121	70%

For more information visit our website:

PLAYERS' STATISTICS

	MARSHALL	OAKES	PIPER	REEVES	ROGERS	ROWETT	SAVAGE	SCOWCROFT	SINCLAIR	STEVENSON	STEWART	STURRIDGE	TAGGART	WILLIAMSON	WISE	WRIGHT	TOTAL	RANK
	29	16	14	1	9	9	35	21	33	0	9	8	0	0	15	0		
	6	5	2	4	4	2	0	3	2	6	3	1	1	1	2	1		
	2654	1436	1256	122	858	823	3085	1774	2867	113	766	569	13	1	1335	4		
	0	1	1	0	0	0	0	5	0	1	0	3	0	0	1	0	30*	19th
	5	5	3	0	2	1	4	18	3	3	0	8	0	0	4	0	143	=18th
	8	6	3	2	2	1	6	21	3	0	3	6	0	0	10	0	167	20th
	38%	45%	50%	0%	50%	50%	40%	46%	50%	100%	0%	57%	0%	0%	29%	0%	46%	6th
	0%	9%	17%	0%	0%	0%	0%	13%	0%	33%	0%	21%	0%	0%	7%	0%	9%	18th
	0	3	1	0	1	0	2	2	0	0	1	0	0	0	0	0	20	=18th
	364	231	37	6	60	100	301	64	407	6	55	20	6	0	226	2	3885	14th
	730	379	218	31	184	180	839	466	580	34	155	122	1	0	466	0	8596	19th
	80%	78%	68%	77%	77%	80%	80%	81%	79%	70%	78%	83%	33%	0%	85%	0%	81%	14th
	59%	55%	54%	50%	71%	52%	65%	61%	55%	53%	56%	62%	75%	0%	70%	100%	61%	19th
	82	155	84	4	60	4	91	11	15	2	37	8	0	0	104	0	972	8th
	28%	26%	18%	25%	25%	0%	16%	27%	20%		22%	13%	0%	0%	27%	0%	25%	10th
	60	28	106	4	34	11	59	22	42	7	35	20	0	0	18	0	853	19th
	78%	93%	66%	50%	71%	91%	73%	73%	83%	71%	77%	45%	0%	0%	83%	0%	73%	1st
	93	51	27	5	10	19	132	27	85	4	31	4	1	0	55	0	985	14th
	77%	80%	78%	60%	80%	68%	68%	74%	71%	100%	74%	100%	0%	0%	73%	0%	73%	15th
	36	9	2	0	5	13	16	3	40	1	5	0	0	0	7	0	276	3rd
	128	41	13	8	28	64	63	15	270	0	25	0	1	0	17	0	1418	9th
	5	5	2	1	2	2	16	6	17	0	0	0	0	0	5	0	131	20th
	29	14	17	4	5	9	68	53	52	1	14	18	1	0	39	0	611	5th
	40	22	27	5	4	4	58	43	21	0	15	14	1	0	26	0	535	13th
	0	2	8	0	1	0	8	8	0	4	2	8	0	0	0	0	114	15th
	3	2	0	1	1	3	14	3	8	0	2	0	0	0	6	0	76	1st
	1	0	0	0	0	0	0	0	0	0	0	0	0	0	1	0	5	=4th

*Including one own goal

CROSSES CAUGHT	CROSSES PUNCHED	CROSSES DROPPED	CATCH SUCCESS	THROWS/ SHORT KICKS	% COMPLETION	LONG KICKS	% COMPLETION
5	1	0	100%	17	100%	63	51%
66	7	5	93%	55	96%	691	52%

www.optaindex.com

PLAYER OF THE SEASON

PLAYER	INDEX SCORE
MUZZY IZZET	688
Callum Davidson	656
Ian Walker	650
James Scowcroft	592
Matt Elliott	591
Lee Marshall	576
Dennis Wise	533*
Frank Sinclair	506
Andy Impey	430
Robbie Savage	366

All players played 75 minutes in at least 15 matches except those marked * who played that amount in 13 games.

Peter Taylor may have been dismissed from his post in September 2001, but at least he could look back and find a few of his own signings ensconced among Leicester's principal players at the season's end. Muzzy Izzet was the noticeable exception in the list.

The Turkey international went one better than in season 2000–01 when he finished second to goalkeeper Tim Flowers in achieving the highest Index score at the club. Izzet provided the drive in the Foxes' engine room, releasing more successful passes than any of his colleagues and firing home four of Leicester's paltry tally of just 30 goals.

As well as providing the attacking impetus, Izzet also displayed steel when Leicester were on the back foot, winning 94 tackles – more than any of his regular team-mates.

Such all-encompassing performances led to Middlesbrough's well-documented interest in the schemer as the 2001–02 season neared its climax.

Taylor's second-ever signing for the Midlands outfit, Callum Davidson, narrowly edged Ian Walker into third place after his efforts in the Foxes' rearguard. The former Blackburn defender missed just eight games during 2001–02 and lunged into more than a century of tackles as his side desperately sought to avoid the drop into the Nationwide League.

As the Foxes' last line of defence, Walker was consistently busy between the posts, managing to keep out 121 of the accurate efforts levelled at his goal – the fourth-highest tally of any Premiership custodian. Relegation may have hurt a player used to life in the top flight, but at least he was a regular at Filbert Street, unlike his last year in north London.

Like Walker, James Scowcroft was brought to Leicester by Taylor in the summer of 2001. He amassed five league goals, grabbing a brace against Chelsea and tested the 'keeper with more shots than any other player at the club, before injury ended his season in March.

FIVE OF THE BEST

Leicester's final season at Filbert Street turned out to be one of upheaval and anticlimax as they finished bottom of the division and consequently slipped through the Premiership trapdoor. Two managerial changes led to 33 different players being utilised during the campaign, yet a winning combination could not be found to reverse the team's flagging fortunes.

TOP GOALSCORERS

	GOALS	GOALS/SHOTS
BRIAN DEANE	6	20%
James Scowcroft	5	13%
Paul Dickov	4	14%
Muzzy Izzet	4	13%
Dean Sturridge	3	21%

Prior to Brian Deane first pulling on the blue shirt in early December 2001, Leicester had plundered an average of 0.6 goals-per-game. However, he notched six goals to earn the accolade of top marksman and the Foxes remained unbeaten whenever he beat the 'keeper. Paul Dickov netted every third game on average to gatecrash the scoring chart, while Dean Sturridge's 21% conversion rate made him the deadliest prospect in front of goal.

While those around him often failed to reach the required standard, Muzzy Izzet remained a consistent performer in the Foxes' engine room. The midfield maestro was the only City player to complete in excess of 900 passes, yet for all his industry he was only credited with one assist. Leicester's distribution rate was the second worst in the Premiership and Robbie Savage, Lee Marshall and Frank Sinclair all failed to achieve the divisional average.

TOP PASSERS

	SUCC PASSES	COMPLETION
MUZZY IZZET	956	75%
Robbie Savage	813	71%
Lee Marshall	738	67%
Frank Sinclair	667	68%
Matt Elliott	656	75%

TOP TACKLERS

	WON	SUCCESS
MUZZY IZZET	94	71%
Robbie Savage	90	68%
Callum Davidson	74	73%
Lee Marshall	72	77%
Frank Sinclair	60	71%

As they fought in vain to retain their top-flight status, Leicester's ball-winning skills actually improved on their 2000–01 performance. Player of the season Muzzy Izzet was the forerunner once more, just six shy of achieving 100 successful tackles. The often-contentious Robbie Savage came a close second, while Callum Davidson was the third Fox to attempt more than a century of challenges. Lee Marshall won the highest proportional rate in the top five.

While losing their Premiership prestige, Leicester seemingly lost their heads too. The Midlands outfit amassed more disciplinary points than any other side with Robbie Savage taking the individual honours at Filbert Street. The Welshman collected 14 bookings – more than any of his colleagues and twice as many as in 2000–01. Muzzy Izzet racked up 98 points, receiving a red card at Bolton, while Dennis Wise's battling displays earned him fourth spot.

DISCIPLINE

	POINTS	FOULS & CARDS
ROBBIE SAVAGE	110	68F, 14Y, 0R
Muzzy Izzet	98	65F, 9Y, 1R
Frank Sinclair	76	52F, 8Y, 0R
Dennis Wise	63	39F, 6Y, 0R
James Scowcroft	62	53F, 3Y, 0R

Filbert Street in 2001–02 than any Leicester player

LIVERPOOL

ADDRESS

Anfield, Anfield Road, Liverpool L4 0TH

CONTACT NUMBERS

Telephone: 0151 263 2361
Fax: 0151 260 8813
Ticket Office: 0151 260 8680
ClubCall: 09068 121184
Superstore: 0151 263 1760
Website: www.liverpoolfc.tv

KEY PERSONNEL

Chairman: D R Moores
Chief Executive: R N Parry BSc, FCA
Directors: N White FSCA, T D Smith,
K E B Clayton FCA, J Burns,
L A Wheatley BSc, FCA
Vice-Presidents: J T Cross, H E Roberts
Club Secretary: W B Morrison
Manager: Gérard Houllier

SPONSORS

Carlsberg

FANZINES

Through the Wind and the Rain,
Red All Over the Land,
The Liverpool Way

COLOURS

Home: Red shirts, red shorts
and red stockings
Away: White shirts, navy shorts
and white stockings

NICKNAME

The Reds

HONOURS

League Champions:
1900–01, 1905–06, 1921–22,
1922–23, 1946–47, 1963–64,
1965–66, 1972–73, 1975–76,
1976–77, 1978–79, 1979–80,
1981–82, 1982–83, 1983–84,
1985–86, 1987–88, 1989–90.
Division Two Champions: 1893–94,
1895–96, 1904–05, 1961–62.
FA Cup Winners: 1965, 1974,
1986, 1989, 1992, 2001.
League Cup Winners: 1981, 1982,
1983, 1984, 1995, 2001
European Cup Winners:
1977, 1978, 1981, 1984
UEFA Cup Winners: 1973, 1976, 2001
European Super Cup Winners:
1977, 2001

RECORD GOALSCORER

Roger Hunt – 245 league goals,
1959–69

BIGGEST WIN

11–0 v Stromsgodset Drammen –
European Cup Winners' Cup 1st round
1st leg, 17 September 1974

BIGGEST DEFEAT

1–9 v Birmingham City – Division Two,
11 December 1954

SEASON REVIEW

After bringing home three trophies in the previous campaign, 2001–02 was always going to be a season filled with high expectation. However, on reflection, the success this time came not in the form of silverware, but in that of progression and growth. The 2001–02 season saw Liverpool return to Europe's premier competition for the first time in 16 years and reach the quarter finals, while simultaneously mounting their most serious title challenge in a decade.

Boss Gérard Houllier showed his ruthless streak when he replaced Sander Westerveld with Polish number one Jerzy Dudek just two games into the season, after the Dutch 'keeper's mistake cost the Reds a point at Bolton. Along with John Arne Riise, the arrival of Dudek helped to reinforce Liverpool's squad over the campaign.

However, Anfield and the football world was rocked on 13 October when Houllier was rushed to hospital at half time during the 1–1 draw with Leeds and underwent a major heart operation. The surgery was a success, but Liverpool would be without their manager until the following March.

Without their leader, assistant manager Phil Thompson took temporary control of team matters and became the link between the players and the convalescing Houllier. The players responded well and by the beginning of December, Liverpool were six points clear at the top of the table after taking 19 points from 21 available in a run that also saw their fourth straight win over rivals Manchester United. The only blip was the Champions League defeat to Barcelona, who were given a standing ovation for an other-worldly performance at Anfield.

However, the Reds' title challenge faltered over the Christmas period and it was poor form in that spell that eventually cost them the title. Between 12 December and 19 January, the team managed just one league win in nine games and crashed out of the FA Cup to Arsenal, with Jamie Carragher dismissed for throwing a coin back into the crowd. Without their manager, many teams would have crumbled, but Liverpool lifted themselves for a trip to Old Trafford and, thanks to a battling display and a Danny Murphy goal, came away with all three points and the golden sky at the end of the storm was in sight.

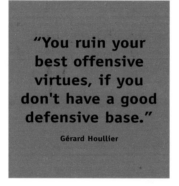

"You ruin your best offensive virtues, if you don't have a good defensive base."

Gérard Houllier

The victory over Manchester United acted as a springboard and off the back of that result, Liverpool went on to beat Leeds 4–0 and then hammer in-form Ipswich 6–0 in what was one of the club's best away performances in the league for some time. Houllier returned to the dugout for the 2–0 victory over Roma in the Champions League that took Liverpool into the quarter finals – one of Anfield's best European nights – and with just two goals conceded in 12 Premiership games the Reds were back on track.

During 2001–02 Liverpool were arguably the hardest working side in the top flight. They went in for more tackles and made more clearances than any other team as they built a solid defensive base and attacked from the back – just like the old days. The result was a total of just 30 goals conceded – fewer than any other side in the division – and 18 clean sheets.

Liverpool eventually ran out of steam at White Hart Lane where they crashed to a 1–0 defeat to Spurs that effectively ended their title charge. But the team refused to stop fighting and secured second place with a classy 5–0 win over Ipswich on the final day of the season.

scoreline than any other club

LIVERPOOL

DATE	OPPONENT	SCORE	ATT.	ANELKA	ARPHEXAD	BABBEL	BARMBY	BERGER	BISCAN	CARRAGHER	DUDEK	FOWLER	GERRARD	HAMANN
18.08.01	West Ham H	2–1	43,935	–	90	45	s34	–	56	90□	–	–	–	90
27.08.01	Bolton W A	1–2	27,205	–	–	45	–	–	–	90	–	64□	90	90
08.09.01	Aston Villa H	1–3	44,102	–	–	–	60□	–	–	90□	90	90	74¹□	90
15.09.01	Everton A	3–1	39,554	–	–	–	–	–	–	90	90	–	85¹	90
22.09.01	Tottenham H	1–0	44,116	–	–	–	90	–	90	90	90	60	–	90
30.09.01	Newcastle A	2–0	52,095	–	–	–	–	–	90	90□	90	90□	–	–
13.10.01	Leeds Utd H	1–1	44,352	–	–	–	s1	–	–	90	90	90	90□	–
20.10.01	Leicester A	4–1	21,886	–	–	–	–	s45	–	90	90	90³	45	–
27.10.01	Charlton A	2–0	22,887	–	–	–	–	s18	–	90	90	s27	90	90
04.11.01	Man Utd H	3–1	44,361	–	–	–	–	s21	–	90	90	s21	90	90
17.11.01	Blackburn A	1–1	28,859	–	–	–	–	62	–	90	90	90	90	90
25.11.01	Sunderland H	1–0	43,537	–	–	–	–	s22	–	90	90	45	90□	44□
01.12.01	Derby Co A	1–0	33,289	–	–	–	–	76	–	90	90	–	90	90
08.12.01	Middlesbro H	2–0	43,674	–	–	–	–	90¹	–	90	90	–	–	90
12.12.01	Fulham H	0–0	37,163	–	–	–	–	66	s10	90	90	–	90	–
16.12.01	Chelsea A	0–4	41,174	–	–	–	–	–	45	90	90	–	90	–
23.12.01	Arsenal H	1–2	44,297	–	–	–	–	90	–	90	90	–	90	–
26.12.01	Aston Villa A	2–1	42,602	s21	–	–	–	90	–	90	90	–	77	90
29.12.01	West Ham A	1–1	35,103	90	–	–	–	90	–	90	90	–	s45	–
01.01.02	Bolton W H	1–1	43,710	s22	–	–	–	85	–	–	90	–	90¹	90
09.01.02	Southampton A	0–2	31,527	90	–	–	–	s12	–	90□	90	–	90	90
13.01.02	Arsenal A	1–1	38,132	85	–	–	–	90	–	90	90	–	90	90□
19.01.02	Southampton H	1–1	43,710	s31	–	–	–	90	–	90	90	–	33	90
22.01.02	Man Utd A	1–0	67,599	s13	–	–	–	s2	–	90□	90	–	90□	90
30.01.02	Leicester H	1–0	42,305	90	–	–	–	86	–	90	90	–	–	90
03.02.02	Leeds Utd A	4–0*	40,216	–	–	–	–	–	–	90□	90	–	89	90
09.02.02	Ipswich A	6–0	25,608	s17	s34	–	–	–	–	–	56	–	82	90
23.02.02	Everton H	1–1	44,371	90¹	–	–	–	–	–	–	90	–	–	90
02.03.02	Fulham A	2–0	21,103	81¹	–	–	s19	–	–	–	90	–	–	90
06.03.02	Newcastle H	3–0	44,204	90	–	–	s8	–	–	–	90	–	–	90¹
16.03.02	Middlesbro A	2–1	31,253	90	–	–	–	–	–	90	90	–	s20	90□
24.03.02	Chelsea H	1–0	44,203	84	–	–	–	–	–	90□	90	–	29	90
30.03.02	Charlton H	2–0	44,094	90	–	–	–	84	–	90	90	–	–	90
13.04.02	Sunderland A	1–0	48,335	90	–	–	–	s1	–	90	90	–	90□	90
20.04.02	Derby Co H	2–0	43,510	66	–	–	–	s7	–	90	90	–	90	90
27.04.02	Tottenham H	0–1	36,017	s26	–	–	–	s22	–	90	90	–	–	90
08.05.02	Blackburn H	4–3	40,663	90¹	–	–	–	–	–	90	90	–	90□	81
11.05.02	Ipswich H	5–0	44,088	s5¹	–	–	–	–	–	90	90	–	33	90

□ Yellow card, ▪ Red card, s Substitute, 90² Goals scored
*including own goal

For more information visit our website:

2001–02 PREMIERSHIP APPEARANCES

HENCHOZ	HESKEY	HYYPIA	KIRKLAND	LITMANEN	McALLISTER	MURPHY	OWEN	REDKNAPP	RIISE	SMICER	VIGNAL	WESTERVELD	WRIGHT	XAVIER	TOTAL
90	–	90	–	90	90	72	90²	s18	s45	–	–	–	–	–	990
90□	s26¹	90	–	–	90	90	90	–	s45	–	–	90	–	–	990
76	90	90	–	–	90	s14	s30	–	61	–	s29□	–	–	–	974
90	90	90	–	–	s12	78□	90¹	–	90¹	s5	90	–	–	–	990
90	s30	90	–	68¹	s6	–	s16	–	90	–	90□	–	–	–	990
90□	90	90	–	–	90	90¹□	–	–	90¹	–	90	–	–	–	990
90	45	90□	–	s45	76	89¹□	–	s14	90	90	–	–	–	–	990
–	83□	90¹	–	s7	90	90	–	79□	90	s11	–	–	90	–	990
90	s7	–	–	83	–	90	63¹	72¹	90	–	–	–	88□	–	988
90	90	90	–	–	–	90	69²	–	90¹	69	–	–	–	–	990
90	s18	90	–	–	90	s28	72¹	–	90	–	–	–	–	–	990
90	90¹	90	–	–	s45	68	–	–	90	77	–	–	s13	–	944
90	90□	90	–	s7	s14	90	83¹□	–	90	–	–	–	–	–	990
90	s12	90	–	90	90	90	78¹	–	90	–	–	–	–	–	990
90	90	90	–	s24	90	80	90	–	90	–	–	–	–	–	990
90	90□	90	–	90	90	90□	–	–	90	–	–	–	s45□	–	990
90□	45	90	–	s45¹	45	90	90	–	90	s45	–	–	–	–	990
90	–	90	–	69¹	s4	s13	90	–	90	86¹	–	–	–	–	990
90	90	90	–	s20	45	59	s31¹	–	90	70	–	–	–	–	990
90	90	90□	–	s5	–	–	90	–	90	68	–	–	90	–	990
90	s33	90	–	90	–	78	–	–	s21	57	–	–	69	–	990
90	s24	90	–	–	s5	66	90	–	90¹	–	–	–	–	–	990
90	90	90	–	–	s18	72	90¹	–	90	s26	–	–	–	–	990
90	90	90	–	–	–	88¹	77	–	90	–	–	–	90	–	990
90	90¹	90	–	–	74	s16	–	–	s4	90□	–	–	90	–	990
90	90²	90	–	–	s1	90	90¹	–	90	–	–	–	90	–	990
90	90²	90¹	–	–	s8	90	90²	–	73	–	–	–	90	90¹	990
90	s35	90	90	–	66	90	90	–	90	s24	–	–	55	90	990
90	90	90□	–	s9¹	–	90	–	–	90	71	–	90□	90	–	990
90	90	90	–	s18	–	90²	72	–	90	82	–	–	–	90	990
90□	90¹	90	–	–	–	90	–	–	90¹	70	–	–	–	90	990
90	90	90	–	s6	–	90	s32	–	90	s61¹	–	–	–	58	990
90	19	90	–	s11	s6	90	79¹	–	90	s71¹□	–	–	–	–	990
90	–	90	–	58	–	s32	89¹	–	90	–	–	–	90□	–	990
90	s24	90	–	s1	–	89	90²	–	90	83	–	–	–	–	990
90	64	90	–	s8	–	82	90	–	90□	90	–	–	–	68	990
90	90¹	90¹	–	–	–	90¹	89	–	90	s1	–	–	–	s9	990
90	90	90	–	–	s8	82	90¹	–	90²	s57¹	–	–	–	85	990

THE MANAGER

GERARD HOULLIER

After the triple cup success of 2001 the new season looked bright for Liverpool. However, just seven games into the season Gérard Houllier was rushed to hospital and underwent a major heart operation that saw him spend the majority of the campaign recuperating away from Anfield.

But the discipline and methods that he had instilled into the players were upheld in his absence by his assistant Phil Thompson and Liverpool maintained a challenge for the Premiership title.

After managing Lens and guiding Paris St. Germain to the French title in 1986, Houllier became Platini's number two in the French national side from 1988 to 1992 and then took over when Platini stepped down.

But France failed to qualify for the 1994 World Cup and Houllier left the post. He returned to the national set up to manage the under-18s, then worked as the head coach of the under-20 team and later became the technical director of the French Football Federation.

He was offered the job of Liverpool manager in 1998 and his reputation and standing among fans and peers has grown since. For his contribution to the game Houllier was awarded the Légion d'Honneur – France's highest civilian honour.

LEAGUE POSITION

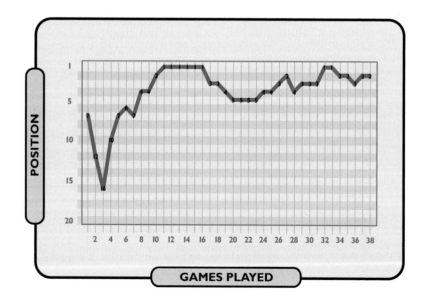

POSITION

GAMES PLAYED

THE GOALS

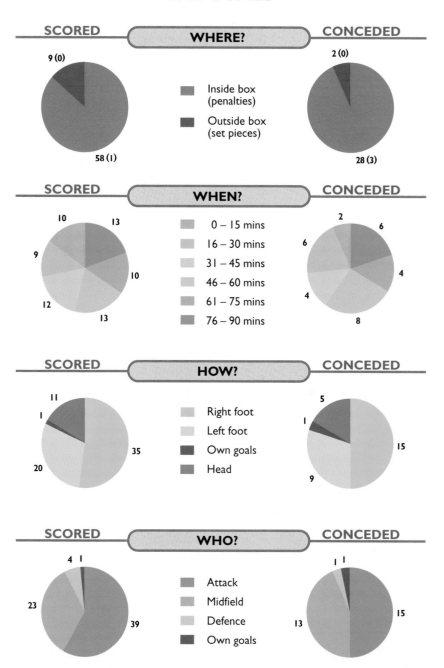

SCORED — **WHERE?** — **CONCEDED**

- Inside box (penalties)
- Outside box (set pieces)

Scored: 9 (0), 58 (1)
Conceded: 2 (0), 28 (3)

SCORED — **WHEN?** — **CONCEDED**

- 0 – 15 mins
- 16 – 30 mins
- 31 – 45 mins
- 46 – 60 mins
- 61 – 75 mins
- 76 – 90 mins

Scored: 13, 10, 13, 12, 9, 10
Conceded: 6, 4, 8, 4, 6, 2

SCORED — **HOW?** — **CONCEDED**

- Right foot
- Left foot
- Own goals
- Head

Scored: 35, 20, 1, 11
Conceded: 15, 9, 1, 5

SCORED — **WHO?** — **CONCEDED**

- Attack
- Midfield
- Defence
- Own goals

Scored: 39, 23, 4, 1
Conceded: 15, 13, 1, 1

tackles than anyone else

LIVERPOOL

	ANELKA	BABBEL	BARMBY	BERGER	BISCAN	CARRAGHER	FOWLER	GERRARD	HAMANN
APPEARANCES									
Start	13	2	2	12	4	33	8	26	31
Sub	7	0	4	9	1	0	2	2	0
Minutes on pitch	1261	90	212	1149	291	2970	667	2142	2735
GOAL ATTEMPTS									
Goals	4	0	0	1	0	0	3	3	1
Shots on target	22	0	1	7	1	2	9	15	9
Shots off target	15	0	1	17	2	4	12	16	15
Shooting accuracy %	59%	0%	50%	29%	33%	33%	43%	48%	38%
Goals/shots %	11%	0%	0%	4%	0%	0%	14%	10%	4%
PASSING									
Goal assists	2	0	0	2	0	1	1	8	4
Long passes	50	10	14	118	19	468	27	517	564
Short passes	297	43	70	368	125	912	156	891	1239
PASS COMPLETION									
Own half %	82%	90%	87%	84%	89%	85%	83%	87%	88%
Opposition half %	60%	75%	80%	69%	65%	69%	57%	66%	81%
CROSSING									
Total crosses	13	4	5	32	4	47	8	93	23
Cross completion %	31%	25%	20%	22%	25%	26%	0%	22%	26%
DRIBBLING									
Dribbles & runs	77	5	7	52	10	27	20	90	69
Dribble completion %	62%	80%	86%	63%	50%	74%	35%	64%	90%
DEFENDING									
Tackles made	23	2	5	69	9	121	6	90	186
Tackles won %	78%	100%	80%	77%	89%	75%	83%	72%	69%
Blocks	0	0	1	5	1	21	2	8	10
Clearances	6	4	3	19	7	288	1	50	45
Interceptions	3	1	2	7	1	23	2	19	48
DISCIPLINE									
Fouls conceded	17	3	7	27	10	32	9	31	51
Fouls won	29	2	1	6	3	32	17	22	60
Offside	37	0	2	1	0	0	15	4	1
Yellow cards	0	0	1	0	0	7	2	5	2
Red cards	0	0	0	0	0	0	0	1	1

GOALKEEPER NAME	START/ (SUB)	TIME ON PITCH	GOALS CONCEDED	MINS/GOALS CONCEDED	SAVES MADE	SAVES/ SHOTS
ARPHEXAD	1 (1)	124	1	124	2	67%
DUDEK	35 (0)	3116	26	120	97	79%
KIRKLAND	1 (0)	90	1	90	2	67%
WESTERVELD	1 (0)	90	2	45	1	33%

For more information visit our website:

PLAYERS' STATISTICS

	HENCHOZ	HESKEY	HYYPIA	LITMANEN	McALLISTER	MURPHY	OWEN	REDKNAPP	RIISE	SMICER	VIGNAL	WRIGHT	XAVIER	TOTAL	RANK
	37	26	37	8	14	31	25	2	34	13	3	10	9		
	0	9	0	13	11	5	4	2	4	9	1	2	1		
	3316	2355	3330	844	1243	2726	2230	183	3129	1304	299	900	760		
	0	9	3	4	0	6	19	1	7	4	0	0	1	67*	4th
	0	19	13	9	8	20	38	1	26	7	0	0	1	208	=5th
	0	23	8	12	10	23	25	1	22	9	2	0	1	218	14th
	0%	45%	62%	43%	44%	47%	60%	50%	54%	44%	0%	0%	50%	49%	2nd
	0%	21%	14%	19%	0%	14%	30%	50%	15%	25%	0%	0%	50%	15%	2nd
	0	7	0	1	4	8	2	0	3	6	0	0	2	51	3rd
	495	93	607	104	247	392	114	17	343	89	51	129	93	4952	2nd
	791	717	932	361	554	990	448	64	942	485	92	235	261	11060	9th
	91%	81%	87%	90%	88%	83%	87%	90%	85%	85%	73%	78%	85%	86%	3rd
	62%	64%	62%	79%	80%	70%	74%	74%	62%	67%	48%	55%	70%	68%	9th
	2	37	4	19	103	95	20	2	154	61	18	13	11	768	19th
	50%	16%	75%	42%	26%	23%	35%	0%	18%	30%	28%	15%	18%	24%	16th
	14	78	16	23	27	122	105	5	174	85	11	12	9	1039	12th
	100%	67%	94%	78%	81%	67%	43%	80%	73%	72%	45%	25%	78%	67%	15th
	97	61	105	13	30	106	20	10	102	62	11	33	27	1190	1st
	72%	67%	70%	85%	87%	74%	75%	70%	74%	68%	73%	76%	85%	73%	13th
	45	8	29	0	6	13	0	0	31	5	1	7	15	208	=11th
	349	30	489	2	22	23	1	2	181	10	26	73	43	1726	1st
	16	4	35	1	6	8	3	1	16	2	6	3	2	209	1st
	28	66	27	6	19	27	11	4	35	25	6	12	17	471	20th
	25	55	45	7	17	40	41	0	64	31	4	17	5	530	15th
	0	24	1	9	5	2	36	0	3	2	1	0	0	143	5th
	4	3	3	0	0	4	1	1	1	2	2	2	1	41	19th
	0	0	0	0	0	0	0	0	0	0	0	1	0	3	=9th

*Including one own goal

CROSSES CAUGHT	CROSSES PUNCHED	CROSSES DROPPED	CATCH SUCCESS	THROWS/SHORT KICKS	% COMPLETION	LONG KICKS	% COMPLETION
2	0	0	100%	1	100%	13	62%
58	28	3	95%	33	91%	588	45%
2	0	0	100%	3	100%	10	40%
2	1	0	100%	6	100%	10	70%

PLAYER OF THE SEASON

PLAYER	INDEX SCORE
SAMI HYYPIA	1,056
Michael Owen	988
John Arne Riise	903
Dietmar Hamann	844
Jamie Carragher	835
Steven Gerrard	821
Jerzy Dudek	811
Danny Murphy	758
Stephane Henchoz	729
Emile Heskey	712

Manager Gérard Houllier said: "You ruin your best offensive virtues, if you don't have a good defensive base", and during the 2001–02 season there were few better defensive bases than the impressive Sami Hyypia.

The giant Finn made 489 clearances during the league season, which was significantly more than any other player in any of the major European top divisions. He also recorded the highest number of defensive clearances for a player in the Champions League. In short, he was solidity personified and one of the main reasons Liverpool kept 18 Premiership clean sheets – a tally no side could better.

Hyypia got stuck into more than 100 tackles and was a commanding presence in the Liverpool defence, yet he has only picked up five league bookings in his three seasons at Anfield. His assuredness, drive and calming influence at the back were some of the reasons he was made club captain following the departures of Robbie Fowler and Jamie Redknapp.

Meanwhile, Michael Owen became the first Englishman to win the European Player of the Year Award since Kevin Keegan in 1979 and ranked second in Opta's Liverpool Index. He scored 19 times – his highest ever league haul – but significantly, he hit the target with 60% of his efforts and scored with 30% of his shots. His hat-trick against Germany also helped England to record a 5–1 win over their rivals.

Ranked third was John Arne Riise – Opta's highest-ranked left-back of the season. Only Owen hit the target with more shots than Riise and his seven goals made him third top-scorer at Anfield. The Norwegian whipped in 128 crosses too and embarked on 174 dribbles and runs – both totals were the highest of any Liverpool player during the 2001–02 Premiership season.

Along with Owen, Jamie Carragher, Steven Gerrard, Danny Murphy and Emile Heskey made it five England internationals featuring in Liverpool's top 10.

4 Liverpool became the first team to beat Manchester

FIVE OF THE BEST

Liverpool's 2001–02 season may not have brought in a haul of silverware like 2000–01, but progression in all areas could well turn out to be a significant victory in the long run. New arrivals at the club made a huge impact while old regulars got better and better and the club achieved their highest finish in the league for more than a decade.

TOP GOALSCORERS

	GOALS	GOALS/SHOTS
MICHAEL OWEN	19	30%
Emile Heskey	9	21%
John Arne Riise	7	15%
Danny Murphy	6	14%
Vladimir Smicer	4	25%

Michael Owen registered his best ever Premiership goal tally with 19. And the little striker saw 30% of his shots hit the back of the net, making him deadlier than van Nistelrooy, Henry, Hasselbaink, Shearer et al. Emile Heskey, despite a barren run mid-season, scored nine times for Liverpool, while left-back John Arne Riise hit seven goals as he turned out to be one of the buys of the season.

Dietmar Hamann marshalled the Liverpool midfield expertly in 2001–02 and no Liverpool player saw more of the ball than the German international. Liverpool's player of the season Sami Hyypia recorded the second most passes, as the newly installed captain was again commanding in defence. His defensive partner Stephane Henchoz was the third-most on-the-ball Red throughout the season and highly accurate with his distribution.

TOP PASSERS

	SUCC PASSES	COMPLETION
DIETMAR HAMANN	1,520	84%
Sami Hyypia	1,190	77%
Stephane Henchoz	1,045	81%
Jamie Carragher	1,044	76%
Steven Gerrard	1,035	74%

TOP TACKLERS

	WON	SUCCESS
DIETMAR HAMANN	129	69%
Jamie Carragher	91	75%
Danny Murphy	78	74%
John Arne Riise	75	74%
Sami Hyypia	73	70%

In keeping with their defensive reputation, no team attempted more tackles than Liverpool during 2001–02 and Dietmar Hamann was the most prolific. The German broke up countless opposition attacks in his holding role while the underrated Jamie Carragher recorded the second-highest success total, after winning three out of four challenges he got stuck into on average. The tireless Danny Murphy came third and his hard work in all areas epitomised Houllier's philosophy.

The huge physical presence of Emile Heskey frightened defences throughout the land, but with his power came a fair few fouls and, although he was only booked three times, he heard the referee's whistle on 66 occasions. Hamann recorded the second-highest total of discipline points, although the fact that he went in for more tackles than any Premiership player apart from Patrick Vieira would account for the odd mistimed challenge.

DISCIPLINE

	POINTS	FOULS & CARDS
EMILE HESKEY	75	66F, 3Y, 0R
Dietmar Hamann	63	51F, 2Y, 1R
Jamie Carragher	53	32F, 7Y, 0R
Steven Gerrard	52	31F, 5Y, 1R
Stephane Henchoz	40	28F, 4Y, 0R

MANCHESTER UNITED

ADDRESS

Old Trafford, Sir Matt Busby Way,
Manchester M16 ORA

CONTACT NUMBERS

Telephone: 0161 868 8000
Fax: 0161 868 8668
Ticket and Match Information:
0161 868 8020
ClubCall: 09068 121 161
Megastore: 0161 868 8567
Museum and Tour Centre:
0161 868 8631
e-mail: webmaster@office.manutd.com
Website: www.manutd.com

KEY PERSONNEL

Chairman: C M Edwards
Chief Executive: P F Kenyon
Deputy Chief Executive: D A Gill
Directors: Sir Bobby Charlton CBE,
J M Edelson, R L Olive
E M Watkins Ll.M
Club Secretary: K R Merrett
Manager: Sir Alex Ferguson CBE

SPONSORS

Vodafone

FANZINES

United We Stand, Red News,
Red Army, Red Attitude

NICKNAME

The Red Devils

COLOURS

Home: Red shirts, white shorts
and black stockings
Away: White shirts, black shorts
and white stockings

HONOURS

League Champions: 1907–08, 1910–11,
1951–52, 1955–56, 1956–57, 1964–65,
1966–67, 1992–93, 1993–94, 1995–96,
1996–97, 1998–99, 1999–2000, 2000–01
Division Two Champions: 1935–36,
1974–75
FA Cup Winners: 1909, 1948, 1963, 1977,
1983, 1985, 1990, 1994, 1996, 1999
League Cup Winners: 1992
European Cup Winners: 1968, 1999
European Cup Winners' Cup Winners: 1991
European Super Cup Winners: 1991
Inter-Continental Cup Winners: 1999

RECORD GOALSCORER

Bobby Charlton – 199 league goals,
1956–73

BIGGEST WIN

10–0 v RSC Anderlecht, European Cup
preliminary round 2nd leg,
26 September 1956

BIGGEST DEFEATS

0–7 v Blackburn Rovers –
Division One, 10 April, 1926
0–7 v Aston Villa – Division One,
27 December 1930
0–7 v Wolverhampton Wanderers –
Division Two, 26 December 1931

SEASON REVIEW

Manchester United began the 2001–02 season as strong favourites to win what would have been a fourth successive Premiership title.

They had spent heavily in the close season, investing £47 million in just two players – Ruud van Nistelrooy and Juan Sebastian Veron.

This was also to be Sir Alex Ferguson's last season in charge after 16 years at the club and his team were expected to send the boss out on a high.

An opening day victory against Fulham appeared to have set the pattern for another successful season, but behind the scenes things were running far from smoothly.

In August, Jaap Stam brought out an autobiography in which he made comments about his manager and team-mates and, while Ferguson never gave this as a reason for the Dutchman's departure, Stam was abruptly sold to Lazio for £16.5m and replaced by veteran Laurent Blanc.

Initially the upheavals didn't seem to have any effect and by late September United were only a point off surprise leaders Bolton.

But United were not playing with their characteristic swagger. The loss of Stam had unsettled the defence and although Blanc was to finish the season strongly, he looked far from comfortable in his first few months at Old Trafford.

The team was also having difficulty adjusting to a new 4-5-1 system that seemed to unbalance United's midfield while also leaving van Nistelrooy an isolated figure up front.

Although the Red Devils progressed to the second phase of the Champions League, they lost twice to Deportivo La Coruna and were far from their best.

> **"Perhaps some of the players took too much for granted and fell into the trap that somehow Manchester United had a divine right to continue winning trophies."**
>
> **Sir Alex Ferguson**

In the Premiership, they lost to Bolton, Liverpool, Arsenal, Chelsea and West Ham. The defence was gifting the opposition chances with Fabien Barthez particularly culpable, especially at Highbury where he presented Thierry Henry with two easy goals.

United found themselves in ninth place, but, to their credit, refused to accept defeat. Victory against Derby on 12 December was the start of a run that saw them win 14 of their next 16 Premiership games.

During this run, Ruud van Nistelrooy scored in eight consecutive league matches, setting a new record, while Andy Cole was sold to Blackburn for £7.5m with Diego Forlan drafted in to replace him.

United were now a point clear at the top of the table and had qualified for the quarter-finals of the Champions League. During the club's resurgence it was also announced that Ferguson was to stay on as United manager and in February he signed a new three-year deal.

But in keeping with United's topsy-turvy campaign, the defending champions lost at Old Trafford in March to Middlesbrough, the team who had also knocked them out of the FA Cup, just when it seemed they were again becoming invincible.

Eliminated from the Champions League by Bayer Leverkusen in the semi-final on away goals, United were left to contemplate a season without trophies.

Their one hope remained the Premiership. But their title dreams were ruined by Arsenal who arrived at Old Trafford needing just a point to secure the Premiership. The fact that the Gunners won 1–0 to sew up the title in United's own backyard was the final ignominy.

Whether or not 2001–02 was just a blip or the end of an era remains to be seen.

MANCHESTER UNITED

DATE	OPPONENT	SCORE	ATT.	BARTHEZ	BECKHAM	BLANC	BROWN	BUTT	CARROLL	CHADWICK	COLE	FORLAN	FORTUNE	GIGGS	IRWIN
19.08.01	Fulham H	3–2	67,534	90	90¹	–	s10	–	–	s13	s55	–	–	90	90
22.08.01	Blackburn A	2–2	29,836	90	90¹	–	90	–	–	–	s16	–	–	90¹	68
26.08.01	Aston Villa A	1–1*	42,632	–	70	–	90	–	90	–	s20	–	–	90	–
08.09.01	Everton H	4–1	67,534	90	s12¹	90	90	–	–	78	90¹	–	90¹	–	–
15.09.01	Newcastle A	3–4	52,056	90	90	90	90	–	–	–	59	–	–	90¹	–
22.09.01	Ipswich H	4–0	67,551	90	–	–	–	90	–	65	90¹	–	90	–	–
29.09.01	Tottenham A	5–3	36,038	90	90¹□	90¹	–	40□	–	–	90¹	–	–	–	45□
13.10.01	Sunderland A	3–1*	48,305	–	–	76	90	90	90	90	90¹	–	–	61¹	–
20.10.01	Bolton W H	1–2	67,559	90	–	–	90	90	–	s23	90	–	–	s23	–
27.10.01	Leeds Utd H	1–1	67,555	90	90□	90	90	75□	–	–	–	–	–	90	–
04.11.01	Liverpool A	1–3	44,361	90	77¹	–	90	90	–	–	–	–	90	–	85
17.11.01	Leicester H	2–0	67,651	90	90	90	90	–	–	–	–	–	s26	64□	45
25.11.01	Arsenal A	1–3	38,174	90□	90□	90□	90	–	–	–	–	–	90	–	–
01.12.01	Chelsea H	0–3	67,544	90	76	90	90	–	–	s1	89	–	67	–	–
08.12.01	West Ham H	0–1	67,582	90	s31	–	–	69□	–	59	s21	–	s8	–	–
12.12.01	Derby Co H	5–0	67,577	83	–	90	–	90	s7	–	–	–	–	–	–
15.12.01	Middlesbro A	1–0	34,358	–	–	90	–	65□	90	–	–	–	–	s25	–
22.12.01	Southampton H	6–1	67,638	90	s24	90	–	90	–	–	–	–	–	s24	–
26.12.01	Everton A	2–0	39,948	90	s34	90	–	56	–	–	–	–	–	90¹	–
30.12.01	Fulham A	3–2	21,159	90	90□	90	–	90□	–	–	–	–	–	90²	–
02.01.02	Newcastle H	3–1	67,646	90	s5	90	–	90	–	–	–	–	–	–	–
13.01.02	Southampton A	3–1	31,858	90	90¹	90□	–	–	–	–	–	–	–	s5	s45
19.01.02	Blackburn H	2–1	67,552	90	90	90	–	s6	–	–	–	–	–	s35	s45□
22.01.02	Liverpool H	0–1	67,599	90	88	90	–	–	–	–	–	–	–	90	–
29.01.02	Bolton W A	4–0	27,350	90	90	72	–	s17	–	–	–	s14	–	90	–
02.02.02	Sunderland H	4–1	67,587	90	90¹	64□	–	s11	–	–	–	s26	–	64	–
10.02.02	Charlton A	2–0	26,475	–	90	90	–	s2	90	–	–	s12	–	88	–
23.02.02	Aston Villa H	1–0	67,592	90	90	90	–	90	–	–	–	–	–	–	86
03.03.02	Derby Co A	2–2	33,041	90	90	–	–	–	–	–	–	s10	–	80	84
06.03.02	Tottenham H	4–0	67,059	90	90²	90	–	s19	–	–	–	90	s19	–	–
16.03.02	West Ham A	5–3	35,281	90	90²	90	–	90¹	–	–	–	s6	s3	–	–
23.03.02	Middlesbro H	0–1	67,683	90	90□	90	–	90	–	–	–	82	s8	90	–
30.03.02	Leeds Utd A	4–3	40,058	90	90□	90	–	90	–	–	–	s15	–	75¹	–
06.04.02	Leicester A	1–0	29,263	–	–	90	s11	90	90	–	–	63	51	s27	79
20.04.02	Chelsea A	3–0	41,725	90	–	90	90	90	–	–	–	s3	42	87	–
27.04.02	Ipswich A	1–0	28,433	–	–	–	90	90	90	79	–	90	–	–	90
08.05.02	Arsenal H	0–1	67,580	90	–	90□	90	–	–	–	–	69	s21	90	–
11.05.02	Charlton H	0–0	67,571	77	–	90	90	–	–	–	–	90	90	s31	68□

□ Yellow card, ■ Red card, s Substitute, 90² Goals scored
*including own goal

For more information visit our website:

2001–02 PREMIERSHIP APPEARANCES

JOHNSEN	KEANE	MAY	NEVILLE G	NEVILLE P	O'SHEA	SCHOLES	SILVESTRE	SOLSKJAER	STAM	STEWART	VAN DER GOUW	VAN NISTELROOY	VERON	WALLWORK	YORKE	TOTAL
–	–	–	90	35	–	90	90	–	90	–	–	77²	80	–	–	990
90	90	–	s22	–	–	74	90□	–	–	–	–	74	90	–	s16	990
90	90	–	90	s45	–	83□	45	s7	–	–	–	90	90□	–	–	990
–	90	–	58	90	–	–	s32	–	–	–	–	s12	90¹	–	78	990
–	89□	–	90□	90	–	s31	–	–	–	–	–	90¹	90¹	–	–	989
90¹	76	90	–	90	–	s25	90	90²	–	–	–	–	s14	–	–	990
90	–	–	90	–	–	90	s45	s50	–	–	–	90¹	90¹	–	–	990
–	–	–	90	s14	–	67	90	90	–	s23	–	–	–	–	s29	990
–	–	79	s11	90	–	67	90	90	–	–	–	–	90¹	–	67	990
–	–	–	90	–	–	90□	90	s15¹	–	–	–	90	90	–	–	990
–	–	–	90	–	s5	s13	90	52	–	–	–	90	90	–	s38	990
–	90	–	90	–	–	90	s45	–	–	–	–	90¹□	–	–	90¹	990
–	90	–	90	s33	–	90¹	57	s12	–	–	–	78	58	–	s32	990
–	90	–	s23	90	–	90□	–	s14	–	–	–	90□	90	–	–	990
–	90□	–	90□	90	90□	90□	90	90	–	–	–	–	–	–	82	990
–	90¹	–	90	–	90	90¹□	90	90²	–	–	–	79¹	90	–	s11	990
–	90□	–	90	s77	13	90	90□	90	–	–	–	90¹	90	–	–	990
–	82¹	–	90	90¹	–	90□	90	66¹	–	–	–	90³	66	s8	–	990
–	90	–	90□	90	–	–	90	90	–	–	–	90¹	90	–	–	990
–	90	–	90	90	–	90	90	–	–	–	–	90¹	–	–	–	990
–	90	–	90	90	–	90²	90	85□	–	–	–	66¹	90	–	s24	990
–	90	–	90	45	–	90	90	90¹	–	–	–	85¹	90	–	–	990
–	90¹	–	90	90	–	90	45	55	–	–	–	90¹	84	–	–	990
–	90	–	90	90	–	90	90	s2	–	–	–	90	90□	–	–	990
–	73	–	90	87	s18	90	90	76³	–	–	–	90¹	–	–	–	987
–	79	–	90	90¹	s26	90	90	90	–	–	–	90²	–	–	–	990
–	90	–	90	90□	–	90	90	78²	–	–	–	67	s23	–	–	990
s4	90	–	90	–	–	–	90	90	–	–	–	90¹	90	–	–	990
90	–	–	90	–	s6	90¹	90	90	–	–	–	90	90¹	–	–	990
90	90□	–	69	s21	–	71□	90	–	–	–	–	90²	71	–	–	990
90	90	–	90□	–	–	90¹	90	84¹□	–	–	–	87	–	–	–	990
90	–	–	90	–	–	s31	90□	–	–	–	–	90□	59□	–	–	990
90	90	–	90	s4	–	90¹□	90	86²	–	–	–	–	–	–	–	990
–	–	–	90	90□	–	90	90	90¹	–	–	–	s39	–	–	–	990
–	–	–	90	s48	–	90¹	90	90¹□	–	–	–	90¹	–	–	–	990
–	90	–	–	90	90	s45	s11	s30	–	45	–	60¹	–	–	–	990
–	90□	–	–	90□	–	90□	90	90	–	–	–	s31	59	–	–	990
–	90	–	–	90□	s22	90	–	90	–	59	s13	–	–	–	–	990

THE MANAGER

SIR ALEX FERGUSON

Despite the likes of Fabio Capello, Marcello Lippi and Sven-Göran Eriksson being linked as replacements for the supposedly-retiring Sir Alex Ferguson, Manchester United announced in February 2002 that the hugely successful Scot was to remain as manager for a further three years.

As if to prove his popularity, Ferguson's decision to stay prompted David Beckham and Roy Keane to sign new contracts themselves, proof, were it needed, that the players were delighted with their manager's decision.

Sadly for the Scot, he had to endure only United's third trophyless season since winning the FA Cup in 1990.

Ferguson had already guided Aberdeen to three Scottish championships and a European Cup Winners' Cup before accepting the manager's job at Old Trafford in 1986.

While it took him four seasons to win some silverware with United, Ferguson's record since 1990 has seen him hailed as arguably the finest British manager of all time.

With seven Premiership titles and a Champions League just some of the many triumphs United have enjoyed under Ferguson, it is clear to see why 2001–02 was such a disappointment to the club.

LEAGUE POSITION

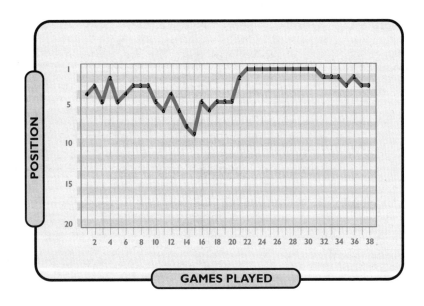

GAMES PLAYED

8 Ruud van Nistelrooy scored in eight consecutive

THE GOALS

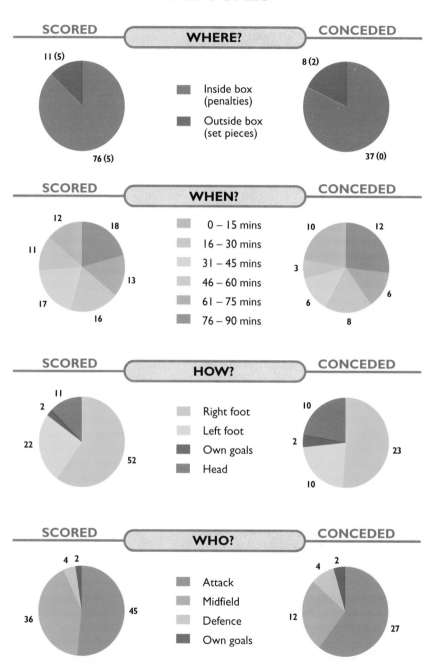

SCORED — **WHERE?** — **CONCEDED**

11 (5)

8 (2)

- ■ Inside box (penalties)
- ■ Outside box (set pieces)

76 (5)

37 (0)

SCORED — **WHEN?** — **CONCEDED**

12   18

11

13

17

16

10   12

3

6

6

8

- ■ 0 – 15 mins
- ■ 16 – 30 mins
- ■ 31 – 45 mins
- ■ 46 – 60 mins
- ■ 61 – 75 mins
- ■ 76 – 90 mins

SCORED — **HOW?** — **CONCEDED**

11

2

22

52

10

2

23

10

- ■ Right foot
- ■ Left foot
- ■ Own goals
- ■ Head

SCORED — **WHO?** — **CONCEDED**

4   2

36

45

4   2

12

27

- ■ Attack
- ■ Midfield
- ■ Defence
- ■ Own goals

Premiership games – setting a new record

MANCHESTER UNITED

	BECKHAM	BLANC	BROWN	BUTT	CHADWICK	COLE	FORLAN	FORTUNE	GIGGS	IRWIN	JOHNSEN
APPEARANCES											
Start	23	29	15	20	5	7	6	8	18	10	9
Sub	5	0	2	5	3	4	7	6	7	2	1
Minutes on pitch	2127	2552	1371	1710	408	710	570	695	1679	830	814
GOAL ATTEMPTS											
Goals	11	1	0	1	0	4	0	1	7	0	1
Shots on target	32	3	0	7	2	11	9	5	19	1	2
Shots off target	38	10	0	11	4	9	16	3	20	0	2
Shooting accuracy %	46%	23%	0%	39%	33%	55%	36%	63%	49%	100%	50%
Goals/shots %	16%	8%	0%	6%	0%	20%	0%	13%	18%	0%	25%
PASSING											
Goal assists	8	0	0	1	2	3	0	0	12	0	0
Long passes	506	284	162	280	22	34	30	46	108	126	56
Short passes	1046	899	411	917	143	182	231	299	565	434	228
PASS COMPLETION											
Own half %	88%	91%	87%	88%	84%	90%	82%	90%	85%	93%	88%
Opposition half %	72%	77%	71%	76%	76%	69%	77%	78%	67%	81%	67%
CROSSING											
Total crosses	253	2	2	23	12	5	17	40	122	25	0
Cross completion %	32%	100%	0%	35%	25%	20%	24%	25%	26%	20%	0%
DRIBBLING											
Dribbles & runs	88	36	19	35	55	24	32	46	186	8	2
Dribble completion %	78%	94%	74%	77%	55%	67%	56%	70%	56%	75%	100%
DEFENDING											
Tackles made	45	65	69	118	11	4	11	23	31	33	17
Tackles won %	58%	74%	75%	69%	82%	100%	91%	61%	68%	73%	59%
Blocks	5	15	11	13	1	0	0	5	5	9	4
Clearances	21	193	124	26	0	0	0	16	8	31	61
Interceptions	7	40	5	17	1	0	1	3	3	4	9
DISCIPLINE											
Fouls conceded	32	39	13	47	5	9	8	16	13	13	15
Fouls won	32	26	19	26	8	15	5	15	25	11	12
Offside	13	0	0	1	1	20	1	3	3	1	0
Yellow cards	6	4	0	5	0	0	0	0	1	3	0
Red cards	0	0	0	0	0	0	0	0	0	0	0

GOALKEEPER NAME	START/ (SUB)	TIME ON PITCH	GOALS CONCEDED	MINS/GOALS CONCEDED	SAVES MADE	SAVES/ SHOTS
BARTHEZ	32 (0)	2860	43	67	88	67%
CARROLL	6 (1)	547	2	274	19	90%
VAN DER GOUW	0 (1)	13	0	N/A	1	100%

For more information visit our website:

PLAYERS' STATISTICS

	KEANE	MAY	NEVILLE G	NEVILLE P	O'SHEA	SCHOLES	SILVESTRE	SOLSKJAER	STAM	STEWART	VAN NISTELROOY	VERON	WALLWORK	YORKE	TOTAL	RANK
	28	2	31	21	4	30	31	23	1	2	29	24	0	4		
	0	0	3	7	5	5	4	7	0	1	3	2	1	6		
	2469	169	2793	2029	360	2757	2800	2062	90	127	2555	2044	8	467		
	3	0	0	2	0	8	0	17	0	0	23	5	0	1	87*	1st
	22	0	0	2	0	42	1	30	0	0	45	23	0	2	258	1st
	22	0	5	7	0	29	10	23	0	1	42	29	0	5	286	1st
	50%	0%	0%	22%	0%	59%	9%	57%	0%	0%	52%	44%	0%	29%	47%	4th
	7%	0%	0%	22%	0%	11%	0%	32%	0%	0%	26%	10%	0%	14%	16%	1st
	5	0	3	0	0	5	5	9	0	0	4	1	0	0	58	1st
	615	19	407	257	53	507	367	116	9	18	90	549	2	29	5085	1st
	1805	58	989	925	97	1444	1144	778	30	66	555	1494	6	239	15140	1st
	92%	95%	90%	88%	87%	91%	84%	88%	97%	93%	88%	91%	100%	86%	89%	1st
	87%	68%	76%	77%	68%	82%	70%	75%	67%	84%	73%	76%	80%	77%	76%	1st
	38	0	71	45	1	32	108	73	0	0	11	72	0	3	955	9th
	29%	0%	31%	18%	0%	25%	27%	32%	0%	0%	9%	32%	0%	0%	28%	1st
	144	1	40	49	6	89	144	75	0	6	115	97	0	23	1322	4th
	87%	100%	83%	84%	100%	80%	74%	57%	0%	50%	50%	82%	0%	61%	71%	5th
	103	4	55	70	9	122	75	47	6	10	22	94	0	6	1051	10th
	75%	100%	76%	73%	56%	70%	68%	64%	100%	50%	82%	68%	0%	67%	71%	20th
	16	1	12	18	3	12	36	5	1	0	0	8	0	2	182	19th
	51	11	213	79	36	8	235	6	3	3	6	10	0	0	1240	20th
	19	2	7	8	5	17	18	5	1	0	1	8	0	0	182	4th
	33	7	31	37	5	35	30	25	0	1	41	30	0	5	490	19th
	27	1	33	9	2	32	39	23	5	3	40	34	0	5	453	20th
	4	0	1	7	0	4	0	12	0	0	64	0	0	4	139	=9th
	4	0	4	4	1	9	3	3	0	0	3	3	0	0	54	14th
	1	0	0	0	0	0	0	0	0	0	0	0	0	0	1	=18th

*Including two own goals

CROSSES CAUGHT	CROSSES PUNCHED	CROSSES DROPPED	CATCH SUCCESS	THROWS/ SHORT KICKS	% COMPLETION	LONG KICKS	% COMPLETION
48	26	6	89%	148	99%	430	61%
17	2	5	77%	43	100%	109	44%
0	0	0	0%	2	100%	1	100%

PLAYER OF THE SEASON

PLAYER	INDEX SCORE
ROY KEANE	1,211
David Beckham	1,177
Ole Gunnar Solskjaer	1,118
Paul Scholes	1,093
Juan Sebastian Veron	1,060
Ruud van Nistelrooy	1,028
Ryan Giggs	1,006
Mikael Silvestre	802
Nicky Butt	782
Laurent Blanc	689

Sir Alex Ferguson described Roy Keane as "probably the most influential player we have ever had at this club", and told how sometimes he felt he needed "another 10 Roy Keanes out there".

High praise indeed and richly deserved, as for the second successive season, Keane was Opta's Manchester United player of the year.

Disappointment in the Premiership was hard enough to take for the Republic of Ireland captain, but defeat in the semi-final of the Champions League left Keane shattered.

Not only had he scored the goal that looked to be taking United to the final, but Keane was out to make amends for missing the 1999 triumph through suspension.

He ended the Premiership campaign with an 89% pass completion rate that, for the second season in a row, no Premiership player could better. He also won 75% of his tackles and chipped in with three goals and five assists.

David Beckham was runner-up to Keane, scoring 11 goals and setting up eight more for team-mates.

Ruud van Nistelrooy may have grabbed most of the headlines, but his strike partner Ole Gunnar Solskjaer enjoyed his most prolific season at United, scoring 25 goals in all competitions.

In the Premiership, the Norwegian scored only two goals fewer from open play than van Nistelrooy, despite spending nearly 500 minutes less on the pitch and he was also more lethal, finding the net with 32% of his attempts.

Juan Sebastian Veron came in for criticism from some sections of the media but, while he may have changed the balance of United's play from time to time, the Argentine showed plenty of flashes of genius and ended the season with an 82% pass completion rate.

Only two defenders appeared on the list, highlighting not just the outstanding attacking players at Ferguson's disposal, but also that 2001–02 was a season to forget from a defensive point of view.

2,163 Roy Keane made more successful

FIVE OF THE BEST

United finished third in the Premiership and were just one goal away from the European Cup final, yet 2001–02 was a disappointing campaign for the club. Sir Alex Ferguson's men finished 10 points behind Arsenal and they will want to ensure that the "shift of power" described by Arsène Wenger lasts for just one season and does not signal the end of United's dominance.

TOP GOALSCORERS

	GOALS	GOALS/SHOTS
RUUD VAN NISTELROOY	23	26%
Ole Gunnar Solskjaer	17	32%
David Beckham	11	16%
Paul Scholes	8	11%
Ryan Giggs	7	18%

Many saw the signing of Ruud van Nistelrooy as one that would secure United another title, but while the club finished trophyless, the Dutchman did not. Van Nistelrooy's 23 goals earned him the PFA Player of the Year award and, by scoring in eight successive matches, he set a Premiership record. Ole Gunnar Solskjaer enjoyed his most prolific season at United and was actually more clinical in front of goal than van Nistelrooy.

For the second successive season, no Premiership player produced more accurate passes than Roy Keane, whose 89% completion rate was two percentage points higher than in the previous campaign. Yet again United finished the season as the Premiership's most accurate passers and no fewer than seven players produced more than 1,000 successful deliveries, including England duo David Beckham and Paul Scholes.

TOP PASSERS

	SUCC PASSES	COMPLETION
ROY KEANE	2,163	89%
Paul Scholes	1,671	86%
Juan Sebastian Veron	1,667	82%
David Beckham	1,185	76%
Gary Neville	1,165	83%

TOP TACKLERS

	WON	SUCCESS
PAUL SCHOLES	85	70%
Nicky Butt	82	69%
Roy Keane	77	75%
Juan Sebastian Veron	64	68%
Wes Brown	52	75%

Paul Scholes has faced regular criticism about his over-zealous and mistimed tackling, but in 2001–02 he won more challenges than any other United player. Nicky Butt enjoyed arguably his best season at the club and was automatically selected for England's World Cup squad, as was Wes Brown, whose return to full fitness was a boost for both United and his country.

Scholes epitomised United's frustration in 2001–02, being booked nine times despite committing just 35 fouls in 35 appearances. Scholes played in a different position for much of the season and it clearly took him time to adjust to his new role. Roy Keane was sent off just once for the third successive season, although this was the only sending-off for a United player – the joint-lowest total in the Premiership.

DISCIPLINE

	POINTS	FOULS & CARDS
PAUL SCHOLES	62	35F, 9Y, 0R
Nicky Butt	62	47F, 5Y, 0R
Roy Keane	51	33F, 4Y, 1R
Laurent Blanc	51	39F, 4Y, 0R
David Beckham	50	32F, 6Y, 0R

MIDDLESBROUGH

SEASON REVIEW

Having parted company with Bryan Robson and Terry Venables, Middlesbrough chairman Steve Gibson appointed Manchester United coach Steve McClaren as Boro manager for 2001–02.

McClaren immediately got to work, selling Christian Karembeu and Keith O'Neill to Greek side Olympiakos and Coventry City respectively.

He then pulled off a major coup in signing England defender Gareth Southgate from Aston Villa for £6.5m to link up with his ex-team-mate Ugo Ehiogu and form a defensive partnership that was a pivotal part of Boro's season.

McClaren also went back to his old club to sign Mark Wilson and Jonathan Greening for a combined fee of £3.5m.

Whatever excitement or anticipation Boro fans might have had soon evaporated though, when they saw their side lose their first four matches to prop up the Premiership.

The new manager clearly had his work cut out and with no more money available for transfers, McClaren seemed to be up against it.

But Boro lost just two of their next 11 league games and, despite elimination from the Worthington Cup, were in a positive frame of mind and now 12th, just four points off a European place.

How grateful McClaren must have been for this good run, as Boro's next five games saw them face Liverpool, Manchester United, Newcastle and Arsenal and after coming away from those fixtures without a single point, Boro ended the calendar year with just goal difference separating them from the drop zone.

By mid-January, Boro were actually in the bottom three, with only two sides having scored fewer goals than them.

McClaren clearly felt the need for more

> **"We are nowhere near what I want. We need to add a lot more quality. I know who I want...so I'm going to have a chat with the chairman."**
>
> **Steve McClaren**

firepower and tried to sign Uruguayan striker Diego Forlan, only to see him eventually move to Manchester United. The Riverside boss then turned his attentions to Dwight Yorke, but this deal stalled when the two parties failed to agree personal terms.

Boro would eventually get their revenge on United in both the Premiership and FA Cup as McClaren accepted that he had to get his side out of trouble with the players at his disposal.

And how his players did him proud. After sensationally knocking Manchester United out of the FA Cup, Boro lost just two of their next 12 league matches, with another victory over United giving McClaren plenty of satisfaction.

This run propelled Boro into the top half of the table, dispelling any fears of relegation and with an FA Cup semi-final against Arsenal to look forward to, the club could at last feel that they were heading in the right direction.

Only an unfortunate own goal from Gianluca Festa settled the semi-final at Old Trafford and although there was immense disappointment at not reaching the FA Cup final, the Boro players took a lot of pride and confidence from a cup run that saw them knock out three of their Premiership rivals.

Despite three straight defeats following the semi-final, Boro remained in mid-table and their finishing position of 12th was an improvement on 2000–01.

McClaren's attempts to trim the wage bill at Boro and put together a squad totally to his liking are likely to improve the longer he stays at the club.

He certainly showed in 2001–02 that he has the mentality and the experience required to steer a team through a difficult period and now he will be hoping to take the club to the next level.

on target than any other side

MIDDLESBROUGH

DATE	OPPONENT	SCORE	ATT.	BERESFORD	BOKSIC	CAMPBELL	CARBONE	COOPER	CROSSLEY	DEANE	DEBEVE	DOWNING	EHIOGU	FESTA	FLEMING	GAVIN	GORDON	GREENING
18.08.01	Arsenal H	0–4	31,557	–	90	–	–	90	–	–	–	–	86□	90	–	–	–	90
21.08.01	Bolton W A	0–1	20,747	–	–	–	–	90	–	90	–	–	90□	90	–	–	–	90
25.08.01	Everton A	0–2	32,829	–	–	–	–	90	–	–	–	–	90	90	–	–	–	90
08.09.01	Newcastle H	1–4	30,044	–	–	–	–	90¹	s57	90	–	–	–	90	–	–	–	90
15.09.01	West Ham H	2–0	25,445	–	–	–	–	71	–	90¹	–	–	90	90	s19	–	–	90□
17.09.01	Leicester A	2–1	15,412	–	–	–	–	90	–	90	–	–	90	90	–	–	–	90¹
23.09.01	Chelsea A	2–2	36,767	–	90¹	–	–	90	90	90□	–	–	–	74	90□	–	–	90
29.09.01	Southampton H	1–3	26,142	–	90¹	–	–	90	–	69	–	–	–	90	90	–	–	90
13.10.01	Charlton A	0–0	20,451	–	89	–	–	–	90	–	–	–	–	90	–	33	–	90
22.10.01	Sunderland H	2–0	28,432	–	86¹	–	–	–	–	–	–	–	–	90	–	–	–	90
27.10.01	Tottenham A	1–2	36,062	–	90¹	–	–	s26	–	–	–	–	–	90	–	–	–	90
03.11.01	Derby Co H	5–1	28,117	–	85¹	–	–	–	–	s5	–	–	–	90	–	–	–	78
17.11.01	Aston Villa A	0–0	35,424	–	90□	–	–	s45□	90	–	–	–	–	90	–	–	–	90□
25.11.01	Ipswich H	0–0	32,586	–	90	–	–	–	90	–	–	–	–	90	–	–	–	90
01.12.01	Blackburn A	1–0	23,849	–	87¹□	–	–	90□	90	–	–	–	–	90	–	s29	–	90
08.12.01	Liverpool A	0–2	43,674	s70	90	–	–	90□	20	–	–	–	–	90	–	–	–	90
15.12.01	Man Utd H	0–1	34,358	–	90	–	–	–	90	–	–	–	–	90	–	–	–	90
26.12.01	Newcastle A	0–3	52,127	–	82	s45	–	–	90	–	–	–	90□	–	–	–	–	90
29.12.01	Arsenal A	1–2	37,948	–	–	s14	–	s31	90	–	–	–	59	–	–	–	–	90□
01.01.02	Everton H	1–0	27,463	–	s7	–	–	–	90	–	–	–	–	90¹	–	s45□	–	45
12.01.02	Fulham A	1–2	18,975	–	–	–	–	90¹	90	–	–	–	–	90	–	–	–	67
19.01.02	Bolton W H	1–1	26,104	–	–	–	–	s51	90	–	–	–	90	–	–	–	–	90
29.01.02	Sunderland A	1–0	44,579	–	–	s8	–	–	90	–	–	–	–	52□	–	90	s34	90□
03.02.02	Charlton H	0–0	24,189	–	–	s45□	–	–	90	–	–	–	–	90	–	90	–	90
09.02.02	Leeds Utd H	2–2	30,221	–	s45	–	90	–	90	–	–	–	–	90	90	45	–	79
19.02.02	Fulham H	2–1	26,235	–	90¹	–	71	–	–	–	–	–	–	90	–	–	–	90
23.02.02	West Ham A	0–1	35,420	–	90	–	90	–	–	–	–	–	89□	–	–	–	–	81□
02.03.02	Leicester H	1–0*	25,734	–	89	–	90□	–	–	–	–	–	–	90	–	–	–	81
06.03.02	Southampton A	1–1	28,931	–	62	–	90	–	–	–	–	–	–	90	60□	–	–	90
16.03.02	Liverpool H	1–2	31,253	–	90	–	90	–	–	–	–	–	–	–	90	–	s17	90
23.03.02	Man Utd A	1–0	67,683	–	79¹	–	90	–	–	–	–	–	–	90	–	–	–	21
30.03.02	Tottenham H	1–1	31,258	–	90	–	90	–	90	–	–	–	–	90	–	–	–	90
01.04.02	Derby Co A	1–0	30,822	–	–	–	90	–	90	–	–	–	–	90	–	–	–	90
06.04.02	Aston Villa H	2–1	26,003	–	–	–	90¹	–	–	–	–	–	–	90¹	–	–	–	90
20.04.02	Blackburn H	1–3	26,932	–	–	–	90	–	–	–	s45	–	–	90□	–	–	–	–
24.04.02	Ipswich A	0–1	25,979	–	–	–	90	90	–	–	90	90	–	–	–	–	–	–
27.04.02	Chelsea H	0–2	28,686	–	–	–	45	90	–	–	s45	s45	90	–	–	–	–	90
11.05.02	Leeds Utd A	0–1	40,218	–	–	–	–	84	–	–	s14	67	90	–	–	–	–	76

□ Yellow card, ■ Red card, s Substitute, 90² Goals scored

*including own goal

For more information visit our website:

2001–02 PREMIERSHIP APPEARANCES

HUDSON	INCE	JOB	JOHNSTON	MARINELLI	MURPHY	MUSTOE	NEMETH	OKON	QUEUDRUE	RICARD	SCHWARZER	SOUTHGATE	STAMP	STOCKDALE	VICKERS	WHELAN	WILKSHIRE	WILSON	WINDASS	TOTAL
–	90□	90□	–	–	–	73	–	–	–	s34	90	90	–	–	–	–	–	s17	56	986
–	90	90	–	–	–	82	–	s8	–	80	90	90	–	–	–	–	–	–	s10	990
–	90	90	–	–	–	s28	s45	62	–	45□	90	90	–	–	62	–	–	–	s28	990
–	90□	s12	78	–	–	90	–	–	–	–	31■	90	–	–	90	–	–	–	33	931
–	90	–	85¹	–	–	90	–	–	–	–	90	90	–	–	–	–	–	s5	90□	990
–	90¹	–	70	s45□	–	78	s12	–	–	–	90	90	–	–	–	–	–	s20	45	990
–	90	–	45	s16	–	78	–	–	–	–	90	90	–	s45¹	–	–	–	s12	–	990
–	–	–	69	s21	–	69	s21	s21	–	–	90	90	–	–	–	–	–	90	–	990
–	90	–	–	s35	–	s57	55	–	90	–	90	–	90	–	–	–	–	90□	s1	990
–	71■	–	s23	67	–	90	73	–	90¹□	–	90	90	–	90	–	–	–	s4	s17	971
–	90	–	s7	90	–	83	64	–	90	–	90	90	–	77	–	–	–	–	s13	990
–	90	–	s12	90²	–	90¹	78¹	–	90	–	90	90	–	90	–	–	–	–	s12	990
–	–	–	90	71	–	90	80	–	45□	–	90	s19	90	–	–	–	–	–	s10	990
s1	–	–	76	89	–	90	75	–	90	–	–	90	–	90	–	–	–	s14	s15	990
–	–	–	90	78	–	90	90	–	61	–	–	90	–	–	–	–	–	s12	s3	990
–	90	–	45	–	–	90	45	–	90□	s45	–	90	–	–	–	–	–	s45	–	990
–	90□	–	–	90	–	90	–	–	90□	64	–	90	–	90	–	s26	–	–	–	990
–	90	–	–	82	–	90	–	s8	90	s8	–	90	–	90	–	45	–	–	–	990
–	90□	–	s20	70	–	90	–	–	90□	90□	–	90	–	90	–	76¹	–	–	–	990
–	90	–	–	83	–	90	–	–	63	90	–	90	s27	90	–	90	–	–	–	990
–	90□	–	–	78	–	90	s12	–	–	50	–	90	s40	90	–	90	–	–	s23□	990
–	90	–	72	90□	–	s18	60	–	39	–	–	90	–	90	–	90¹	–	–	s30	990
–	90	–	–	–	–	s17	–	–	90	–	–	90	73	90	–	82¹□	–	–	56	952
–	90	–	–	s27	–	–	–	–	90	–	–	90	90	45	–	90	–	–	63	990
–	90¹□	–	–	–	–	s45	–	–	90	–	–	90	45	–	–	90	–	s11¹	–	990
–	90	–	–	–	s29	61	s19¹	–	90□	–	90	90	–	90	–	71	–	s19	–	990
–	90□	–	–	–	s9	88□	s9	–	90	–	90	90	–	90□	–	81	–	s2	–	989
–	90□	–	–	–	s19	90	s1	–	90	–	90	90	–	90	–	71	–	s9	–	990
–	–	–	–	–	–	90	–	–	90□	–	90	–	s28	–	90¹	90	–	–	–	960
–	90	–	–	s8	–	73	s17	–	90	–	90	90¹	–	82	–	73	–	–	–	990
–	90□	–	–	–	–	90	–	–	90□	–	90	90	–	90	90	s69	–	s11	–	990
–	–	–	–	s32	–	90	–	–	90¹	–	90	–	90	–	89	58	–	s1	–	990
–	90	–	–	–	–	90¹	–	–	90	–	90	–	90	–	90	90	–	–	–	990
–	–	90	–	–	–	90	–	–	90	–	90	–	11	90	–	s79	–	–	–	990
–	90	–	45	s45	–	76□	s14¹	–	88■	–	90	90	–	90	–	–	45□	–	90	988
s4	90□	–	68□	s22	–	–	90	–	90	–	90	90	–	86	–	–	–	–	–	990
–	90□	–	–	–	–	45	s45	–	90	–	–	90	–	90□	–	90□	–	–	45	990
–	90	–	–	–	s6	90	90	–	–	90	–	90	–	90	–	90	–	–	s23	990

THE MANAGER

STEVE McCLAREN

Steve McCLaren took charge of Middlesbrough in June 2001, replacing the previous season's managerial partnership of Bryan Robson and Terry Venables.

McCLaren's first taste of top-flight management came at Derby County, where he was assistant to Jim Smith. Among his admirers was Alex Ferguson, who offered him the assistant manager's job at Old Trafford midway through the 1998–99 season following Brian Kidd's departure from Manchester United to take charge of Blackburn Rovers.

In his first season under Ferguson, McCLaren won the 'treble' and followed that up with two more Premiership titles.

In November 2000, McCLaren and Peter Taylor were asked by the Football Association to take joint charge of England in a friendly away to Italy – arguably the proudest moment of McCLaren's career.

The two managers picked a relatively young squad, a move that laid the foundations for future England coach Sven-Göran Eriksson and McCLaren remained on the coaching staff going into the 2002 World Cup finals.

Boro chairman Steve Gibson had no hesitation in appointing McCLaren as his new manager and while 2001–02 wasn't the club's best ever in the Premiership, he has already shown that he is one of the best young coaches around.

LEAGUE POSITION

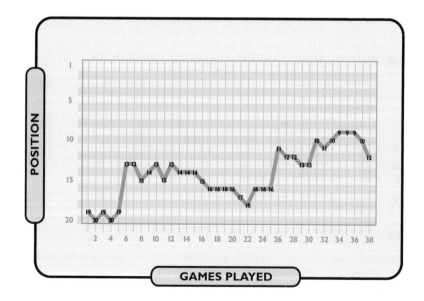

POSITION

GAMES PLAYED

35 Boro's Steve McClaren used more players

THE GOALS

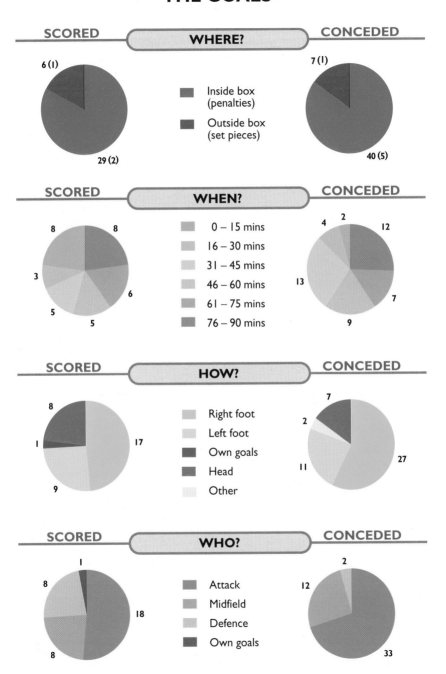

SCORED — **WHERE?** — **CONCEDED**

- Inside box (penalties)
- Outside box (set pieces)

Scored: 6 (1), 29 (2)
Conceded: 7 (1), 40 (5)

SCORED — **WHEN?** — **CONCEDED**

- 0 – 15 mins
- 16 – 30 mins
- 31 – 45 mins
- 46 – 60 mins
- 61 – 75 mins
- 76 – 90 mins

Scored: 8, 8, 6, 5, 5, 3
Conceded: 2, 12, 7, 9, 13, 4

SCORED — **HOW?** — **CONCEDED**

- Right foot
- Left foot
- Own goals
- Head
- Other

Scored: 8, 17, 9, 1
Conceded: 7, 2, 27, 11

SCORED — **WHO?** — **CONCEDED**

- Attack
- Midfield
- Defence
- Own goals

Scored: 1, 8, 18, 8
Conceded: 2, 12, 33

in the Premiership than any other manager

MIDDLESBROUGH

	BOKSIC	CAMPBELL	CARBONE	COOPER	DEANE	DEBEVE	DOWNING	EHIOGU	FESTA	FLEMING	GAVIN	GORDON	GREENING	HUDSON	INCE
APPEARANCES															
Start	20	0	13	14	6	1	2	29	8	8	5	0	36	0	31
Sub	2	4	0	4	1	3	1	0	0	0	4	1	0	2	0
Minutes on pitch	1791	112	1106	1388	524	194	202	2574	652	704	458	34	3048	5	2771
GOAL ATTEMPTS															
Goals	8	0	1	2	1	0	0	1	1	0	0	0	1	0	2
Shots on target	24	0	8	3	4	1	0	1	1	0	0	0	7	0	11
Shots off target	21	0	12	5	6	3	1	8	1	2	1	0	19	0	28
Shooting accuracy %	53%	0%	40%	38%	40%	25%	0%	11%	50%	0%	0%	0%	27%	0%	28%
Goals/shots %	18%	0%	5%	25%	10%	0%	0%	11%	50%	0%	0%	0%	4%	0%	5%
PASSING															
Goal assists	1	0	5	0	0	1	0	0	0	0	0	0	1	0	2
Long passes	50	5	143	205	20	33	8	222	61	70	45	3	288	0	390
Short passes	455	26	473	457	165	67	59	500	157	234	87	1	1054	1	1088
PASS COMPLETION															
Own half %	79%	86%	87%	88%	95%	91%	89%	82%	81%	85%	76%	50%	86%	0%	88%
Opposition half %	65%	50%	69%	67%	59%	74%	78%	60%	54%	81%	44%	0%	72%	100%	70%
CROSSING															
Total crosses	40	2	88	23	0	4	23	3	6	14	4	0	81	0	98
Cross completion %	20%	0%	30%	30%	0%	50%	22%	33%	0%	36%	25%	0%	20%	0%	29%
DRIBBLING															
Dribbles & runs	92	2	80	17	11	9	20	24	15	18	2	0	157	0	62
Dribble completion %	52%	0%	64%	88%	55%	89%	50%	92%	80%	89%	100%	0%	68%	0%	81%
DEFENDING															
Tackles made	13	1	30	17	5	5	0	55	12	29	16	2	96	1	112
Tackles won %	77%	100%	70%	76%	100%	100%	0%	75%	100%	66%	63%	100%	79%	100%	71%
Blocks	2	1	1	22	0	0	0	42	9	3	9	0	16	0	24
Clearances	0	2	1	85	9	3	0	355	67	20	57	1	45	1	59
Interceptions	0	1	1	6	0	1	0	16	9	2	5	0	6	0	18
DISCIPLINE															
Fouls conceded	14	2	25	27	16	3	2	34	9	9	8	0	49	0	52
Fouls won	20	5	31	17	9	1	5	31	11	9	2	0	68	0	78
Offside	39	1	17	0	7	0	1	1	0	1	0	0	11	0	0
Yellow cards	2	1	1	3	1	0	0	2	1	0	2	0	5	0	11
Red cards	0	0	0	0	0	0	0	2	2	0	0	0	0	0	1

GOALKEEPER NAME	START/ (SUB)	TIME ON PITCH	GOALS CONCEDED	MINS/GOALS CONCEDED	SAVES MADE	SAVES/ SHOTS
BERESFORD	0 (1)	70	2	35	2	50%
CROSSLEY	17 (1)	1517	18	84	59	77%
SCHWARZER	21 (0)	1831	27	68	65	71%

For more information visit our website:

PLAYERS' STATISTICS

	JOB	JOHNSTON	MARINELLI	MURPHY	MUSTOE	NEMETH	OKON	QUEUDRUE	RICARD	SOUTHGATE	STAMP	STOCKDALE	VICKERS	WHELAN	WILKSHIRE	WILSON	WINDASS	TOTAL	RANK
	3	13	12	0	31	11	1	28	6	37	3	26	2	18	6	2	8		
	1	4	8	5	5	10	3	0	3	0	3	2	0	1	1	8	19		
	282	985	1197	95	2771	995	99	2366	506	3330	294	2343	152	1452	515	309	795		
	0	1	2	0	2	3	0	2	0	1	0	1	0	4	0	0	1	35*	17th
	2	2	13	0	5	8	0	8	4	4	1	1	0	11	2	2	4	127	20th
	3	2	6	1	3	9	0	15	4	8	1	3	0	18	5	0	11	196	18th
	40%	50%	68%	0%	63%	47%	0%	35%	50%	33%	50%	25%	0%	38%	29%	100%	27%	39%	19th
	0%	25%	11%	0%	25%	18%	0%	9%	0%	8%	0%	25%	0%	14%	0%	0%	7%	11%	14th
	0	0	3	0	1	1	0	3	0	0	1	0	0	0	0	0	0	19	20th
	15	53	78	9	290	48	28	390	22	477	23	209	15	56	40	38	77	3802	17th
	82	275	424	35	918	284	62	742	121	657	73	558	36	429	149	96	256	10064	14th
	85%	81%	89%	82%	88%	85%	88%	75%	77%	79%	81%	75%	78%	82%	73%	90%	76%	83%	11th
	73%	69%	75%	67%	78%	67%	74%	57%	71%	57%	58%	66%	63%	69%	56%	69%	68%	66%	14th
	2	25	96	3	2	19	0	55	6	5	13	41	0	16	12	7	6	694	20th
	0%	28%	28%	0%	50%	16%	0%	15%	0%	20%	31%	22%	0%	0%	8%	0%	17%	23%	17th
	23	68	118	1	21	39	2	67	22	60	14	29	0	53	10	6	11	1067	11th
	48%	63%	62%	100%	71%	67%	100%	78%	41%	88%	50%	90%	0%	58%	40%	83%	64%	68%	12th
	6	25	19	4	116	15	5	103	6	92	12	76	1	16	16	3	12	921	19th
	50%	60%	68%	100%	77%	80%	100%	72%	67%	67%	75%	80%	100%	75%	81%	100%	92%	74%	7th
	1	3	1	0	23	5	0	14	2	48	1	35	1	13	2	0	2	280	2nd
	0	9	4	2	56	1	0	161	1	436	2	113	11	5	10	3	6	1564	4th
	1	1	3	2	8	2	0	22	1	18	2	8	2	4	1	0	1	142	15th
	7	14	24	0	40	12	1	37	18	40	6	25	3	33	8	8	25	552	13th
	12	27	29	2	34	15	1	53	19	38	3	14	0	19	11	6	21	605	2nd
	6	4	4	0	1	7	0	4	0	0	0	0	0	25	1	0	11	141	7th
	1	1	2	0	2	0	0	8	2	0	0	2	0	2	1	1	2	53	15th
	0	0	0	0	0	0	0	0	0	0	0	0	0	0	0	0	0	7	=1st

*Including one own goal

CROSSES CAUGHT	CROSSES PUNCHED	CROSSES DROPPED	CATCH SUCCESS	THROWS/ SHORT KICKS	% COMPLETION	LONG KICKS	% COMPLETION
1	2	0	100%	0	0%	15	40%
36	26	6	86%	19	95%	343	41%
52	20	7	88%	23	91%	435	50%

PLAYER OF THE SEASON

PLAYER	INDEX SCORE
GARETH SOUTHGATE	768
Ugo Ehiogu	765
Franck Queudrue	711
Paul Ince	637
Alen Boksic	631
Mark Schwarzer	631
Robbie Mustoe	533
Robbie Stockdale	527
Jonathan Greening	477
Noel Whelan	471*

All players played 75 minutes in at least 15 matches except those marked * who played that amount in 14 games.

Nobody was surprised when Sven-Göran Eriksson included Middlesbrough defender Gareth Southgate in his 2002 World Cup squad.

The former Crystal Palace centre-back formed an excellent partnership with Ugo Ehiogu in the heart of Boro's defence and ended the 2001–02 season as Opta's Middlesbrough player of the season.

Southgate made 436 clearances – more than any of his team-mates – and he and Ehiogu were responsible for more than half of all Boro's defensive clearances throughout the season.

Ehiogu was second in the list and the former Aston Villa defender could count himself unlucky not to have joined Southgate in Japan and Korea.

Boro's third highest-rated player of the season was another defender, highlighting how new boss Steve McClaren made Boro a harder team to break down and score against.

Franck Queudrue was brought in on loan from Lens, but impressed sufficiently for Boro to make his move permanent in a £2.5m deal at the end of the season.

Queudrue was one of only three Boro players to attempt more than 100 tackles and, despite a red card at home to Blackburn, endeared himself to the fans.

Another loan signing, Benito Carbone, would have been fourth on the list, but the Italian did not spend long enough on the pitch to qualify.

Carbone scored just once in 1,106 minutes for the club, and despite five assists – more than any other Boro player – he was sent back to Bradford City at the end of the campaign.

Elsewhere, Robbie Mustoe ended the season with an 83% pass completion rate – more accurate than any of his team-mates.

And Robbie Stockdale's fine form didn't go unnoticed. His tackle success rate of 80% was the best at the club and new Scotland manager Berti Vogts selected the defender to play against Nigeria and earn his first cap.

694 Middlesbrough players were responsible for the

FIVE OF THE BEST

The arrival of Steve McClaren signalled a new era for Middlesbrough. Although the new manager's main aim was to develop the squad to his own tastes and make them a harder side to beat, Boro flirted with relegation yet again. But McClaren did enough to suggest that he can turn the club around and make them a regular top 10 side.

TOP GOALSCORERS

	GOALS	GOALS/SHOTS
ALEN BOKSIC	8	18%
Noel Whelan	4	14%
Szilard Nemeth	3	18%
Colin Cooper	2	25%
Robbie Mustoe	2	25%

Alen Boksic was Boro's top Premiership scorer for the second successive season, although his return of eight goals was not as high as in 2000–01. However, he scored with the same percentage of shots, indicating he had fewer chances rather than a dip in standards. The next four players on the list scored just 11 goals between them and it was easy to see why McClaren tried to sign Diego Forlan and Dwight Yorke.

Paul Ince was linked with a move away from The Riverside in 2001–02, yet Boro couldn't have done without their captain, who produced more successful passes than any of his team-mates. Three of the next four players in the chart were signed by McClaren, a sign that given financial backing, he can be more successful with signings than his predecessors.

TOP PASSERS

	SUCC PASSES	COMPLETION
PAUL INCE	1,147	78%
Jonathan Greening	1,038	77%
Robbie Mustoe	1,000	83%
Gareth Southgate	782	69%
Franck Queudrue	729	64%

TOP TACKLERS

	WON	SUCCESS
ROBBIE MUSTOE	89	77%
Paul Ince	79	71%
Jonathan Greening	76	79%
Franck Queudrue	74	72%
Gareth Southgate	62	67%

Often underrated, Robbie Mustoe failed to appear in just two Premiership matches in 2001–02 and won more tackles than any other Boro player. Paul Ince and Jonathan Greening were next on the list, highlighting how Boro's midfield battled for every ball to try and regain possession. Boro's tackle success rate was three percentage points higher than in 2000–01, something that McClaren can take credit for.

Since returning to the Premiership in 1997, Paul Ince had gone 135 league games without being sent off, but the run came to an end at home to Sunderland. The fact that no team earned more red cards than Boro shows that he was not the only culprit though. Franck Queudrue only committed 34 fouls, but received eight yellow cards, while Ugo Ehiogu was sent off twice – which didn't help his England chances.

DISCIPLINE

	POINTS	FOULS & CARDS
PAUL INCE	91	52F, 11Y, 1R
Franck Queudrue	67	37F, 8Y, 1R
Jonathan Greening	64	49F, 5Y, 0R
Ugo Ehiogu	52	34F, 2Y, 2R
Robbie Mustoe	46	40F, 2Y, 0R

fewest number of crosses in the Premiership

NEWCASTLE UNITED

ADDRESS

St James' Park,
Newcastle-upon-Tyne NE1 4ST

CONTACT NUMBERS

Telephone: 0191 201 8400
Fax: 0191 201 8600
Ticket Office: 0191 261 1571
ClubCall: 09068 121190
St James' Park Shop: 0191 201 8426
Website: www.nufc.co.uk

KEY PERSONNEL

President: Sir John Hall
Patron: T Bennett
Honorary President: Bob Young
Chairman: W F Shepherd
Deputy Chairman: D S Hall
Directors: A O Fletcher, R Jones,
L Wheatley
Director of Football Administration:
R Cushing
Manager: Sir Bobby Robson CBE

SPONSORS

NTL

FANZINES

The Mag,
True Faith

COLOURS

Home: Black and white striped shirts,
black shorts and black stockings
Away: Heron and raven shirts, heron
and raven shorts and heron and raven
stockings

NICKNAME

The Magpies

HONOURS

League Champions: 1904–05, 1906–07,
1908–09, 1926–27
Division One Champions: 1992–93
Division Two Champions: 1964–65
FA Cup Winners: 1910, 1924, 1932,
1951, 1952, 1955
Fairs Cup Winners: 1969

RECORD GOALSCORER

Jackie Milburn –
177 league goals, 1946–57

BIGGEST WIN

13–0 v Newport County – Division Two,
5 October 1946

BIGGEST DEFEAT

0–9 v Burton Wanderers – Division Two,
15 April 1895

SEASON REVIEW

Newcastle United exceeded all expectations with a fourth-place finish in 2001–02. The Magpies might even have won the title if their squad had been stronger, but although the major prize in domestic football evaded them, Bobby Robson's men firmly re-established themselves as one of the Premiership's leading sides.

Participation in the Intertoto Cup meant that the Magpies started their season early and after draws against Chelsea and Sunderland they chalked up their first win of the season against Middlesbrough.

That match saw Newcastle come from a goal down to win 4–1. This was to be a feature of their season. Plenty of teams breached Newcastle's defence, but scoring first was never a guarantee of victory against Bobby Robson's resilient side, who came from behind to win 10 times in 2001–02 – making them the Premiership's comeback kings.

Victories continued to be interspersed with defeats, but Newcastle were handily placed in sixth position, just three points off the top, when Derby visited St James' Park. The Magpies won that game courtesy of an Alan Shearer penalty and embarked on a seven-game unbeaten run which saw them underline their credentials as potential championship contenders.

The most memorable result in this sequence of fine performances came at Highbury. Newcastle finally ended a run of 30 games without a victory in London with a controversial 3–1 win over Arsenal that lifted the Magpies to the top of the table.

They followed that with another comeback to seal an amazing 4–3 victory over Leeds at Elland Road and, as the busy Christmas period drew to a close, Newcastle found themselves three points clear at the top of the league.

> ## "We are on the edge of achieving something quite remarkable."
>
> **Bobby Robson**

The form of Alan Shearer and summer signing Craig Bellamy had been key to this run. The two frontmen formed an excellent partnership, allying power and pace to devastating effect and terrifying some of the Premiership's best defences. By the time Bellamy succumbed to injury, the two players had scored 25 goals between them.

Unfortunately, Bellamy's absence seemed to knock the stuffing out of the Magpies. He managed just one substitute appearance in Newcastle's last 11 games, during which time the team took just 16 points and faded from the title race.

Newcastle's FA Cup hopes were also dashed as they lost out to Arsenal in a sixth round replay. But with Chelsea and Leeds failing to capitalise on the Magpies' loss of form, Newcastle still had enough in reserve to secure fourth place and guarantee themselves a shot at Champions League qualification in 2002–03.

Bobby Robson was pleasantly surprised by his team's success, but confessed that he would need to strengthen his squad to build on their achievements. He has already added England under-21 star Jermaine Jenas to his ranks and will probably turn his attention to the defence next.

For all their ability going forward, Newcastle conceded too many goals to sustain a lasting title challenge. Their final tally of nine clean sheets was fewer than any other team in the top seven. Without the brilliance of Shay Given, they might even have conceded more.

This doesn't change the fact that Newcastle enjoyed a superb campaign. They were one of the most attractive sides to watch in 2001–02 and were once again the favourite team of many neutrals. If they can address their defensive shortcomings, the Magpies might surprise a few more people in 2002–03.

NEWCASTLE UNITED

DATE	OPPONENT	SCORE	ATT.	ACUNA	AMEOBI	BARTON	BASSEDAS	BELLAMY	BERNARD	CORT	DABIZAS	DISTIN	DYER
19.08.01	Chelsea A	1–1	40,124	83¹	71	90	85	90	–	–	90	–	–
26.08.01	Sunderland H	1–1	52,021	s48	75	90▫	–	90¹	–	–	90	–	–
08.09.01	Middlesbro A	4–1	30,004	90	s10	78	–	81▫	–	–	90¹	–	–
15.09.01	Man Utd H	4–3*	52,056	90▫	–	s45	–	89	–	–	90¹	s1	–
23.09.01	West Ham A	0–3	28,840	90	s14	58	–	90	–	–	90	s32	–
26.09.01	Leicester H	1–0	49,185	90▫	s3	–	–	90	–	–	90▫	–	–
30.09.01	Liverpool H	0–2	52,095	57	s16	–	–	90▫	–	–	90	–	–
13.10.01	Bolton W A	4–0	25,631	s1	s3	–	–	87¹▫	–	–	86	s4	–
21.10.01	Tottenham H	0–2	50,593	75	s9	–	s15	90▫	–	–	90▫	90	–
27.10.01	Everton A	3–1	37,524	90¹▫	–	–	–	90¹	–	–	90	–	–
03.11.01	Aston Villa H	3–0	51,057	–	–	–	–	90²	s5	–	90	–	–
17.11.01	Fulham A	1–3	21,159	–	s1	–	–	90	–	–	75▫	s15	–
24.11.01	Derby Co H	1–0	50,070	–	–	–	–	90	–	–	90	–	–
01.12.01	Charlton A	1–1	24,151	–	s1	–	–	89▫	–	–	90	–	–
09.12.01	Ipswich A	1–0	24,748	–	–	–	–	90	s31	–	90	–	s9
15.12.01	Blackburn H	2–1	50,064	–	59	–	–	–	90¹	–	–	90	s45
18.12.01	Arsenal A	3–1	38,012	–	–	–	–	72▫▫Δ	90	–	90	s4	86
22.12.01	Leeds Utd A	4–3	40,287	–	–	–	–	89¹	s11	–	44	s46	90
26.12.01	Middlesbro H	3–0	52,127	–	–	–	–	90¹	s11¹	–	–	90	84
29.12.01	Chelsea H	1–2	52,123	–	–	–	–	90	s27	–	–	90	90
02.01.02	Man Utd A	1–3	67,646	–	s8	–	–	82	s8	–	90	90	90
12.01.02	Leeds Utd H	3–1*	52,130	–	–	–	–	90¹▫	–	–	90▫	s4	90¹
19.01.02	Leicester A	0–0	21,354	–	–	–	–	90	–	–	90	90▫	90
30.01.02	Tottenham A	3–1	35,798	90¹	–	–	–	90¹	–	–	90	90▫	–
02.02.02	Bolton W H	3–2	52,094	s9	–	–	–	90¹	–	–	90	90	–
09.02.02	Southampton H	3–1	51,857	–	–	–	–	90	–	–	90	82	–
24.02.02	Sunderland A	1–0	48,290	–	s1	–	–	90▫	–	–	90¹	90	–
02.03.02	Arsenal H	0–2	52,067	–	65	–	–	–	–	s8	90	90	–
06.03.02	Liverpool A	0–3	44,204	s53	–	–	–	–	s14	76	90	90	–
16.03.02	Ipswich H	2–2	51,115	90	s13	–	–	–	–	77	90▫	90	s25
30.03.02	Everton H	6–2	51,921	s12	–	–	–	–	s16¹	74¹	90	90	78
01.04.02	Aston Villa A	1–1	36,597	s6	–	–	–	–	s6	84	90	90	90
08.04.02	Fulham A	1–1	50,017	–	–	–	–	–	–	68	s1	90	90¹
13.04.02	Derby Co H	3–2	31,031	–	–	–	–	–	s24	59	90	90▫	90¹
20.04.02	Charlton H	3–0	51,360	–	–	–	–	–	s11▫	–	s19	90	90
23.04.02	Blackburn A	2–2	26,712	–	–	–	–	s18	s45	–	90	90	90
27.04.02	West Ham H	3–1	52,127	–	–	–	–	–	90	s6	90	s45▫	84
11.05.02	Southampton A	1–3	31,973	–	–	–	–	–	90	–	90▫	90	59

▫ Yellow card, ▪ Red card, s Substitute, 90² Goals scored

*including own goal, + card rescinded, Δ no suspension served, card remained on record

For more information visit our website:

2001–02 PREMIERSHIP APPEARANCES

ELLIOTT	GIVEN	GRIFFIN	HUGHES	JENAS	LEE	LUA-LUA	McCLEN	O'BRIEN	ROBERT	SHEARER	SOLANO	SPEED	TOTAL
90	90	s5	90□	–	90□	s19	–	s7□	90□	–	–	–	990
40	90	–	90	–	90	–	–	s50	90□	s15	90	42	990
90	90□	–	90	–	90□	s9	–	s12	90¹	80²	90	–	990
90□	90	90	–	–	45¹	–	–	90	90¹	90	90	–	990
90	90	–	–	–	90	–	–	90	90	90	76	–	990
90	90	90	–	–	90	–	–	90	90	87	90¹	–	990
90	90	90	–	–	90	–	–	90	90	90	74	s33	990
90	90	–	90	–	90	–	–	90	90¹	90¹	90¹	89□	990
–	90	–	81	–	–	s15	–	90	90	90	75	90	990
90	90	–	90	–	–	s1	–	90	90	90□	89¹□	90	990
90	90	–	90	–	90	–	–	90	85	90¹	90	90	990
90□	90	–	90	–	89□	s13	–	90□	90□	90□	77	90¹	990
90	90□	–	90	–	90	s1	–	90	89	90¹	90	90	990
90	90	–	90	–	90	s3	–	90	87	88□+	90	90¹□	988
90	90	–	90	–	90	–	–	90	59¹	90	81¹	90	990
90	90	–	90	–	45	s31	–	90	–	90	90	90¹	990
58	90	–	90	–	–	s32	–	90¹	s32¹	90¹	58	90□	972
90¹□	90	–	90	–	–	s1	–	90	79	90¹	90¹	90	990
90	90	–	90	–	s11	s6	–	90	79	90¹	79	90	990
63	90	–	90	–	–	s16	–	90	90	90¹	74	90	990
90	90	–	90	–	90	–	–	–	–	90¹	82□	90	990
90	90	–	90	–	–	–	–	86	90□	90	90	90	990
90	90	–	90	–	–	–	–	–	90	90	90□	90	990
45	90	–	90	–	–	–	90	90	s45	90¹	90	–	990
–	90	–	90	–	–	–	81	90	90	90²	90	90	990
s8	90	–	90	s13	–	–	77	90	90¹	90²	90	90	990
–	90	–	90	90	–	–	–	90	89	90	90	90	990
–	90	–	82	90	–	s25	–	90	90	90	90	90	990
–	90	–	90	90	–	–	–	90	90	90	90	37	990
–	90	–	90	65	–	s13	–	90	90¹	90¹	77	–	990
–	90	–	90	90	–	s16	–	90¹	74	90¹	90²	–	990
–	90	–	90	90	–	–	–	90	84	90¹	90	–	990
90	90	–	90	s22	–	–	–	89	90□	90	90	90	990
–	90	–	90	s17	–	s31¹	–	66	90¹	73	90	90	990
90	90	–	90	s11	–	90¹	–	71	79	90¹	79	90¹	990
45□	90	–	90	–	–	72	–	–	90□	90²	90	90	990
–	90	–	90	s6	–	84¹	–	45	90¹	90¹	90	90	990
–	90	–	90	s31	–	90	–	–	90	90¹	90	90	990

THE MANAGER

BOBBY ROBSON

Bobby Robson has been involved in football for 52 years and at 69 years of age showed no sign of slowing down.

After a playing career which took in spells at Fulham and West Brom, as well as 20 appearances for England, Robson cut his managerial teeth at Craven Cottage before taking over the hotseat at Ipswich.

He took the Portman Road club to FA and UEFA Cup glory before taking on the England job, guiding his country to the quarter-finals of the 1986 World Cup and the semi-finals in 1990.

After leaving England, Robson enjoyed huge success abroad, winning league titles in Holland and Portugal while managing PSV Eindhoven, Sporting Lisbon and Porto. That success earned him the Barcelona job and, although he failed to win the Primera Liga, the Catalan giants did win two trophies during his time at the club, including the European Cup Winners' Cup.

Following a brief spell back in charge of PSV, Robson finally fulfilled a lifelong ambition in 1999 by taking over at Newcastle, the club he had supported as a boy.

Since his arrival, Robson has rejuvenated the Magpies, guiding them to fourth place in 2001–02 and earning the club a shot at the Champions League.

LEAGUE POSITION

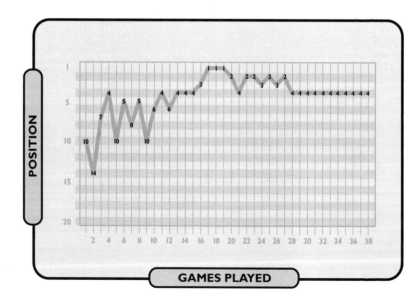

POSITION

GAMES PLAYED

7 Alan Shearer took more penalties than

THE GOALS

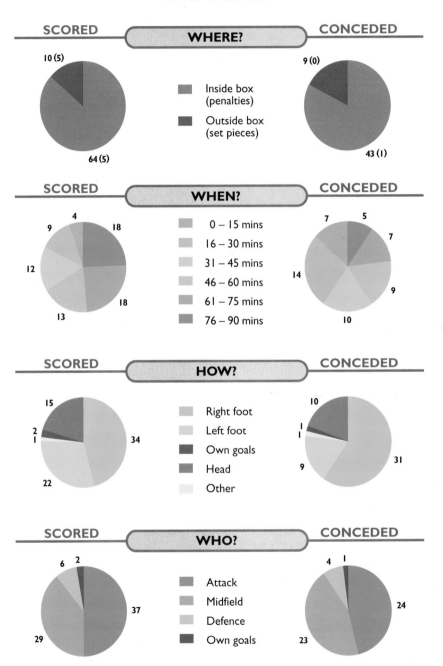

anyone else in the top flight.

NEWCASTLE UNITED

	ACUNA	AMEOBI	BARTON	BASSEDAS	BELLAMY	BERNARD	CORT	DABIZAS	DISTIN
APPEARANCES									
Start	10	4	4	1	26	4	6	33	20
Sub	6	11	1	1	1	12	2	2	8
Minutes on pitch	974	349	361	100	2317	569	452	2925	1943
GOAL ATTEMPTS									
Goals	3	0	0	0	10	3	1	3	0
Shots on target	6	3	0	0	39	4	3	9	3
Shots off target	5	5	1	1	31	4	9	17	5
Shooting accuracy %	55%	38%	0%	0%	56%	50%	25%	35%	38%
Goals/shots %	27%	0%	0%	0%	14%	38%	8%	12%	0%
PASSING									
Goal assists	0	0	0	0	4	0	1	0	0
Long passes	81	7	64	8	117	53	12	337	270
Short passes	319	100	185	44	842	181	151	985	603
PASS COMPLETION									
Own half %	88%	77%	90%	82%	90%	78%	87%	85%	82%
Opposition half %	78%	62%	67%	63%	80%	70%	74%	69%	63%
CROSSING									
Total crosses	2	6	8	0	94	26	3	8	23
Cross completion %	0%	17%	13%	0%	20%	19%	33%	25%	26%
DRIBBLING									
Dribbles & runs	4	22	9	3	199	43	7	56	38
Dribble completion %	50%	55%	89%	33%	63%	77%	86%	91%	89%
DEFENDING									
Tackles made	28	6	8	5	32	21	4	100	95
Tackles won %	71%	67%	50%	80%	69%	86%	100%	73%	72%
Blocks	5	0	4	0	4	3	0	26	22
Clearances	8	3	20	0	2	17	3	329	176
Interceptions	6	0	0	0	0	4	0	37	16
DISCIPLINE									
Fouls conceded	21	9	6	0	42	12	4	78	20
Fouls won	10	11	3	8	49	18	4	64	22
Offside	1	5	1	0	49	2	8	0	2
Yellow cards	3	0	1	0	8	1	0	6	4
Red cards	0	0	0	0	1	0	0	0	0

+ one card rescinded

GOALKEEPER NAME	START/ (SUB)	TIME ON PITCH	GOALS CONCEDED	MINS/GOALS CONCEDED	SAVES MADE	SAVES/ SHOTS
GIVEN	38 (0)	3420	52	66	124	70%

For more information visit our website:

PLAYERS' STATISTICS

	DYER	ELLIOTT	GRIFFIN	HUGHES	JENAS	LEE	LUA-LUA	McCLEN	O'BRIEN	ROBERT	SHEARER	SOLANO	SPEED	TOTAL	RANK
	15	26	3	34	6	15	4	3	31	34	36	37	28		
	3	1	1	0	6	1	16	0	3	2	1	0	1		
	1370	2149	275	3043	615	1270	568	248	2766	3041	3223	3171	2451		
	3	1	0	0	0	1	3	0	2	8	23	7	4	74*	3rd
	5	2	0	0	3	2	10	1	3	37	44	21	17	212	4th
	7	7	0	4	6	7	8	0	8	48	40	26	26	265	2nd
	42%	22%	0%	0%	33%	22%	56%	100%	27%	44%	52%	45%	40%	44%	9th
	25%	11%	0%	0%	0%	11%	17%	0%	18%	9%	27%	15%	9%	15%	4th
	4	4	0	4	1	2	3	0	0	11	4	9	2	49	4th
	119	353	65	378	74	253	35	38	278	245	164	449	405	4416	6th
	606	642	99	1131	236	625	245	133	690	1035	771	1340	1016	12147	4th
	90%	80%	87%	85%	79%	90%	86%	87%	80%	78%	84%	82%	88%	84%	6th
	81%	67%	69%	75%	75%	78%	77%	84%	62%	71%	67%	72%	75%	71%	3rd
	25	54	3	79	1	10	26	2	4	340	67	345	14	1140	2nd
	20%	20%	0%	28%	0%	40%	27%	50%	0%	26%	24%	34%	29%	27%	4th
	71	50	6	64	21	20	79	3	39	257	51	106	38	1190	8th
	77%	62%	17%	72%	76%	70%	67%	67%	77%	57%	45%	71%	87%	67%	14th
	29	78	13	63	17	54	22	9	101	46	35	86	98	954	17th
	83%	74%	92%	76%	53%	80%	64%	78%	76%	61%	74%	80%	64%	73%	14th
	2	20	3	32	3	6	0	1	37	3	8	16	11	206	13th
	3	118	12	108	5	10	2	3	270	11	35	33	65	1324	14th
	4	13	0	11	3	8	0	0	18	3	2	13	11	149	11th
	14	29	5	11	4	21	18	2	27	38	85	64	46	558	11th
	21	18	6	35	10	15	10	2	38	75	79	49	24	577	4th
	11	0	0	0	0	0	7	0	1	4	30	7	2	130	12th
	0	4	0	1	0	3	0	0	3	7	2	3	3	51	16th
	0	0	0	0	0	0	0	0	0	0	1+	0	0	2	=15th

*Including two own goals

CROSSES CAUGHT	CROSSES PUNCHED	CROSSES DROPPED	CATCH SUCCESS	THROWS/ SHORT KICKS	% COMPLETION	LONG KICKS	% COMPLETION
54	41	4	93%	103	98%	657	63%

PLAYER OF THE SEASON

PLAYER	INDEX SCORE
CRAIG BELLAMY	1,009
Alan Shearer	899
Laurent Robert	852
Nikos Dabizas	820
Nolberto Solano	806
Gary Speed	762
Shay Given	750
Sylvain Distin	711
Robbie Elliott	703
Andy O'Brien	681

There were a few eyebrows raised when Newcastle parted with £6 million for Coventry's Craig Bellamy. The young Welsh striker had been a disappointment since moving from Norwich to Highfield Road, failing to make a real impact in Coventry's ill-fated 2000–01 Premiership campaign.

Bobby Robson clearly felt Bellamy had more to offer though and, after a campaign in which he scored 13 goals and picked up the PFA Young Player of the Year award, Bellamy more than repaid his manager's faith.

Bellamy was Opta's Newcastle player of the season, finishing ahead of his strike partner Alan Shearer in the rankings. Shearer also had a fantastic campaign, top-scoring for the Magpies and falling just one goal short of the coveted Golden Boot – particularly frustrating after a deflected strike against Manchester United was taken off him by the Premiership's dubious goals panel. He scored more penalties than anyone else in the Premiership and also converted more headers into goals than any other player.

The former England captain was supplied with a steady stream of chances by Newcastle's two exciting wingers Laurent Robert and Nolberto Solano, both of whom featured highly in Opta's top 10.

Solano delivered more crosses than any other Premiership player, setting up nine goals in the process. Robert provided even more assists, 11 in total.

Nikos Dabizas was the Magpies' highest-rated defender, completing more clearances than any of his team-mates at the back. If he failed to deal with the opposition, Newcastle could usually rely on their excellent goalkeeper Shay Given to bail them out of trouble.

Given successfully parried 70% of all accurate opposition shots in a solid season between the sticks.

Kieron Dyer did not feature. The England star was sidelined for much of the campaign with injury and did not play enough time to qualify for Opta's top 10.

5 Laurent Robert scored more free kicks

FIVE OF THE BEST

Rejuvenated Newcastle enjoyed a tremendous season, scoring plenty of goals on their way to Champions League qualification. Inspired by the strike partnership of Alan Shearer and Craig Bellamy, the Magpies played some of the most entertaining football in the Premiership, exceeding all expectations with a fourth-placed finish.

TOP GOALSCORERS

	GOALS	GOALS/SHOTS
ALAN SHEARER	23	27%
Craig Bellamy	10	14%
Laurent Robert	8	9%
Nolberto Solano	7	15%
Gary Speed	4	9%

Alan Shearer and Craig Bellamy were as effective as any strike partnership during the 2001–02 season. Bellamy's injury lay-off was a bitter blow to Newcastle, but the duo still managed 33 goals between them. There were also important contributions from midfield where Laurent Robert, Nolberto Solano and Gary Speed all weighed in with their fair share of goals. Shearer's goals-to-shots ratio of 27% was among the best in the Premiership.

Nolberto Solano was Newcastle's creator-in-chief during 2001–02. The Peruvian international set up nine goals and created plenty more chances with his accurate crossing and passing. Solano also made more successful passes than any of his team-mates completing 75% in total. Gary Speed kept things simple to record the highest pass completion rate in Newcastle's midfield, while Aaron Hughes and Nikos Dabizas distributed the ball effectively at the back.

TOP PASSERS

	SUCC PASSES	COMPLETION
NOLBERTO SOLANO	1,339	75%
Aaron Hughes	1,199	79%
Gary Speed	1,137	80%
Nikos Dabizas	1,044	79%
Laurent Robert	927	72%

TOP TACKLERS

	WON	SUCCESS
ANDY O'BRIEN	77	76%
Nikos Dabizas	73	73%
Nolberto Solano	69	80%
Sylvain Distin	68	72%
Gary Speed	63	64%

Former Bradford man Andy O'Brien has become a firm favourite at Newcastle and he showed his commitment by winning more tackles than anyone else at the club during the 2001–02 season. Nikos Dabizas wasn't far behind his fellow defender, but surprisingly it was Nolberto Solano who recorded the best tackle success rate among the club's top-five ball winners. Sylvain Distin impressed everyone at the club with some tough-tackling displays and won more challenges than Gary Speed.

No one would call Alan Shearer a dirty player, but the number nine's physical style saw him concede more free kicks than any of his team-mates during the 2001–02 season. Shearer's red card against Charlton was later rescinded, while Craig Bellamy's against Arsenal incurred no ban. Bellamy was shown more yellow cards than anyone else at Newcastle, as his spiky temperament often saw him on the wrong side of referees.

DISCIPLINE

	POINTS	FOULS & CARDS
ALAN SHEARER	97	85F, 2Y, 1R
Nikos Dabizas	96	78F, 6Y, 0R
Nolberto Solano	73	64F, 3Y, 0R
Craig Bellamy	72	42F, 8Y, 1R
Laurent Robert	59	38F, 7Y, 0R

SOUTHAMPTON

COLOURS

Home: Red and white striped shirts,
black shorts and white stockings
Away: Black shirts, black shorts and
black stockings

NICKNAME

The Saints

HONOURS

Division Three (South) Champions:
1921–22
Division Three Champions: 1959–60
FA Cup Winners: 1976

RECORD GOALSCORER

Mike Channon – 185 league goals,
1966–77, 1979–82

BIGGEST WIN

9–3 v Wolverhampton Wanderers –
Division Two, 18 September 1965

BIGGEST DEFEATS

0–8 v Tottenham Hotspur – Division
Two, 28 March 1936
0–8 v Everton – Division One,
20 November 1971

SEASON REVIEW

After losing the services of their manager and best defender to the lure of Tottenham Hotspur within the space of five months, the last thing Southampton needed was a poor start to the 2001–02 season.

But that is exactly what they got, suffering defeat in all of their opening three games against Leeds, Chelsea and Spurs without so much as a single goal for consolation. Even the move from The Dell to an impressive new stadium in St. Mary's failed to lift spirits on the south coast. Southampton were a club seriously down in the dumps.

So, following a 2–0 defeat at West Ham in October, Saints chairman Rupert Lowe moved in to rectify the sorry situation by sacking manager Stuart Gray – who he had only put in full-time charge some 10 weeks earlier – and replacing him with Gordon Strachan, the former Coventry boss.

Strachan wasn't the first choice of the majority of Southampton fans and in the early weeks of his tenure, the doubters looked like they were going to be proved right. The Saints let slip a 3–1 lead against Ipswich to draw 3–3 in Strachan's first game in charge and followed that result up with three straight defeats. But the tide was about to turn.

The first signs of a revival came in the home match against Charlton in November when Marian Pahars headed in the winner to earn the club a first win at their new home at the sixth attempt. Two weeks later, they travelled to fellow strugglers Leicester and produced an excellent 4–0 win with Swedish midfielder Anders Svensson – one of the club's two major summer signings, Rory Delap being the other – scoring his first two Premiership goals for the Saints.

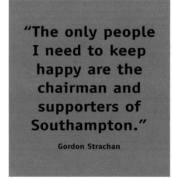

> "The only people I need to keep happy are the chairman and supporters of Southampton."
>
> **Gordon Strachan**

Over the next couple of months, Southampton pulled themselves well clear of trouble by beating Sunderland, Tottenham and then – consecutively and with impressive performances – Chelsea away and Liverpool at home.

Powerful striker James Beattie scored three times in those two games and, with a handful of international friendlies coming up, he was being tipped for a first full England cap. Sadly, a nasty injury sustained in the 3–1 defeat to Manchester United in January ruled Beattie out for the best part of three months and the opportunity passed him by.

However, left-back Wayne Bridge had better luck. He made his international debut against Holland in February and won two more caps before the season's end to force his way into the World Cup squad – the first Southampton player to do so since Peter Shilton in 1986.

Back in the Premiership, following a 3–1 win at Ipswich that included a goal of the season contender from unsung hero Chris Marsden, the Saints' form began to wane. A string of disappointing draws at home, coupled with defeat at Blackburn, meant that the lingering fear of relegation still hovered over the south coast club.

But a 2–0 home win over Derby, followed by a 1–1 draw at Charlton, made the Saints mathematically safe with a month or so to spare – quite an achievement considering they made such a poor start to the campaign. They also survived while picking up just 36 yellow cards – the lowest tally in the division.

The club's first year at St. Mary's was wrapped up with a last-day win over Newcastle and a testimonial for Matt Le Tissier, who retired from playing after 16 years of fantastic service.

SOUTHAMPTON

DATE	OPPONENT	SCORE	ATT.	BEATTIE	BENALI	BLEIDELIS	BRIDGE	DAVIES	DELAP	DELGADO	DODD	DRAPER	EL KHALEJ	FERNANDES	JONES	LE TISSIER
18.08.01	Leeds Utd A	0–2	39,715	s18	s6	–	90	90□	90	–	–	–	–	–	90	–
25.08.01	Chelsea H	0–2	31,107	s19	–	–	90	90	90	–	–	–	–	–	90	–
09.09.01	Tottenham A	0–2	33,668	s17	–	–	90	90	90	–	–	s17	90	–	90	–
15.09.01	Bolton W A	1–0	24,378	90	–	–	90	90	90	–	–	–	69□	–	90	–
24.09.01	Aston Villa H	1–3	26,794	90	s24	–	90	77	53■	–	–	–	90	–	90	s13
29.09.01	Middlesbro A	3–1	26,142	90^2	s23	–	90	90	52□	–	–	–	90	–	90	–
13.10.01	Arsenal H	0–2	29,759	90	–	–	90	90	–	–	s51	–	90	–	90	–
20.10.01	West Ham A	0–2	25,842	90	–	–	90	68	90	–	90	90□	90	–	90	–
24.10.01	Ipswich H	3–3	29,614	90^1□	–	–	90	–	70	–	s34	–	90□	–	90	–
27.10.01	Fulham A	1–2	18,771	71^1□	–	–	90	s19	90	–	90	–	90	–	90	–
03.11.01	Blackburn H	1–2	30,523	90	–	–	90	–	90	–	90	–	90	–	90	–
17.11.01	Derby Co A	0–1	32,063	66	–	–	90	–	s10	–	90	–	–	–	90	s24
24.11.01	Charlton H	1–0	31,198	90	–	–	90	s5	–	–	90	–	–	–	90	–
02.12.01	Everton A	0–2	28,138	90	–	–	90	s22	–	–	90	–	–	–	90	–
08.12.01	Leicester A	4–0	20,321	90^1	–	–	90	–	s3	–	90	–	–	–	90	–
15.12.01	Sunderland H	2–0*	29,459	90	–	–	90	–	–	–	90	–	–	–	90	–
22.12.01	Man Utd A	1–6	67,638	90	–	–	90	59□	s9	–	90	–	–	–	90	–
26.12.01	Tottenham H	1–0	31,719	90^1	–	–	90	–	90	–	90	–	–	–	90	–
29.12.01	Leeds Utd H	0–1	31,622	90	–	–	90	–	90	–	90	–	–	s12	90	–
01.01.02	Chelsea A	4–2	35,156	90^2	–	–	90	–	90	90□	–	–	–	–	90	–
09.01.02	Liverpool H	2–0*	31,527	90^1	–	–	90	–	35	–	90	–	–	–	90	–
13.01.02	Man Utd H	1–3	31,858	26^1	–	–	90	–	–	s64	90	–	60	–	90	–
19.01.02	Liverpool A	1–1	43,710	–	–	–	90	90^1□	–	–	90	–	–	76	90	s1
30.01.02	West Ham H	2–0	31,879	–	–	s1	90	83^1	–	–	90	–	–	89^1	90	s7
02.02.02	Arsenal A	1–1	38,024	–	–	–	90	67□	–	–	90□	–	–	s15	90	0□
09.02.02	Newcastle A	1–3	51,857	–	–	–	90	90□	s42	–	90	–	–	–	90	–
23.02.02	Bolton W H	0–0	31,380	–	–	–	90	–	88■	–	90	–	–	89	–	–
02.03.02	Ipswich A	3–1	25,440	–	–	–	90	90	90^1	–	–	–	–	–	90	–
06.03.02	Middlesbro H	1–1	28,931	–	–	–	90	90	90	–	–	–	–	–	90	–
16.03.02	Leicester H	2–2	30,012	s27	–	–	90	63	–	–	–	–	s67	s27	90	–
23.03.02	Sunderland A	1–1	46,120	–	–	–	90	72	–	–	s18	–	–	–	90	–
30.03.02	Fulham H	1–1	31,616	–	–	–	90	s16	90^1□	–	90	–	–	–	90	–
01.04.02	Blackburn A	0–2	28,851	–	–	–	90	58	90	–	90□	–	–	58	90	–
06.04.02	Derby Co H	2–0	29,263	90	–	–	90	–	90	–	90	–	90	–	90	–
13.04.02	Charlton A	1–1*	26,557	90□	–	–	90	–	90	–	90	–	90	–	90	–
20.04.02	Everton H	0–1	31,785	90	–	–	90	–	90□	–	68	–	–	s45	90	–
27.04.02	Aston Villa A	1–2	35,255	90^1	–	–	90	s10	90	–	90	–	s45	45	–	–
11.05.02	Newcastle H	3–1	31,973	90^1	–	–	90	–	90	–	90	–	55■	s20	–	–

□ Yellow card, ■ Red card, s Substitute, 90^2 Goals scored

*including own goal

2001–02 PREMIERSHIP APPEARANCES

LUNDEKVAM	MARSDEN	McDONALD	MONK	MOSS	MURRAY	OAKLEY	ORMEROD	PAHARS	PETRESCU	RICHARDS	RIPLEY	ROSLER	SVENSSON	TELFER	TESSEM	WILLIAMS	TOTAL
89□	79□	–	–	–	–	90	–	72	–	90	–	84	90	–	s11	–	989
90	71	–	–	–	–	90	–	71	–	90	s19	80	90	–	s10	–	990
–	–	–	–	–	s8	90	–	73	–	90	–	90	73	–	82	–	990
90	s4	–	–	–	–	90	–	s21[1]	–	90	–	–	90	–	86	–	990
90	–	s13	–	–	–	90	–	77[1]	–	–	–	–	90	–	66	–	953
90	90	s13	–	–	–	90	–	77[1]	–	–	s38	–	67	–	–	–	990
39	60□	–	90□	–	–	54	–	90	–	–	s36	–	54	–	s36	–	960
90	90	–	–	–	–	–	–	76	–	–	s14	–	s22	–	–	–	990
90	90[1]	–	–	–	–	90	–	90[1]	s20	–	56	s7	–	–	83	–	990
36	–	–	–	–	–	90□	–	90	s34	–	–	–	90	–	56	s54	990
–	90	–	–	–	–	90	–	90[1]	–	–	–	–	–	90	–	90□	990
90	90	–	–	–	–	90	–	85[1]	–	–	–	–	80	90	–	90□	990
90	68	–	–	–	–	90	–	90	–	–	–	–	90	90	–	90□	990
90	90	–	–	–	–	87	–	90[1]	–	–	–	–	90[2]	90	–	90	990
90	90□	–	–	–	–	90	s6	84[1]	–	–	–	–	90	90	–	90	990
90	90	–	–	–	–	–	s31	90[1]	–	–	–	–	81	90	–	90	990
90	90	–	–	–	–	–	s9	81	–	–	–	–	90	90	–	90	990
90	90	–	–	–	–	–	–	90	–	–	–	–	90	78□	–	90	990
90	90[1]	–	–	–	–	–	s8	82[1]	–	–	–	–	90	90	–	90	990
90	90	–	–	–	–	s55	s14	76	–	–	–	–	90	90	–	90	990
90	90□	–	–	–	–	–	s30	90	–	–	–	–	90	90	–	90	990
90	90	–	–	–	–	–	–	89	–	–	–	–	90	90	s14	90	990
90	–	–	–	–	–	81	–	90	–	–	–	–	90	90	s9	90	990
90	90	–	–	–	–	75	–	90	–	–	–	–	90	90	s23[1]	90	990
90	90	–	–	–	–	74	–	90[1]	–	–	–	–	90	48	s16	90	990
90	90	–	–	–	–	–	s67	23	–	–	–	–	90	s1	90	90	988
90	90[1]	–	–	–	–	90	78[1]	–	–	–	–	–	90	90	s12	90□	990
90□	90	–	–	–	–	90	90	s23	–	–	–	–	67[1]	90	–	90	990
23	90	–	–	–	–	90	90	90[2]	–	–	–	–	63	90	–	90	990
90□	72□	–	–	–	–	90	90	90□	–	–	–	–	90	90	s18[1]	90	990
90	–	–	–	–	–	90	90	74	–	–	–	–	73	90	s17	90	990
90	–	–	–	–	–	90	90	s32	–	–	–	–	–	90	s32	90	990
–	49	–	–	–	–	90[1]	s19	71[1]	–	–	–	–	–	90	s41	90□	990
–	–	–	–	–	–	9	s23	67	–	–	–	–	90	90	s81□	90	990
90	–	–	–	–	–	–	s22	90□	–	–	–	–	90	90	45	90	990
90	–	–	–	90	–	–	80	–	–	–	–	–	90	90	s45□	45	990
90	–	–	s30	90	–	62	60	–	–	–	–	–	70[1]	90[1]	s28	–	955

THE MANAGER

GORDON STRACHAN

Gordon Strachan was a surprise choice to replace sacked Southampton boss Stuart Gray in October, considering that he himself had only just been relieved of the managerial duties at Coventry City, with whom he was relegated in 2000–01.

But the brave decision of Saints chairman Rupert Lowe paid off as Strachan guided the club away from the relegation zone and into mid-table, while overseeing the development of an exciting young team.

Strachan – who enjoyed a great deal of success in his playing career with Aberdeen, Manchester United and Leeds – cut his managerial teeth at Highfield Road after originally moving to the club in the dual role of player and assistant to Ron Atkinson. He took over the hot seat in 1996 and his team had a couple of flirts with relegation before going down in 2001.

In fairness to Strachan, he had enjoyed a fair amount of success at Coventry, signing the likes of Darren Huckerby, George Boateng and Robbie Keane before moving them on for big fees. But the relationship between manager and fans turned sour towards the end of his five-year tenure and a change was probably best for all parties.

LEAGUE POSITION

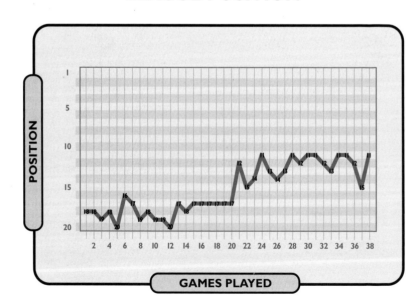

POSITION

GAMES PLAYED

3 Southampton won fewer matches by a

THE GOALS

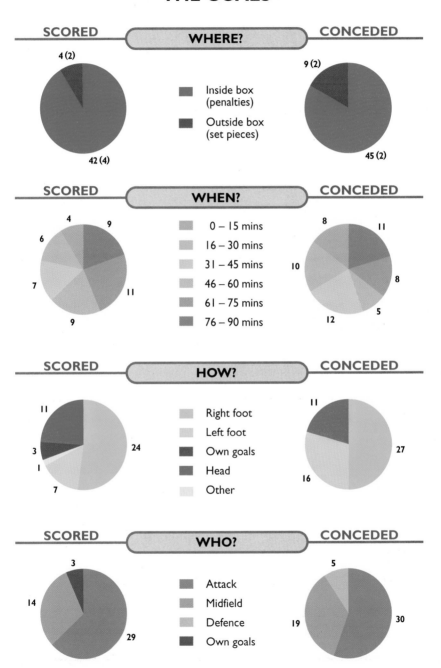

SCORED **WHERE?** **CONCEDED**

4 (2)

- Inside box (penalties)
- Outside box (set pieces)

42 (4)

9 (2)

45 (2)

SCORED **WHEN?** **CONCEDED**

4 9
6
7 11
9

- 0 – 15 mins
- 16 – 30 mins
- 31 – 45 mins
- 46 – 60 mins
- 61 – 75 mins
- 76 – 90 mins

8 11
10 8
5
12

SCORED **HOW?** **CONCEDED**

11
3 24
1
7

- Right foot
- Left foot
- Own goals
- Head
- Other

11
27
16

SCORED **WHO?** **CONCEDED**

3
14
29

- Attack
- Midfield
- Defence
- Own goals

5
30
19

one-goal margin than any other team

SOUTHAMPTON

	BEATTIE	BENALI	BLEIDELIS	BRIDGE	DAVIES	DELAP	DELGADO	DODD	DRAPER	EL KHALEJ	FERNANDES	LE TISSIER	LUNDEKVA...
APPEARANCES													
Start	24	0	0	38	18	24	0	26	1	12	6	0	34
Sub	4	3	1	0	5	4	1	3	1	2	5	4	0
Minutes on pitch	2134	53	1	3420	1519	2072	64	2421	107	1136	536	45	2887
GOAL ATTEMPTS													
Goals	12	0	0	0	2	2	0	0	0	0	1	0	0
Shots on target	33	0	0	4	10	10	1	0	1	1	3	0	3
Shots off target	37	0	0	8	10	22	3	3	1	3	3	1	4
Shooting accuracy %	47%	0%	0%	33%	50%	31%	25%	0%	50%	25%	50%	0%	43%
Goals/shots %	17%	0%	0%	0%	10%	6%	0%	0%	0%	0%	17%	0%	0%
PASSING													
Goal assists	5	0	0	2	0	2	0	4	0	1	0	0	0
Long passes	75	10	1	462	91	147	1	448	15	97	60	4	273
Short passes	563	22	1	929	422	543	19	791	38	203	170	15	586
PASS COMPLETION													
Own half %	81%	94%	0%	75%	79%	77%	100%	78%	83%	75%	81%	80%	80%
Opposition half %	58%	80%	100%	64%	57%	60%	83%	65%	62%	62%	67%	64%	52%
CROSSING													
Total crosses	47	0	0	171	47	37	0	88	3	4	46	10	11
Cross completion %	23%	0%	0%	26%	28%	16%	0%	23%	67%	25%	17%	10%	18%
DRIBBLING													
Dribbles & runs	70	0	0	168	90	52	1	25	1	14	23	3	30
Dribble completion %	57%	0%	0%	80%	48%	77%	0%	84%	100%	71%	78%	0%	83%
DEFENDING													
Tackles made	24	5	0	82	63	86	0	67	1	46	21	2	41
Tackles won %	75%	60%	0%	80%	71%	71%	0%	75%	0%	83%	86%	100%	85%
Blocks	2	2	0	31	3	8	0	32	0	11	1	0	41
Clearances	22	0	0	154	22	68	0	110	2	138	8	0	320
Interceptions	2	1	0	11	5	18	0	14	2	10	7	0	13
DISCIPLINE													
Fouls conceded	73	0	0	20	46	41	0	34	3	25	12	0	22
Fouls won	76	2	0	30	30	29	0	23	1	32	3	2	27
Offside	17	0	0	4	3	2	1	0	0	0	0	0	3
Yellow cards	3	0	0	0	5	3	0	3	1	2	0	1	2
Red cards	0	0	0	0	0	2	0	0	0	1	0	0	1

GOALKEEPER NAME	START/ (SUB)	TIME ON PITCH	GOALS CONCEDED	MINS/GOALS CONCEDED	SAVES MADE	SAVES/ SHOTS
JONES	36 (0)	3240	51	64	105	67%
MOSS	2 (0)	180	3	60	10	77%

For more information visit our website:

PLAYERS' STATISTICS

	MARSDEN	McDONALD	MONK	MURRAY	OAKLEY	ORMEROD	PAHARS	PETRESCU	RICHARDS	RIPLEY	ROSLER	SVENSSON	TELFER	TESSEM	WILLIAMS	TOTAL	RANK
	27	0	1	0	26	8	33	0	4	1	3	33	27	7	27		
	1	2	1	1	1	10	3	2	0	4	1	1	1	15	1		
	2293	26	120	8	2235	899	2754	54	360	163	261	2810	2377	901	2439		
	3	0	0	0	1	1	14	0	0	0	0	4	1	2	0	46*	=10th
	12	0	0	0	9	3	37	0	2	0	3	15	6	4	4	161	=15th
	8	1	0	0	17	21	29	1	2	1	2	31	9	5	3	225	13th
	60%	0%	0%	0%	35%	13%	56%	0%	50%	0%	60%	33%	40%	44%	57%	42%	16th
	15%	0%	0%	0%	4%	4%	21%	0%	0%	0%	0%	9%	7%	22%	0%	11%	12th
	0	0	0	0	1	2	5	0	0	1	0	5	2	0	2	32	=12th
	261	1	7	7	295	38	138	4	45	5	13	270	264	56	344	3897	13th
	782	9	24	6	884	228	762	25	86	34	60	904	896	222	513	9791	17th
	85%	100%	100%	67%	85%	77%	85%	100%	81%	93%	71%	80%	84%	75%	79%	80%	16th
	70%	78%	60%	30%	73%	68%	70%	76%	56%	71%	62%	70%	69%	65%	47%	64%	18th
	64	1	0	0	33	16	107	0	0	13	3	98	167	30	9	1005	6th
	30%	0%	0%	0%	21%	6%	22%	0%	0%	15%	33%	21%	25%	37%	44%	24%	13th
	46	4	0	0	41	35	158	1	2	10	5	99	46	27	15	973	13th
	70%	50%	0%	0%	68%	60%	67%	0%	100%	70%	100%	63%	74%	48%	93%	68%	9th
	88	0	2	0	83	13	42	2	11	5	1	120	51	41	82	982	15th
	72%	0%	100%	0%	70%	69%	69%	50%	82%	80%	0%	73%	71%	73%	76%	74%	8th
	8	0	3	0	10	0	1	0	5	1	0	4	4	1	37	205	14th
	40	0	8	0	20	1	0	4	39	0	4	30	48	16	260	1396	11th
	7	0	1	0	11	3	1	0	5	1	0	7	7	2	11	139	17th
	64	3	1	0	31	12	48	0	1	0	17	46	28	25	39	593	7th
	28	0	0	0	21	21	46	0	7	3	8	44	17	15	47	519	16th
	3	0	0	0	0	22	61	0	0	0	2	3	0	8	0	129	13th
	4	0	1	0	1	0	2	0	0	0	0	0	1	2	5	36	20th
	1	0	0	0	0	0	0	0	0	0	0	0	0	0	0	5	=4th

*Including three own goals

CROSSES CAUGHT	CROSSES PUNCHED	CROSSES DROPPED	CATCH SUCCESS	THROWS/ SHORT KICKS	% COMPLETION	LONG KICKS	% COMPLETION
56	32	6	90%	33	91%	701	43%
5	0	1	83%	4	100%	54	44%

PLAYER OF THE SEASON

PLAYER	INDEX SCORE
JAMES BEATTIE	833
Marian Pahars	771
Paul Williams	659
Jason Dodd	632
Claus Lundekvam	607
Anders Svensson	599
Paul Jones	547
Rory Delap	542
Wayne Bridge	541
Chris Marsden	518

Southampton's James Beattie scored 10 goals in as many games towards the end of the year 2000 to establish himself as a Premiership striker of vast potential. But the goals dried up somewhat after that prolific spell and 2001–02 was seen by many as a make-or-break season in Beattie's Premiership career.

He ended up passing the test with flying colours, scoring a dozen goals to finish second to Marian Pahars in the St. Mary's Stadium scoring charts, despite missing a large chunk of the season due to a serious ankle injury.

The former Blackburn Rovers youngster also created five strikes for team-mates and caused havoc for a number of defences with his heading ability – indeed, just four other Premiership strikers bettered his tally of 164 aerial flick-ons.

Pahars was the other player to shine for Southampton in attack in 2001–02. The little Latvian frontman hit 14 goals himself – including two from the penalty spot – and set up five others.

And while those two were doing the damage at one end of the pitch, the likes of Paul Williams, skipper Jason Dodd and Claus Lundekvam were keeping things tight at the back.

By making 260 clearances, Williams – a free transfer capture from Gordon Strachan's former club Coventry – particularly impressed and proved to be an excellent replacement for Dean Richards who left for Tottenham Hotspur in September.

Others to make the Saints' top 10 performers chart were Swedish midfielder Anders Svensson and England left-back Wayne Bridge, both of whom capped their impressive seasons by making it into their respective World Cup squads.

However, Rory Delap missed the cut for the Republic of Ireland despite some great end-of-season form, during which he scored a goal of the year contender in the 1–1 draw against Fulham.

Chris Marsden also had a solid season and completed the top 10 at St. Mary's.

3,420 Wayne Bridge played the maximum amount of minutes

FIVE OF THE BEST

After the worst possible start to the 2001–02 season, Southampton fans genuinely feared that their team would be playing out of the top flight for the first time since 1978. But following the appointment of Gordon Strachan in October, the men from St. Mary's set about securing their Premiership survival, with a number of young players in key positions.

TOP GOALSCORERS

	GOALS	GOALS/SHOTS
MARIAN PAHARS	14	21%
James Beattie	12	17%
Anders Svensson	4	9%
Chris Marsden	3	15%
Jo Tessem	2	22%

Arguably the Saints' brightest star in 2001–02 was Latvian Marian Pahars. With 14 goals, he finished as the club's leading scorer for the second time in three seasons and was also the most clinical taker of chances, converting 21% of his shots. James Beattie ran his little strike partner close, scoring 12 times from 70 efforts, but his season was disrupted by a serious ankle injury sustained against Manchester United in January.

The 2001–02 campaign was a momentous one for left-back Wayne Bridge. For the second season running, he was one of just a handful of players to play every minute of every Premiership game and he also won his first England cap in February. In addition, he made more successful passes than anyone else at Southampton just ahead of Matt Oakley who, like Bridge, came up through the club's youth ranks.

TOP PASSERS

	SUCC PASSES	COMPLETION
WAYNE BRIDGE	942	68%
Matt Oakley	917	78%
Paul Telfer	863	74%
Anders Svensson	861	73%
Jason Dodd	858	69%

TOP TACKLERS

	WON	SUCCESS
ANDERS SVENSSON	87	73%
Wayne Bridge	66	80%
Chris Marsden	63	72%
Paul Williams	62	76%
Rory Delap	61	71%

Signing midfield man Anders Svensson for just £500,000 was probably the shrewdest move of Stuart Gray's tenure as Southampton manager. The Sweden international was a consistent figure in the Saints' midfield and ended up winning 87 challenges – more than any of his team-mates by some distance. Midfielder Chris Marsden and defenders Wayne Bridge and Paul Williams fought it out for second place in the tackling table.

Chris Marsden completed a regular season of football for the Saints in 2001–02 for the first time since arriving from Birmingham in 1999. He produced some fine displays and scored a couple of crucial goals, but was also the team's joint-dirtiest player according to the stats. Marsden was booked four times and saw red against Arsenal putting him level on Opta disciplinary points with powerhouse striker James Beattie.

DISCIPLINE

	POINTS	FOULS & CARDS
CHRIS MARSDEN	82	64F, 4Y, 1R
James Beattie	82	73F, 3Y, 0R
Rory Delap	62	41F, 3Y, 2R
Kevin Davies	61	46F, 5Y, 0R
Paul Williams	54	39F, 5Y, 0R

SUNDERLAND

ADDRESS

The Stadium of Light, Stadium Park,
Sunderland SR5 1SU

CONTACT NUMBERS

Telephone: 0191 551 5000
Fax: 0191 551 5123
Ticket Office: 0191 551 5151
Ticket Office Fax: 0191 551 5150
ClubCall: 09068 121 140
Club Shop: 0191 551 5050
Club Shop Fax: 0191 551 5123
e-mail: communications@safc.com
Website: www.safc.com

KEY PERSONNEL

Chairman: R S Murray
Vice-Chairman: J M Fickling
Sales and Marketing Director: J Slater
Communications Director: L Callaghan
Financial Director: P Walker
Director of Football Operations:
M Blackbourne
Property Director: G Daville
Company Secretary: J Purdon
Manager: Peter Reid

SPONSORS

Reg Vardy

FANZINES

The Wearside Roar
A Love Supreme
Sex and Chocolate

COLOURS

Home: Red and white striped shirts,
black shorts and black stockings
Away: Blue and navy striped shirts,
blue shorts and blue stockings

NICKNAMES

The Black Cats

HONOURS

League Champions: 1891–92, 1892–93
1894–95, 1901–02, 1912–13, 1935–36
Division One Champions:
1995–96, 1998–99
Division Two Champions: 1975–76
Division Three Champions: 1987–88
FA Cup Winners: 1937, 1973

RECORD GOALSCORER

Charlie Buchan –
209 league goals, 1911–25

BIGGEST WIN

11–1 v Fairfield – FA Cup 1st round,
2 February 1895

BIGGEST DEFEATS

0–8 v West Ham United –
Division One, 19 October 1968
0–8 v Watford – Division One,
25 September, 1982
0–8 v Sheffield Wednesday –
Division One, 26 December 1911

SEASON REVIEW

After finishing seventh in each of the previous two Premiership campaigns, it was no surprise that the 2001–02 season was considered such a disappointment for Sunderland. The loss of key players, poor league form, embarrassing cup exits and a controversial direct playing style all combined to leave the club's traditionally loyal fans questioning the direction of the team for the first time in Peter Reid's seven-year reign.

It had all started brightly enough, with Kevin Phillips firing the club to an opening day win over Ipswich. But the Black Cats then lost to newly-promoted Fulham and were affected by key midfield man Don Hutchison's defection to West Ham.

Having spent much of the summer bolstering his attacking options, Reid may have felt that the squad could cope with the loss. However, French forwards Lilian Laslandes and David Bellion failed to make the impact expected of them and Reid was forced to rely on the stuttering front pairing of Phillips and veteran Niall Quinn for goals.

Former France international Laslandes was a particular disappointment. He arrived in the north east from Bordeaux with a £3.6 million price tag and a reputation as a neat finisher with a strong aerial game – factors which would seem to have earmarked him as Quinn's natural successor.

But after he had failed to score in his first five months in England, he was loaned out to FC Köln in Germany, where he endured another goalless spell. All in all, Laslandes attempted 13 shots in 2001–02 without scoring.

While Sunderland's attacking play often left their supporters disgruntled, the team were still able to grind out results with regularity. Reid's men became the first team to defeat Leeds in the league when they fought out an impressive 2–0 win at the Stadium of Light in November and throughout the campaign, the Black Cats managed to keep an impressive total of 11 clean sheets.

Indeed, after Sunderland had managed four shut-outs in five games in December, the club moved up into the top half of the table. The last of those games was a thrilling 3–0 win over Blackburn, which had the fans anticipating a push for a European place in the second half of the season.

But unfortunately Sunderland's campaign went downhill soon after, starting with a 5–0 drubbing at the hands of Ipswich in their next game.

The Black Cats went on to score only 12 goals in their final 19 league matches. That left them with a total of just 29 efforts for the 2001–02 campaign – an all-time Premiership low – which was perhaps unsurprising as they scored with only 7% of their shots – the worst conversion rate in the division.

Reid tried to halt the decline by bringing in internationals such as Jason McAteer, Claudio Reyna, Joachim Bjorklund and Patrick Mboma. But the team's poor form continued.

The manager admitted the issue when stating; "Our problem has been obvious: goals. No disrespect to the strikers, it has been a lack of goals throughout the team." But despite Reid's assertion, Sunderland's forwards managed only 18 goals all season – the lowest total of any strike force in the division.

With Phillips again being linked with a move away from the club and Quinn nearing retirement age, a major restructuring project will need to be undertaken if the Black Cats are to be competitive in the Premiership in the near future.

> **"There is no point disguising the fact that it has been a very disappointing and difficult season for everyone. We've all been there and we've all seen it."**
>
> **John Fickling**

SUNDERLAND

DATE	OPPONENT	SCORE	ATT.	ARCA	BELLION	BJORKLUND	BUTLER	CRADDOCK	GRAY	HAAS	HUTCHISON	KILBANE	KYLE	LASLANDES
18.08.01	Ipswich H	1–0	47,370	85	–	–	–	90	90	90	–	90	–	72
22.08.01	Fulham A	0–2	20,197	–	s15	–	–	90□	90	90	90	90	–	70
26.08.01	Newcastle A	1–1	52,021	–	s21	–	–	90	90	90□	69	90	–	–
08.09.01	Blackburn H	1–0	45,103	90□	–	–	–	90	90	90	–	s14	–	62
16.09.01	Aston Villa A	0–0	31,668	90	–	–	–	90	90	90□	–	90	–	s8
19.09.01	Tottenham H	1–2	47,310	90	–	–	–	90	90	90	–	78	–	s12
22.09.01	Charlton H	2–2	46,825	90	–	–	–	90	90	90□	–	–	–	90□
29.09.01	Bolton W A	2–0	24,520	90	–	–	–	90¹	90	–	–	90	–	–
13.10.01	Man Utd H	1–3	48,305	90	s45	–	–	90	90	–	–	45	–	–
22.10.01	Middlesbro A	0–2	28,432	90	s14	–	–	90	90	90	–	–	–	s1
27.10.01	Arsenal H	1–1	48,029	90	–	–	–	90□	90	75□	–	–	–	–
03.11.01	Leicester A	0–1	20,573	90□	–	–	–	83	90	90	–	–	–	–
18.11.01	Leeds Utd H	2–0	48,005	90¹	–	–	–	–	90	90	–	–	–	s21
25.11.01	Liverpool A	0–1	43,537	58	–	–	s32	–	90	90□	–	–	–	s14
01.12.01	West Ham H	1–0	47,437	90	–	–	s72□	–	90	90□	–	–	–	s32
09.12.01	Chelsea H	0–0	48,017	90□	–	–	–	–	90	–	–	90	–	68
15.12.01	Southampton A	0–2	29,459	–	–	–	–	90□	90	90	–	81	–	s23
22.12.01	Everton H	1–0	48,013	90	–	–	–	–	90	90	–	–	s11	–
26.12.01	Blackburn A	3–0	29,869	78	–	–	–	–	90	90	–	s12¹	s22□	–
29.12.01	Ipswich A	0–5	24,517	90	–	–	–	–	45	90	–	s45	s45	–
01.01.02	Aston Villa H	1–1	45,324	90	–	–	–	–	90	90	–	–	–	–
12.01.02	Everton A	0–1	30,736	45	s45	–	–	90	90	90□	–	90	–	–
19.01.02	Fulham H	1–1	45,124	–	–	–	–	90	90	90	–	90	–	–
29.01.02	Middlesbro H	0–1	44,579	s21	s9	–	–	90	90	81	–	90	–	–
02.02.02	Man Utd A	1–4	67,587	s45	–	90□	–	90	90	61	–	90	–	–
09.02.02	Derby Co A	1–0	31,771	80	s10	76	–	90	90	90	–	–	s4	–
24.02.02	Newcastle H	0–1	48,290	–	–	90	s20	90	90	90	–	90□	–	–
02.03.02	Tottenham A	1–2	36,062	–	–	59	–	90	90	90	–	90	–	–
05.03.02	Bolton W H	1–0	43,011	–	–	–	–	90	90	90	–	90	–	–
16.03.02	Chelsea A	0–4	40,218	–	s24	–	–	90	90	90	–	90	–	–
23.03.02	Southampton H	1–1	46,120	–	s45	–	–	90	90	–	–	61	–	–
30.03.02	Arsenal A	0–3	38,042	–	–	90	s45	90	90	–	–	s14	–	–
01.04.02	Leicester H	2–1	44,950	–	–	90	–	90	90□	–	–	90□	–	–
07.04.02	Leeds Utd A	0–2	39,195	–	s10	90	–	90	–	–	–	90	–	–
13.04.02	Liverpool H	0–1	48,335	–	–	90	–	80	–	–	–	90	s10	–
20.04.02	West Ham A	0–3	33,319	–	–	90□	s36	90	–	–	–	90	s32	–
27.04.02	Charlton A	2–2	26,614	–	–	90	90	90	77	–	–	90¹□	–	–
11.05.02	Derby Co H	1–1	47,989	–	–	90	90	90	90	–	–	90	–	–

□ Yellow card, ■ Red card, s Substitute, 90² Goals scored

For more information visit our website:

2001–02 PREMIERSHIP APPEARANCES

MACHO	MBOMA	McATEER	McCANN	McCARTNEY	PHILLIPS	QUINN	RAE	REYNA	SCHWARZ	SORENSEN	THIRLWELL	THOME	VARGA	WILLIAMS	TOTAL
–	–	–	90□	–	90¹	s18	s5	–	90	90	–	90	–	–	990
–	–	–	90	90□	90	s20	–	–	75	90	–	–	–	–	990
–	–	–	90□	–	90¹	90	s1	–	89	90	–	90	–	–	990
–	–	–	90	90□	90	s28¹	76	–	90	90	–	–	–	–	990
90	–	–	90□	90	90□	82	–	–	90□	–	–	–	–	–	990
90	–	–	90	57	90¹	90	–	–	90□	–	–	–	–	s33	990
90	–	–	90	–	90	90²	–	–	90	–	–	–	–	90	990
–	–	–	90□	–	90¹	90	–	–	90	90	–	–	90	90	990
–	–	–	–	–	90¹	90	–	–	90	90	90	–	90	90	990
–	–	90	90	–	90	89□	–	–	76□	90	–	–	90	–	990
–	–	90	77	–	90	s15	–	–	90¹□	90	–	90	90	s13	990
–	–	90□	90□	s7	90	s25	–	–	90	90	–	90	65	–	990
–	–	87	90	s3	90¹	69□	–	–	–	90	90	90	–	90	990
–	–	90□	90	s18	90	90	–	–	–	90	76	90□	–	72	990
–	–	18	90	–	90¹	58	–	–	–	90	90□	90	–	90	990
–	–	–	90	90	90	s22	–	–	–	90	90	90	–	90	990
–	–	90	90□	–	90	s9	–	90	–	90	67	–	–	90	990
–	–	90□	90	–	90	79	–	90¹	–	90	–	90	–	90	990
–	–	90	90	–	90	68²	–	90	–	90	–	90□	–	90	990
–	–	45	90	s45	90	45	–	90	–	90	–	90□	–	90	990
–	–	90	90	–	90	90	–	23	–	90	s67□	90¹	–	90	990
–	–	57	90	–	90	s33	–	–	–	90	90	–	90	–	990
–	–	90□	89	–	90¹	90	–	–	90□	90	–	–	90	s1□	990
–	–	69	–	–	90	90	–	90	90	90	–	–	90	–	990
90	–	61	–	s29	90¹	s29	–	90□	–	–	–	–	45□	90	990
–	–	90	–	–	90□	86¹	–	90	90	90	–	–	–	s14	990
–	s45	90□	–	–	90	45	–	90	70	90	–	–	–	–	990
–	73¹	90□	–	90	90	s17	–	54	s31	90	–	–	–	s36	990
–	89	90¹	–	90	90□	s1	–	–	90□	90	–	–	–	90	990
–	90	–	90	90□	–	s11	–	–	66	90	79	–	–	90□	990
–	84□	90¹	90□	45	90	s6	–	90	–	90	s29	–	–	90	990
–	21	45□	90□	–	76	s69	–	90□	–	90	90	–	–	90	990
–	–	90	90	–	90	90	–	85²	–	90	s5	–	–	90□	990
–	s45	90	90□	90	45	90	–	90	–	90	–	–	–	80	990
–	–	90	90	90	90	90	–	89□	–	90	–	–	–	90	989
–	–	–	90	90	72	58	–	90	s18□	90	54	–	–	90	990
–	s9	90□	–	s13	81¹	90□	–	–	–	90	90	–	–	90	990
–	s18	90	–	–	90¹	72	–	90	–	90	–	–	–	90	990

THE MANAGER

PETER REID

A fiery midfielder for Everton, Manchester City and England during his playing days, as a manager Peter Reid has always tried to get his sides to play a passionate style of football that reflects his personality.

He was handed his first coaching job at Maine Road in 1990 and as player-manager twice led City to fifth place in the top flight, before being surprisingly sacked in 1993. The club have not managed to reach those heights again in the years since Reid's departure.

Reid was eventually appointed as Sunderland manager in 1995 and has since been responsible for taking the club from the lower reaches of Division One to a place among English football's elite. During that time, he has enjoyed a period of unequivocal backing from the club's fans, board and players and guided the club to consecutive seventh place finishes in the Premiership in 1999–2000 and 2000–01.

But the team's decline in 2001–02 seemed to have a major impact on Reid's standing in the north east. For the first time in the manager's reign, there was discord among the supporters, with many fans calling for Reid's resignation during a campaign spent struggling against the drop.

LEAGUE POSITION

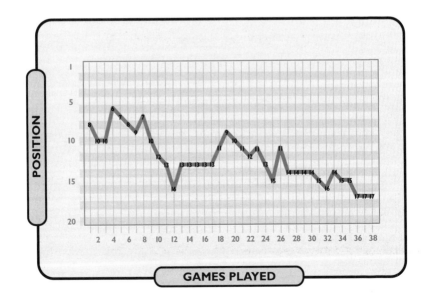

4 Sunderland players scored more own goals past

THE GOALS

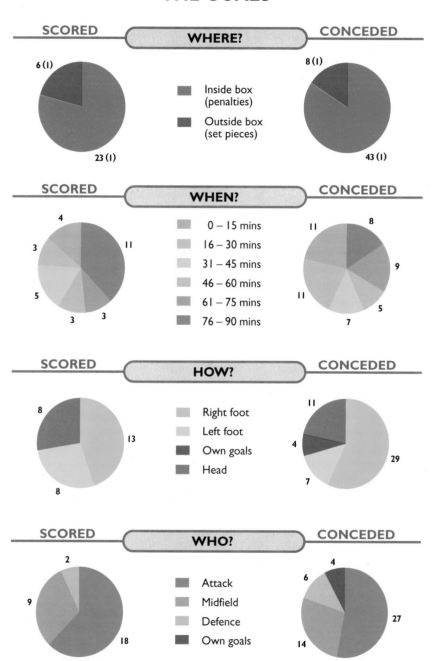

WHERE?
SCORED — CONCEDED

- Inside box (penalties)
- Outside box (set pieces)

SCORED: 6 (1), 23 (1)
CONCEDED: 8 (1), 43 (1)

WHEN?
SCORED — CONCEDED

- 0 – 15 mins
- 16 – 30 mins
- 31 – 45 mins
- 46 – 60 mins
- 61 – 75 mins
- 76 – 90 mins

SCORED: 4, 11, 3, 5, 3, 3
CONCEDED: 8, 11, 9, 11, 5, 7

HOW?
SCORED — CONCEDED

- Right foot
- Left foot
- Own goals
- Head

SCORED: 8, 13, 8, 8
CONCEDED: 11, 29, 7, 4

WHO?
SCORED — CONCEDED

- Attack
- Midfield
- Defence
- Own goals

SCORED: 2, 9, 18
CONCEDED: 4, 6, 27, 14

their goalkeeper than any other team

SUNDERLAND

	ARCA	BELLION	BJORKLUND	BUTLER	CRADDOCK	GRAY	HAAS	HUTCHISON	KILBANE	KYLE	LASLANDES
APPEARANCES											
Start	20	0	11	2	30	35	27	2	24	0	5
Sub	2	9	1	5	0	0	0	0	4	6	7
Minutes on pitch	1762	193	990	385	2683	3092	2377	159	2150	124	473
GOAL ATTEMPTS											
Goals	1	0	0	0	1	0	0	0	2	0	0
Shots on target	10	2	0	3	4	2	1	1	10	2	6
Shots off target	14	2	2	6	6	11	6	1	18	1	7
Shooting accuracy %	42%	50%	0%	33%	40%	15%	14%	50%	36%	67%	46%
Goals/shots %	4%	0%	0%	0%	10%	0%	0%	0%	7%	0%	0%
PASSING											
Goal assists	4	0	0	1	0	0	1	0	0	0	0
Long passes	174	11	58	40	398	505	271	8	131	7	27
Short passes	500	52	217	150	607	1235	856	53	665	34	120
PASS COMPLETION											
Own half %	74%	62%	77%	74%	78%	80%	79%	85%	82%	86%	69%
Opposition half %	67%	56%	50%	70%	56%	69%	67%	61%	64%	59%	61%
CROSSING											
Total crosses	161	22	0	24	3	175	75	3	113	4	11
Cross completion %	31%	18%	0%	29%	67%	21%	27%	67%	25%	25%	18%
DRIBBLING											
Dribbles & runs	120	30	5	44	13	159	74	9	145	2	3
Dribble completion %	61%	47%	100%	75%	85%	84%	66%	22%	54%	50%	67%
DEFENDING											
Tackles made	63	8	34	11	91	89	82	5	45	1	5
Tackles won %	81%	63%	91%	73%	76%	74%	82%	60%	84%	100%	60%
Blocks	6	0	13	0	43	26	16	1	8	0	1
Clearances	3	1	84	3	355	115	90	6	33	1	0
Interceptions	3	1	3	3	14	12	13	2	6	0	0
DISCIPLINE											
Fouls conceded	30	2	16	1	38	32	43	6	22	8	14
Fouls won	29	4	11	14	31	39	38	5	36	3	7
Offside	6	0	0	0	0	3	1	1	4	3	4
Yellow cards	3	0	2	1	3	1	7	0	3	1	1
Red cards	0	0	0	0	0	0	0	0	0	0	0

GOALKEEPER NAME	START/ (SUB)	TIME ON PITCH	GOALS CONCEDED	MINS/GOALS CONCEDED	SAVES MADE	SAVES/ SHOTS
MACHO	4 (0)	360	8	45	13	62%
SORENSEN	34 (0)	3060	43	71	105	71%

For more information visit our website:

PLAYERS' STATISTICS

	MBOMA	McATEER	McCANN	McCARTNEY	PHILLIPS	QUINN	RAE	REYNA	SCHWARZ	THIRLWELL	THOME	VARGA	WILLIAMS	TOTAL	RANK
	5	26	29	12	37	24	1	17	18	11	12	9	23		
	4	0	0	6	0	14	2	0	2	3	0	0	5		
	474	2092	2596	1117	3244	2224	82	1421	1595	1007	1080	740	2139		
	1	2	0	0	11	6	0	3	1	0	1	0	0	29	20th
	3	13	7	0	66	23	0	12	6	0	1	1	2	175	12th
	9	14	18	3	72	25	1	13	1	2	5	0	3	240	9th
	25%	48%	28%	0%	48%	48%	0%	48%	86%	0%	17%	100%	40%	42%	15th
	8%	7%	0%	0%	8%	13%	0%	12%	14%	0%	17%	0%	0%	7%	20th
	0	3	1	0	4	3	0	1	4	0	0	0	0	22	=16th
	22	274	362	190	200	76	25	206	180	108	193	142	308	4353	7th
	114	806	1087	330	842	706	32	600	503	390	296	205	648	11142	8th
	89%	84%	83%	80%	84%	71%	82%	83%	85%	84%	80%	86%	77%	80%	15th
	46%	72%	71%	63%	68%	60%	59%	75%	72%	80%	57%	69%	64%	66%	13th
	4	191	60	31	73	8	7	72	32	9	3	0	28	1109	3rd
	50%	30%	28%	16%	33%	25%	57%	22%	22%	11%	33%	0%	46%	27%	5th
	15	80	50	41	126	21	2	54	21	12	14	9	24	1075	10th
	53%	68%	54%	76%	71%	48%	50%	93%	76%	75%	100%	89%	88%	69%	7th
	6	67	160	51	22	14	3	39	89	57	39	27	72	1083	7th
	83%	79%	73%	78%	73%	79%	33%	64%	69%	70%	74%	81%	81%	76%	2nd
	0	9	13	12	0	6	1	7	4	5	10	6	30	217	10th
	6	32	44	90	1	29	2	11	12	18	123	85	138	1349	13th
	0	16	25	11	0	4	0	7	8	5	6	7	15	161	10th
	11	47	72	14	45	65	2	21	42	14	24	12	35	616	3rd
	8	31	29	17	66	64	3	21	21	1	19	4	26	538	12th
	7	3	0	0	72	33	0	1	0	0	0	0	1	139	=9th
	2	8	9	3	3	3	0	2	7	2	3	1	3	68	6th
	0	0	0	0	0	0	0	1	0	0	0	0	0	1	=18th

CROSSES CAUGHT	CROSSES PUNCHED	CROSSES DROPPED	CATCH SUCCESS	THROWS/ SHORT KICKS	% COMPLETION	LONG KICKS	% COMPLETION
6	0	1	86%	8	88%	75	63%
81	19	14	85%	73	95%	621	61%

PLAYER OF THE SEASON

PLAYER	INDEX SCORE
KEVIN PHILLIPS	859
Thomas Sorensen	741
Jody Craddock	734
Niall Quinn	683
Jason McAteer	679
Michael Gray	656
Darren Williams	568
Bernt Haas	564
Gavin McCann	533
Julio Arca	519

The 2001–02 campaign was not one Sunderland fans will look back on fondly. But despite a disappointing personal season, Kevin Phillips was certainly one of the key reasons why Peter Reid's side managed to avoid the drop.

Phillips scored crucial goals throughout 2001–02, including his 50th Premiership goal for the club against Leeds in November. Overall, the former Watford striker's efforts directly earned the club 10 points and without those, the Black Cats would have been relegated.

Indeed, while Phillips' goal tally of 11 was perhaps lower than would be expected of a player of his calibre, the fact that the figure constituted more than a third of the club's efforts for the season – 38% – showed how much Sunderland relied upon his predatory instincts.

Those skills saw Phillips fire 66 accurate shots on goal, which was more than he managed in the 1999–2000 campaign when he netted 30 times in the league. Phillips' total of 138 shots was also more than any other player in the Premiership managed in 2001–02.

The player Opta rated as Sunderland's best in 2000–01, Dane Thomas Sorensen, was again one of the club's most consistent performers in 2001–02. He was one of 11 Premiership 'keepers to make more than a century of saves, blocking 71% of the efforts fired at his goal. Sorensen's fine reflexes helped him keep 10 clean sheets – the equal sixth-highest total among Premiership 'keepers.

Other defensive players Jody Craddock, Michael Gray, Darren Williams and Bernt Haas also benefited from the team's fine defensive record to make Opta's Sunderland top 10.

Niall Quinn ranked in fourth place, having overcome fitness problems to fire six crucial goals, while fellow Irish international Jason McAteer made a promising start after moving from Blackburn, getting forward to send in 191 crosses for the Black Cats – more than any other player at the club.

FIVE OF THE BEST

If the 2000–01 campaign had been a season of underachievement for Sunderland, 2001–02 was one of great disappointment. Peter Reid's charges struggled to live up to their potential and the team's original aim of qualifying for European competition quickly changed to mere Premiership survival – a feat that was not achieved until the final day of the campaign.

TOP GOALSCORERS

	GOALS	GOALS/SHOTS
KEVIN PHILLIPS	11	8%
Niall Quinn	6	13%
Claudio Reyna	3	12%
Jason McAteer	2	7%
Kevin Kilbane	2	7%

Sunderland were the least prolific side in the Premiership in 2001–02, so the goals of Kevin Phillips became ever more crucial to the club's fortunes. The England international's 11 strikes were instrumental in helping the Black Cats avoid the drop, with strike partner Niall Quinn netting only six times in an inconsistent season. Unfortunately, no other player in the squad was able to score more than three league goals.

For the second consecutive season, club captain Michael Gray was the club's most prolific passer of the ball, as his bursts forward from left-back remained an integral part of the team's attacking play. Gray made a total of 1,274 successful passes, while newcomer Bernt Haas reached 813 on the opposite flank. Sandwiched between the two full-backs were midfielders Gavin McCann and Jason McAteer, who were both accurate with 76% of their distribution.

TOP PASSERS

	SUCC PASSES	COMPLETION
MICHAEL GRAY	1,274	73%
Gavin McCann	1,097	76%
Jason McAteer	818	76%
Bernt Haas	813	72%
Kevin Phillips	749	72%

TOP TACKLERS

	WON	SUCCESS
GAVIN McCANN	117	73%
Jody Craddock	69	76%
Bernt Haas	67	82%
Michael Gray	66	74%
Stefan Schwarz	61	69%

Battling midfielder Gavin McCann again finished the season with more than a century of tackles to his name and his total of 117 successful challenges was by far the highest figure at Sunderland. Despite his industrious performances, McCann slipped out of the England reckoning as Sunderland's poor form continued throughout the campaign. Swiss defender Haas marked his first season at Sunderland with an excellent 82% tackle success rate.

Sunderland picked up more Opta disciplinary points than any other side in 2000–01, but made a conscious effort to clean up their act in 2001–02, becoming the last side in the Premiership to receive a red card – Claudio Reyna receiving his marching orders against Liverpool as late as mid-April. Gavin McCann's tough-tackling nature resulted in him picking up nine bookings, illustrating why he ended the year as the club's most indisciplined player.

DISCIPLINE

	POINTS	FOULS & CARDS
GAVIN McCANN	99	72F, 9Y, 0R
Niall Quinn	74	65F, 3Y, 0R
Jason McAteer	71	47F, 8Y, 0R
Bernt Haas	64	43F, 7Y, 0R
Stefan Schwarz	63	42F, 7Y, 0R

TOTTENHAM HOTSPUR

ADDRESS

White Hart Lane, Bill Nicholson Way,
748 High Road, Tottenham,
London N17 0AP

CONTACT NUMBERS

Telephone: 020 8365 5000
Fax: 020 8365 5175
Spurs Ticketline: 08700 112222
Spurs Line: 09068 100 500
(all calls charged at 60p a minute)
Spurs Megastore: 020 8365 5042
e-mail: mail@spurs.co.uk
Website: www.spurs.co.uk

KEY PERSONNEL

Club President: Bill Nicholson OBE
Chairman: Daniel Levy
Executive Directors: D J Pleat (Football
Director), P L Viner (Finance Director),
P Z Kemsley (Property Director)
Non-Executive Directors: D Buchler
(Vice Chairman), M S Peters MBE
Club Secretary: John Alexander
Manager: Glenn Hoddle

SPONSORS

2001–02 Holsten
2002–03 Thomson Holidays

FANZINES

Cock A Doodle Doo
My Eyes Have Seen The Glory

COLOURS

Home: White shirts, navy shorts
and navy stockings
Away: Sky blue shirts, white shorts
and white stockings

NICKNAMES

Spurs

HONOURS

League Champions: 1950–51, 1960–61
Division Two Champions:
1919–20, 1949–50
FA Cup Winners: 1901, 1921, 1961,
1962, 1967, 1981, 1982, 1991
League Cup Winners: 1971, 1973, 1999
European Cup Winners' Cup Winners:
1963
UEFA Cup Winners: 1972, 1984

RECORD GOALSCORER

Jimmy Greaves –
220 league goals, 1961–70

BIGGEST WIN

13–2 v Crewe Alexandra – FA Cup 4th
round replay, 3 February 1960

BIGGEST DEFEAT

0–8 v Cologne – UEFA Intertoto Cup,
22 July 1995

SEASON REVIEW

Disappointment has become a way of life for Tottenham Hotspur fans in recent years. But the fact that Spurs supporters still felt the players had underachieved, despite their best Premiership finish in six years and reaching the Worthington Cup final, is surely a positive sign of the impact made by Glenn Hoddle.

Pre-season preparations had not started well. Sol Campbell's defection to arch-rivals Arsenal had the supporters seething and fans favourite Stephen Carr picked up an injury that was to keep him out for the entire campaign.

Some astute summer signings raised morale in the White Hart Lane crowd though, with Gus Poyet, Christian Ziege and Kasey Keller bringing some much-needed experience to the squad. Former favourite Teddy Sheringham returned from Manchester United as Player of the Year to become Hoddle's captain.

But fans still worried that without Campbell the defence would be lightweight. This fear was compounded just weeks into the season, when Gary Doherty was put out of action for seven months with a broken leg.

At that stage, Tottenham had won only one of their opening five league games. So, when Campbell's replacement Goran Bunjevcevic was also ruled out for the majority of the campaign days later, the board reluctantly shelled out £8.1m for Southampton's Dean Richards.

This appeared to give the club some measure of defensive stability, with Richards and Ledley King forming a fine understanding. Indeed, Spurs won three of their next four away matches – against West Ham, Newcastle and Sunderland – which was more than they managed in the entire 2000–01 campaign.

When Sheringham grabbed a late winner against Bolton at the start of December, Tottenham lay in fifth place – just two points behind second-placed Arsenal.

Hoddle certainly had Spurs playing some attractive football and with talented midfielders Simon Davies, Ziege and Darren Anderton providing dangerous deliveries, they were always a threat going forward. Overall, Tottenham were accurate with 28% of their crosses in 2001–02 and no Premiership side could better that figure.

Unfortunately, that was as good as it got. An inconsistent spell around the turn of the year saw Tottenham lose winnable matches against Charlton, Southampton and Ipswich (twice) to leave the club floundering in the mid-table mediocrity that has become so familiar to their supporters.

Up front, record signing Sergei Rebrov endured a torrid time, scoring just one Premiership goal all season and spending most of his time on the bench. The Ukrainian was not the only culprit though, as the whole team were accurate with just 39% of their shots – the worst figure in the league – meaning that much of their fine approach play went to waste.

Two exciting cup runs provided some respite. The Worthington Cup seemed to offer Spurs their most realistic route into European football and when they demolished Chelsea 5–1 in the semi-final second leg, most pundits made them favourites to win the final.

However, more poor finishing – particularly from Les Ferdinand – saw Blackburn Rovers take the trophy, while an embarrassing 4–0 defeat to Chelsea saw Spurs' FA Cup hopes disappear soon after.

Despite those setbacks, the season ended positively with the free transfer signings of Jamie Redknapp and Milenko Acimovic. With Carr and Doherty on the way back and the likes of Davies, King and Anthony Gardner all showing great promise, fans may see a clearer sign of Hoddle's grand scheme in the near future.

> **"We have felt there has been a resurgence of interest in the club and the type of football we are producing. Now we have to marry that success with wins on the field."**
>
> **David Pleat**

TOTTENHAM HOTSPUR

DATE	OPPONENT	SCORE	ATT.	ANDERTON	BUNJEVCEVIC	CLEMENCE	DAVIES	DOHERTY	ETHERINGTON	FERDINAND	FREUND	GARDNER	IVERSEN	KELLER
18.08.01	Aston Villa H	0–0	36,059	s23	90	90□	–	90□	–	22	67	–	s68	–
20.08.01	Everton A	1–1	29,503	90¹	90	s14	–	64■+	–	–	76	–	90	–
25.08.01	Blackburn A	1–2	24,992	86	–	7	s4	90	–	–	s83	–	90	–
09.09.01	Southampton H	2–0	33,668	80	90	–	90¹	90	–	90	90	–	–	–
16.09.01	Chelsea H	2–3	36,037	90	59	–	90	–	–	90□	85□	–	–	–
19.09.01	Sunderland A	2–1	47,310	82	–	–	90	–	–	69	90	–	–	–
22.09.01	Liverpool A	0–1	44,116	90	–	–	74	–	–	90	90□	–	–	–
29.09.01	Man Utd H	3–5	36,038	84	–	–	–	–	–	90¹	90□	–	–	–
15.10.01	Derby Co H	3–1	30,148	90	–	–	–	–	–	87¹	90	–	–	–
21.10.01	Newcastle A	2–0*	50,593	89	–	–	s40	–	–	79	90□	–	–	–
27.10.01	Middlesbro H	2–1	36,062	90	–	–	–	–	–	90¹	90	–	–	–
04.11.01	Leeds Utd A	1–2	40,203	90¹	–	–	s3	–	–	90	87	–	–	–
17.11.01	Arsenal H	1–1	36,049	90	–	–	s5	–	–	70□	85	–	–	–
24.11.01	West Ham A	1–0	32,780	90	–	–	90	–	–	90¹	90□	–	–	–
03.12.01	Bolton W H	3–2	32,971	90	s45	–	90	–	–	s45¹	45	–	–	–
08.12.01	Charlton A	1–3	25,125	90	45	–	67	–	–	–	–	–	s45	–
15.12.01	Fulham H	4–0	36,054	90¹	–	–	90¹	–	–	63¹□	90□	–	–	–
22.12.01	Ipswich H	1–2	36,040	90□	–	–	76¹	–	–	s22	90	s45	–	–
26.12.01	Southampton A	0–1	31,719	90	–	–	s14	–	–	90	71	76□	–	–
29.12.01	Aston Villa A	1–1	41,134	90	–	–	–	–	–	82¹□	90	s6	–	90
01.01.02	Blackburn H	1–0	35,131	90	–	–	–	–	–	90	90	–	–	90
12.01.02	Ipswich A	1–2	25,077	90	–	–	s45	–	s4	28	–	–	s62	–
19.01.02	Everton H	1–1	36,056	90	–	–	90	–	s14	45¹	–	90	s45	–
30.01.02	Newcastle H	1–3	35,798	90	–	–	70	–	s20	–	–	–	90¹	–
02.02.02	Derby Co A	0–1	27,721	s25	–	–	65	–	s45	–	–	–	90	–
09.02.02	Leicester H	2–1	35,973	90¹	–	–	90¹	–	90	83	–	–	90	–
02.03.02	Sunderland H	2–1	36,062	–	–	–	90	–	–	76¹	–	s1	–	–
06.03.02	Man Utd A	0–4	67,599	–	–	–	90	–	s4	s45	–	–	–	–
13.03.02	Chelsea A	0–4	39,652	–	–	–	90	–	–	81	–	s22	–	–
18.03.02	Charlton H	0–1	29,602	90	–	–	90	–	s16	45	–	90□	s45	–
24.03.02	Fulham A	2–0	15,885	75	–	–	s15	–	–	–	–	90□	90	–
30.03.02	Middlesbro A	1–1	31,258	78	–	–	s12	–	90	–	–	90	90¹	90
01.04.02	Leeds Utd H	2–1	35,167	62	–	s7	90	–	83□	–	–	90	90¹	90
06.04.02	Arsenal A	1–2	38,186	90	–	–	s45	–	s12	–	–	90	54	90
13.04.02	West Ham H	1–1	36,083	90	–	–	90	s6	–	–	–	90	s45	90
20.04.02	Bolton W A	1–1	25,817	90	–	–	90	s5	–	–	–	90□	45¹□	90
27.04.02	Liverpool H	1–0	36,017	90	–	90	90	–	–	–	–	90	90	90
11.05.02	Leicester A	1–2	21,716	90	–	74	71	s16	s19	–	–	90	90	90

□ Yellow card, ■ Red card, s Substitute, 90² Goals scored

*including own goal, + card rescinded

For more information visit our website:

2001–02 PREMIERSHIP APPEARANCES

KING	LEONHARDSEN	PERRY	POYET	REBROV	RICHARDS	SHERINGHAM	SHERWOOD	SULLIVAN	TARICCO	THATCHER	THELWELL	ZIEGE	TOTAL
90	–	s9	90	90	–	–	–	90	81	–	–	90□	990
90	–	–	66□	–	–	90□	–	90	90	–	–	90□	940
90	–	90	90	s23	–	90	–	90	67□	–	–	90¹	990
90	s10	–	–	–	–	90	–	90	90	–	–	90¹	990
90	–	90	–	s5	–	90²	–	90	90	–	s31	90	990
90	s8	90□	90	s21	–	90¹	–	90	90	–	–	90¹□	990
90	–	90	90	s16	–	90	–	90	90	–	–	90	990
90	–	90□	90□	s6	90¹	90	–	90	90	–	–	90¹	990
90	–	90	90¹	s3	90	90	–	90	90	–	–	90¹	990
90	–	90	90¹	s11	90	90	s1	90	50	–	–	90	990
90	–	90	90	–	90	90¹	–	90	75	s15	–	90	990
90	–	90	87¹	s3	90	90□	–	90	90	–	–	90□	990
90	–	90	90¹	s20	90	90□	–	90	90	–	–	90	990
90	s37	90□	53	–	90	90	–	90	–	–	–	90	990
90	s2	45	90¹	88	90	90¹	–	90	–	–	–	90	990
90	–	90	90¹	90	90	90	s23	90	90□	–	–	–	990
90	–	90□	90	s27¹	90	90	–	90	90	–	–	–	990
90	–	45	s14	68	90	54□	–	90	90	–	–	90	954
90	–	–	87	s3	90□	90	s19	90	90□	–	–	90	990
90	–	90	90	s8	90□	90	–	–	90	–	–	84□	990
90	–	90	85	–	90¹	90	s5	–	90	–	–	90	990
90	–	90	90¹□	90	90	–	90	90	86	–	–	45	990
–	76	90	–	s3	90	90	90	90	87	–	–	–	990
90	s3	90	87	s3	90□	87	90	90	90	–	–	–	990
90	90	90	90	s10	90	90	80□	90	45□	–	–	–	990
90	–	–	–	s7	90	–	90	90	90	66	s24	–	990
90	–	–	90¹	s14	90	90	90	90	89	90	–	90	990
90	–	s24	66□	45	90	90	90□	90	41□	90	–	86□	941
90	–	s45□	90	s9	45	90	90□	90	59□	68□	–	90	959
90	–	90	90	74	–	–	90	90	–	–	–	90	990
90	–	90	90¹	–	–	90¹	90□	90	–	90	–	90	990
90	–	90□	90□	72	–	s18	90	–	–	90□	–	–	990
–	–	90	s28	s2	90	88¹	90	–	–	90□	–	–	990
45	–	90□	90□	s36	90	90¹□	90□	–	–	–	–	78	990
–	–	90	90	45	–	90¹	90	–	–	90	–	84	990
–	–	90□	90	s40	–	90	90	–	90	90	–	–	990
–	–	90□	90¹	–	–	90	–	–	90	90	–	–	990
–	–	90	90	–	–	90¹	–	–	90	90	–	–	990

THE MANAGER

GLENN HODDLE

In his first full season in charge at Tottenham, Glenn Hoddle's attempts to bring the glory days back to White Hart Lane met with mixed results.

The former England international's memorable playing career at the club saw him win a host of individual accolades, while Spurs also went through a period of considerable success winning the UEFA Cup in 1984 and the FA Cup twice. But as a manager, Hoddle's achievements have been more varied.

He would point to the fact that he made a positive impact at each of his postings. In club football, Hoddle guided Swindon to the Premiership for the first time in their history, he put Chelsea back on the footballing map and was also the most successful post-war manager at Southampton, in terms of percentage of games won in the top flight.

On the international scene, Hoddle also achieved some notable results after being made England manager in 1996. His exciting side won Le Tournoi in 1997 and then acquitted themselves well at the World Cup a year later before Hoddle resigned amid controversy in 1999.

However, after missing out on the Worthington Cup in 2002, Hoddle has now gone more than a decade as a manager without picking up a major trophy.

LEAGUE POSITION

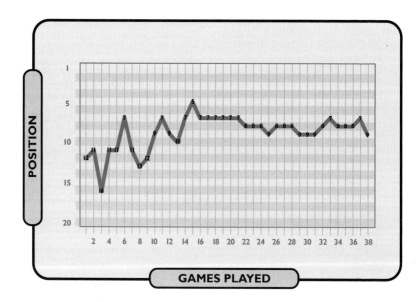

70% of the goals Tottenham conceded came in the

THE GOALS

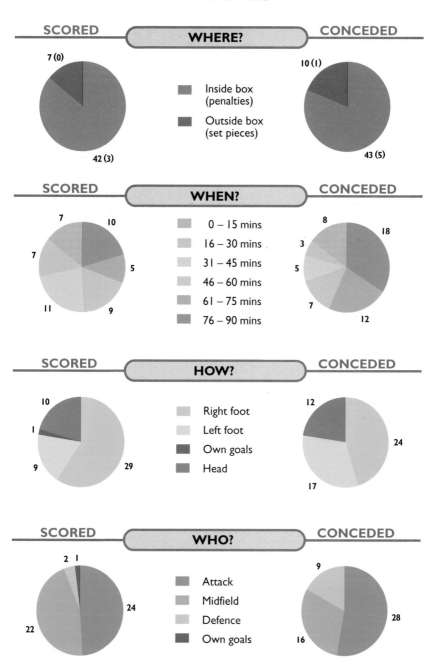

WHERE?

SCORED — CONCEDED

- Inside box (penalties)
- Outside box (set pieces)

Scored: 7 (0), 42 (3)
Conceded: 10 (1), 43 (5)

WHEN?

SCORED — CONCEDED

- 0 – 15 mins
- 16 – 30 mins
- 31 – 45 mins
- 46 – 60 mins
- 61 – 75 mins
- 76 – 90 mins

Scored: 7, 10, 7, 5, 11, 9
Conceded: 8, 18, 3, 5, 7, 12

HOW?

SCORED — CONCEDED

- Right foot
- Left foot
- Own goals
- Head

Scored: 10, 1, 9, 29
Conceded: 12, 24, 17

WHO?

SCORED — CONCEDED

- Attack
- Midfield
- Defence
- Own goals

Scored: 2, 1, 24, 22
Conceded: 9, 28, 16

second half – the highest proportion in the Premiership

TOTTENHAM HOTSPUR

	ANDERTON	BUNJEVCEVIC	CLEMENCE	DAVIES	DOHERTY	ETHERINGTON	FERDINAND	FREUND	GARDNER
APPEARANCES									
Start	33	5	4	22	4	3	22	19	11
Sub	2	1	2	9	3	8	3	1	4
Minutes on pitch	2934	419	282	2046	361	397	1752	1679	1050
GOAL ATTEMPTS									
Goals	3	0	0	4	0	0	9	0	0
Shots on target	8	0	1	9	0	4	19	1	2
Shots off target	16	3	3	12	1	2	30	7	5
Shooting accuracy %	33%	0%	25%	43%	0%	67%	39%	13%	29%
Goals/shots %	13%	0%	0%	19%	0%	0%	18%	0%	0%
PASSING									
Goal assists	5	1	0	3	0	1	2	0	0
Long passes	639	66	38	164	29	20	76	189	112
Short passes	1402	125	116	726	86	140	576	659	246
PASS COMPLETION									
Own half %	83%	91%	86%	82%	88%	85%	81%	83%	79%
Opposition half %	73%	70%	80%	71%	72%	71%	68%	78%	67%
CROSSING									
Total crosses	277	6	1	60	1	21	5	27	9
Cross completion %	30%	33%	0%	27%	100%	24%	80%	30%	11%
DRIBBLING									
Dribbles & runs	77	13	6	155	5	43	45	18	19
Dribble completion %	60%	92%	83%	52%	60%	58%	67%	83%	84%
DEFENDING									
Tackles made	134	11	10	62	17	7	29	49	44
Tackles won %	67%	64%	70%	71%	76%	57%	72%	71%	77%
Blocks	15	3	2	4	5	1	1	10	17
Clearances	24	45	11	19	52	3	15	45	126
Interceptions	13	2	2	7	0	1	0	8	6
DISCIPLINE									
Fouls conceded	40	1	4	21	12	7	49	39	19
Fouls won	24	7	9	19	4	5	36	21	9
Offside	0	0	0	5	0	0	28	1	0
Yellow cards	1	0	1	0	1	1	4	6	4
Red cards	0	0	0	0	1+	0	0	0	0

+ one card rescinded

GOALKEEPER NAME	START/ (SUB)	TIME ON PITCH	GOALS CONCEDED	MINS/GOALS CONCEDED	SAVES MADE	SAVES/ SHOTS
KELLER	9 (0)	810	9	90	40	82%
SULLIVAN	29 (0)	2610	44	59	104	70%

For more information visit our website:

PLAYERS' STATISTICS

	IVERSEN	KING	LEONHARDSEN	PERRY	POYET	REBROV	RICHARDS	SHERINGHAM	SHERWOOD	TARICCO	THATCHER	THELWELL	ZIEGE	TOTAL	RANK
	12	32	2	30	32	9	24	33	15	30	11	0	27		
	6	0	5	3	2	21	0	1	4	0	1	2	0		
	1309	2835	226	2688	2823	932	2115	2947	1388	2480	959	55	2357		
	4	0	0	0	10	1	2	10	0	0	0	0	5	49*	8th
	17	1	2	0	27	11	7	40	1	2	1	0	13	166	=13th
	19	7	1	0	49	13	12	50	4	7	1	0	22	264	3rd
	47%	13%	67%	0%	36%	46%	37%	44%	20%	22%	50%	0%	37%	39%	20th
	11%	0%	0%	0%	13%	4%	11%	11%	0%	0%	0%	0%	14%	11%	11th
	1	0	1	0	4	3	1	3	0	1	1	0	6	33	=10th
	49	332	20	325	238	55	251	313	351	288	119	8	268	4421	5th
	361	871	77	611	1102	328	480	1428	662	865	212	17	667	11840	6th
	84%	81%	75%	81%	82%	80%	82%	86%	84%	81%	76%	88%	79%	82%	12th
	67%	71%	75%	62%	70%	74%	64%	71%	75%	74%	61%	78%	61%	70%	4th
	30	17	8	7	31	31	4	39	24	104	13	0	213	928	11th
	43%	29%	25%	14%	23%	29%	25%	15%	29%	28%	15%	0%	25%	28%	2nd
	21	63	6	12	43	19	13	31	23	63	13	1	67	764	20th
	71%	95%	83%	100%	70%	79%	85%	68%	91%	81%	85%	100%	79%	72%	3rd
	9	92	8	137	75	17	62	33	58	72	34	1	109	1071	8th
	78%	80%	25%	71%	69%	71%	74%	67%	72%	76%	79%	100%	78%	73%	18th
	3	49	0	38	13	0	34	7	10	21	17	1	16	267	4th
	19	236	1	268	58	3	276	12	50	87	92	10	69	1616	3rd
	0	17	0	25	10	3	17	3	11	11	9	0	17	162	9th
	10	15	7	36	43	22	31	36	22	44	13	2	41	514	18th
	22	39	5	36	54	24	34	45	12	50	8	0	12	484	19th
	16	1	2	0	6	15	0	29	0	1	0	0	6	110	18th
	1	0	0	9	6	0	3	4	5	4	3	0	6	59	=9th
	0	0	0	0	1	0	0	1	0	2	0	0	0	5	=4th

*Including one own goal

CROSSES CAUGHT	CROSSES PUNCHED	CROSSES DROPPED	CATCH SUCCESS	THROWS/ SHORT KICKS	% COMPLETION	LONG KICKS	% COMPLETION
36	5	1	97%	16	100%	236	48%
49	10	3	94%	75	97%	568	55%

PLAYER OF THE SEASON

PLAYER	INDEX SCORE
TEDDY SHERINGHAM	811
Gustavo Poyet	803
Dean Richards	776
Neil Sullivan	764
Christian Ziege	764
Les Ferdinand	742
Darren Anderton	708
Chris Perry	706
Ledley King	694
Simon Davies	608

If Glenn Hoddle's appointment as Tottenham manager was the return of the Messiah, the homecoming of favoured acolyte Teddy Sheringham proved to be just as popular among the fans at N17.

After four supremely successful seasons at Manchester United, Sheringham returned to White Hart Lane to lead Hoddle's troops in 2001–02. The England international fired 10 league goals, while he also netted a further three strikes in cup competitions.

However, the most crucial goal of Sheringham's season came while playing for England. Coming off the bench in the World Cup qualifier against Greece, the veteran scored the fastest substitute goal in international history after six seconds on the pitch to help secure England's passage to the Far East.

Former Chelsea hero Gustavo Poyet also made an instant impact after his switch from Stamford Bridge, finishing as the club's joint-top scorer in the Premiership along with Sheringham.

Another new signing, Dean Richards, proved that Hoddle's faith in his abilities was not unfounded. Despite only joining Spurs at the end of September, the powerful defender finished the campaign with 276 defensive clearances – more than any other Tottenham player.

Hoddle can also take great credit for Darren Anderton's resurrection as a Premiership force. The injury-prone midfielder's famed familiarity with the White Hart Lane treatment room had many fans writing him off as a spent force.

But crucially, Anderton made 35 league appearances in 2001–02 – more than he had made in any of the previous six campaigns – and his cultured performances in the centre of the Spurs midfield seemed to epitomise the style and flair that Hoddle promised to bring back to the Lane.

Youngsters Ledley King and Simon Davies also made great strides, with both players earning regular first-team places as well as gaining international recognition with England and Wales respectively.

FIVE OF THE BEST

With Glenn Hoddle's restructuring plan still in its early stages, the 2001–02 campaign was always going to be one of transition for Tottenham Hotspur. The team produced some promising performances, most notably in cup competitions, but inconsistency continued to blight Spurs' progress and they were unable to maximise their potential.

TOP GOALSCORERS

	GOALS	GOALS/SHOTS
GUSTAVO POYET	10	13%
Teddy Sheringham	10	11%
Les Ferdinand	9	18%
Christian Ziege	5	14%
Simon Davies	4	19%

While Gustavo Poyet and Teddy Sheringham were Tottenham's top scorers in the Premiership, Les Ferdinand was by far the club's deadliest striker. The former England man scored with 18% of his shots and would surely have ended 2001–02 with more than nine goals, had injury not curtailed his season in March. Honourable mentions go to Christian Ziege and Simon Davies, who both got forward to score with some regularity, despite usually playing as wing-backs.

One of the most positive aspects of Spurs' season in 2001–02 was the re-emergence of Darren Anderton. Persuaded to sign an extended contract in the summer, the England international went on to become a crucial player for Spurs, making 1,557 successful passes – the eighth-highest figure in the Premiership. Germany international Christian Ziege's injury woes meant that he did not figure in Tottenham's top five, but he still managed to set up a club-high total of six goals.

TOP PASSERS

	SUCC PASSES	COMPLETION
DARREN ANDERTON	1,557	76%
Teddy Sheringham	1,320	76%
Gustavo Poyet	987	74%
Ledley King	909	76%
Mauricio Taricco	879	76%

TOP TACKLERS

	WON	SUCCESS
CHRIS PERRY	97	71%
Darren Anderton	90	67%
Christian Ziege	85	78%
Ledley King	74	80%
Mauricio Taricco	55	76%

Chris Perry finished the 2001–02 campaign as Tottenham's top tackler for the third season in a row since joining the club from Wimbledon. By winning 90 challenges, Darren Anderton proved that he was back to his competitive best after so many years plagued with fitness problems, while promising young defender Ledley King was arguably the most improved player of the year, winning a club-high 80% of his tackles.

Mauricio Taricco hit the headlines for the wrong reasons in March 2002, when he was sent off in consecutive fixtures against Chelsea and Manchester United. Many fans felt that the Argentine received his just desserts, after escaping punishment for an horrific challenge on Everton's Thomas Gravesen earlier in the season. Gus Poyet was controversially dismissed in that clash against Everton though, meaning his disciplinary record was Spurs' second worst behind Taricco's.

DISCIPLINE

	POINTS	FOULS & CARDS
MAURICIO TARICCO	68	44F, 4Y, 2R
Gustavo Poyet	67	43F, 6Y, 1R
Chris Perry	63	36F, 9Y, 0R
Les Ferdinand	61	49F, 4Y, 0R
Christian Ziege	59	41F, 6Y, 0R

WEST HAM UNITED

ADDRESS

Boleyn Ground, Green Street,
Upton Park, London E13 9AZ

CONTACT NUMBERS

Telephone: 020 8548 2748
Fax: 020 8548 2758
Ticket Office: 020 8548 2700
HammersLine: 0906 586 1966
(calls cost 60p per minute)
Club Merchandise: 020 8548 2722
Website: www.whufc.com

KEY PERSONNEL

Chairman: Terence Brown
Vice-Chairman: Martin Cearns
Directors: Terence Brown,
Martin Cearns, Paul Aldridge (Managing),
Charles Warner, Nick Igoe
Football Secretary: Peter Barnes
Manager: Glenn Roeder

SPONSORS

Dr Martens

FANZINES

On The Terraces
On A Mission
Over Land And Sea

COLOURS

Home: Claret shirts with sky blue
sleeves, white shorts and white
stockings
Away: Sky blue shirts, sky blue shorts
and sky blue stockings

NICKNAMES

The Hammers
The Irons

HONOURS

Division Two Champions:
1957–58, 1980–81
FA Cup Winners: 1964, 1975, 1980
European Cup Winners' Cup Winners:
1964–65

RECORD GOALSCORER

Vic Watson – 298 league goals, 1920–35

BIGGEST WIN

10–0 v Bury – League Cup 2nd round
2nd leg, 25 October 1983

BIGGEST DEFEAT

2–8 v Blackburn Rovers – Division One,
26 December 1963

SEASON REVIEW

A new era dawned on West Ham United in the summer of 2001 as former first-team coach Glenn Roeder became the club's new manager. He replaced the popular figure of Harry Redknapp, who left the club at the tail end of the 2000–01 campaign.

Despite the likes of Steve McClaren and Alan Curbishley being linked with the vacant managerial position, the club eventually promoted from within and gave Roeder his first managerial role for five years since he was sacked by Watford.

And within a few weeks of the start of the new season, there were calls for the Hammers' board to dispense with Roeder's services. This followed a disastrous start to the campaign, which saw the team drop into the bottom three after two heavy away defeats at Everton and Blackburn.

In fact, bookmakers stopped taking bets on Roeder getting the sack, but he defended himself by saying: "I hope I will be given the chance and the time – but whether it is me or someone else, they won't have a magic wand to turn it around straight away."

The 2–0 win over Southampton in late October was enough to save his skin, but resulted in his opposite number Stuart Gray being forced to walk the plank.

The following weekend, the Hammers claimed their first away win for eight months as they defeated Ipswich Town in front of the live television cameras. The victory was also memorable for Jermain Defoe's first-ever Premiership goal.

Stand-in striker Paul Kitson then took centre-stage with a thrilling hat-trick at Charlton, but it was not enough to give the team all three points. The Addicks snatched a draw thanks to a spectacular

> **"The dust has hardly settled on this season and already the speculation has started. It is a back-handed compliment, I suppose."**
>
> **Glenn Roeder**

90th-minute equaliser through Jonatan Johansson's bicycle kick.

Tottenham's visit to Upton Park coincided with the opening of the new Dr. Martens Stand and the first appearance of Opta Index's Hammer of the year, David James. An injury sustained playing for England before the season had started delayed James' debut between the sticks for three months. However it was not the best of starts for the goalkeeper as a Les Ferdinand tap-in gave the visitors maximum points.

But a fortnight later James was celebrating his first win for the club – at Old Trafford of all places. Defoe upstaged all the attacking talent on the pitch by leaping like a salmon to head past Fabien Barthez.

Into 2002 and the Hammers gained revenge for that 7–1 drubbing at Ewood Park in October with a 2–0 win over Blackburn. But four days later, the club suffered what was to be their biggest disappointment of 2001–02, when they lost 3–2 to Chelsea in an FA Cup fourth round replay at Upton Park.

Manchester United's visit to Upton Park in March was one of the most exciting games of the season. Unfortunately for the Hammers the visitors triumphed by five goals to three.

However, the team responded well with 13 points out of a possible 15 in their next five games and striker Frédéric Kanouté put it down to the new regime. He said, "It is definitely more professional now. A lot of things have changed."

A 2–1 win over Bolton on the final day of the season ensured Roeder's work was rewarded with the Hammers ending the campaign in seventh spot – above rivals Tottenham – for the third-highest finish in the club's history.

WEST HAM UNITED

DATE	OPPONENT	SCORE	ATT.	BYRNE	CAMARA	CARRICK	COLE	COURTOIS	DAILLY	DEFOE	DI CANIO	FOXE	GARCIA	HISLOP	HUTCHISON
18.08.01	Liverpool A	1–2	43,935	–	–	90	79	s11	90□	s18	90¹□	–	–	90	–
25.08.01	Leeds Utd H	0–0	24,517	–	–	90	90	–	90	s20	90	–	–	90	–
08.09.01	Derby Co A	0–0	27,802	–	–	90	85	–	90□	s10	80	–	–	90	90□
15.09.01	Middlesbro A	0–2	25,445	–	–	90□	90	–	90	s45	–	–	–	90	90
23.09.01	Newcastle H	3–0	28,840	–	–	90	–	87	90	s7	90¹	–	–	90	90¹
29.09.01	Everton A	0–5	32,049	s13	–	90	–	77	90	–	90	–	–	90	90
14.10.01	Blackburn A	1–7	22,712	–	–	90¹	–	–	45	–	90□	s45	–	90	90
20.10.01	Southampton H	2–0	25,842	–	–	90	–	86	90	–	90	–	–	90	90
24.10.01	Chelsea H	2–1	26,520	–	–	90¹	–	45	90	s45	90	–	–	90	90
28.10.01	Ipswich A	3–2	22,834	–	–	90□	–	–	90	s2¹	88¹	90	–	90	90
03.11.01	Fulham H	0–2	26,217	–	–	90	–	61	90	s29	90	90□	–	90	90
19.11.01	Charlton A	4–4	23,198	–	–	90	s27	–	90	s12¹	90	90	–	90	63
24.11.01	Tottenham H	0–1	32,780	–	–	–	90□	–	90	90	–	–	–	90	–
01.12.01	Sunderland A	0–1	47,437	–	–	90	79	–	90	90	–	–	–	90	–
05.12.01	Aston Villa A	1–1	28,377	–	–	90	90	–	90	90¹	90□	–	–	90	90
08.12.01	Man Utd A	0–1	67,582	–	s6	90	90	–	90	84¹	90□	–	–	90□	–
15.12.01	Arsenal H	1–1	34,523	–	–	90□	90□	–	90	s45	90□	–	–	90	–
22.12.01	Leicester A	1–1	20,131	–	–	90	90□	–	90	88	90¹	–	–	90	–
26.12.01	Derby Co H	4–0	31,397	–	–	90	90	–	90	s16¹	89¹	–	–	90	–
29.12.01	Liverpool H	1–1	35,103	–	–	90	90	–	90	90	–	–	–	90	–
01.01.02	Leeds Utd A	0–3	39,320	–	–	–	90	–	90	75	–	–	s7	90	–
12.01.02	Leicester H	1–0	34,698	–	–	–	90	–	90□	s19	90¹	s5	–	90	–
20.01.02	Chelsea A	1–5	40,035	–	–	90	90	s25	90	s10¹	70□	–	–	90	–
30.01.02	Southampton A	0–2	31,879	–	–	45	90	–	90	s24	90	–	–	66□	–
02.02.02	Blackburn H	2–0	35,307	–	–	90	90	–	90	s18	90	–	–	58	–
09.02.02	Bolton W A	0–1	24,342	–	–	–	90	–	90	90	–	90□	77	–	–
23.02.02	Middlesbro H	1–0	35,420	–	–	90□	–	–	90	90	–	–	s2	–	41
02.03.02	Aston Villa A	1–2	37,341	–	–	90	–	–	90	90	90¹	–	67	–	–
06.03.02	Everton H	1–0	29,883	–	–	–	90	–	90	s6	90	–	s9	–	–
16.03.02	Man Utd H	3–5	35,281	–	–	90	90	–	90	s16¹	90	–	–	–	–
30.03.02	Ipswich H	3–1	33,871	–	–	90	90	–	90	s14¹	89¹	–	–	–	–
01.04.02	Fulham A	1–0	19,416	–	–	90	90	–	90□	s5	67	–	–	–	–
06.04.02	Charlton H	2–0	32,389	–	–	90	89	–	90	s20	70¹	–	–	–	–
13.04.02	Tottenham A	1–1	36,083	–	–	90	–	–	90	90	–	–	–	–	–
20.04.02	Sunderland H	3–0	33,319	–	–	90	90	–	90	80¹	–	–	s10	–	–
24.04.02	Arsenal A	0–2	38,038	–	–	90□	90	–	90	s11	–	–	–	–	–
27.04.02	Newcastle A	1–3	52,127	–	–	90	90	–	90	90¹	–	–	s7	–	–
11.05.02	Bolton W H	2–1	35,546	–	–	89	90□	–	90	90	–	–	s1	–	–

□ Yellow card, ■ Red card, s Substitute, 90² Goals scored

For more information visit our website:

2001-02 PREMIERSHIP APPEARANCES

JAMES	KANOUTE	KITSON	LABANT	LOMAS	McCANN	MINTO	MONCUR	PEARCE	REPKA	SCHEMMEL	SINCLAIR	SOMA	SONG	TODOROV	WINTERBURN	TOTAL
–	–	–	–	–	s20	–	70□	–	–	90	90□	–	90	72□	90	990
–	–	–	–	–	s6	–	84□	–	–	90	90	–	90□	70□	90	990
–	54	–	–	–	–	–	s5	–	–	90	90	–	90	s36	90	990
–	–	–	–	–	–	–	64	–	79□	90	90	s8	45	s26	82□	979
–	83[1]	–	–	–	–	–	s3□	–	90	90□	90	–	–	–	90□	990
–	79	s11	–	–	–	–	–	–	–	90	90	s26	90	–	64	990
–	90□	–	–	–	s45	–	45□	–	61□	90	90	90	–	–	–	961
–	90[2]	–	–	–	–	–	s4	–	90	90	90	–	–	–	90	990
–	81[1]	s9	–	–	–	–	–	–	–	90	90	–	–	–	90	990
–	90[1]	–	–	–	–	90	–	–	–	90	90	–	–	–	90□	990
–	90	–	–	–	–	–	–	–	–	90	90	–	–	–	90	990
–	–	78[3]	–	s27	–	63□	–	–	90	90□	90	–	–	–	–	990
90	–	90	–	53	–	90	s37□	–	90	90	90	–	–	–	–	990
90	–	90	–	–	–	89	s11	–	90	90	90	–	–	s1	–	990
90	–	–	–	–	–	–	–	–	90	90	90	–	–	–	90□	990
90	–	–	–	–	–	–	–	–	90	90□	90	–	–	–	90	990
90	45[1]	–	–	–	–	–	–	–	90□	90	90	–	–	–	90	990
90	–	s2	–	–	–	–	–	–	90	90	90□	–	–	–	90	990
90	74	–	–	–	–	–	s1	–	90□	90[1]	90[1]	–	–	–	90	990
90	90	–	–	–	–	–	–	–	90	90	90[1]□	–	–	–	90	990
90	83□	–	–	–	–	90	–	–	90□	90	90	–	–	s15	90	990
90	71	–	–	–	–	85	–	–	90	90	90	–	–	–	90	990
90	80	–	–	–	–	–	–	–	90	90	65□	–	–	–	90	970
90	90	–	90	90	–	–	s45□	–	90□	90	–	–	–	–	–	990
90	72[1]	–	s32	90	–	–	s3	–	90	90□	87[1]□	–	–	–	90	990
90	90□	s13	90	90□	–	90	–	–	–	90	–	–	–	–	–	990
90	90[1]	–	s49□	88	–	–	90	90	90	–	–	–	–	–	90	990
90	–	–	s23	–	–	–	–	90□	90	90	90	–	–	–	90	990
90	84	–	90	–	–	–	–	90	90	81	90[1]	–	–	–	90	990
90	90[1]	–	90	90[1]	–	–	–	–	90□	90□	–	–	–	–	74	990
90	76	–	–	90[1]	–	–	s1	–	90	90	90	–	–	–	90	990
90	85[1]	–	23	90	–	–	s23	s67	90	90	90	–	–	–	–	990
90	90[1]	–	–	90□	–	–	s1	–	90	90	90	–	–	–	90	990
90	90	–	60	90	–	–	–	90[1]	90	90	90	–	–	–	s30	990
90	–	–	s5	90[1]	–	–	–	90□	90□	85□	90[1]	–	–	–	90	990
90	79	–	s73	90□	–	–	–	90	90	17	90	–	–	–	90	990
90	90□	–	83	90	–	–	–	90□	90	–	72	–	–	–	s18	990
90	89	–	–	90[1]	–	–	s1	90[1]	90□	–	90	–	–	–	90	990

THE MANAGER

GLENN ROEDER

When Glenn Roeder was promoted from first-team coach to West Ham manager in June 2001, he described it as the proudest day of his life. The east Londoner, who grew up supporting the Hammers, said: "When Harry Redknapp brought me in to join the coaching staff, I never dreamed that I would be his successor."

However, not many fans were pleased with the decision as they were expcting a big-name appointment, not a man whose managerial credentials to date included unspectacular spells at Gillingham and Watford, where he was sacked in 1996. And many pundits were soon tipping West Ham for the drop.

But after a shaky start to the campaign that saw the team slip into the bottom two, Roeder soon managed to turn the season around with three consecutive wins in late October and the side were never in danger after that.

Roeder, who was part of the England coaching set-up under Glenn Hoddle, was initially handed a one-year deal, given his inexperience at the top level. But he was soon rewarded with a three-year extension to his contract, tying him to Upton Park until the end of the 2004–05 campaign.

LEAGUE POSITION

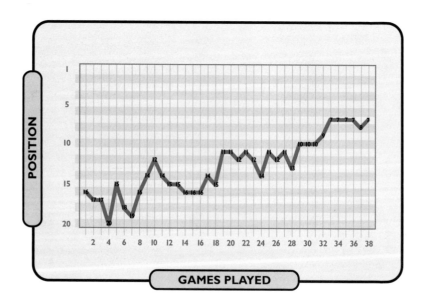

POSITION

GAMES PLAYED

6 Jermain Defoe scored more goals coming off the

THE GOALS

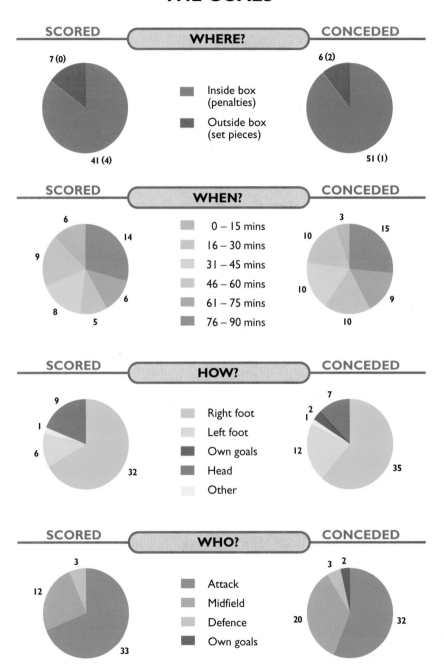

SCORED — **WHERE?** — **CONCEDED**

7 (0)
41 (4)

6 (2)
51 (1)

- Inside box (penalties)
- Outside box (set pieces)

SCORED — **WHEN?** — **CONCEDED**

6
14
9
6
8
5

3
15
10
10
9
10

- 0 – 15 mins
- 16 – 30 mins
- 31 – 45 mins
- 46 – 60 mins
- 61 – 75 mins
- 76 – 90 mins

SCORED — **HOW?** — **CONCEDED**

9
1
6
32

7
2
1
12
35

- Right foot
- Left foot
- Own goals
- Head
- Other

SCORED — **WHO?** — **CONCEDED**

3
12
33

3
2
20
32

- Attack
- Midfield
- Defence
- Own goals

WEST HAM UNITED

	BYRNE	CAMARA	CARRICK	COLE	COURTOIS	DAILLY	DEFOE	DI CANIO	FOXE	GARCIA	HUTCHISON	KANOUTE	KITSON
APPEARANCES													
Start	0	0	30	29	5	38	14	26	4	2	24	27	3
Sub	1	1	0	1	2	0	21	0	2	6	0	0	4
Minutes on pitch	13	6	2654	2609	392	3375	1619	2263	410	180	2028	2215	293
GOAL ATTEMPTS													
Goals	0	0	2	0	0	0	10	9	0	0	1	11	3
Shots on target	0	0	9	22	2	7	28	33	0	0	11	27	6
Shots off target	0	0	26	23	6	6	20	22	1	3	15	55	3
Shooting accuracy %	0%	0%	26%	49%	25%	54%	58%	60%	0%	0%	42%	33%	67%
Goals/shots %	0%	0%	6%	0%	0%	0%	21%	16%	0%	0%	4%	13%	33%
PASSING													
Goal assists	0	0	2	3	1	1	0	6	0	0	2	3	0
Long passes	1	0	395	296	16	320	27	206	48	17	222	88	9
Short passes	5	3	827	890	91	557	329	943	79	62	805	689	71
PASS COMPLETION													
Own half %	100%	0%	89%	85%	76%	83%	79%	85%	85%	70%	84%	77%	76%
Opposition half %	80%	0%	68%	71%	71%	57%	67%	70%	64%	56%	67%	61%	68%
CROSSING													
Total crosses	0	0	42	56	21	4	19	218	1	5	30	50	5
Cross completion %	0%	0%	36%	29%	14%	0%	26%	30%	0%	20%	23%	30%	0%
DRIBBLING													
Dribbles & runs	0	1	53	193	23	21	64	159	6	9	82	175	2
Dribble completion %	0%	100%	74%	70%	48%	95%	58%	62%	83%	67%	65%	48%	100%
DEFENDING													
Tackles made	0	0	96	105	8	69	23	43	9	6	94	28	1
Tackles won %	0%	0%	69%	69%	75%	86%	87%	74%	89%	83%	68%	79%	100%
Blocks	0	0	13	10	2	42	0	3	7	0	10	2	0
Clearances	0	0	47	42	6	408	4	7	53	5	61	23	4
Interceptions	0	0	19	11	1	17	2	2	8	1	9	6	0
DISCIPLINE													
Fouls conceded	0	1	25	43	4	66	30	32	5	6	55	58	11
Fouls won	0	0	30	80	9	17	31	45	4	6	55	58	4
Offside	0	0	0	4	1	0	28	21	0	2	3	34	4
Yellow cards	0	0	4	5	0	4	0	5	2	0	3	4	0
Red cards	0	0	0	0	0	0	0	1	0	0	0	0	0

GOALKEEPER NAME	START/ (SUB)	TIME ON PITCH	GOALS CONCEDED	MINS/GOALS CONCEDED	SAVES MADE	SAVES/ SHOTS
HISLOP	12 (0)	1080	25	43	44	64%
JAMES	26 (0)	2340	32	73	109	77%

For more information visit our website:

PLAYERS' STATISTICS

	LABANT	LOMAS	McCANN	MINTO	MONCUR	PEARCE	REPKA	SCHEMMEL	SINCLAIR	SOMA	SONG	TODOROV	WINTERBURN	TOTAL	RANK
	7	14	0	5	7	8	31	35	34	1	5	2	29		
	5	1	3	0	12	1	0	0	0	2	0	4	2		
	708	1248	71	422	663	787	2750	3063	3014	124	405	220	2608		
	0	4	0	0	0	2	0	1	5	0	0	0	0	48	9th
	1	7	0	0	4	3	1	5	16	0	0	1	2	185	8th
	5	7	1	0	4	2	4	5	28	1	1	2	2	242	=7th
	17%	50%	0%	0%	50%	60%	20%	50%	36%	0%	0%	33%	50%	43%	14th
	0%	29%	0%	0%	0%	40%	0%	10%	11%	0%	0%	0%	0%	11%	10th
	2	0	0	1	0	0	0	6	7	0	0	0	1	35	9th
	105	141	10	42	125	75	293	329	195	15	33	4	262	3721	18th
	214	415	24	109	239	149	683	1117	1173	41	70	46	836	10526	13th
	70%	85%	78%	79%	84%	78%	85%	85%	78%	97%	81%	77%	82%	83%	9th
	62%	72%	75%	64%	75%	61%	61%	73%	69%	67%	43%	62%	76%	67%	12th
	67	17	0	4	9	3	1	132	122	0	1	0	21	828	17th
	19%	35%	0%	25%	22%	0%	0%	20%	30%	0%	0%	0%	33%	27%	6th
	11	23	0	10	15	7	21	87	188	3	2	7	52	1222	7th
	82%	87%	0%	50%	100%	86%	95%	93%	68%	100%	100%	57%	79%	68%	10th
	28	37	1	13	39	8	75	108	80	2	11	2	86	973	16th
	79%	65%	100%	77%	62%	75%	75%	73%	75%	100%	55%	100%	71%	73%	17th
	1	4	0	10	3	8	46	25	8	0	5	0	23	222	9th
	19	32	1	21	6	46	341	98	63	11	52	3	122	1540	5th
	6	2	0	4	8	5	27	23	12	1	9	1	24	198	3rd
	8	13	0	8	20	12	41	53	38	0	6	12	23	570	9th
	11	24	1	4	12	4	43	23	53	1	2	5	31	557	8th
	0	1	0	0	0	0	0	6	16	0	0	2	0	122	14th
	1	3	0	1	6	3	7	6	5	0	1	2	4	66	7th
	0	0	0	0	0	0	2	0	0	0	0	0	0	3	=9th

CROSSES CAUGHT	CROSSES PUNCHED	CROSSES DROPPED	CATCH SUCCESS	THROWS/SHORT KICKS	% COMPLETION	LONG KICKS	% COMPLETION
33	8	5	87%	36	100%	252	54%
66	32	7	90%	41	95%	552	49%

PLAYER OF THE SEASON

PLAYER	INDEX SCORE
DAVID JAMES	991
Paolo Di Canio	868
Jermain Defoe	816
Frédéric Kanouté	784
Joe Cole	719
Trevor Sinclair	699
Tomás Repka	686
Christian Dailly	661
Don Hutchison	647
Nigel Winterburn	638

David James was Glenn Roeder's first major signing after being appointed West Ham boss.

The Hammers paid Aston Villa £3.25 million to secure the England 'keeper's services in July 2001 and he proved to be a great acquisition. Not only was he named Opta's West Ham player of the season, but he was also the top-ranking custodian in the Premiership overall.

His 77% saves-to-shots ratio was among the best for a regular goalkeeper and he managed nine clean sheets – seven of them on home soil. There had been fears that he would miss the entire season after suffering a bad knee injury in an international friendly against Holland on the eve of the 2001–02 campaign.

But he recovered to claim the goalkeeping jersey from former number one Shaka Hislop in late November and went on to make 109 saves – just two short of the total amassed by England colleague Nigel Martyn who was an ever-present in the Premiership. He also made 66 catches.

In second place in the end-of-season Index for West Ham was Paolo Di Canio. The Italian maestro, who had some memorable spats with James before the goalkeeper's arrival at Upton Park, was one of the Hammers' chief providers in 2001–02 with six assists.

He was said to be close to joining Manchester United in January 2001 in order to boost the Red Devils' Champions League campaign, but the move failed to materialise much to the delight of the West Ham faithful.

Young striker Jermain Defoe had a memorable first season in the Premiership and he finised as the club's second-top scorer with 10 goals, including the winner at Old Trafford. Roeder was careful not to burn him out and often rested him from certain games.

However, Defoe was more than useful coming off the bench to score six goals in 21 substitute appearances, making him the most prolific replacement in the division during 2001–02.

FIVE OF THE BEST

West Ham United had a very satisfactory Premiership campaign, defying many of the so-called media "experts" who tipped them for the drop. The Hammers' superb home form — which saw them amass 40 points out of a maximum 57 — was second only to Liverpool's record at Anfield. Glenn Roeder will aim for his team to try and break into the top six in 2002–03.

TOP GOALSCORERS

	GOALS	GOALS/SHOTS
FREDERIC KANOUTE	11	13%
Jermain Defoe	10	21%
Paolo Di Canio	9	16%
Trevor Sinclair	5	11%
Steve Lomas	4	29%

Frédéric Kanouté may have struggled with injury at times, but the French hotshot still managed to finish 2001–02 as the Hammers' top-scorer netting 11 goals. The sought-after forward found the back of the net every 201 minutes on average and was ably supported by teenage sensation Jermain Defoe. The rookie striker had a fantastic term scoring with more than 20% of his attempts at goal in his first full campaign in the Premiership.

French full-back Sébastien Schemmel was the only Hammers man to complete more than a thousand successful passes throughout the 2001–02 season and proved to be a real snip at just £465,000 from Metz. Meanwhile England internationals Michael Carrick and Trevor Sinclair were both effective distributors of the ball in the Premiership, completing 76% and 72% of their passes respectively throughout the course of the campaign.

TOP PASSERS

	SUCC PASSES	COMPLETION
S SCHEMMEL	1,119	77%
Trevor Sinclair	980	72%
Michael Carrick	933	76%
Joe Cole	902	76%
Nigel Winterburn	864	79%

TOP TACKLERS

	WON	SUCCESS
S SCHEMMEL	79	73%
Joe Cole	72	69%
Michael Carrick	66	69%
Don Hutchison	64	68%
Nigel Winterburn	61	71%

Popular defender Sébastien Schemmel made life difficult for his opponents by winning 79 of his attempted challenges in the top flight and would have chalked up more had ligament damage sustained at Arsenal in April not halted his campaign prematurely. Joe Cole's all-round game improved in 2001–02 as he won 26 more tackles than the previous term, illustrating how much valuable work the England star did for the team.

Scotland captain Christian Dailly was the only Hammers player to be ever-present in 2001–02, but all that time on the pitch saw him chalk up the most fouls too. Defensive partner Tomás Repka endured a nightmare start to his career in English football with two red cards in his opening three games, but he recovered well to form a great understanding with Dailly at the heart of the West Ham rearguard.

DISCIPLINE

	POINTS	FOULS & CARDS
CHRISTIAN DAILLY	78	66F, 4Y, 0R
Tomás Repka	74	41F, 7Y, 2R
Sébastien Schemmel	71	53F, 6Y, 0R
Frédéric Kanouté	70	58F, 4Y, 0R
Don Hutchison	64	55F, 3Y, 0R

more often than any other player

BIRMINGHAM CITY

ADDRESS

St Andrew's Stadium,
Birmingham B9 4NH

CONTACT NUMBERS

Telephone: 0121 772 0101
Fax: 0121 766 7866
Ticket Office: 0121 722 0101 Ext. 5
Ticket Information Line: 09068 332 988
Club Shop: 0121 772 0101 Ext. 8
ClubCall: 09068 12 11 88
e-mail: bob@bcfcpromo.fsnet.co.uk
Website: www.bcfc.com

KEY PERSONNEL

Presidents: David Sullivan, Ralph Gold,
David Gold
Chairman: David Gold
Vice Chairman: Jack Wiseman
Managing Director: Karren Brady
Directors: Bradley Gold,
Michael Wiseman, Alan Jones
Henri Brandman
Executive Directors: Joanne Allsopp
Jason Holloway, Steve Pain
Club Secretary: Alan G Jones BA, MBA
Manager: Steve Bruce

SPONSORS

Phones 4U

FANZINES

The Zulu,
Made in Brum

COLOURS

Home: Blue shirts, white shorts
and blue stockings
Away: Yellow shirts, yellow shorts and
yellow stockings

NICKNAMES

Blues

HONOURS

Division Two Champions:
1892–93, 1920–21, 1947–48,
1954–55, 1994–95
League Cup Winners: 1963
Leyland DAF Cup Winners: 1991
Auto Windscreens Shield Winners: 1995

RECORD GOALSCORER

Joe Bradford – 249 league goals,
1920–35

BIGGEST WIN

12–0 v Walsall T Swifts – Division Two,
December 17 1892

BIGGEST DEFEAT

1–9 v Sheffield Wednesday – Division
One, 13 December 1930
1–9 v Blackburn Rovers – Division One,
5 January 1895

SEASON REVIEW

Birmingham City's defeat to Preston North End in the 2000–01 play-offs was the Midlands club's third successive loss at the semi-final stage of the competition. Yet again, Trevor Francis had to rally his troops for a new season with the club still in Division One.

An opening day 3–1 reversal at Wimbledon was hardly the ideal start, although it gave the fans the chance to see summer signings Nico Vaesen and Tommy Mooney in action.

To their credit, Birmingham bounced back by winning their next four league matches. Those victories, however, were swiftly followed by a run of six games without a win, culminating in a comprehensive 6–0 Worthington Cup defeat at Manchester City. This result cost Francis his job five days later, despite a 3–1 success at Barnsley.

With the hunt now on for a new manager, Steve Barron and Mick Mills – members of Francis's backroom staff – were put in charge of team affairs. A 0–0 draw at Nottingham Forest and home wins against Bradford and Gillingham gave the players a timely boost – Brazilian striker Marcelo in particular. The former Sheffield United man went on a run of 12 goals in 14 appearances – including a hat-trick against Bradford City – between Francis's last game and the 3–0 win at Stockport on 29 December.

Despite the reasonable record of Barron and Mills, it became clear that former Birmingham player and Crystal Palace manager Steve Bruce was the board's number one choice to take over. However, Palace refused to accept his resignation and it was only after a protracted legal battle that Bruce finally joined City – the day after the Blues had beaten Palace 1–0 at St Andrew's.

> "I'm looking forward to smelling the hot-dogs. I haven't been in the Premiership since 1996 and I miss the big grounds and the big games. You can smell the hot-dogs at the big games."
>
> **Steve Bruce**

Bruce introduced new faces to revitalise the push for promotion, but the good form of Manchester City, Wolves and West Bromwich Albion made the play-offs the only realistic target.

It took a 10-match unbeaten run, culminating in a 2–0 win in the final game at home to Sheffield United to achieve a fifth-place finish and a play-off semi-final with Millwall.

The first leg at St Andrew's ended in a 1–1 draw, with Dion Dublin's late equaliser cancelling out Bryan Hughes's goal for City. An injury-time winner from Stern John proved to be the only goal of the second leg and sent a joyous Birmingham on to face Norwich City in the final.

There was very little to separate the two sides in Cardiff until Iwan Roberts's header gave Norwich the lead in the opening minute of the first period of extra-time. But Geoff Horsfield's equaliser took the game to penalties.

Birmingham's spot-kicks were faultless, while their opponents failed to beat Vaesen with two of their four attempts. With the score at 3–2 in Birmingham's favour, 18-year-old Darren Carter – a Blues fan all his life – stepped up and converted his kick to secure a place in the 2002–03 Premiership.

In his short time at the club Bruce earned the club promotion via the play-offs, justifying his controversial decision to move to St Andrew's.

But Bruce is unlikely to move on again. "For the first time in my managerial career I am comfortable with the people I am working for," he claimed.

And his relationship with the board will improve further if he can establish the club in the top flight after so many years in the lower leagues.

spot than any other Division One team

BIRMINGHAM CITY

DATE	OPPONENT	SCORE	ATT.	BAK	BENNETT	BRAGSTAD	BURROWS	CARTER	DEVLIN	EADEN	FERRARI	FLEMING	FURLONG	GILL	GRAINGER	HOLDSWORTH	HORSFIELD	HUGHES B	HUGHES
11.08.01	Wimbledon A	1–3	9,142	–	–	–	–	–	–	90	–	–	s25□	70	55	s35	65	s20[1]	–
19.08.01	Millwall H	4–0	19,091	–	–	–	–	–	–	90[1]	–	–	s19	90	90	–	88[1]	90[2]	–
25.08.01	Walsall A	2–1	7,245	–	–	–	–	–	–	90	–	–	s8	90	34□	–	65[1]	90	–
27.08.01	Stockport H	2–1	18,478	–	–	–	–	–	–	90	–	–	s15	62□	90[1]	–	75	90	–
08.09.01	Sheff Wed H	2–0	19,421	–	–	–	90	90	–	90	–	–	s28	90	–	–	88	90[1]	–
15.09.01	Man City A	0–3	31,714	–	90	–	–	–	45	–	–	s12	90	90	–	90	90	–	–
18.09.01	Burnley H	2–3	18,426	–	45	–	–	–	–	–	–	s8	90	90□	–	90	90	–	–
23.09.01	Preston H	0–1	23,004	–	–	–	–	–	90	–	–	–	90	90□	90	90	90	–	–
26.09.01	Watford A	3–3	13,091	–	–	–	–	–	45	–	–	–	90	90[1]	90□	90[1]	90[1]	–	–
29.09.01	Crewe A	0–0	7,314	–	–	–	–	–	90	–	–	–	–	90	90	58	90	–	–
13.10.01	Barnsley A	3–1	11,910	–	–	–	–	–	90	–	–	s12[1]□	90	90	–	78[1]	56	–	–
17.10.01	Nottm For A	0–0	18,210	–	–	–	–	–	10	–	–	s60□	90	90	–	30	–	–	–
20.10.01	Bradford H	4–0	25,011	–	–	–	s1	–	–	–	s1	–	90	90	90	–	–	–	–
23.10.01	Gillingham H	2–1	27,101	–	–	–	–	–	–	–	s2	–	90□	90	–	90[2]	–	–	–
26.10.01	Grimsby A	1–3	5,419	–	–	–	s31	–	–	90	–	–	–	59	90□	–	90	–	–
30.10.01	Portsmouth A	1–1	15,612	–	–	–	–	–	–	90	–	–	–	90	–	90	–	–	–
04.11.01	Rotherham H	2–2*	28,436	–	–	–	–	–	–	90	s17	–	–	90□	–	90[1]	–	–	–
07.11.01	West Brom H	0–1	23,554	–	–	–	–	–	–	90	s15	–	–	90	–	90	–	–	–
17.11.01	Sheff Utd A	0–4	15,686	–	–	–	–	–	–	90	–	90	–	90□	–	90	–	–	–
25.11.01	Coventry H	2–0	18,279	–	90	–	90□	–	–	90	–	90□	–	90□	–	90□	–	–	–
30.11.01	Gillingham A	1–1	8,575	–	90	–	90	–	–	90	–	90	–	66	–	80□	–	–	–
08.12.01	Norwich H	4–0	17,310	–	90	–	90	–	–	90	–	90	–	–	–	–	–	–	–
11.12.01	C Palace H	1–0	20,119	–	90	–	90	–	–	90	–	90	–	–	–	–	–	–	–
16.12.01	Wolves A	1–2	21,482	–	90	–	90□	–	–	84	–	90	–	–	s36	–	s18	–	–
22.12.01	Walsall H	1–0	20,127	–	90	–	90	–	–	90	–	–	–	90	–	90	s19	–	–
26.12.01	Sheff Wed A	1–0	24,335	–	90	–	–	–	–	–	–	–	–	90	–	90[1]	s39	–	–
29.12.01	Stockport A	3–0	5,827	s32	90	–	–	–	–	–	–	–	–	90□	–	80□	–	–	–
01.01.02	Nottm For H	1–1	19,770	s6	90	–	90	–	–	–	–	–	–	66	–	90□	–	–	–
10.01.02	Millwall A	1–1	11,856	64□	90	–	90	–	–	90	–	–	–	–	–	82□	s20	–	–
19.01.02	Wimbledon H	0–2	17,766	90	90	–	s54	–	–	–	–	–	–	90□	–	90	90	–	–
29.01.02	West Brom A	0–1	25,266	–	90	–	–	90	–	90	–	–	63	–	90	–	–	90	–
16.02.02	Barnsley H	1–0	19,208	–	–	–	–	90	90	–	–	–	–	–	90	–	90	–	–
23.02.02	Watford H	3–2	18,059	–	90	–	–	90	71□	s19	–	–	–	–	90	–	90□	–	–
26.02.02	Burnley A	1–0	13,504	–	90	–	–	90	79	s11	–	–	–	–	90	–	–	–	90
02.03.02	Preston A	0–1	15,543	–	90	–	–	90	90	–	–	–	–	–	90	–	s11	90	–
05.03.02	Man City H	1–2	24,160	–	90	–	–	90	90	–	–	–	–	–	73	–	90	–	–
09.03.02	Wolves H	2–2	22,104	–	90	–	–	90	90[1]	–	–	–	–	–	90	–	90	90	–
12.03.02	Bradford A	3–1	13,105	–	–	–	–	90	90□	s11	–	–	–	–	90	s2[1]□	90	–	–
15.03.02	Norwich A	1–0	18,258	–	–	–	–	–	90	s1	–	–	–	–	90□	s8	90	–	–
24.03.02	Coventry A	1–1	17,945	–	–	–	–	90	45	–	–	–	–	–	77□	s13[1]	70	–	–
30.03.02	Grimsby H	4–0	23,249	–	–	–	s12	–	s16	–	–	–	–	–	–	s24	90[2]	78	–
01.04.02	C Palace A	0–0	19,598	–	–	–	–	–	s5	–	–	–	–	–	–	75	85□	90	–
07.04.02	Portsmouth H	1–1	25,030	–	–	–	–	–	s9	–	–	–	–	90	–	s27□	90	90	–
10.04.02	Crewe H	3–1	28,615	–	–	–	–	90[1]	90	–	–	–	–	–	–	90	90	–	–
13.04.02	Rotherham A	2–2*	10,536	–	–	–	–	–	90	–	–	–	–	–	90[1]	–	90	90	–
21.04.02	Sheff Utd H	2–0	29,178	–	–	–	–	90	59	–	–	–	–	–	90[1]	–	89[1]	90□	–

□ Yellow card, ■ Red card, s Substitute, 90[2] Goals scored, *including own goal

For more information visit our website:

2001–02 DIVISION ONE APPEARANCES

HUTCHINSON	HYDE	JOHN	JOHNSON A	JOHNSON D	JOHNSON M	KELLY	KENNA	LAZARIDIS	LUNTALA	MARCELO	McCARTHY	MOONEY	O'CONNOR	PURSE	SONNER	TEBILY	VAESEN	VICKERS	WILLIAMS	WOODHOUSE	TOTAL
–	–	–	–	–	90	–	–	90	–	–	–	90	90	90□	90	–	90	–	–	–	990
–	–	–	–	–	90□	–	–	90	–	–	–	71	72	90	s18	–	90□	–	–	s2	990
–	–	–	s25	–	90	90	–	38	–	–	–	82¹	90	90	s51■	–	–	–	–	–	933
–	–	–	s31	–	90	90	–	90	–	–	–	59¹	90	90□	s28	–	–	–	–	–	990
–	–	–	62¹	–	90	90	–	–	s2	s1	–	–	90	–	–	–	–	–	–	89	990
s45	–	–	78	–	90	90	–	s45	–	–	–	–	90	–	–	–	–	–	–	45	990
s45	–	–	90²	–	90	90	–	82	–	–	–	–	45	–	90	–	–	–	–	s45	990
s28	–	–	90□	–	62	42	–	45	–	–	–	–	–	–	90	–	s48	–	–	s45	990
–	–	–	81	–	90	–	–	45	–	s9	–	s45	–	–	s45	–	90	–	–	90	990
–	–	–	90	–	90	–	s32	s11	s32	–	58	–	–	79	–	–	90	–	–	90	990
–	–	–	–	–	90	–	90	s24	66¹	–	–	90	90	–	–	–	90	–	–	s34	990
–	–	–	–	–	90	–	–	90	90	–	–	90□	90	s80□	–	–	90	–	–	90	990
–	–	–	–	–	90	–	89	90	89³	–	–	72	90	90¹	–	–	90	–	–	s18	990
–	–	–	–	–	90	–	90	90	88	–	–	90	90	73	–	–	90	–	–	s17	990
–	–	–	–	–	90	–	90	72	90¹	–	–	–	90□	90	–	–	90	–	–	s18	990
–	–	–	–	–	90	–	90	90	90¹	–	–	–	90	90	–	–	90□	–	–	–	990
–	–	–	73	–	90	–	90	s1	–	–	–	90	90	90	–	–	90	–	–	89	990
–	–	–	90	–	90	–	–	s15	–	–	75	75□	90	77■	–	–	90	–	–	90	977
–	–	–	s45	–	–	–	45	45□	–	90□	90□	90	–	–	–	90	90	–	s45□	–	990
–	–	–	–	–	–	–	s3	90²	–	–	90	87	–	–	90	90	–	–	990
–	–	–	s1	–	s24	–	–	89¹	–	–	s10	90	90	–	–	90	90□	–	990
–	–	–	s9	–	–	–	90	90	90¹	–	81³	90□	90□	–	–	90	–	–	990
–	s45□	–	–	–	–	–	90	90	90	–	90¹	45	90	–	–	90	–	–	990
–	–	–	s6	–	–	–	90	54	90¹□	–	72	–	90□	–	–	90	90□	–	990
–	–	–	s8□	–	–	–	90	–	82□	–	–	90	90¹	–	–	90	71	–	990
–	–	–	s29	–	–	90	51	–	–	61	90	90	90	–	–	90	90	–	990
–	s10	–	s21	–	–	90	–	–	69¹	90	90¹	58	90□	–	–	90¹	90	–	990
–	84	–	s33	–	s24	–	90	–	90	57	90¹	90	–	–	–	90	–	990
–	–	–	s8	–	–	–	90	–	70	–	90¹	90□	90	–	–	90	s3■	–	967
–	–	–	–	–	–	90	s45	–	70	s20	90	45	90□	–	–	36	–	–	990
–	–	90	–	90	–	81	90	–	s9	–	s27□	90	–	–	–	–	–	990
–	90¹	–	–	–	90	s18	–	–	72	–	90	–	–	90	–	990
s7	90	–	90	–	90	83	–	90²	–	90¹□	–	90¹□	–	–	90	–	990
–	90	–	90	90□	s39□	–	90¹	–	90□	–	–	51	990
–	79	s2	88□	90	s32	–	90	–	90□	–	–	58	990
s17	73	s17	90¹	90	–	90	–	90	–	90□	–	–	990
–	90¹	–	90	90	–	73	90	–	–	s17	990
–	79¹	58	90	90	s32	–	69	90¹	–	90	–	990
–	82¹	–	90	90	–	89	90	–	90	90□	990
–	90	s45	90	90	s20	–	90	–	90	90	–	990
–	66¹	74¹	90	90	90	–	90	90	990
–	90	90	90	s35	–	s15	90	90	55	90	990
–	81¹	90□	21	90	90	–	63	s69	90	90	990
–	70¹	s20	–	90	s10	–	80¹	90	90	90	990
–	90	90□	–	90	–	90	90	90	990
–	78	s1	s31	–	90	–	90	77■	90	90	s12	977

THE MANAGER

STEVE BRUCE

Few managers had a more eventful 2001–02 season than Steve Bruce.

The former Manchester United captain, whose managerial career had already included spells with Sheffield United and Huddersfield Town, ended his short association with Wigan Athletic in May 2001 to link up with Crystal Palace and their ambitious chairman Simon Jordan.

Under Bruce, the Eagles established themselves in the top six of the first division, but in October it became clear, following Trevor Francis's dismissal at Birmingham, that the Midlands club wanted Bruce to take over.

Bruce was keen on the move, but Jordan refused to accept the ex-Blues player's resignation and took him to the High Court. The Eagles chairman secured a ruling that meant Bruce had to stay at Palace until he had served a nine-month notice period, as per his contract.

Eventually, the various parties settled their differences and Bruce was unveiled as Birmingham manager on 12 December, the day after their home league fixture with Palace.

In half a season at St Andrew's, Bruce got the club promoted via the play-offs, an achievement which had eluded his predecessor Trevor Francis, who, in a strange twist of fate, took over the Selhurst Park hot-seat.

LEAGUE POSITION

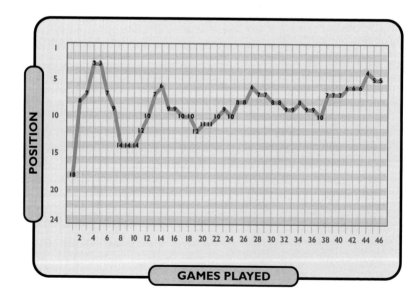

GAMES PLAYED

7 Birmingham scored fewer goals between the 76th

THE GOALS

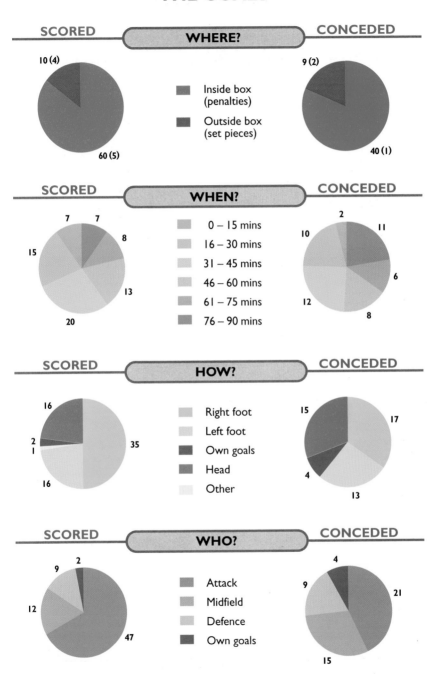

SCORED — **WHERE?** — **CONCEDED**

Inside box (penalties)
Outside box (set pieces)

Scored: 10 (4), 60 (5)
Conceded: 9 (2), 40 (1)

SCORED — **WHEN?** — **CONCEDED**

0 – 15 mins
16 – 30 mins
31 – 45 mins
46 – 60 mins
61 – 75 mins
76 – 90 mins

Scored: 7, 7, 8, 15, 13, 20
Conceded: 2, 11, 10, 6, 12, 8

SCORED — **HOW?** — **CONCEDED**

Right foot
Left foot
Own goals
Head
Other

Scored: 16, 2, 1, 35, 16
Conceded: 15, 17, 4, 13

SCORED — **WHO?** — **CONCEDED**

Attack
Midfield
Defence
Own goals

Scored: 2, 9, 12, 47
Conceded: 4, 9, 21, 15

and 90th minutes than anyone else in Division One

MANCHESTER CITY

ADDRESS

Maine Road, Moss Side,
Manchester M14 7WN

CONTACT NUMBERS

Contact Numbers
Telephone: 0161 232 3000
Fax: 0161 232 8999
Ticket Office: 0161 226 2224
Dial-A-Seat: 0161 828 1200
ClubCall: 09068 12 11 91
Superstore: 0161 232 1111
Mail Order: 0161 828 1201
e-mail: mcfc@mcfc.co.uk
Website: www.mcfc.co.uk

KEY PERSONNEL

Chairman: D Bernstein
Directors: C Bird, B Bodek, A Lewis
A Mackintosh, D Tueart, J Wardle
Club Secretary: B Halford
Manager: Kevin Keegan

SPONSORS

2001-02 Eidos 2002-03 First Advice

FANZINES

Bert Trautmann's Helmet
King of the Kippax
This Charming Fan
Chips 'n Gravy
City Til I Cry

COLOURS

Home: Laser blue shirts, white shorts
and navy stockings
Away: Silver shirts, black shorts and
luminous yellow stockings

NICKNAMES

Blues, Citizens

HONOURS

League Champions: 1936-37, 1967-68
Division One Champions: 2001-02
Division Two Champions: 1898-99,
1902-03, 1909-10, 1927-28,
1946-47, 1965-66
FA Cup Winners: 1904, 1934,
1956, 1969
League Cup Winners: 1970, 1976
European Cup Winners' Cup Winners:
1970

RECORD GOALSCORER

Tommy Johnson - 158 league goals
1919-30

BIGGEST WIN

10-1 v Huddersfield Town – Division
Two, 7 November 1987
10-1 v Swindon Town – FA Cup 4th
round, 29 January 1930

BIGGEST DEFEAT

1-9 v Everton – Division One,
3 September 1906

SEASON REVIEW

Kevin Keegan had a busy summer in 2001 following his appointment as Manchester City manager in succession to Joe Royle. The former England coach's close season signings included the experienced Stuart Pearce from West Ham and Celtic playmaker Eyal Berkovic.

Both new boys scored in City's opening game, a 3–0 home win over Watford and the attacking football Keegan's men played was a sign of things to come as their first 10 league matches included 47 goals, 27 in City's favour.

There were big victories during this sequence, such as the 5–2 win over Crewe Alexandra and the 6–2 drubbing of Sheffield Wednesday, but 4–0 losses at West Brom and at home to Wimbledon suggested that City's defensive frailties could be exposed.

After a lean season in the Premiership, Shaun Goater was scoring goals at a rapid rate – his hat-trick against Gillingham on 3 November was his second of the league campaign – and one of the reasons for his prolific record was the excellent service supplied by the City midfield.

Following his arrival in mid-September, Algerian Ali Benarbia set the pulses racing with his creativity and eye for goal, swiftly becoming one of the most admired players in the division.

Reversals at Portsmouth and Crystal Palace were the only league defeats City suffered from November to January, a record that firmly established them as promotion candidates. The 3–1 New Year's Day win at Sheffield United was particularly significant as it elevated the Maine Road club to the top of Division One for the first time since their 4–2 win at Burnley in August.

Having beaten Swindon Town in the FA Cup third round, City were handed a trip to

> **"There have been a few false dawns here. They have to trust that this is not another one. We will be going for it in the Premiership."**
>
> **Kevin Keegan**

Premiership strugglers Ipswich Town for their next tie, a match ideally suited to show how much progress had been made under Keegan. George Burley's side were emphatically beaten 4–1, with Berkovic staking a claim for goal of the season with a scintillating volley struck from the edge of the area direct from a Benarbia corner.

City's cup adventure ended when Newcastle United beat them 1–0 in the next round, but this hiccup did little to dampen their promotion crusade.

Their form in the final third of the season was little short of exceptional – one defeat in 15 games – and with Wolves winning just two of their league fixtures in March, Keegan's men were able to stay in top spot for the remainder of the campaign following their 3–1 success at Crewe.

A 2–0 win in the battle of the top two at Molineux on 1 April put City one point away from securing promotion, which was eventually achieved when Wolves lost 1–0 at Millwall four days later.

City were crowned champions following their 5–1 drubbing of Barnsley at Maine Road, with recent £5m recruit Jon Macken grabbing a brace and Darren Huckerby netting his second hat-trick in three games. They were handed the trophy after the 3–1 defeat of Portsmouth on the final day of the season and appropriately Benarbia, Berkovic and Division One top scorer Goater were all named in the PFA's Division One Team of the Season.

The title was won in typical Keegan fashion, as the man himself was quick to point out: "More than 100 goals scored and 50 conceded – I guess you could say that is my style".

But it remains to be seen whether such open football will work in the Premiership during the 2002–03 campaign.

MANCHESTER CITY

DATE	OPPONENT	SCORE	ATT.	BENARBIA	BERKOVIC	CHARVET	COLOSIMO	DICKOV	DUNNE	EDGHILL	ETUHU	GOATER	GRANT	GRANVILLE	HAALAND	HORLOCK	HOWEY
11.08.01	Watford H	3–0	33,939	–	76[1]	90	–	s1	90	–	–	89[1]	–	90	–	–	90
18.08.01	Norwich A	0–2	18,745	–	20	90	–	–	90	–	–	90	–	90□	–	s21	90
25.08.01	Crewe H	5–2	32,844	–	–	79	–	–	90	–	–	90[2]	s45	90□	–	s45	90
27.08.01	Burnley A	4–2	19,602	–	–	–	–	–	90	90□	–	90[3]	90□	90	–	90	90
08.09.01	West Brom A	0–4	23,524	–	–	–	s12	s26	90	78	–	90	90	64	–	64□	90
15.09.01	Birmingham H	3–0	31,714	75	–	–	–	s10	90[1]	90□	90	80[2]	–	90	–	s15	90□
19.09.01	Coventry A	3–4*	18,804	90[1]	–	–	s45	–	–	90	45□	90	–	90	–	s45[1]	90
22.09.01	Sheff Wed A	6–2	25,731	80[1]	–	–	–	s45	45	90	–	74[2]	90[1]	–	s10	–	90□
25.09.01	Walsall H	3–0	31,525	78[1]	–	–	–	–	90	–	90	71[1]	–	71	–	s12	90
29.09.01	Wimbledon H	0–4	32,989	90	–	–	s21	–	45	–	63	90	–	90	–	s27	90
13.10.01	Stockport H	2–2	34,214	90[1]	s27	–	–	–	80	–	90□	90[1]	–	63	–	–	90
16.10.01	Sheff Utd H	0–0	32,454	90	s15	–	s8	–	90□	–	90□	90	–	–	–	76□	75
21.10.01	Preston A	1–2	21,014	74	s15□	–	s1	s11	90□	–	90	90□	–	90	–	–	–
23.10.01	Grimsby H	4–0	30,797	59	s31	–	–	s14	81	–	–	76[1]	–	–	–	90	90[1]
28.10.01	Nottm For A	1–1	28,226	90	–	–	–	–	90	–	90□	90[1]	–	s33	–	90	90
31.10.01	Barnsley A	3–0	15,159	90	71	–	–	s12	90	–	–	78[1]	–	s2	–	–	90
03.11.01	Gillingham H	4–1	33,067	90	81	–	s26	–	64	–	s4	90[3]	–	–	–	s9	86
17.11.01	Portsmouth A	1–2	19,103	90□	–	–	–	–	90	–	–	40	–	–	–	90	90□
24.11.01	Rotherham H	2–1	34,223	90[1]	–	–	–	–	90	–	–	–	–	–	–	s16	45
01.12.01	Grimsby A	2–0	7,960	90	90	–	–	–	90	–	–	90[1]	–	–	–	90	–
04.12.01	Millwall H	3–2	13,026	90	–	–	–	–	90□	–	–	90[1]	–	s1	–	90	–
08.12.01	C Palace A	1–2	22,080	90	–	–	–	–	90	–	–	90[1]	–	–	–	90	–
11.12.01	Wolves H	1–0	33,639	67	84	–	–	–	90	–	–	90	s45	–	–	90[1]	–
16.12.01	Bradford H	3–1	30,749	90	–	–	–	–	90	90	78	67	–	–	s12	90[1]	–
26.12.01	West Brom H	0–0	34,407	90	84□	–	–	–	–	49□	–	52	–	–	s16	90□	74
29.12.01	Burnley H	5–1	34,250	90	90[1]	–	–	–	s69	80	–	65	–	–	–	90	90
01.01.02	Sheff Utd A	3–1	26,291	–	83[1]	–	–	–	90	90□	–	87[1]	–	–	s7	90	90
13.01.02	Norwich H	3–1	31,794	90	86[2]	–	–	–	90	–	–	62	–	–	–	90□	21
20.01.02	Watford A	2–1	17,074	82	90	–	–	–	90	–	–	89	–	–	–	90□	–
30.01.02	Millwall H	2–0	30,238	7□	90	–	–	s1	90	–	–	89[2]	–	–	–	90	–
03.02.02	Wimbledon A	1–2	10,664	90[1]	77□	–	–	–	90	s13	–	90	–	–	–	90	–
10.02.02	Preston H	3–2	34,220	84	80□	–	–	–	90	–	–	–	–	–	–	90	90
23.02.02	Walsall A	0–0	7,618	–	90	–	–	–	90	–	–	90	–	–	–	90	90
27.02.02	Sheff Wed H	4–0	33,682	–	78[1]	–	–	–	90	s45	–	90[1]	–	–	–	90[1]	90
03.03.02	Coventry H	4–2	33,335	90	26	–	–	–	–	–	–	90□	–	–	–	90	90
05.03.02	Birmingham A	2–1	24,160	90	–	–	–	–	90	–	–	90	–	–	–	90[1]	71
08.03.02	Bradford A	2–0	18,168	90	–	–	–	–	90	–	–	80	–	–	–	90	–
12.03.02	Crewe A	3–1	10,092	90[1]	–	–	–	–	90	–	–	90[1]	–	–	–	90	–
16.03.02	C Palace H	1–0	33,637	90□	–	–	–	–	90	–	–	72	–	–	–	90[1]	–
19.03.02	Stockport A	1–2	9,537	90	–	–	–	–	90	–	–	33□	–	–	–	90	90
23.03.02	Rotherham A	1–1	11,426	90[1]	31	–	–	–	90□	–	–	90	–	–	–	90	90
30.03.02	Nottm For H	3–0	34,345	90	–	–	–	–	69	–	–	73	–	–	–	90	90
01.04.02	Wolves A	2–0	28,015	90	–	–	–	–	90	–	–	–	–	–	–	90	90
06.04.02	Barnsley H	5–1	33,628	90	–	–	–	–	90	–	–	–	–	–	–	90	66
13.04.02	Gillingham A	3–1	9,494	90	–	–	–	–	86	–	–	90[1]	–	–	–	90[1]	90
21.04.02	Portsmouth H	3–1	34,657	90	s20	–	–	–	90	–	–	64[1]	–	–	–	90	56[1]

□ Yellow card, ■ Red card, s Substitute, 90[2] Goals scored, *including own goal

For more information visit our website:

2001–02 DIVISION ONE APPEARANCES

HUCKERBY	JENSEN	JIHAI	KILLEN	MACKEN	MEARS	METTOMO	MIKE	NASH	NEGOUAI	PEARCE	RITCHIE	SHUKER	TIATTO	TOURE	WANCHOPE	WEAVER	WHITLEY	WIEKENS	WRIGHT-PHILLIPS	TOTAL
s1	–	–	–	–	–	–	–	90	–	90¹	–	–	90	–	89	–	s14	90	–	990
–	–	–	–	–	–	–	–	28	–	90¹	–	–	90	–	89■	s62	s49	90	–	989
s11	–	–	–	–	–	–	–	90	–	90¹	–	–	90	90²	90	–	–	45	45	990
–	–	–	–	–	–	–	–	90	–	90¹	–	–	90	90¹	90	–	–	–	–	990
90	–	–	–	–	–	–	–	90	–	90	–	–	90	–	90	–	s26	–	–	990
s10	–	–	–	–	–	–	–	90	–	90	–	–	90	80	90	–	–	–	–	990
–	–	–	–	–	–	–	–	90	–	–	–	45	90■	–	90	–	90	–	–	990
s16	–	–	–	–	–	–	–	90	–	–	–	–	90■	90²	90	–	90■	–	–	990
s19	–	–	–	–	–	–	–	90	–	–	s19	–	90■	90¹	90	–	90	–	–	990
90	–	–	–	–	–	–	–	90	–	–	–	–	90	s45	90	–	69	–	–	990
90■	–	–	–	–	s26	–	–	90	–	–	–	–	90■	–	90	–	64	s10	–	990
–	–	–	–	–	90■	–	–	90	–	–	–	–	90■	–	90	–	–	82	–	976
89¹	–	–	–	–	90	–	–	–	79	–	–	–	90	–	90	–	90	–	–	989
90²	–	–	–	–	90■	–	–	90	–	–	–	–	90	–	90	–	–	–	s9	990
90	–	–	–	–	90■	–	–	90	–	–	–	–	90	–	90	–	57	–	–	990
90¹	–	–	–	–	90	–	–	–	88¹	–	s19	–	90	–	90	–	–	90	–	990
90¹	–	–	–	–	90	–	–	90	–	–	–	–	90	–	90	–	–	90	–	990
90¹	–	–	–	–	90	s50■	–	90	90	–	–	–	–	–	–	–	–	90	–	990
90	–	–	s11	–	90	79	–	90¹	90■	–	–	74	–	–	90	–	s45	90■	–	990
90¹	–	–	–	–	90	–	90	90	–	–	–	90	–	–	–	–	90	90	–	990
90¹	–	–	–	–	90	–	90	–	–	–	–	–	89■	–	–	–	90■	90¹■	–	990
90	–	–	–	–	90	–	90	s25	–	–	–	90	–	–	–	–	65	90	–	990
90■	–	–	–	–	90	–	90	s23	–	s6	–	45	–	–	–	–	90	85¹	–	990
–	–	–	–	–	90	–	90	–	–	s6	–	–	–	s23	–	90	90	s38	–	949
s25¹	–	–	–	–	90	–	90	–	–	–	–	90	–	90³	–	–	21	s10	–	990
s3	–	–	–	–	90	–	90	–	–	–	s21	69	–	90■	–	–	–	90¹	–	990
s28	–	s4	–	–	–	–	90	–	90	s69	–	12■	–	90¹■	–	–	–	90■	–	912
s1	s8	–	–	–	–	–	90	90	–	–	–	90	–	90¹	–	–	90	90	–	990
90	90	–	–	–	–	–	–	90	–	–	–	–	–	–	–	90	90	90	–	907
90	90	–	–	–	–	–	–	s8	89■	–	–	–	–	–	–	90	82	90	–	989
90	90	–	–	–	–	–	–	–	90	s6	–	s10	–	90¹	90	–	s8	82¹	–	990
79	90	–	s11	–	–	–	–	–	90	–	–	90	–	–	90	–	–	90	–	990
90¹	90	–	–	–	–	–	–	–	90	s12	–	90	–	–	90	–	–	–	45	990
90¹	s64	s14	–	–	76	–	–	–	76	s14	–	90¹	–	–	90	–	–	–	90²	990
90	90¹	–	–	–	s19	–	–	s57	90■	–	–	90	–	–	–	33	–	–	90■	990
90¹	90	–	s10¹	–	–	–	–	90	90	–	–	90■	–	–	–	–	90	90	–	990
90¹	90■	–	–	–	–	–	–	90	90	–	–	90■	–	–	–	–	90	45	–	990
90	90	s45■	s18	–	–	–	–	90	–	–	–	–	45	–	–	–	90	90	–	990
–	90	–	–	–	–	s45	–	90¹	–	–	–	–	–	–	–	–	90	45	–	933
90	90	s59	–	–	–	–	–	90	90	–	–	–	–	–	–	–	–	90	–	990
90³	90	90	s17	s6	s21■	–	–	90	84	–	–	–	–	–	–	–	–	90	–	990
90■	90	90■	90■	–	–	–	–	90	–	–	–	–	–	–	–	–	–	–	90²■	990
90³	90	s14	–	90²	s22	–	–	90	68	–	–	76	–	–	–	–	s24	90	–	990
s27¹	90	s14	63	–	s4	–	–	90	90	–	–	76■	–	–	–	–	–	90	–	990
90	90	–	s26¹	–	–	–	–	90	90	–	–	70	–	–	–	–	s34	90	–	990

THE MANAGER

KEVIN KEEGAN

Kevin Keegan's managerial career began at Newcastle United in February 1992, with the Magpies facing relegation from the old Division Two. He steered them to survival and the following season gained promotion to the Premiership as Division One champions.

Once in the top flight, Newcastle entertained everyone with their attractive football, which so nearly resulted in Keegan's men winning the 1995–96 Premiership title, when they finished second to Manchester United.

Keegan surprisingly resigned in January 1997 and was next employed at Fulham, where he helped lay the foundations for the success the club have since enjoyed under Jean Tigana.

He left Craven Cottage in May 1999 to become England Coach, but, as he later admitted, was found tactically lacking at the highest level.

Keegan took over as manager of Manchester City in the summer of 2001. It was imperative that he succeeded in his first season at Maine Road to prove his managerial credentials after such a wretched spell at international level.

He did this emphatically, winning the Division One title with the emphasis – as usual – on positive, attacking play. It will be interesting to see if this tactic is as successful in the 2002–03 Premiership campaign.

LEAGUE POSITION

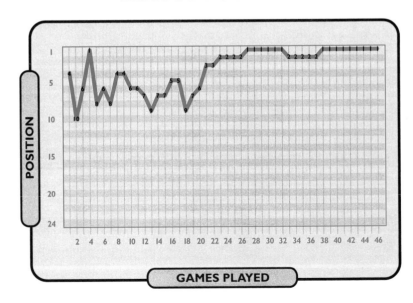

POSITION

GAMES PLAYED

1 City lost just one league game

THE GOALS

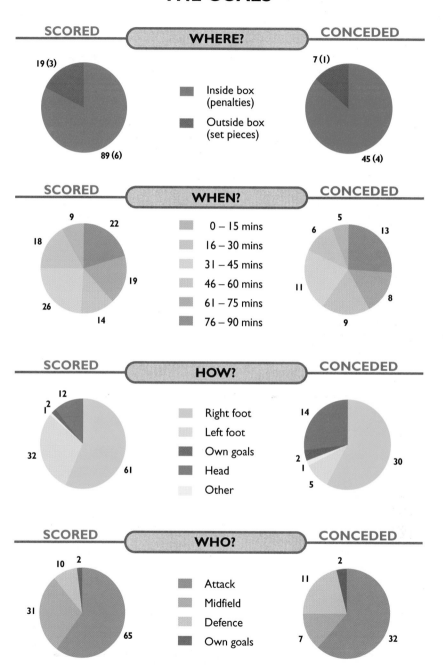

SCORED — **WHERE?** — **CONCEDED**

19 (3)

- Inside box (penalties)
- Outside box (set pieces)

89 (6)

7 (1)

45 (4)

SCORED — **WHEN?** — **CONCEDED**

9 · 22 · 18 · 19 · 26 · 14

- 0 – 15 mins
- 16 – 30 mins
- 31 – 45 mins
- 46 – 60 mins
- 61 – 75 mins
- 76 – 90 mins

5 · 13 · 6 · 11 · 8 · 9

SCORED — **HOW?** — **CONCEDED**

12 · 2 · 1 · 32 · 61

- Right foot
- Left foot
- Own goals
- Head
- Other

14 · 2 · 1 · 30 · 5

SCORED — **WHO?** — **CONCEDED**

10 · 2 · 31 · 65

- Attack
- Midfield
- Defence
- Own goals

2 · 11 · 7 · 32

at Maine Road – 4–0 to Wimbledon

WEST BROMWICH ALBION

ADDRESS

The Hawthorns, West Bromwich,
West Midlands B71 4LF

CONTACT NUMBERS

Telephone: 0121 525 8888
Fax: 0121 553 6634
Ticket Office: 0121 525 8888
Club Shop: 0121 525 2145
ClubCall: 09068 12 11 93
e-mail: enquiries@wbafc.co.uk
Website: www.wba.co.uk

KEY PERSONNEL

President: Sir F A Millichip
Vice President:: J G Silk
Acting Chairman: C Stapleton
Directors: J W Brandrick,
B Hurst, B McGing, J Peace
Chief Executive: J D Wile
Manager: Gary Megson

SPONSORS

West Bromwich Building Society

FANZINES

Grorty Dick

COLOURS

Home: Navy and white striped shirts,
white shorts and navy stockings
Away: Green and yellow striped shirts,
green shorts and yellow stockings

NICKNAMES

Albion, Baggies, Throstles

HONOURS

Division One Champions: 1919–20
Division Two Champions:
1901–02, 1910–11,
FA Cup Winners: 1888, 1892, 1931,
1954, 1968
League Cup Winners: 1966

RECORD GOALSCORER

Vic Watson – 298 league goals,
1920–35

BIGGEST WIN

12–0 v Darwen – Division One,
4 April 1892

BIGGEST DEFEAT

3–10 v Stoke City –
Division One, 4 February 1937

SEASON REVIEW

Following their semi-final defeat at the hands of Bolton Wanderers in the 2000–01 play-offs, West Bromwich Albion approached the 2001–02 season determined to put together another promotion challenge.

After a disappointing start, Gary Megson recruited Darren Moore, Andy Johnson and – on loan – Sunderland's Danny Dichio. However, it was the summer signing from Carlisle, Scott Dobie, who led the autumn revival with seven goals in his first 10 matches, aided by timely strikes from veteran Bob Taylor.

A run of six 1–0 wins in eight games, between 31 October and 12 December ensured that Albion were firmly among the play-off places ahead of the busy Christmas period.

> "We've proved the critics wrong once and we'll do it again".
>
> **Gary Megson**

A 4–0 win over Stockport on New Year's Day, including two from Dichio – now signed permanently – proved to be the perfect warm-up exercise for Albion's third round FA Cup match at Sunderland. The home side were beaten 2–1, earning the Baggies a fourth round tie with Leicester City at the Hawthorns.

January's clash with Walsall was overshadowed by the death of Jeff Astle, on the eve of the fixture. The Saddlers were defeated 1–0 and scorer Jason Roberts fittingly revealed a T-shirt bearing a picture of the Albion legend following his strike.

This victory was the first of four successive league wins and goalkeeper Russell Hoult stretched his run of clean sheets to seven league and cup matches before Millwall gave Albion a taste of their own medicine by winning 1–0 at the New Den.

Megson rallied his troops however, and they bounced back with their biggest win of the season – a 5–0 drubbing of struggling Portsmouth. Now in third place,

could Albion put enough pressure on Wolves and Manchester City to snatch an automatic promotion place?

Defeat at Preston was their final league loss of the campaign, while Albion's FA Cup run ended at home to Fulham in round six.

The league fixture in mid-March at Sheffield United made the headlines after some explosive incidents. The Blades had three men sent off and then suffered two injuries, leaving referee Eddie Wolstenholme with no option other than to abandon the game. West Brom were 3–0 leaders at the time and, following an inquiry, the result was allowed to stand.

With Albion's form improving and Wolves on the slide, it was only a matter of time before Dave Jones's men were overtaken. Eventually Albion moved into second place with a 1–1 draw at home to Rotherham. A nerve-wracking 1–0 win at Bradford in their next game meant that they would be promoted to the Premiership in second place, if they defeated visitors Crystal Palace on the last day.

A Moore goal after 17 minutes settled Albion's nerves and Taylor's 54th minute poacher's strike secured West Brom's Premiership place, after a 16-year absence.

Megson – who achieved so much on a far smaller budget than that of counterparts Kevin Keegan and Dave Jones – was deservedly awarded the Division One Manager of the Year award, while Hoult, Moore and Neil Clement were named in the PFA's Division One Team of the Season.

West Brom's record of 15 1–0 wins indicated that their defence will relish the challenge of Premiership football. Reinforcements to the forward line however, will be a necessity if Albion are to cause their top-flight opponents problems at the other end of the pitch.

WEST BROMWICH ALBION

DATE	OPPONENT	SCORE	ATT.	APPLETON	BALIS	BENJAMIN	BUTLER	CHAMBERS A	CHAMBERS J	CLEMENT	CUMMINGS	DICHIO	DOBIE	FOX
11.08.01	Walsall A	1–2	9,181	90	90	–	78	–	–	90¹	s12	–	90	s25
18.08.01	Grimsby H	0–1	17,971	90□	90	–	–	–	–	90	83	–	90	90
25.08.01	Sheff Wed A	1–1	18,844	90	–	–	s63	s30□	–	90	27	90¹□	67	–
27.08.01	Gillingham H	1–0	18,180	90□	83	–	90	s22	s7	90	–	90¹	89	–
08.09.01	Man City H	4–0	23,524	90□	–	–	90	89	s1	90¹	–	69□	s41¹	–
15.09.01	Watford A	2–1	15,726	90	–	–	63□	90□	s1	–	90	–	76²	–
18.09.01	Preston H	2–0	18,289	90	–	–	90	89	–	90	s1	–	90²	s25
22.09.01	Wimbledon H	0–1	19,222	90	–	–	90	90	–	90	–	–	90	s45
25.09.01	Portsmouth A	2–1	17,287	90	–	–	90	s8	–	90¹	90	–	90¹	–
29.09.01	Burnley H	1–0	21,442	90	–	–	–	–	–	90	–	–	90¹	–
11.10.01	Millwall A	0–2	17,335	45□	–	–	–	s45	–	–	s45	–	90	90
16.10.01	Stockport A	2–1	6,052	90	–	–	–	–	–	90	–	–	90	–
19.10.01	Norwich A	0–2	20,465	88	–	–	–	s2	90	68	s22	–	90	s21
25.10.01	Wolves H	1–1	26,143	90	–	–	–	–	–	90¹□	–	–	49	s45
28.10.01	Barnsley A	2–3	12,490	90	s27	–	s11	–	–	90¹	–	–	–	s45
31.10.01	C Palace A	1–0	17,273	90□	–	–	–	–	–	90	s11	–	–	–
04.11.01	Nottm For H	1–0	18,281	90	90	–	–	–	–	90	–	–	90	–
07.11.01	Birmingham A	1–0	23,554	90	61	–	90	–	s29	90	–	–	90	–
17.11.01	Rotherham A	1–2	8,509	–	90	–	s14	–	–	76□	–	–	90	s45
24.11.01	Bradford H	1–0	18,910	–	82□	–	–	90	–	90	s1	–	90	–
02.12.01	Wolves A	1–0	27,515	–	90	–	–	90	–	90	–	90	90	–
08.12.01	Sheff Utd H	0–1	19,462	–	90	–	–	90	–	90	s8	90	51	s21
12.12.01	Coventry H	1–0*	22,543	–	90	–	–	90	–	90□	–	90	89	–
15.12.01	Crewe A	1–1	8,154	–	90	–	–	73□	–	90	–	90	–	–
22.12.01	Sheff Wed H	1–1	20,340	–	90	–	–	–	–	90	–	90	90	s29¹
26.12.01	Man City A	0–0	34,407	–	90	–	s45	–	–	90	90	61	s29	s16
29.12.01	Gillingham A	1–2	9,912	–	45	–	4□	–	–	90	90□	90	s45	s27
01.01.02	Stockport H	4–0	20,541	–	90	–	s13	–	–	90	–	79²	90	–
12.01.02	Grimsby A	0–0	6,011	–	55	–	–	54	–	90	–	90	s36	–
20.01.02	Walsall H	1–0	20,290	–	90	–	–	s2	–	90	–	71□	s19	–
29.01.02	Birmingham H	1–0	25,266	–	83	–	–	54	–	90	–	54	s36	s36
03.02.02	Burnley A	2–0	15,846	–	83	–	–	90	–	90	–	90	s4	–
10.02.02	Norwich H	1–0	19,115	–	81	–	–	90	–	90	–	80¹□	s10	–
19.02.02	Millwall A	0–1	13,716	–	s45	–	90	–	–	90	–	s45	45	s33
23.02.02	Portsmouth H	5–0	21,028	–	90¹	–	90□	90	–	85	s5	–	83¹	–
26.02.02	Preston A	0–1	14,487	–	90	–	84	61	–	90	–	–	90□	s29
02.03.02	Wimbledon A	1–0	8,363	–	90	–	90	90	–	90	–	78¹	90	–
05.03.02	Watford H	1–1	19,580	–	90	–	66	58□	–	90	–	90¹	90	s24
16.03.02	Sheff Utd A	3–0△	17,692	–	82	–	s14	56	–	82	–	82	82²	–
22.03.02	Nottm For A	1–0	24,788	–	90	–	–	90□	–	90	–	59	90	–
26.03.02	Crewe H	4–1*	21,303	–	89	–	–	90	–	90	–	90¹	75	s1
30.03.02	Barnsley H	3–1	23,167	–	90	s45¹	–	45	–	90	–	90¹	75	s15
01.04.02	Coventry A	1–0	21,513	–	90	s22□	–	87	–	90	–	62	s28	–
07.04.02	Rotherham H	1–1	22,376	–	90	–	–	s18	–	90	–	90	s32	–
13.04.02	Bradford A	1–0	20,209	–	90¹	s25	–	65□	–	90	–	74	90	–
21.04.02	C Palace H	2–0	26,712	–	90	–	–	90	–	90	–	89	s23	s1

□ Yellow card, ■ Red card, s Substitute, 90² Goals scored, * including own goal

For more information visit our website:

2001–02 DIVISION ONE APPEARANCES

GILCHRIST	HOULT	JENSEN	JOHNSON	JORDAO	LYTTLE	McINNES	MOORE	QUINN	ROBERTS	ROSLER	SIGURDSSON	TAYLOR	VARGA	TOTAL
90□	90	–	–	65	–	90□	–	s6	–	–	90	84	–	990
90	90	–	–	s7	–	90	–	s14	–	–	90	76	–	990
90	90	–	–	90	90□	60	–	–	–	–	90	s23	–	990
90	90	–	–	s1	–	90□	–	–	–	–	90	68	–	990
90	90	–	–	90	90¹□	–	–	49	–	–	90□	s21	–	990
90	90	–	–	89	90	s27	s14	–	–	–	90	63□	–	963
90	90	–	–	90	90	–	–	–	–	–	90	65	–	990
25	90	–	s65	–	45	–	–	s16	–	–	74	90	–	990
–	90	–	90□	–	90	90	–	–	–	–	90□	82	–	990
90	90	–	90	–	90	90	90	s7□	–	–	90	83	–	990
90	–	90	90	–	45	90	30	–	–	–	90	s60	–	990
90	90	–	90	–	90	90	90□	–	–	–	90	90²	–	990
90	90	–	69	–	–	90□	90□	–	–	–	90	90□	–	990
90	90	–	45	–	90	90	90	s41□	–	–	90	90	–	990
90	90	–	79¹	–	63	90	90	90	–	–	45	89△	–	989
90	90	–	90	–	90	90	90	–	–	79□	90	90¹	–	990
90	90	–	s36	–	–	90	90	–	–	90¹□	90	54	–	990
90	90	–	90¹	–	–	90	–	–	–	67	90	s23	–	990
90□	90	–	90	45	s45	90	90¹	–	–	90	45	–	–	990
90	90	–	–	90	s8	90¹	90	–	–	89	90	–	–	990
90	90	–	–	90¹□	–	90	90	–	–	–	–	–	–	990
82	90	–	69	–	–	90	90	–	–	–	90	s39	–	990
90	90	–	s24	66	–	90	90	–	–	–	90□	s1	–	990
90	90	–	s17	90¹	–	90	90	–	s22	–	90□	68	–	990
39	90	–	90	61	–	90	90	–	s51	–	90	–	–	990
–	90	–	90□	74	–	90	45	–	90□	–	90	–	–	990
–	90	–	90¹	6	s84	90	90	–	63	–	–	–	–	904
90	90	–	90¹	–	–	90	90	–	77¹	–	90	s11	–	990
90	90	–	90	–	s35	90	90	–	90	–	90□	–	–	990
90	90	–	90	88□	–	90	90	–	89¹□	–	90	s1	–	990
90	90	–	90	–	s7	90	90	–	90¹	–	90□	–	–	990
90	90	–	90	–	s7	90	90	–	86²□	–	90	–	–	990
90	90	–	90	–	s9	90	90	–	90	–	90	–	–	990
90	90	–	90	57□	45	90	–	–	90	–	90	–	–	990
90	90	–	87	s3	–	90	–	–	90²	–	90¹	s7	–	990
90	90	–	90	–	s6	90	–	–	44	–	90	s46	–	990
90	90	–	90	90	–	–	–	–	–	–	90□	s12	–	990
90	90	–	90	s32	–	58	–	–	–	–	90	s32	–	990
82	82	–	71	s11	–	82¹	82	–	–	–	68□	s26	–	902
90	90	–	–	90	–	90	90	–	–	–	90	s31¹	–	990
90	90	–	–	90²	–	90	90	–	–	–	82	s15	s8	990
63	90	–	–	90¹	s27	90	90	–	–	–	–	–	90	990
90	90	–	–	90	s3	90	90	–	–	–	–	62¹	90	984
53	90	–	58	90	–	90	90	–	–	–	s37	72¹	90	990
90	90	–	90	–	–	90	90□	–	–	–	90	s16	–	990
90	90	–	73	s17	–	90	90¹	–	–	–	90	67¹	–	990

△ Match abandoned after 82 minutes. WBA awarded 3–0 win

THE MANAGER

GARY MEGSON

Gary Megson could not have had a tougher introduction to management than his first post at Norwich. The Canaries were in turmoil following their relegation from the Premiership and Megson's reign only lasted from December until the end of the 1995–96 campaign.

After a year in charge at Blackpool, Megson moved to Stockport. His first season at Edgeley Park saw the newly-promoted Hatters finish eighth in Division One and he swiftly became one of the game's most sought-after young managers.

Stoke City was Megson's next destination, but his tenure at the Britannia Stadium was ended when the club was taken over by an Icelandic consortium.

Megson arrived at West Brom in March 2000, with Albion fighting for Division One survival. Not only did they stay up, but the following season they finished sixth before losing to Bolton in the play-offs.

The 2001–02 campaign ended in success, however, with the Baggies securing automatic promotion ahead of Black Country rivals Wolves.

Megson now has the tough task of guiding Albion to safety in his first season as a Premiership manager, a challenge he will no doubt approach with the grit and determination that has characterised his career.

LEAGUE POSITION

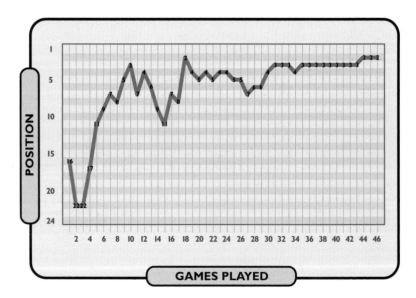

POSITION

GAMES PLAYED

11 West Brom conceded the fewest goals

THE GOALS

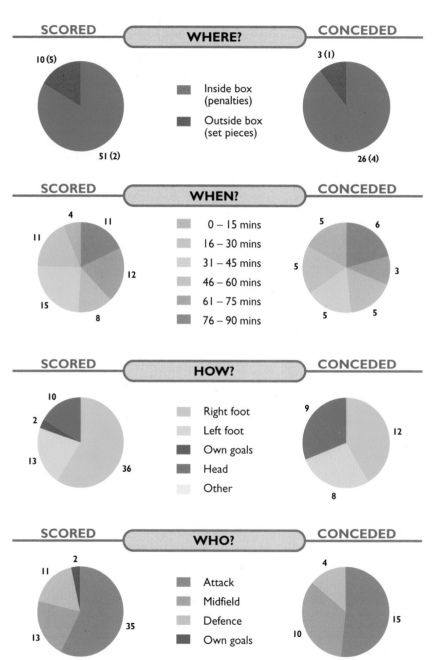

WHERE?

SCORED — CONCEDED

- Inside box (penalties)
- Outside box (set pieces)

Scored: 10 (5), 51 (2)
Conceded: 3 (1), 26 (4)

WHEN?

SCORED — CONCEDED

- 0 – 15 mins
- 16 – 30 mins
- 31 – 45 mins
- 46 – 60 mins
- 61 – 75 mins
- 76 – 90 mins

Scored: 4, 11, 11, 12, 15, 8
Conceded: 5, 6, 5, 3, 5, 5

HOW?

SCORED — CONCEDED

- Right foot
- Left foot
- Own goals
- Head
- Other

Scored: 10, 2, 13, 36
Conceded: 9, 12, 8

WHO?

SCORED — CONCEDED

- Attack
- Midfield
- Defence
- Own goals

Scored: 2, 11, 13, 35
Conceded: 4, 15, 10

at home of any Division One side

COMPARATIVE TABLES

Debates will inevitably rage about which team is the best, which players are better than others and which referee is the strictest in the league.

Now you can settle all those arguments with the definitive guide to the 2001–02 Premiership season. Our comparative tables show how teams fared in relation to each other, how the top 20 players ranked in certain categories and who were the top players of the season.

This section is divided up to analyse key aspects of the game.

THE TEAMS

All the Premiership teams are compared and contrasted over a number of categories. Find out which team were the best and worst passers, tacklers and defenders, plus which sides had the best and worst disciplinary records.

THE PLAYERS

The top 20 players in each category are compared and contrasted to highlight the best goalscorers, passers, tacklers and goalkeepers, as well as the players with the best and worst disciplinary records.

THE INDEX

Who was the best player in each position and who was the most influential player of the season? The Opta Index takes an objective view.

TEAMS OF THE SEASON

Everybody's favourite pastime – with a twist. Opta select their teams of the season based on actual performance in key areas.

REFEREES

An in-depth look at the disciplinary record of the 2001–02 season in terms of the fouls and penalties awarded and yellow and red cards issued by referees.

FA PREMIERSHIP
SEASON 2001–2002

	PLD	HOME					AWAY					PTS	GD
		W	D	L	F	A	W	D	L	F	A		
Arsenal	38	12	4	3	42	25	14	5	0	37	11	87	43
Liverpool	38	12	5	2	33	14	12	3	4	34	16	80	37
Man Utd	38	11	2	6	40	17	13	3	3	47	28	77	42
Newcastle	38	12	3	4	40	23	9	5	5	34	29	71	22
Leeds Utd	38	9	6	4	31	21	9	6	4	22	16	66	16
Chelsea	38	11	4	4	43	21	6	9	4	23	17	64	28
West Ham	38	12	4	3	32	14	3	4	12	16	43	53	–9
Aston Villa	38	8	7	4	22	17	4	7	8	24	30	50	–1
Tottenham	38	10	4	5	32	24	4	4	11	17	29	50	–4
Blackburn	38	8	6	5	33	20	4	4	11	22	31	46	4
Southampton	38	7	5	7	23	22	5	4	10	23	32	45	–8
Middlesbro	38	7	5	7	23	26	5	4	10	12	21	45	–12
Fulham	38	7	7	5	21	16	3	7	9	15	28	44	–8
Charlton	38	5	6	8	23	30	5	8	6	15	19	44	–11
Everton	38	8	4	7	26	23	3	6	10	19	34	43	–12
Bolton W	38	5	7	7	20	31	4	6	9	24	31	40	–18
Sunderland	38	7	7	5	18	16	3	3	13	11	35	40	–22
Ipswich	38	6	4	9	20	24	3	5	11	21	40	36	–23
Derby Co	38	5	4	10	20	26	3	2	14	13	37	30	–30
Leicester	38	3	7	9	15	34	2	6	11	15	30	28	–34

19 Arsenal went the entire season

THE TEAMS

How did your team rate against the other Premiership sides in key categories? You will find the answer in this section. All 20 teams are featured in each table and are ranked according to a key category, which will be explained beneath each chart.

The tables will show you the main areas of strength and weakness within each team and will go some way to explaining why certain teams were successful and why others struggled, over the course of the 2001–02 season.

For example, on page 240 you will see that Sunderland managed a goals-to-shots ratio of just 7.0% compared with Arsenal's 15.4%. This shows how the Black Cats had to attempt more than twice as many shots to score a goal as the Premiership champions, which was clearly a key factor in the relative success of each team.

You can discover which team scored the most headed goals, which won the most tackles, which earned the most disciplinary points and which side suffered most at the hands of their opponents.

There is an explanation beneath each of the charts showing how the ranking is calculated and how to access the information.

The most important table of all, of course, is the Premiership league table.

Opposite you will see how all 20 teams finished in the 2001–02 Premiership season and a breakdown of their home and away records.

Arsenal won the title by seven points from Liverpool in second, who qualified for the Champions League. Third-placed Manchester United and fourth-placed Newcastle United also qualified for the 2002-03 Champions League, but they will enter the competition only if they progress past a qualifying round. If they are eliminated at that stage, they will enter the UEFA Cup.

Leeds United's fifth position secured them a spot in the UEFA Cup alongside sixth-placed Chelsea and Worthington Cup winners Blackburn Rovers. Aston Villa and Fulham will enter the Intertoto Cup in a bid to reach the UEFA Cup.

Leicester City were the first side to be relegated when they lost to Manchester United on 6 April. They were joined by Derby County two weeks later and Ipswich Town on the last day of the season, ending a six-year and a two-season sojourn in the top flight respectively.

GOALSCORING

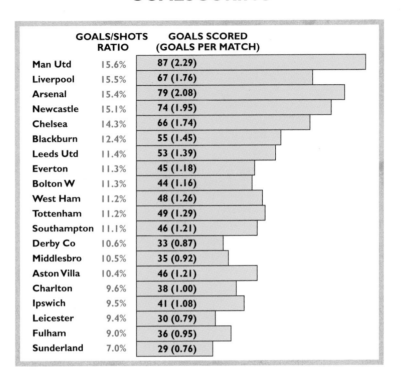

	GOALS/SHOTS RATIO	GOALS SCORED (GOALS PER MATCH)
Man Utd	15.6%	87 (2.29)
Liverpool	15.5%	67 (1.76)
Arsenal	15.4%	79 (2.08)
Newcastle	15.1%	74 (1.95)
Chelsea	14.3%	66 (1.74)
Blackburn	12.4%	55 (1.45)
Leeds Utd	11.4%	53 (1.39)
Everton	11.3%	45 (1.18)
Bolton W	11.3%	44 (1.16)
West Ham	11.2%	48 (1.26)
Tottenham	11.2%	49 (1.29)
Southampton	11.1%	46 (1.21)
Derby Co	10.6%	33 (0.87)
Middlesbro	10.5%	35 (0.92)
Aston Villa	10.4%	46 (1.21)
Charlton	9.6%	38 (1.00)
Ipswich	9.5%	41 (1.08)
Leicester	9.4%	30 (0.79)
Fulham	9.0%	36 (0.95)
Sunderland	7.0%	29 (0.76)

Ian Pearce's late winner for West Ham against Bolton Wanderers on the final day of the season was the 1,000th goal to be scored in the 2001–02 Premiership and the final total of 1,001 goals was marginally up on the 992 netted in the 2000–01 season.

Defensive frailties may have let Manchester United down during the course of the season, but goalscoring-wise they were as lethal as ever. The Red Devils once again topped the scoring charts – just as they have done for the previous seven seasons – with 87 goals.

United not only scored more than anyone else in the league, but they also proved to be the most clinical from the chances they created. The likes of Ruud van Nistelrooy and Ole Gunnar Solskjaer possessed fantastic strike rates and, combined with a midfield packed with creativity, it meant trouble for opposing defences, with 15.6% of all chances ending up as goals.

Liverpool were only marginally less economical in front of goal than their great rivals, but they will be keen to start creating more chances, finishing the season with 20 fewer goals than United.

Arsenal hit the record books during 2001–02, scoring in every single league game on their way to the title, making them the first Premiership side to ever do so. Arsenal also joined United in being the only side to average more than two goals per game.

Sunderland's flirtation with relegation stemmed from the fact that they performed the worst in front of goal. A lean season for Kevin Phillips left the Black Cats with few other striking options. They managed to put away just 7% of the chances they created and scored fewer goals than any other team.

SHOOTING

	SHOOTING ACCURACY	Shots on target	Shots off target
Arsenal	49.7%	255	258
Liverpool	48.8%	208	218
Leeds Utd	48.3%	217	232
Man Utd	47.4%	258	286
Everton	47.4%	184	204
Leicester	46.1%	143	167
Derby Co	45.8%	143	169
Chelsea	45.7%	208	247
Newcastle	44.4%	212	265
Charlton	44.0%	161	205
Aston Villa	43.9%	189	242
Blackburn	43.8%	184	236
Bolton W	43.5%	166	216
West Ham	43.3%	185	242
Sunderland	42.2%	175	240
Southampton	41.7%	161	225
Fulham	40.9%	160	231
Ipswich	40.9%	177	256
Middlesbro	39.3%	127	196
Tottenham	38.6%	166	264

KEY ■ Shots on target ☐ Shots off target

Arsenal's players were the most accurate in front of goal in the 2001–02 Premiership, with almost half of their efforts forcing opposition 'keepers to take action.

Considering that the Gunners fired in well over 500 shots during the course of the season, that meant opposing custodians had a lot of work to do and it was no wonder that Arsène Wenger's men managed to score in every single game. This was the second successive season where Arsenal proved to be the team with the greatest accuracy.

Only Manchester United managed to conjure up a higher number of goal attempts than Arsenal in 2001–02, but the Red Devils' efforts were more wayward with only 47.4% finding the target. Both Liverpool and Leeds United managed a greater accuracy than that and the four clubs who recorded the highest shooting accuracy figures all finished in the Premiership's top five.

While Arsenal were successfully able to pick their spot, north London rivals Tottenham Hotspur lacked direction in front of goal. Just 38.6% of their efforts were on target and, alongside Middlesbrough, they were the only other top-flight club whose shooting accuracy fell below 40%.

Relegated east Midlands duo Leicester City and Derby County were both reasonably accurate, but the fact that they only managed 310 and 312 shots on goal respectively told its own tale as to why they went down.

Overall, there were fewer goal attempts in the Premiership in 2001–02 than in the previous campaign, but the level of accuracy remained consistent with an average of 44.44% of shots being on target – compared to 44.45% in 2000–01.

on goal than any other side

PASSING

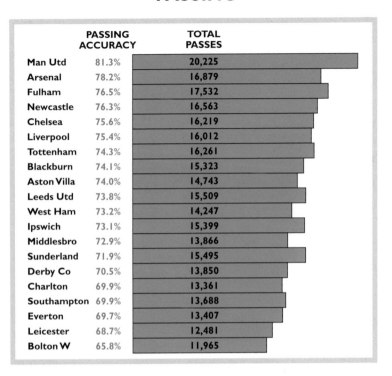

	PASSING ACCURACY	TOTAL PASSES
Man Utd	81.3%	20,225
Arsenal	78.2%	16,879
Fulham	76.5%	17,532
Newcastle	76.3%	16,563
Chelsea	75.6%	16,219
Liverpool	75.4%	16,012
Tottenham	74.3%	16,261
Blackburn	74.1%	15,323
Aston Villa	74.0%	14,743
Leeds Utd	73.8%	15,509
West Ham	73.2%	14,247
Ipswich	73.1%	15,399
Middlesbro	72.9%	13,866
Sunderland	71.9%	15,495
Derby Co	70.5%	13,850
Charlton	69.9%	13,361
Southampton	69.9%	13,688
Everton	69.7%	13,407
Leicester	68.7%	12,481
Bolton W	65.8%	11,965

The superior passing ability of Manchester United dominated the Premiership once again in 2001–02 and this was the fourth season in succession that Sir Alex Ferguson's men topped the distribution charts.

A dominant midfield comprising the likes of Roy Keane, David Beckham, Paul Scholes and Ryan Giggs was always going to dominate any passing charts, but the addition of Juan Sebastian Veron helped United improve even further on 2000–01's figures.

The Red Devils made more than 20,000 passes during the course of the season, retaining possession with 81.3% of those deliveries compared to 78.6% in 2000–01. The accuracy of their ball playing was also over three percentage points higher than nearest rivals Arsenal whose 78.2% completion rate was an improvement on the previous campaign.

Fulham arrived in the Premiership having won the first division at a canter and Jean Tigana's men achieved this by playing some attractive passing football. It was a style they stuck with in their first season back in the top flight for 34 years and only Manchester United attempted more passes.

Fellow new boys Bolton Wanderers adopted a wholly different style in their attempt to retain Premiership status. Sam Allardyce's men were very direct and while they ultimately succeeded in staying up, the accuracy of their passing let them down with only 65.8% of their distribution finding a fellow team member.

Bottom club Leicester City also struggled to find too much accuracy with their passing, but the other two relegated sides – Derby County and Ipswich Town – both managed a pass completion rate of better than 70% despite their lowly league positions.

66% Bolton Wanderers had the worst

PASSING IN OPPOSITION HALF

	PASSING ACCURACY	PASSES ATTEMPTED
Man Utd	75.6%	11,747
Arsenal	72.8%	9,942
Newcastle	71.1%	10,094
Tottenham	69.5%	10,172
Aston Villa	69.3%	9,397
Fulham	68.8%	10,032
Chelsea	68.7%	9,111
Blackburn	68.3%	9,381
Liverpool	67.6%	9,312
Leeds Utd	67.6%	9,132
Ipswich	67.5%	9,882
West Ham	66.8%	8,693
Sunderland	66.4%	9,433
Middlesbro	65.9%	8,040
Derby Co	64.9%	8,233
Charlton	64.5%	8,631
Everton	63.8%	8,411
Southampton	63.6%	8,497
Leicester	60.6%	7,448
Bolton W	58.4%	7,395

One of the reasons why the Premiership was regarded as among the most exciting leagues in the world in 2001–02 was because of the top teams' commitment to playing attacking football, retaining possession and taking the game to the opposition.

Just as in 2000–01, it was Manchester United who dominated most matches, as the passing in the opposition half table illustrated. The Red Devils made almost 12,000 of their passes in enemy territory and more than three-quarters of these were successful as United forced opponents onto the back foot.

Not surprisingly, champions Arsenal were also very effective in their opponents' half of the field and the accuracy of the Gunners' passing was also an improvement on the previous season's showing, although they did attempt fewer passes in total than in 2000–01.

Bobby Robson's Newcastle United side had a very attacking look about it and they fought their way into the Champions League by making more than 10,000 passes in the opposition half. The Magpies, Arsenal and Manchester United were the only three teams to achieve an average accuracy of better than 70%, while Tottenham Hotspur – under the guidance of Glenn Hoddle, a great passer himself – also excelled in distributing more than 10,000 passes in opposition territory throughout the campaign.

Meanwhile, it was Bolton Wanderers who struggled the most further up field and they ended up with the worst accuracy in the division. As they achieved their aim of staying in the top flight, Trotters supporters will not have been too concerned, but just 58.4% of their passes were completed in the opposition half of the field.

passing accuracy in the Premiership

SHORT PASSING

	PASSING ACCURACY	SHORT PASSES
Man Utd	84.2%	15,140
Arsenal	80.4%	12,363
Newcastle	79.6%	12,147
Fulham	79.3%	13,108
Liverpool	79.2%	11,060
Chelsea	78.5%	11,979
Blackburn	78.1%	11,030
Ipswich	77.8%	11,050
Middlesbro	77.5%	10,064
Aston Villa	77.4%	10,686
Tottenham	77.3%	11,840
Leeds Utd	77.0%	11,367
West Ham	76.8%	10,526
Sunderland	75.2%	11,142
Charlton	75.1%	9,795
Derby Co	74.8%	9,985
Southampton	74.5%	9,791
Leicester	73.7%	8,596
Everton	73.3%	9,535
Bolton W	71.4%	8,407

When teams conceded possession to either Manchester United or Arsenal in 2001–02, it became extremely difficult for them to win it back. The two Premiership giants excelled when making short passes and were the only sides who boasted a completion rate in excess of 80% during the campaign.

Opta Index define a short pass as one played over a distance of 25 yards or less and for the fourth consecutive season it was United who led the way in the discipline.

Captain Roy Keane set a great example by playing 1,608 short passes – more than any other individual in the top flight. The Irishman was ably supported by England man Paul Scholes and Argentinian schemer Juan Sebastian Veron – both of whom were in a select group of players in the Premiership to complete more than a thousand short passes.

Double-winners Arsenal marginally improved their rate from 2000–01 and were grateful for the influence of Patrick Vieira, whose constant supply of distribution helped the Gunners top the 80% completion barrier.

Meanwhile, Newcastle United's improvement in their short distribution record was a factor as they reached the heights of Champions League qualification for the first time in five years.

Fulham, meanwhile, were often accused of passing the ball too much in 2001–02 and this claim was supported by the stats which showed that only Manchester United attempted more short passes than the Cottagers.

It was pleasing on the eye, but unlike Newcastle – who had Alan Shearer's 23 goals – the Londoners were often inclined to overpass, rather than take responsibility for a shot.

2,163 Roy Keane was the only Premiership player

LONG PASSING

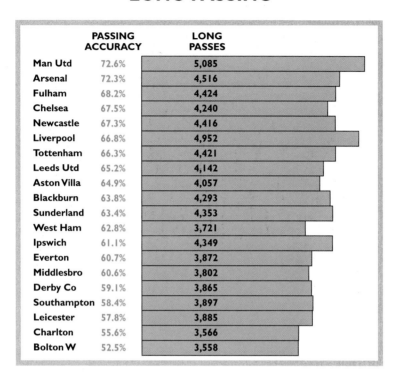

	PASSING ACCURACY	LONG PASSES
Man Utd	72.6%	5,085
Arsenal	72.3%	4,516
Fulham	68.2%	4,424
Chelsea	67.5%	4,240
Newcastle	67.3%	4,416
Liverpool	66.8%	4,952
Tottenham	66.3%	4,421
Leeds Utd	65.2%	4,142
Aston Villa	64.9%	4,057
Blackburn	63.8%	4,293
Sunderland	63.4%	4,353
West Ham	62.8%	3,721
Ipswich	61.1%	4,349
Everton	60.7%	3,872
Middlesbro	60.6%	3,802
Derby Co	59.1%	3,865
Southampton	58.4%	3,897
Leicester	57.8%	3,885
Charlton	55.6%	3,566
Bolton W	52.5%	3,558

Ipswich Town were among the five most accurate long-ball distributors in the 2000–01 season as they impressively qualified for the UEFA Cup. But in 2001–02, the Tractor Boys' passing rate seriously declined and that was a contributory factor to their bottom-three placing.

George Burley's side fell from being the fifth-most accurate distributors in 2000–01 to the unlucky 13th spot in 2001–02 after completing a below average 61% of their long balls – those that cover a distance of more than 25 yards.

Manchester United were the only side to attempt more than 5,000 raking passes and they were just marginally more accurate than Arsenal, whose completion rate was an improvement on the 2000–01 campaign.

Just up the Seven Sisters Road, Tottenham Hotspur supporters would have been pleased to see their team improve its long distribution accuracy by a massive seven percentage points from 2000–01. That is no doubt a reflection on Glenn Hoddle's passing principles compared to the more direct style of previous incumbent George Graham.

By steering clear of injury and maintaining a high level of form, midfielder Darren Anderton was Spurs' key man. He helped improve the team's long-pass tally with his 458 successful efforts – more than any other Englishman in the Premiership.

Across the capital, the likes of Sean Davis and Steve Finnan were vital in helping Fulham complete an impressive 68% of their passes upfield, but in contrast, Bolton Wanderers, Charlton Athletic and Leicester City all struggled to make long passes count and often saw the ball coming straight back at them.

to complete more than 2,000 passes

CROSSING

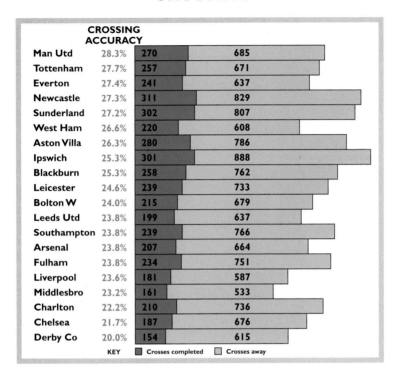

	CROSSING ACCURACY	Crosses completed	Crosses away
Man Utd	28.3%	270	685
Tottenham	27.7%	257	671
Everton	27.4%	241	637
Newcastle	27.3%	311	829
Sunderland	27.2%	302	807
West Ham	26.6%	220	608
Aston Villa	26.3%	280	786
Ipswich	25.3%	301	888
Blackburn	25.3%	258	762
Leicester	24.6%	239	733
Bolton W	24.0%	215	679
Leeds Utd	23.8%	199	637
Southampton	23.8%	239	766
Arsenal	23.8%	207	664
Fulham	23.8%	234	751
Liverpool	23.6%	181	587
Middlesbro	23.2%	161	533
Charlton	22.2%	210	736
Chelsea	21.7%	187	676
Derby Co	20.0%	154	615

KEY   ▉ Crosses completed   ▉ Crosses away

With a squad including the likes of David Beckham and Ryan Giggs, you would expect Manchester United to appear near the top of any crossing table in the Premiership and so it was in 2001–02 with Ruud van Nistelrooy the main beneficiary.

When the Dutchman moved to Old Trafford in the summer of 2001, he must have been relishing the service he was going to receive from the flanks and he wasn't to be disappointed as United provided the most accurate crosses in the top flight. Twenty-eight per cent of their centres found a colleague – a distinct improvement on their completion rates of the previous three seasons.

Like Sir Alex Ferguson, Glenn Hoddle encouraged his Tottenham Hotspur players to whip plenty of balls in the box and they did him proud in his first full season in charge by finding another white shirt with 27.7% of their crosses – the second best rate in the Premiership.

But for sheer number of balls crossed into the box, it was relegated Ipswich Town who led the way with 1,189 attempted. Unfortunately, the majority of those amounted to very little as Town's strikers were unable to fully capitalise on the service.

Another relegated side, Derby County, proved to be the least accurate crossing team, which is something Italian hitman Fabrizio Ravanelli would have been frustrated about.

Another disappointed Italian was Chelsea boss Claudio Ranieri. His side possessed one of the best strike partnerships around in Jimmy Floyd Hasselbaink and Eidur Gudjohnsen, but they received poor service from the flanks during 2001–02, with only 21.7% of Chelsea's crosses being accurate.

71% Manchester United had the worst tackle

TACKLING

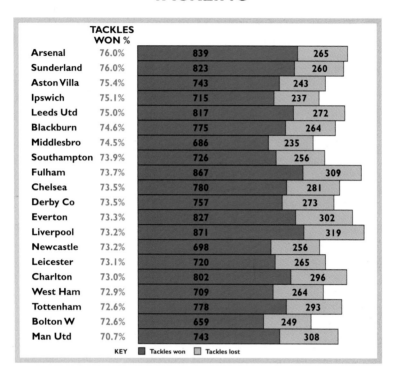

	TACKLES WON %	Tackles won	Tackles lost
Arsenal	76.0%	839	265
Sunderland	76.0%	823	260
Aston Villa	75.4%	743	243
Ipswich	75.1%	715	237
Leeds Utd	75.0%	817	272
Blackburn	74.6%	775	264
Middlesbro	74.5%	686	235
Southampton	73.9%	726	256
Fulham	73.7%	867	309
Chelsea	73.5%	780	281
Derby Co	73.5%	757	273
Everton	73.3%	827	302
Liverpool	73.2%	871	319
Newcastle	73.2%	698	256
Leicester	73.1%	720	265
Charlton	73.0%	802	296
West Ham	72.9%	709	264
Tottenham	72.6%	778	293
Bolton W	72.6%	659	249
Man Utd	70.7%	743	308

KEY   ■ Tackles won   ▢ Tackles lost

Arsenal's attacking play in 2001–02 was a joy to watch at times and understandably grabbed much of the attention, as they scooped the Premiership and FA Cup double for the second time under Arsène Wenger.

But crucially, the Gunners coupled their slick forward play with a ruthless streak which saw them make almost 100 tackles more in 2001–02 than they had managed in the previous campaign, when they finished second in the league.

So, while the flair of Thierry Henry, Dennis Bergkamp and Robert Pires was easy on the eye, the grit and determination of midfield men Patrick Vieira, Ray Parlour and Edu was equally vital in breaking up opposition forays and setting counter attacks in motion.

The Gunners won 76% of all their challenges, a rate more than three percentage points better than they managed in 2000–01 and it was a figure that only Sunderland – under the demanding management of Peter Reid – were able to match.

Overall though, it was Liverpool who made the greatest number of tackles in the Premiership, with the Merseysiders attempting a total of 1,190 challenges over the course of the season. German midfielder Dietmar Hamann typified the spirit and defensive resolve at Anfield by making 186 of those tackles – more than anyone else at the club – from his holding role in front of the back four.

Surprisingly, Manchester United posted the lowest tackle success rate in the top flight, coming out on top with just 70.7% of their attempted challenges. That was despite the gritty influence of feisty skipper Roy Keane and the hard work put in by his midfield sidekicks Paul Scholes and Nicky Butt.

CLEARANCES

	TOTAL CLEARANCES	Headed clearances	Other clearances
Liverpool	1,726	994	732
Everton	1,658	967	691
Middlesbro	1,564	860	704
Tottenham	1,616	848	768
Leeds Utd	1,502	820	682
West Ham	1,540	818	722
Charlton	1,482	794	688
Blackburn	1,411	777	634
Derby Co	1,501	767	734
Southampton	1,396	763	633
Leicester	1,418	742	676
Sunderland	1,349	739	610
Fulham	1,318	738	580
Ipswich	1,303	738	565
Newcastle	1,324	729	595
Chelsea	1,371	727	644
Arsenal	1,257	723	534
Aston Villa	1,318	722	596
Bolton W	1,290	694	596
Man Utd	1,240	679	561

KEY ☐ Headed clearances ☐ Other clearances

Liverpool's centre-backs Sami Hyypia and Stéphane Henchoz have formed one of the most formidable central defensive partnerships in Premiership history. And against some of Europe's finest attackers – both domestically and in the Champions League in 2001–02 – the duo's uncompromising style of play gave the Reds an excellent platform on which to build.

Hyypia and Henchoz were responsible for making a large number of the Reds' 1,726 clearances – the highest total in the Premiership. They also dominated their aerial battles with strikers the length and breadth of the country, giving some great protection to Jerzy Dudek's goal. And with Gérard Houllier setting his side up to sit back and hit out on the break, the strength of his defenders was of crucial importance.

Liverpool's Merseyside rivals Everton also showed rugged determination in clearing their lines at the back, while Middlesbrough and Tottenham Hotspur – who invested heavily in their defence – were grateful for a high number of clearances, too.

Traditionally, Manchester United are more accustomed to dominating games than soaking up pressure and, consequently, they haven't had to make too many clearances over recent seasons. But in 2001–02, the Red Devils were forced to clear their lines far more often than they had in 2000–01 – some 191 times more, in fact.

The likes of Arsenal, Chelsea and Newcastle United – teams who spent more time attacking than defending – all had a relatively low number of clearances to their names. Conversely, Bolton Wanderers came under a great deal of pressure from opponents, but made far fewer clearances than other teams that struggled.

994 Liverpool made more headed clearances

CHANCES ALLOWED

	SHOTS ALLOWED	Goals conceded	Saves made
Arsenal	110	36	74
Liverpool	132	30	102
Leeds Utd	148	37	111
Chelsea	152	38	114
Man Utd	153	45	108
Aston Villa	161	47	114
Fulham	164	44	120
Everton	165	57	108
Sunderland	169	51	118
Southampton	169	54	115
Middlesbro	173	47	126
Newcastle	176	52	124
Blackburn	182	51	131
Charlton	189	49	140
Bolton W	191	62	129
Tottenham	197	53	144
Leicester	199	64	135
Ipswich	205	64	141
West Ham	210	57	153
Derby Co	225	63	162

KEY ☐ Goals conceded ☐ Saves made

The best teams are always built on the foundation of a strong defence – or so the saying goes – but that requires more than a goalkeeper who can pull off saves. If the defenders are able to deny their opponents the time and space to even create goalscoring opportunities, then it makes the job that much easier for the man between the sticks.

To that end, it was David Seaman, Richard Wright and Stuart Taylor at Arsenal who enjoyed the most comfortable 2001–02 campaign, as the trio of custodians had to face just 110 accurate shots between them – an improvement on the previous term's total when they were confronted with a season-low 116 attempts.

Seventy four of those shots in 2001–02 were kept out, meaning that Arsenal boss Arsène Wenger possessed the only set of 'keepers in the Premiership who were forced into fewer than 100 saves.

Liverpool, meanwhile, conceded the fewest goals in the 2001–02 Premiership and faced only 132 shots in all. Other top six clubs – Leeds United, Chelsea and Manchester United – also kept their opponents' goal attempts down to a minimum, although fourth-placed Newcastle United were not as tight at the back and Shay Given may well feel that he was given rather too much work to do as he faced 176 shots.

At the opposite end of the spectrum, Derby County presented their opponents with the most scoring opportunities – something that did them no favours as they strove to beat the drop. Ipswich and Leicester also allowed more shots than they could cope with, but Glenn Roeder's West Ham United performed remarkably to finish in seventh place despite facing a sizeable 210 shots.

DISCIPLINE – FOULS CONCEDED

	DISCIPLINARY POINTS	Foul committed = 1pt	Yellow card = 3pts	Red card = 6pts
Leicester	869	611	76	5
Arsenal	864	615	71	6
Leeds Utd	862	625	69	5
Everton	826	637	57	3
Sunderland	826	616	68	1
Blackburn	809	608	59	4
Bolton W	804	588	58	7
Derby Co	788	551	73	3
West Ham	786	570	66	3
Chelsea	771	546	69	3
Charlton	766	559	63	3
Middlesbro	753	552	53	7
Southampton	731	593	36	5
Fulham	724	547	55	2
Newcastle	723	558	51	2
Tottenham	721	514	59	5
Aston Villa	700	556	44	2
Man Utd	658	490	54	1
Ipswich	658	520	44	1
Liverpool	612	471	41	3

KEY: Foul committed = 1pt · Yellow card = 3pts · Red card = 6pts

Disciplinary matters were never far away from the headlines in 2001–02 with the players and referees under scrutiny more than ever before. Several incidents prompted the FA to use video evidence to help with disciplinary judgements and a number of red cards were rescinded, while other players were brought to book for matters that were not initially witnessed by the matchday referee or his assistants.

According to the Opta scoring system, bottom side Leicester City were adjudged to have the poorest disciplinary record, with the Foxes receiving 76 yellow and five red cards during their forlorn fight to beat the drop. Robbie Savage was the chief culprit picking up 14 cautions – more than any other player in the Premiership.

But success on the field does not necessarily mirror a team's disciplinary record, as champions Arsenal were the second most-indisciplined team according to Opta. The Gunners were regularly embroiled in controversy over discipline, with Thierry Henry, Patrick Vieira and Martin Keown all hauled in front of the FA at some point during the campaign.

In total Arsène Wenger's men had six players sent off in the Premiership along with another six in cup competitions, making a total of 44 dismissals since the French manager took charge at Highbury. Crucially though, no Gunner saw red in the team's record-breaking run-in of 13 straight wins.

The Premiership's cleanest team were Liverpool who committed fewer fouls and earned fewer yellow cards than any other team. In 2000–01, the best-behaved side were Ipswich Town and they maintained their clean-cut image in 2001–02 to earn the second lowest number of disciplinary points and a place in the UEFA Cup.

80 Liverpool became the first team to reach **80** points

DISCIPLINE – FOULS WON

Team	DISCIPLINARY POINTS	Foul committed = 1pt	Yellow card = 3pts	Red card = 6pts
Arsenal	898	625	75	8
Fulham	876	636	72	4
Newcastle	851	608	69	6
Middlesbro	827	632	61	2
Leeds Utd	826	598	72	2
West Ham	802	577	69	3
Blackburn	795	585	62	4
Leicester	788	566	62	6
Aston Villa	778	571	61	4
Sunderland	764	560	60	4
Ipswich	757	586	49	4
Everton	746	566	48	6
Derby Co	737	572	51	2
Chelsea	734	551	57	2
Liverpool	720	549	53	2
Charlton	691	508	55	3
Southampton	690	549	43	2
Bolton W	664	505	45	4
Tottenham	663	510	49	1
Man Utd	644	473	53	2

KEY — Foul committed = 1pt — Yellow card = 3pts — Red card = 6pts

Title winners Arsenal may have possessed one of the Premiership's poorest disciplinary records in 2001–02, but they were also the team subjected to the worst disciplinary abuse according to the stats.

The Gunners were the most sinned-against team, with more players receiving cards in games against the Highbury outfit than any other team. A total of eight players were given their marching orders when playing Arsène Wenger's men, while a further 75 were cautioned.

During the 2000–01 season, Wenger claimed that teams were afraid to tackle rivals Manchester United and that the Red Devils enjoyed a respect that was not given to his side. Interestingly, the statistics for 2001–02 showed that this was the case once again as United emerged as the least sinned-against side. They were the only team to be fouled on fewer than 500 occasions and their total of 473 free-kicks won was significantly down on the previous campaign.

In contrast, Fulham received some rough treatment on their return to the top flight, and were fouled more than any other side. Striker Louis Saha bore the brunt of the fury, winning 97 free-kicks – more than any other player in the Premiership. His strike partner Barry Hayles was the joint-fourth-most fouled player behind Arsenal's Patrick Vieira and Damien Duff of Blackburn Rovers.

Overall, the number of yellow cards issued in 2001–02 was down for the third season in a row, with the tally falling to 1,166 from 1,210 the previous campaign. That was despite the fact that there were a greater number of fouls committed during 2001–02.

There were, however, seven more red cards than in the previous season.

in a 38-game season and not win the league.

GOALS CONCEDED

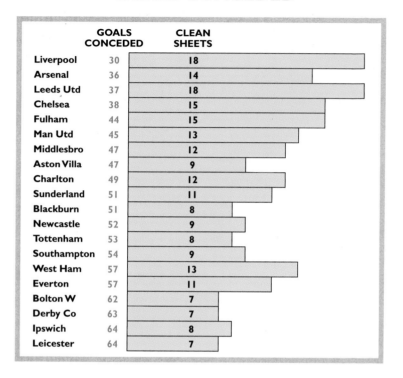

	GOALS CONCEDED	CLEAN SHEETS
Liverpool	30	18
Arsenal	36	14
Leeds Utd	37	18
Chelsea	38	15
Fulham	44	15
Man Utd	45	13
Middlesbro	47	12
Aston Villa	47	9
Charlton	49	12
Sunderland	51	11
Blackburn	51	8
Newcastle	52	9
Tottenham	53	8
Southampton	54	9
West Ham	57	13
Everton	57	11
Bolton W	62	7
Derby Co	63	7
Ipswich	64	8
Leicester	64	7

For the second time in three seasons, it was Liverpool who boasted the Premiership's tightest defence, with Gérard Houllier and Phil Thompson's men letting in just 30 goals during the course of the 2001–02 campaign.

The Reds used a trio of different goalkeepers in their opening three games, but Jerzy Dudek established himself between the sticks after that and the Poland international went on to have a fine first season of Premiership football. He kept 17 clean sheets during the term and built up an excellent understanding with defensive lynchpins Sami Hyypia and Stéphane Henchoz. Full-backs Jamie Carragher, John Arne Riise and Abel Xavier also played important roles.

Arsenal's defensive capabilities have been renowned for years and although there were some new faces around in season 2001–02, as opposed to the familiar "old guard", the result was pretty much the same. The Gunners conceded less than one goal per game on average – a marginal improvement on their performance in 2000–01.

One defence that was significantly poorer in season 2001–02 was that of Manchester United, which was beaten on 45 occasions in the league. In 2000–01, it was the Red Devils who boasted the Premiership's finest defensive record, conceding just 31 goals on their way to winning a seventh Premiership title. But, by selling Jaap Stam, United lost some defensive cohesion and they conceded 14 more goals in 2001–02 than they did in the previous campaign.

All of the relegated sides were particularly weak in defence. Leicester City, Derby County and Ipswich Town possessed the three worst defensive records in the Premiership and paid the price.

34 There were 34 0–0 draws

SHUT OUTS

FAILING TO SCORE		KEEPING A CLEAN SHEET	
	MATCHES		**MATCHES**
Leicester	19	Leeds Utd	18
Derby Co	17	Liverpool	18
Charlton	16	Chelsea	15
Sunderland	16	Fulham	15
Fulham	15	Arsenal	14
Everton	14	Man Utd	13
Ipswich	14	West Ham	13
Middlesbro	14	Charlton	12
Bolton W	13	Middlesbro	12
Aston Villa	11	Everton	11
Blackburn	11	Sunderland	11
Southampton	11	Aston Villa	9
West Ham	11	Newcastle	9
Leeds Utd	10	Southampton	9
Chelsea	9	Blackburn	8
Tottenham	7	Ipswich	8
Man Utd	6	Tottenham	8
Newcastle	6	Bolton W	7
Liverpool	4	Derby Co	7
Arsenal	0	Leicester	7

Leicester City failed to score in half of their 38 league fixtures in 2001–02 and that inability to find the back of the net was a major factor in seeing the Foxes relegated back to Division One, following a six-year spell in the Premiership.

A serious dearth of goals from strikers such as Ade Akinbiyi proved costly, as did a barren two-month spell between late September and November, when the Foxes plundered just two goals in nine games.

Their east Midlands rivals Derby County did not fare much better in front of goal and drew a blank in 17 of their matches. Experienced Italian marksman Fabrizio Ravanelli was prolific in the early stages of the term, but scored just once after Christmas as the rest of the team struggled to find the net too.

Conversely, Arsenal became the first team to score in every game of a league season since Preston North End in 1888–89 as they made their way to their 12th title success.

While the Gunners were the masters of scoring, Liverpool were kings of keeping goals out and goalkeeper Jerzy Dudek was instrumental in the Reds' success. The former Feyenoord shot-stopper kept 17 clean sheets in his 35 Premiership appearances and was subbed in the Reds' other shut-out.

Only Leeds United and their ever-present 'keeper Nigel Martyn bettered that record. The veteran registered 18 shut-outs and kept exciting England under-21 prospect Paul Robinson on the sidelines for the entire campaign.

Classy defenders Marcel Desailly, John Terry and William Gallas were important figures as Chelsea chalked up 15 clean sheets and their west London neighbours Fulham did well to equal that tally considering their 13th-placed finish.

COMEBACKS

LOST AFTER LEADING		WON AFTER BEING BEHIND	
	MATCHES		MATCHES
Tottenham	5	Newcastle	10
Bolton W	4	Arsenal	5
Middlesbro	4	Man Utd	4
Everton	3	Aston Villa	3
Ipswich	3	Bolton W	2
West Ham	3	Charlton	2
Arsenal	2	Chelsea	2
Aston Villa	2	Leeds Utd	2
Chelsea	2	Leicester	2
Derby Co	2	Tottenham	2
Leeds Utd	2	Blackburn	1
Leicester	2	Everton	1
Man Utd	2	Fulham	1
Southampton	2	Ipswich	1
Blackburn	1	Liverpool	1
Charlton	1	Middlesbro	1
Fulham	1	Southampton	1
Liverpool	0	Derby Co	0
Newcastle	0	Sunderland	0
Sunderland	0	West Ham	0

Following four consecutive bottom-half Premiership finishes, Newcastle United weren't widely expected to be challenging for a place in the UEFA Cup, let alone the Champions League, in 2001–02.

But Bobby Robson instilled a never-say-die spirit into his squad and it paid off as they earned 10 Premiership victories in games in which they had trailed at some point, to help them attain an impressive fourth-placed finish.

Incredibly, Newcastle triumphed in twice as many games from losing positions as their nearest challengers in the art, Arsenal.

And the Gunners were among the Toon's comeback scalps, as they hit three in reply to Robert Pires's opener at Highbury to inflict the champions' final Premiership defeat of the season in December.

In the following match, the north-east giants travelled to face Leeds United –

themselves very much title contenders at that stage – and hit back from 3–1 down to take the points in one of the season's most exciting games.

Another contender for Premiership match of the season was the encounter between Tottenham Hotspur and Manchester United at White Hart Lane in September. Spurs went in at half-time 3–0 ahead and cruising, but were stunned as the Red Devils came out for the second half and hit five with no reply.

That was one of the five games Tottenham lost having been ahead in 2001–02 – more than any other team. Others who felt the heartbreak were Bolton and Middlesbrough, who both let leads slip on four occasions each.

Among the sides who never lost having been ahead were Newcastle, Liverpool and, surprisingly, Sunderland who were economical with their goals.

NARROW MARGINS

WON BY A SINGLE GOAL		LOST BY A SINGLE GOAL	
	MATCHES		MATCHES
Arsenal	11	Derby Co	14
Liverpool	11	Blackburn	11
Leeds Utd	9	Ipswich	11
Middlesbro	9	Tottenham	11
Newcastle	9	Everton	9
Tottenham	9	Leicester	9
Man Utd	8	Middlesbro	9
West Ham	8	Aston Villa	8
Aston Villa	7	Sunderland	8
Bolton W	7	Bolton W	7
Everton	7	Fulham	7
Sunderland	7	Man Utd	6
Charlton	6	Southampton	6
Chelsea	6	Charlton	5
Blackburn	5	Chelsea	5
Derby Co	5	West Ham	5
Ipswich	5	Leeds Utd	4
Fulham	4	Liverpool	3
Leicester	4	Arsenal	1
Southampton	3	Newcastle	1

One-nil to the Arsenal – the victory chant frequently heard at Highbury during previous successful campaigns – was only apt on three occasions in 2001–02. However, the Gunners still pulled off 11 Premiership wins by a single goal margin – the joint-highest tally along with runners-up Liverpool.

Three of Arsenal's narrow triumphs were achieved by a 2–1 scoreline, in consecutive matches over the festive period – including the win at Anfield that Arsène Wenger later cited as being the turning point of their season.

Liverpool were the masters of the 1–0 in 2001–02; winning by that score on seven occasions – most notably against Manchester United at Old Trafford, when Danny Murphy's clever chipped goal was enough to clinch the victory.

Meanwhile, the only side not to win a league match 1–0 in 2001–02 were Claudio Ranieri's Chelsea.

Other teams to scrape home on a regular basis included top-six outfits Leeds United and Newcastle United, both of whom enjoyed one-goal-margin-wins on nine occasions.

At the other end of the table the small margin between success and failure was illustrated perfectly. Ipswich Town were the victims of a few smash-and-grab encounters, going down to 11 one-goal losses, as they suffered the dramatic and expensive consequences of relegation to Nationwide League Division One. An extra goal in a few of those games could have kept Ipswich up.

Derby County supporters won't need telling that their side lost more Premiership games than anyone else in 2001–02. 14 of their 24 defeats – more than half – were by a margin of just one goal and nine by a 1–0 scoreline.

WHERE GOALS SCORED

	GOALS FROM OUTSIDE BOX	Outside box (set-pieces)	Inside box (penalties)
Aston Villa	6.5%	3(0)	43(2)
Leicester	6.7%	2(0)	28(2)
Charlton	7.9%	3(1)	35(0)
Southampton	8.7%	4(2)	42(4)
Arsenal	11.4%	9(1)	70(6)
Derby Co	12.1%	4(2)	29(2)
Man Utd	12.6%	11(5)	76(5)
Liverpool	13.4%	9(0)	58(1)
Newcastle	13.5%	10(5)	64(5)
Fulham	13.9%	5(0)	31(1)
Tottenham	14.3%	7(0)	42(3)
West Ham	14.6%	7(0)	41(4)
Leeds Utd	15.1%	8(2)	45(1)
Everton	15.6%	7(1)	38(3)
Ipswich	17.1%	7(0)	34(1)
Middlesbro	17.1%	6(1)	29(2)
Sunderland	20.7%	6(1)	23(1)
Chelsea	24.2%	16(1)	50(4)
Blackburn	27.3%	15(0)	40(1)
Bolton W	27.3%	12(6)	32(0)

KEY ▪ Outside box (set-pieces) ▪ Inside box (penalties)

For long-range goals in 2001–02, Lancashire was the place to be, as promoted rivals Bolton Wanderers and Blackburn Rovers scored 12 and 15 times from outside the area respectively.

Those rasping efforts from distance accounted for 27.3% of the goals both teams scored – the joint-highest proportion in the Premiership.

Overall, Chelsea scored from long range most frequently with Dutchmen Jimmy Floyd Hasselbaink and Boudewijn Zenden responsible for half of the Blues' 16 strikes from outside the box. But with six, Newcastle United's Laurent Robert was the Premiership's most prolific player from distance, thanks largely to his prowess at set-piece situations.

At the other end of the scale, wooden-spoon winners Leicester managed the fewest goals from outside the area – just two – with Brian Deane and Stefan Oakes the men responsible.

Aston Villa's return from long range was also below par, but they compensated for that by netting 43 – or 93.5% – of their goals from inside the area. With big Peter Crouch in attack, Villa may take the direct route to success again in 2002–03 under Graham Taylor.

Among the other teams to score a large percentage of their goals from close range were Charlton Athletic, who did so despite being only one of two teams – the other being Bolton – not to score a penalty in 2001–02. The Addicks had three opportunities to put that right, but Graham Stuart, Jason Euell and Paul Konchesky all missed from the spot.

Newcastle striker Alan Shearer was more successful from 12 yards. The former England skipper converted five spot kicks – more than anyone else in the top flight during the campaign.

6 Bolton scored six goals direct from

WHERE GOALS CONCEDED

GOALS FROM OUTSIDE BOX

Team	%	Outside box (set-pieces)	Inside box (penalties)
Liverpool	6.7%	2(0)	28(3)
West Ham	10.5%	6(2)	51(1)
Leeds Utd	10.8%	4(0)	33(1)
Ipswich	10.9%	7(1)	57(5)
Blackburn	11.8%	6(2)	45(1)
Fulham	13.6%	6(1)	38(0)
Everton	14.0%	8(1)	49(1)
Aston Villa	14.9%	7(1)	40(3)
Middlesbro	14.9%	7(1)	40(5)
Leicester	15.6%	10(4)	54(5)
Sunderland	15.7%	8(1)	43(1)
Bolton W	16.1%	10(2)	52(2)
Charlton	16.3%	8(1)	41(3)
Southampton	16.7%	9(2)	45(2)
Newcastle	17.3%	9(0)	43(1)
Derby Co	17.5%	11(4)	52(3)
Man Utd	17.8%	8(2)	37(0)
Chelsea	18.4%	7(1)	31(3)
Tottenham	18.9%	10(1)	43(5)
Arsenal	22.2%	8(1)	28(3)

KEY ▮ Outside box (set-pieces) ▮ Inside box (penalties)

For the third season out of four, Arsenal conceded proportionately more goals from outside the penalty area than any other side in the Premiership.

That wasn't necessarily a bad thing though. It showed that opposing teams had to try their luck from distance against the Gunners, as the defensive wall formed by the likes of Sol Campbell, Martin Keown and Tony Adams did not allow opponents to get close to goal at regular intervals.

Although it perhaps indicated a weakness that Arsenal's goalkeepers had in saving long-distance shots, that did not ultimately bother the Highbury faithful too much, following their team's league and FA Cup success.

The Gunners' north London rivals Tottenham Hotspur also conceded a high ratio of their goals from outside the box in 2001–02, but overall, relegated Derby County were the most susceptible to long-range blockbusters, shipping 11.

Conversely, Liverpool chiefs Gérard Houllier and Phil Thompson saw just two shots from outside the area beat their goalkeepers – one of which was hit by Dean Holdsworth past Sander Westerveld in Bolton Wanderers' shock early-season win over the Reds.

Outside of the Premiership's top two, Leeds United had the best defensive record, thanks in no small part to the heroics of ever-present goalkeeper Nigel Martyn. The England man's goal was one of only three in the top flight never penetrated by a direct free kick.

The only two teams who went the entire 2001–02 campaign without conceding a goal from the penalty spot were Manchester United and Fulham, whose respective custodians, Fabien Barthez and Edwin van der Sar, saved a spot-kick apiece.

HOW GOALS WERE SCORED

Team	Headed Goals %					
Aston Villa	32.6%	15		8		22
Leicester	30.0%	9		5		15
Ipswich	29.3%	12		6		22
Sunderland	27.6%	8		8		13
Bolton W	25.0%	11		5		27
Southampton	23.9%	11	3	7		24
Middlesbro	22.9%	8		9		17
Fulham	22.2%	8		12		14
Charlton	21.1%	8	3	6		21
Tottenham	20.4%	10		9		29
Newcastle	20.3%	15	2	22		34
Leeds Utd	18.9%	10	2	21		20
West Ham	18.8%	9		6		32
Blackburn	18.2%	10	3	17		25
Everton	17.8%	8		14		22
Liverpool	16.4%	11		20		35
Man Utd	12.6%	11	2	22		52
Chelsea	12.1%	8		18		39
Derby Co	12.1%	4		17		12
Arsenal	8.9%	7		19		52

KEY ■ Headers ■ Own goals □ Other □ Left foot □ Right foot

Long-ball traditionalists Graham Taylor and Dave Bassett only managed Aston Villa and Leicester City respectively, for limited periods of the 2001–02 season, but their two teams still happened to be the ones who scored the highest proportion of headed goals in the Premiership.

Fifteen of Villa's goals – around one third of their total efforts – were nodded home during the league campaign. Targetman Dion Dublin got four of those, as did Colombian ace Juan Pablo Angel, while beanpole striker Peter Crouch rose to head in a couple following his £5 million arrival from Division One strugglers Portsmouth.

The only side to claim as many headed goals as Villa were Newcastle United, for whom Alan Shearer got six – more than any other player in the Premiership. But Leicester managed proportionately more, with headers accounting for 30% of their overall tally. Former Ipswich Town striker James Scowcroft was the Foxes' most prolific player in the air, netting three times with his head.

For the fourth season in a row, champions Arsenal finished bottom of the headed goal chart, with just nine per cent of their 79 Premiership strikes coming as a result of their aerial ability.

The Gunners stars were far more comfortable using their right feet and, with 52, netted more goals off that side than any other team. However, 67% of West Ham's goals-for column came as a result of right-footed shots – the top flight's highest ratio.

The team most reliant on left-footed goals were relegated Derby County. Veteran Italian striker Fabrizio Ravanelli netted five with his left peg, as did Malcolm Christie, who was equally comfortable finishing chances with either foot.

HOW GOALS WERE CONCEDED

Team	HEADED GOALS %	Headers	Own goals	Other	Left foot	Right foot
Arsenal	27.8%	10	2	8		16
Chelsea	26.3%	10		5		23
Leicester	25.0%	16	1	15		32
Leeds Utd	24.3%	9	2	14		12
Bolton W	24.2%	15	3	21		23
Tottenham	22.6%	12		17		24
Man Utd	22.2%	10	2	10		23
Sunderland	21.6%	11	4	7		29
Everton	21.1%	12	1	11		33
Southampton	20.4%	11		16		27
Ipswich	20.3%	13	1	1	15	34
Newcastle	19.2%	10	1	1	9	31
Charlton	18.4%	9	1	11		28
Blackburn	17.6%	9		20		22
Liverpool	16.7%	5	1	9		15
Aston Villa	14.9%	7	2	8		30
Middlesbro	14.9%	7	2	11		27
West Ham	12.3%	7	2	1	12	35
Derby Co	9.5%	6	1	17		39
Fulham	9.1%	4	1	15		24

KEY: Headers · Own goals · Other · Left foot · Right foot

Fifty-three per cent of the 1,001 goals scored in the 2001–02 Premiership came from right-footed shots, a slight rise on the 50% ratio of the 2000–01 campaign.

By conceding just 12, Leeds showed that they were the team most comfortable in dealing with the threat of their right-footed opponents, while Aston Villa were at the other end of the scale – 64% of the goals they shipped were as a result of right-foot shots.

Fulham were champions of making sure that the teams they were playing weren't allowed the opportunities to score headed goals. Only four of the Premiership strikes that the Cottagers conceded were nodded in – a fact that compliments the way in which their giant goalkeeper Edwin van der Sar dealt with the crosses and corners fired into his penalty area and also the aerial strength of centre-backs Andy Melville and Alain Goma.

On the other hand, Leicester City were the weakest side when it came to dealing with crosses. Sixteen of the 64 goals the relegated Foxes let in came via headers – a tally that probably wouldn't have been so great had dominating skipper Matt Elliott remained fit for selection for the whole of the season.

As well as scoring the lowest proportion on goals from headers, Arsenal conceded the highest proportion – some 27.8%.

Meanwhile, by conceding 21, Sam Allardyce's Bolton showed that they were the team most susceptible to left-footed shots, while Chelsea's goal was penetrated by a mere five left-peg strikes.

The only team to let in more than one goal in the 'other' category – those scrambled efforts that find their way in off a thigh or chest – were Middlesbrough, who conceded two.

goals than any other player.

WHEN GOALS WERE SCORED

	FIRST HALF GOALS %	0–15 mins	16–30 mins	31–45 mins	46–60 mins	61–75 mins	76–90 mins	SECOND HALF GOALS %
Newcastle	33.8%	4	9	12	13	18	18	66.2%
Derby Co	36.4%	5	3	4	6	5	10	63.6%
Southampton	37.0%	4	6	7	9	11	9	63.0%
Everton	37.8%	5	4	8	12	7	9	62.2%
Blackburn	38.2%	4	8	9	10	9	15	61.8%
Charlton	39.5%	3	6	6	7	6	10	60.5%
Sunderland	41.4%	4	3	5	3	3	11	58.6%
Ipswich	43.9%	9	4	5	8	6	9	56.1%
Leeds Utd	45.3%	10	12	2	9	10	10	54.7%
Middlesbro	45.7%	8	3	5	5	6	8	54.3%
Man Utd	46.0%	12	11	17	16	13	18	54.0%
Liverpool	46.3%	10	9	12	13	10	13	53.7%
Arsenal	46.8%	11	12	14	11	12	19	53.2%
West Ham	47.9%	6	9	8	5	6	14	52.1%
Chelsea	48.5%	5	9	18	6	9	19	51.5%
Fulham	50.0%	4	5	9	7	7	4	50.0%
Leicester	50.0%	4	10	1	3	6	6	50.0%
Tottenham	51.0%	7	7	11	9	5	10	49.0%
Bolton W	59.1%	8	5	13	3	6	9	40.9%
Aston Villa	60.9%	10	10	8	6	6	6	39.1%

KEY ▢ 0–15 mins ▢ 16–30 mins ▢ 31–45 mins ▢ 46–60 mins ▢ 61–75 mins ▢ 76–90 mins

On average, 55% of the goals scored in the 2001–02 season came in the second half of matches.

But not where Bobby Robson's Newcastle United were concerned. Like their manager, the Toon's players had the greatest staying power in the Premiership and notched over 66% of their league goals in the second half of games.

Their most profitable period was the last half-hour when they registered 36 of their overall 74-goal tally. That stamina also helped the Magpies achieve 10 wins from games in which they had trailed – the most in the division.

Southampton and Everton also scored a high percentage of their goals in the second half of games – no doubt the half-time team talks of fiery Scots Gordon Strachan, Walter Smith and latterly David Moyes had a part to play in this particular phenomenon.

Aston Villa meanwhile, were the Premiership's most productive team in the first half of matches during 2001–02. The Villans hit 61% of their goals before the break, but, as a consequence, their record in the second half of games was proportionally the poorest in the entire top flight.

Not surprisingly, given their attacking prowess, Manchester United got off to the most flying starts during the campaign, scoring 12 times within the opening 15 minutes of their matches. They also netted 17 times in the quarter-hour leading up to the break – once again, the best tally in the league.

By contrast, Alan Curbishley's Charlton scored the fewest early goals in the Premiership. They bagged just three in the first 15 minutes throughout the season and Sunderland were on the receiving end of two of those strikes.

9 Chelsea scored more goals after the 90

WHEN GOALS WERE CONCEDED

	FIRST HALF GOALS %	0–15 mins	16–30 mins	31–45 mins	46–60 mins	61–75 mins	76–90 mins	SECOND HALF GOALS %
Tottenham	30.2%	8	3	5	7	12	18	69.8%
Derby Co	33.3%	9	8	4	12	14	16	66.7%
Chelsea	34.2%	6	5	2	5	9	11	65.8%
Leeds Utd	37.8%	3	3	8	9	4	10	62.2%
Liverpool	40.0%	2	6	4	8	4	6	60.0%
West Ham	40.4%	3	10	10	10	9	15	59.6%
Middlesbro	40.4%	2	4	13	9	7	12	59.6%
Everton	42.1%	8	8	8	10	10	13	57.9%
Man Utd	42.2%	10	3	6	8	6	12	57.8%
Aston Villa	42.6%	8	5	7	7	10	10	57.4%
Blackburn	43.1%	5	6	11	9	11	9	56.9%
Bolton W	43.5%	5	7	15	10	10	15	56.5%
Ipswich	45.3%	7	11	11	10	9	16	54.7%
Arsenal	47.2%	3	4	10	8	3	8	52.8%
Leicester	50.0%	8	10	14	9	8	15	50.0%
Southampton	55.6%	8	10	12	5	8	11	44.4%
Fulham	56.8%	8	8	9	7	5	7	43.2%
Sunderland	56.9%	11	11	7	5	9	8	43.1%
Charlton	59.2%	12	9	8	4	6	10	40.8%
Newcastle	59.6%	7	14	10	9	7	5	40.4%

KEY ▢ 0–15 mins ▢ 16–30 mins ▢ 31–45 mins ▢ 46–60 mins ▢ 61–75 mins ▢ 76–90 mins

Any Manchester United fans turning up late to Premiership games in 2001–02 were running the risk of missing some exciting goal action – although it wasn't always at the right end of the pitch as far as they were concerned.

Because while Sir Alex Ferguson's men scored 12 times in the opening 15 minutes of their matches – more than anyone else – they were also one of the teams most likely to concede a goal in the opening stages of games.

In fact, only Charlton with 12 against and Sunderland with 11 against, let in a higher number of early goals than the Red Devils, who were also highly susceptible late on, conceding a dozen goals in the final 15-minute period.

Proportionally, Tottenham's defence was the most secure in the first 45 minutes of Premiership fixtures, as they were beaten just 16 times – 30% of their overall goals-against column – before the break.

However, no team showed as much vulnerability in the closing stages of games, as the White Hart Lane men let slip 18 goals between the 76th and 90th minutes – perhaps an indication that the ageing limbs of some Spurs stars didn't always hold out until the final whistle.

The side with the best defensive record in the second half of games was Newcastle who let in just 40% of their goals after the interval and only five in the closing quarter of an hour of their encounters. Other teams who fared particularly well once the second period was underway were Charlton, Sunderland and Fulham, who all ended up in the bottom 10. That trio's problems mainly came in the first halves of their matches.

Strangely, Derby County scored more goals than any other team straight after the half-time break.

minutes were up than any other team

WHO SCORED THE "GOALS FOR"

	% GOALS BY ATTACKERS	Attack	Midfield	Defence	Own goals
Derby Co	75.8%	25	6	2	
Leicester	70.0%	21	8	1	
West Ham	68.8%	33	12	3	
Chelsea	68.2%	45	15	5	
Aston Villa	65.2%	30	14	1	1
Fulham	63.9%	23	12	1	
Southampton	63.0%	29	14		3
Sunderland	62.1%	18	9	2	
Arsenal	60.8%	48	26	5	
Charlton	60.5%	23	7	5	3
Liverpool	58.2%	39	23	4	1
Leeds Utd	56.6%	30	15	6	2
Man Utd	51.7%	45	36	4	2
Middlesbro	51.4%	18	8	8	1
Ipswich	51.2%	21	16	4	
Bolton W	50.0%	22	19	2	1
Newcastle	50.0%	37	29	6	2
Tottenham	49.0%	24	22	2	1
Everton	46.7%	21	9	14	1
Blackburn	43.6%	24	26	2	3

KEY ■ Attack ■ Midfield □ Defence ■ Own goals

Blackburn Rovers may have struggled at the wrong end of the Premiership for the majority of the campaign, but the performances of their midfield players were excellent throughout 2001–02.

The likes of Tugay, Craig Hignett and highly-rated duo David Dunn and Damien Duff all contributed heavily on the goalscoring front, helping Rovers return a total of 26 strikes from midfield. That figure accounted for 47% of the team's overall tally of goals for the season – the highest proportion in the Premiership.

On the other hand, Derby County's midfielders scored just six goals between them in 2001–02 – the poorest return of any top flight engine room. However, the Rams' strikers – nine-goal men Fabrizio Ravanelli and Malcolm Christie in the main – netted 76% of their team's goals, which was the highest ratio in the division.

The most prolific defence in the Premiership belonged to Everton. That was due in part to David Unsworth's ability to strike a ball from distance, but full-back Steve Watson and Scotland stopper David Weir also made significant contributions, scoring four apiece.

Four teams went the entire campaign without having a defender score, including relegated Leicester City. That was quite a surprise considering that the Foxes' rearguard men had contributed seven strikes in 2000–01, with the likes of Matt Elliott and Gerry Taggart netting a couple each. Their absence due to injury at various times cost the team dearly.

No Aston Villa defender found the net either, despite the fact that veteran goalkeeper Peter Schmeichel showed them how it was done in the 3–2 defeat at Everton in October. By doing so, the big Dane became the first ever 'keeper to score in the Premiership.

WHO SCORED THE "GOALS AGAINST"

% GOALS BY ATTACKERS

Team	%	Attack	Midfield	Defence	Own goals
Chelsea	73.7%	28	8	2	
Middlesbro	70.2%	33	12	2	
Blackburn	66.7%	34	15	2	
Leicester	64.1%	41	21	1	
Charlton	63.3%	31	15	2	1
Aston Villa	61.7%	29	13	3	2
Bolton W	61.3%	38	15	6	3
Man Utd	60.0%	27	12	4	2
Ipswich	59.4%	38	19	6	
Fulham	56.8%	25	15	3	1
West Ham	56.1%	32	20	3	2
Southampton	55.6%	30	19	5	
Everton	54.4%	31	21	5	
Leeds Utd	54.1%	20	12	3	2
Sunderland	52.9%	27	14	6	4
Tottenham	52.8%	28	16	9	
Liverpool	50.0%	15	13	1	1
Derby Co	47.6%	30	28	4	1
Newcastle	46.2%	24	23	4	1
Arsenal	41.7%	15	15	4	2

KEY ■ Attack ■ Midfield □ Defence ■ Own goals

Chelsea hoped that 2001–02 would be the season that finally saw them emerge from their also-ran status to become genuine championship contenders. But the Blues didn't get their wish and a major reason for that was their defence's inability to cope with opposing strikeforces.

Seventy-three per cent of the goals that Chelsea conceded were scored by frontmen – proportionately the highest rate in the Premiership. Conversely, they had no problem dealing with the runs and shots of opposition midfield players and conceded just eight goals from that area – the lowest amount in the division.

Arsenal's defence was the most successful when it came to containing strikers, although they had some trouble dealing with runners from the centre of the pitch, conceding 42% of their goals to midfielders.

One area in which rock-bottom Leicester City excelled in 2001–02 was keeping things tight at set-pieces. That is illustrated by the fact that just one of the 64 goals they conceded in the Premiership was netted by a defender – Liverpool's Sami Hyypia in the 4–1 rout at Filbert Street in October.

By contrast, Tottenham Hotspur had big problems stopping their opponents' backline players from coming forward to score. On nine occasions, Glenn Hoddle saw his team concede goals to defenders – although that's a figure that included long-range efforts from the likes of Leeds United man Ian Harte and Middlesbrough's Franck Queudrue.

Sunderland could stake a claim for being the unluckiest team of the season. They were the only side to score four own goals past their goalkeeper, with defender Jody Craddock responsible twice, in 2–0 away defeats to Southampton and Leeds.

goals than any other midfielder

GOALSCORING

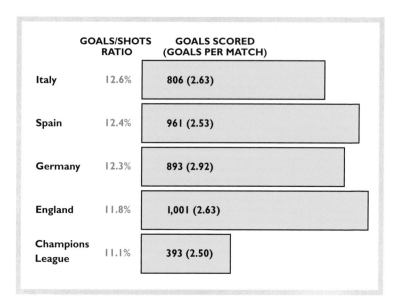

	GOALS/SHOTS RATIO	GOALS SCORED (GOALS PER MATCH)
Italy	12.6%	806 (2.63)
Spain	12.4%	961 (2.53)
Germany	12.3%	893 (2.92)
England	11.8%	1,001 (2.63)
Champions League	11.1%	393 (2.50)

With Arsenal finding the net in every single one of their league fixtures and Manchester United scoring on 87 occasions, you may have thought that the English Premiership was the place to be for goals in the 2001–02 season.

But that was not the case, as the teams in the Bundesliga served up an average of 2.92 goals per game in 2001–02, making Germany's top flight the most prolific among Europe's leading leagues. Runners-up Bayer Leverkusen found the net more often than their rivals, scoring 77 times and managing at least four goals in no fewer than nine of their games.

Of the 306 matches played in the Bundesliga, just 23 finished goalless, while Borussia Dortmund's Marcio Amoroso and Martin Max of 1860 Munich benefited from the free-scoring nature of the division, netting 18 apiece to end as joint-top marksmen.

Meanwhile, the players of Italy's Serie A were the most proficient finishers in Europe in 2001–02 – converting an average of 12.6% of their shots into goals. Often typecast as a league where tactical probing rather than goalmouth action prevails,

champions Juventus and Internazionale helped dispel the myth by averaging more than 1.8 strikes per game each. Juve also possessed Serie A's joint-leading scorer in Frenchman David Trezeguet, who returned an exceptional tally of 24 goals – none of which were penalties – in 34 appearances. Piacenza's Dario Hubner equalled that total; another remarkable feat considering his side struggled in the bottom half of the table.

Across mainland Europe, Spain's Primera Liga played host to some of the world's most exciting talents, but it wasn't always a thrill-a-minute judging by the total of 34 scoreless draws in 2001–02 – the same amount as the English Premiership witnessed.

The Champions League saw just 2.5 goals per game – a lower ratio than any of Europe's main domestic divisions – illustrating that while the best attackers were on show, the quality of the teams meant there were few easy victories. Victors Real Madrid proved they were the best in 2001–02 by scoring 35 times and Manchester United's Dutch striker Ruud van Nistelrooy – with 10 – excelled as the Champions League's top goalscorer.

PENALTY TAKING

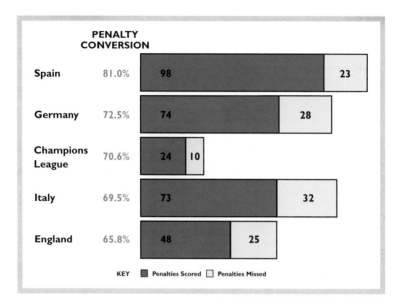

PENALTY CONVERSION

League	%	Penalties Scored	Penalties Missed
Spain	81.0%	98	23
Germany	72.5%	74	28
Champions League	70.6%	24	10
Italy	69.5%	73	32
England	65.8%	48	25

KEY ■ Penalties Scored □ Penalties Missed

England coach Sven-Göran Eriksson and his Italy counterpart Giovanni Trapattoni would not have been encouraged by the standard of penalty taking in their respective domestic leagues in the build-up to a World Cup campaign.

Failure from the spot was particularly widespread in the Premiership, where just 65.8% of penalties were converted – a massive 12-percentage-point reduction on the 2000–01 season.

Even more worrying for Eriksson was the high rate of spot kicks spurned by English players in the Premiership – home-grown stars netted just 17 of the 29 penalties they took – a 58.6% conversion rate – and England international strikers Alan Shearer and Kevin Phillips were as guilty as anyone, failing twice each for Newcastle and Sunderland respectively.

In Italy, the situation wasn't a great deal better. Serie A penalty takers only found the net with 69.5% of their efforts from 12 yards, missing 32 in total. Torino striker Marco Ferrante was particularly profligate, flunking four chances from the penalty spot.

Spain's Primera Liga saw by far the highest number of penalties in 2001–02, with 121 being awarded over the course of the season. It was also the league to be in for successfully converted spot kicks – 98 of those taken ended up in the net. Real Madrid and Portugal winger Luis Figo set the standard by posting a 100% success rate from his five penalty kicks.

In Germany – a country famed for its ice-cool conversion of penalties – the standard of spot kicks was decidedly average in the 2001–02 Bundesliga. Of the 102 taken, 72.5% were scored, and that was a ratio significantly boosted by the efforts of Borussia Dortmund striker Marcio Amoroso, who scored seven times from 12 yards out, making him the most prolific penalty taker in the major European leagues.

The accuracy in the Champions League was also fairly average with 70.6% of the penalties going in. Manchester United were awarded the most chances from the spot, five in total – the same amount as they were handed in the Premiership. On the other hand, Bolton and Blackburn were the teams in the English top flight to be given the fewest spot kicks – just one apiece.

in the Premiership were missed

PASSES COMPLETED

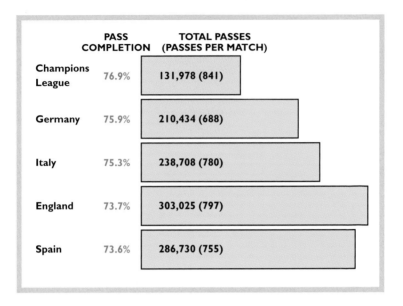

	PASS COMPLETION	TOTAL PASSES (PASSES PER MATCH)
Champions League	76.9%	131,978 (841)
Germany	75.9%	210,434 (688)
Italy	75.3%	238,708 (780)
England	73.7%	303,025 (797)
Spain	73.6%	286,730 (755)

The standard of football in the English Premiership has improved significantly over the last few years, but the quality of passing in the division in 2001–02 was still some way short of that seen in some other top European leagues.

For example, the players in the German Bundesliga completed 75.9% of their overall passes in 2001–02 – an accuracy ratio more than two percentage points higher than that of the Premiership. The passing in Italy's top flight was also technically superior to that in England, with Serie A teams finding a team-mate 75.3% of the time.

But compared to those leagues, there were more passes per game on average in the Premiership and the division was also ahead of the Spanish Primera Liga in terms of successful distribution.

The top passing team in England, by some distance, were Manchester United, despite their failed attempt to retain the league crown. They made more passes and enjoyed a higher accuracy record than any other side and they also boasted the country's most prolific passer – Roy Keane.

German outfit Schalke, Italian giants Juventus and Spaniards Real Madrid were the top passing teams in their respective domestic leagues, although only in Juve's case did the ability to dominate games result in title success.

Real Madrid were also the best passers in the Champions League and did manage to triumph in that competition. Vicente Del Bosque's men completed an impressive 82% of their passes on their way to winning the trophy for a ninth time by defeating Bayer Leverkusen at Hampden Park.

However, it was Real's big rivals Barcelona who supplied the tournament's number one passer, in midfielder Xavi. He laid off a massive 1,031 balls before the Catalans' semi-final exit.

Not surprisingly, the overall distribution accuracy rate of 76.9% in the Champions League was greater than that of any domestic division in 2001–02, as the competition, by its nature, separated the wheat from the chaff. Teams new to the tournament in 2002–03 will have to adapt quickly.

DISCIPLINE

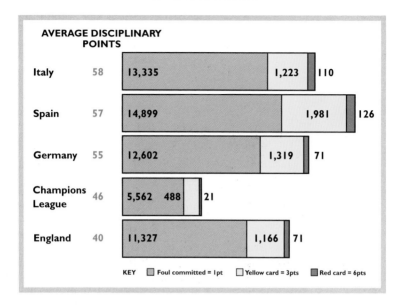

AVERAGE DISCIPLINARY POINTS

Country	Points	Foul committed = 1pt	Yellow card = 3pts	Red card = 6pts
Italy	58	13,335	1,223	110
Spain	57	14,899	1,981	126
Germany	55	12,602	1,319	71
Champions League	46	5,562	488	21
England	40	11,327	1,166	71

KEY ■ Foul committed = 1pt □ Yellow card = 3pts ■ Red card = 6pts

Talk of cynical fouls, red-card controversy and downright cheating was never far from the pages of English newspapers in the 2001–02 season.

But based on Opta's disciplinary system of one point for a foul, three for a yellow card and six for a red, the Premiership was actually the most serene place, compared to the other top leagues in Europe.

Match referees in England dished out a combination of 1,237 yellow and red cards in 2001–02, which may sound a lot but was substantially lower than the card totals in Spain, Germany and Italy.

When fouls are also taken into account, Italy's Serie A was ranked by the Opta points system as the most indisciplined competition, with the main culprits being relegated Verona.

They racked up a massive tally of 860 fouls as well as 83 yellow and eight red cards during a miserable 2001–02 campaign, which ended in last-day disaster as they dropped into Serie B.

But it was Verona's local rivals Chievo who employed the player with the worst fouling record, in Bernardo Corradi. The striker put himself about a bit too much, committing 121 misdemeanours.

Disciplinary problems were also rife in the Spanish Primera Liga. An amazing 126 red cards were shown during the season – some 55 more than in the Premiership, where the same number of games were played. Among the main offenders in Spain were Tenerife, who gave away more fouls than any other side and Rayo Vallecano who picked up 11 dismissals.

Surprisingly, former Tottenham Hotspur and Everton midfielder Vinny Samways was one of La Liga's most indisciplined players, amassing 17 cautions for Las Palmas in 2001–02 – three more than the most booked player in the English Premiership, Robbie Savage.

Along with Savage's Leicester City side, Premiership champions Arsenal also posted a poor disciplinary record and had three players – Thierry Henry, Martin Keown and Patrick Vieira – called to FA headquarters to answer misconduct charges. Liverpool and Manchester United set a better example, accruing just four red cards between them in 2001–02.

than in any other major domestic league

THE PLAYERS

The top scorer is easy enough for anyone to monitor — but who was the top tackler, the most prolific passer, the best crosser or the best shot-stopper? And which players had the best and worst disciplinary records in the league in 2001–02?

The answers to these and many more questions are contained in this section - and only Opta can provide this information, because of the unique way in which they monitor every single touch of the ball.

But it is not just quantity that counts — it is quality too. So, although many of the categories are sorted on the total number of successful outcomes, you can also see percentage completion rates to judge for yourself how good players really are by comparison.

The bar charts show several pieces of information. For example, in the chart that shows which player had the most shots in total, on page 274, you will also be able to see the player who had the most shots on target. In addition, the figure shown alongside the bars indicates how accurate their shooting was.

There is an explanation beneath each of the charts, showing how the ranking is calculated and what it means.

The Golden Boot was won by Thierry Henry, who finished the season with 24 Premiership goals. Three men, Alan Shearer, Ruud van Nistelrooy and 2000–01's top marksman Jimmy Floyd Hasselbaink, finished the season with 23 goals.

It was a good season for goalscoring, with England star Michael Owen achieving a personal best 19 league goals, while Manchester United's Norwegian forward Ole Gunnar Solskjaer chipped in with an impressive 17.

Fredrik Ljungberg was the top-scoring midfielder, netting 12 times in the Premiership, closely followed by David Beckham, whose tally of 11 goals was a personal best for a single season.

70% Tottenham conceded the biggest percentage

FASTEST / LATEST GOALS
IN 2001–02 PREMIERSHIP

		PLAYER	MATCH	TIME MINS SECS	
FASTEST	1	Alan Smith	Newcastle v LEEDS UTD	0	29
	2	Ruud van Nistelrooy	MAN UTD v Southampton	0	30
	3	David Unsworth	EVERTON v Fulham	0	31
	4	Dion Dublin	West Ham v ASTON VILLA	0	51
	5	Marcus Bent	Charlton v IPSWICH	0	53
LATEST	1	Juan Pablo Angel	ASTON VILLA v Tottenham	94	23
	2	Dennis Bergkamp	Fulham v ARSENAL	94	14
	3	David Dunn	Charlton v BLACKBURN	94	13
	4=	Michael Ricketts	BOLTON W v Leicester	93	48
	4=	Michael Ricketts	BOLTON W v Everton	93	48

Kick-off, a few passes, give it away, get it back and spring the offside trap – 29 seconds gone and Leeds United scored the fastest goal of the season.

They may have ended up losing the match away to Newcastle, but the speed with which Leeds stung their opponents deserved acclaim in itself.

Alan Smith was certainly in the nick of time – Ruud van Nistelrooy was just a second behind with his goal against Southampton. The Dutch striker latched onto the end of a Paul Scholes pass to fire past Paul Jones – the first of six occasions on which the Saints 'keeper picked the ball out of the back of his net that afternoon.

Perhaps the most unlikely scorer of a goal within half a minute (or so) of the kick-off was Everton's David Unsworth who was just a second behind the Manchester United hitman. Unsworth benefited greatly from David Moyes' appointment as he enjoyed a lengthy run in the side – could this be explained by the powerful defender's goal in the first minute of the new manager's debut in charge of the Toffeemen?

Late goals were also plentiful during 2001-02, but the deepest into stoppage time came at Villa Park, where Juan Pablo Angel put away a penalty at the death to salvage a point for the home side against Tottenham Hotspur.

Indeed, Dennis Bergkamp may have a case should he decide to complain about the delay preceding Angel's spot-kick, as it denied the Arsenal man the latest goal with his 95th-minute effort at Craven Cottage. But then again, he does have a couple of medals to make up for the disappointment.

of goals in the second half of games.

GOALS – FREE-KICKS, PENALTIES, HEADERS, GOALS FROM OUTSIDE THE BOX

With the vast array of talent on show in the Premiership, there was little wonder that goals of every shape and size were banged away regularly, for our delectation. Certain players were adept at putting away particular types of goals while others went for an all-round onslaught – here is the breakdown of the top exponents of each type of striking art.

There were 73 spot-kicks awarded during 2001–02 – five more than in the previous campaign. Forty-eight were put away, while 16 were kept out by the goalkeeper, leaving nine players rueing a penalty off-target. The only player to net five penalties was Alan Shearer, although it could have been seven had he not failed with a pair of attempts. Three players tied for second place including Golden Boot winner Thierry Henry. The Frenchman was less successful in the Champions League where he scored just two of his four attempts.

PENALTIES

PLAYER	PENALTY GOALS
Alan Shearer	5
Paolo Di Canio	4
Thierry Henry	4
Ruud van Nistelrooy	4
Jimmy Hasselbaink	3
Teddy Sheringham	3

SET-PIECES

PLAYER	SET-PIECE GOALS
Laurent Robert	5
David Beckham	4
Per Frandsen	3
Youri Djorkaeff	2
Ian Harte	2
Fabrizio Ravanelli	2

Five was again the top score for converted free-kicks, as it was during 2000-01, but this time it was Newcastle's Laurent Robert who put away a quintet of efforts. The previous winner, David Beckham, managed four, although he of course saved his most celebrated effort for the national side, when he scored against Greece to take England to the World Cup. Bolton's Per Frandsen was the only other player to net at least three – his only goals of the campaign coming from dead-ball situations.

Alan Shearer added to his success from spot-kicks with the most headed goals during 2001-02, scoring six times to out-nod everyone else by two clear strikes. There were 193 headed goals in total during the course of the season – a far lower proportion of the total Premiership goal tally than in the previous season, perhaps explained by a fairly disappointing 11% chance conversion rate overall. Six players finished joint-second with four headed goals apiece, but for the second season in a row Duncan Ferguson did not score with his head.

HEADED GOALS

PLAYER	HEADED GOALS
Alan Shearer	6
Juan Pablo Angel	4
Dion Dublin	4
Jimmy Hasselbaink	4
Marian Pahars	4
Niall Quinn	4
Marcus Stewart	4

GOALS FROM OUTSIDE THE BOX

PLAYER	LONG-RANGE GOALS
Laurent Robert	6
David Beckham	5
Jimmy Hasselbaink	5
Damien Duff	4
David Dunn	4
Ian Harte	4
Thierry Henry	4

Completing the Newcastle clean sweep, Laurent Robert registered more goals from outside the area than any other Premiership player during 2001-02. David Beckham was again deposed from his number one spot from the 2000–01 campaign, although the Manchester United man still put away the second-highest tally with five, rivalled by Chelsea's Jimmy Floyd Hasselbaink. However, few could touch the brilliance of some of the Dutchman's long-rangers. Blackburn's David Dunn and Damien Duff were among four players with four long-distance strikes apiece.

GOALSCORERS

Although most goalscorers will happily put away their strikes at any ground and at any time during a match, occasionally a player will prefer the confines of his own stadium, or have a penchant for leaving it late to score. Here Opta reveal who prefers to shy away from their own fans' expectations, or who liked to leave it late to make their mark.

HOME

PLAYER	HOME GOALS
Jimmy Hasselbaink	14
Ruud van Nistelrooy	14
Thierry Henry	12
Alan Shearer	12
2 players on	10

Jimmy Floyd Hasselbaink and Ruud van Nistelrooy both scored 61% of their goals on their own grounds – a greater proportion than any of the other Premiership strikers during 2001-02. Thierry Henry and Alan Shearer also enjoyed playing in familiar surroundings, bagging 12 home goals apiece. Overall, 56% of goals were scored by the home team – 9% of those by the top four league goalscorers.

With Arsenal remaining unbeaten away for the whole of the season while scoring in every match, it was no surprise to see Thierry Henry at the top of the away goalscorers table. The Frenchman scored half of his goals on opposition turf, beating Alan Shearer and Ole Gunnar Solskjaer into joint-second. Indeed, the Norwegian was more than happy to delight travelling fans, netting 65% of his strikes away from home.

AWAY

PLAYER	AWAY GOALS
Thierry Henry	12
Alan Shearer	11
Ole Solskjaer	11
3 players on	9

FIRST GOALSCORERS

PLAYER	FIRST GOALS
Jimmy Hasselbaink	8
Fredrik Ljungberg	8
Michael Owen	8
Ruud van Nistelrooy	7
4 players on	6

That all-important first goal settled no fewer than 65 Premiership matches during 2001-02, proving once again how crucial it can be. There was a three-way tie for the bookies' favourite bet – Jimmy Floyd Hasselbaink and Michael Owen were keen to open the scoring, but perhaps the most surprising joint-winner was midfielder Fredrik Ljungberg. No fewer than four of the Swede's eight openers came in Arsenal's last six matches of the season.

Michael Owen bagged the final goal in Premiership matches more times than any other player, with nine final efforts to his name. West Ham were unlikely to be too happy about this – Owen scored the last goal in both games against the Hammers, stealing a win and a draw for Liverpool. Thierry Henry and Ruud van Nistelrooy proved their concentration did not lapse late on with five goals apiece, while Alan Shearer showed that he was a man to watch for the full 90 minutes.

LAST GOALSCORERS

PLAYER	LATE GOALS
Michael Owen	9
Thierry Henry	8
Ruud van Nistelrooy	8
Alan Shearer	7
8 players on	6

goals than any other player

GOALSCORING

Player	Goals/Shots Ratio	Headers	Shots
Thierry Henry	17.9%		24
Alan Shearer	27.4%	6	17
Ruud van Nistelrooy	26.4%	3	20
Jimmy Hasselbaink	18.7%	4	19
Michael Owen	30.2%	3	16
Ole Solskjaer	32.1%	3	14
Robbie Fowler	16.5%	3	12
Marian Pahars	21.2%	4	10
Eidur Gudjohnsen	20.9%		14
Andrew Cole	21.3%	4	9
Fredrik Ljungberg	26.1%		12
Juan Pablo Angel	18.2%	4	8
James Beattie	17.1%	3	9
Michael Ricketts	16.7%	3	9
Darius Vassell	16.7%	1	11
Jason Euell	17.5%		11
David Beckham	15.7%		11
Mark Viduka	13.9%	3	8
Frédéric Kanouté	13.4%	3	8
Kevin Phillips	8.0%	2	9

KEY: Headers, Shots

When Thierry Henry joined Arsenal in August 1999, he was used to playing out wide, rather than up front, but Arsène Wenger transformed the former Monaco and Juventus player into a world-class striker.

Henry scored twice on the final day of Arsenal's double-winning campaign to finish as the Premiership's top scorer.

This gave the Frenchman 58 goals in 99 Premiership appearances during his Highbury career, a superb strike rate.

Alan Shearer vindicated his decision to retire from international football, to concentrate on playing for Newcastle United, by finishing the season just one goal behind Henry.

Shearer ended 2001–02 with six headed goals – the most in the Premiership – to help his side qualify for the 2002–03 Champions League.

Dutch pair Jimmy Floyd Hasselbaink and Ruud van Nistelrooy also scored 23 goals, with the latter having to make do with the PFA Player of the Year award, in an otherwise trophy-less season for Manchester United.

Leeds had a season they would rather forget, but there was no doubting what a fantastic buy Robbie Fowler was. He also had the accolade of scoring more times at Filbert Street than any Leicester player, with four goals.

Juan Pablo Angel scored just once in 2000-01, but answered his critics with 12 goals for Aston Villa in 2001–02.

Fredrik Ljungberg was the highest-scoring midfielder with 12 goals, followed by David Beckham – setting up a key battle in the World Cup.

The likes of Darius Vassell and Michael Ricketts impressed at club level to earn international recognition, while Andy Cole ended his international career by retiring after missing out on England's 2002 World Cup squad.

0 Diego Forlan played 570 minutes without

MINUTES PER GOAL

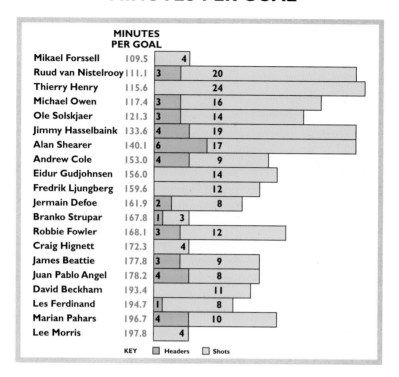

	MINUTES PER GOAL	Headers	Shots
Mikael Forssell	109.5		4
Ruud van Nistelrooy	111.1	3	20
Thierry Henry	115.6		24
Michael Owen	117.4	3	16
Ole Solskjaer	121.3	3	14
Jimmy Hasselbaink	133.6	4	19
Alan Shearer	140.1	6	17
Andrew Cole	153.0	4	9
Eidur Gudjohnsen	156.0		14
Fredrik Ljungberg	159.6		12
Jermain Defoe	161.9	2	8
Branko Strupar	167.8	1	3
Robbie Fowler	168.1	3	12
Craig Hignett	172.3		4
James Beattie	177.8	3	9
Juan Pablo Angel	178.2	4	8
David Beckham	193.4		11
Les Ferdinand	194.7	1	8
Marian Pahars	196.7	4	10
Lee Morris	197.8		4

KEY ▓ Headers ☐ Shots

With a four-way tie for top goalscorer averted by Thierry Henry's second against Everton on the final day of the campaign, it was perhaps surprising that Mikael Forssell of Chelsea ended up as the striker who made the most of his time on the pitch during 2001-02.

The Finn bagged four strikes from 20 attempts, averaging a goal every 109.5 minutes. Having beaten Ruud van Nistelrooy into second place – the Dutchman had to wait over a minute and a half more to score each of his 23 goals – Forssell looks certain to threaten Jimmy Floyd Hasselbaink and Eidur Gudjohnsen for their places in the Blues' starting XI in the near future.

After Forssell and van Nistelrooy come the usual suspects – Henry was the third-most frequent scorer with Michael Owen not far behind. But unexpectedly, given their own 23-goal hauls, Hasselbaink and Alan Shearer are behind the Liverpool man as well as Ole Gunnar Solskjaer.

Indeed, Shearer had to wait almost a full half an hour more to score on average than van Nistelrooy, despite the two players bringing home the bacon the same number of times.

The top-ranking midfielder sneaked into the top 10 – Fredrik Ljungberg's scintillating end to the season was capped by a goal every 159.6 minutes on average. The only other midfield player to make the top 20 was the England captain – David Beckham had to wait more than three hours on average for each of his 11 goals.

Meanwhile, 2000-01's most-frequent scorer, Branko Strupar, had the same problem as previously – injury prevented the Belgian demonstrating his clinical finishing more than a handful of times.

Derby would have been grateful for a few more appearances by Strupar and Lee Morris, who scored every 197.8 minutes on average.

SHOOTING

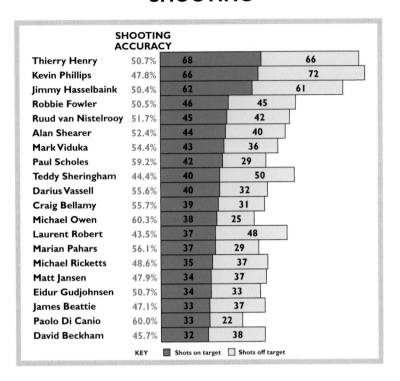

SHOOTING ACCURACY

Player	Accuracy	Shots on target	Shots off target
Thierry Henry	50.7%	68	66
Kevin Phillips	47.8%	66	72
Jimmy Hasselbaink	50.4%	62	61
Robbie Fowler	50.5%	46	45
Ruud van Nistelrooy	51.7%	45	42
Alan Shearer	52.4%	44	40
Mark Viduka	54.4%	43	36
Paul Scholes	59.2%	42	29
Teddy Sheringham	44.4%	40	50
Darius Vassell	55.6%	40	32
Craig Bellamy	55.7%	39	31
Michael Owen	60.3%	38	25
Laurent Robert	43.5%	37	48
Marian Pahars	56.1%	37	29
Michael Ricketts	48.6%	35	37
Matt Jansen	47.9%	34	37
Eidur Gudjohnsen	50.7%	34	33
James Beattie	47.1%	33	37
Paolo Di Canio	60.0%	33	22
David Beckham	45.7%	32	38

KEY ■ Shots on target □ Shots off target

For the second successive season, Thierry Henry had more shots on target than any other player.

The Arsenal striker scored with 24 of his 68 efforts on target, ending the 2001–02 campaign as the Premiership's top scorer.

Kevin Phillips had just two accurate shots fewer than the Frenchman, but also fired 72 efforts off target – the most in the Premiership.

The Sunderland striker's 138 shots in total was more than any player has managed in a single season since Opta began compiling records and while his goal return of 11 didn't match his totals in previous seasons, they more than helped Peter Reid's side survive relegation.

Chelsea's Jimmy Floyd Hasselbaink was the only other player to fire more than 100 shots in total and, but for injury in the last two games of the season, may well have ended the season as top scorer for the second year in a row.

Manchester United's season may have been disappointing, but Paul Scholes still managed more efforts on target than any other midfielder and was one of six players on the list to be selected for England's World Cup squad.

The only side, other than Manchester United, to have three players on the list was Newcastle United, whose attacking and entertaining style of play not only won many admirers, but also a place in the qualification round for the 2002-03 Champions League.

Strike pair Alan Shearer and Craig Bellamy fired in 83 shots on target between them, while French winger Laurent Robert added a further 37, albeit with the lowest shooting accuracy of any player on the list.

Southampton were another side who entertained and were rewarded with a finishing place of 11th. Both Marian Pahars and James Beattie made the list.

15 Robert Pires set up the most

GOAL ASSISTS

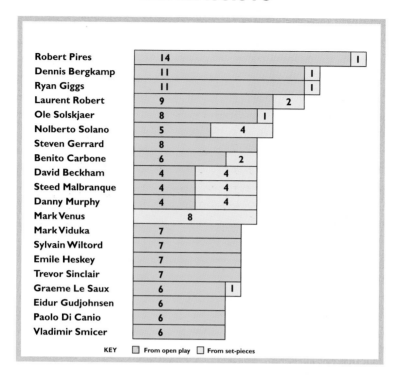

Robert Pires	14	1
Dennis Bergkamp	11	1
Ryan Giggs	11	1
Laurent Robert	9	2
Ole Solskjaer	8	1
Nolberto Solano	5	4
Steven Gerrard	8	
Benito Carbone	6	2
David Beckham	4	4
Steed Malbranque	4	4
Danny Murphy	4	4
Mark Venus	8	
Mark Viduka	7	
Sylvain Wiltord	7	
Emile Heskey	7	
Trevor Sinclair	7	
Graeme Le Saux	6	1
Eidur Gudjohnsen	6	
Paolo Di Canio	6	
Vladimir Smicer	6	

KEY ▢ From open play ▢ From set-pieces

As seems to be the way with new recruits at Highbury, Robert Pires suddenly hit form during his second season at the club.

The Frenchman was ruled out of the final eight league games of the season with a knee injury, but not before he had provided a Premiership-best 15 goal assists for his colleagues on their way to the title. His unselfishness was undeniably the key to many a Gunners victory during the campaign and his haul matched the best by any Premiership player since Opta began compiling statistics.

There was a tie for the runners-up spot. Pires's team-mate Dennis Bergkamp rediscovered his creativity to set up a colleague 12 times – a figure matched by Manchester United's Ryan Giggs.

Two other United stars made the top 10 – Ole Gunnar Solskjaer capped a fine first season without his loathed 'super-sub' tag with nine assists, while last term's top provider, David Beckham, sneaked in at joint-ninth with eight.

French star Laurent Robert answered his critics with 11 crisp deliveries to his name, beating Liverpool's main man, England injury-victim Steven Gerrard, by three.

The top 20 was filled with attack-minded players, with one notable exception in the form of the only defender to continually supply killer balls. It may have turned out to be a disappointing season for Ipswich, but if Mark Venus can retain the form that saw him provide team-mates with eight assists, he will surely be vital to Town's bid to return to the top flight at the first attempt.

Interestingly, Liverpool star Emile Heskey – the target of some criticism – proved himself an able provider at Premiership level. He set up seven goals during the season, the same amount as other unselfish strikers; Mark Viduka of Leeds and Arsenal's Sylvain Wiltord.

PASSING

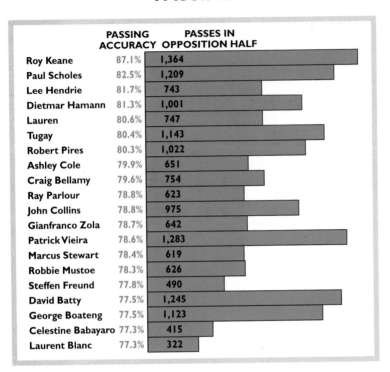

	PASSING ACCURACY	PASSES IN OPPOSITION HALF
Roy Keane	87.1%	1,364
Paul Scholes	82.5%	1,209
Lee Hendrie	81.7%	743
Dietmar Hamann	81.3%	1,001
Lauren	80.6%	747
Tugay	80.4%	1,143
Robert Pires	80.3%	1,022
Ashley Cole	79.9%	651
Craig Bellamy	79.6%	754
Ray Parlour	78.8%	623
John Collins	78.8%	975
Gianfranco Zola	78.7%	642
Patrick Vieira	78.6%	1,283
Marcus Stewart	78.4%	619
Robbie Mustoe	78.3%	626
Steffen Freund	77.8%	490
David Batty	77.5%	1,245
George Boateng	77.5%	1,123
Celestine Babayaro	77.3%	415
Laurent Blanc	77.3%	322

In a season of disappointment for Sir Alex Ferguson, he was able to take a crumb of comfort from the fact that Manchester United's passing game remained the best in the Premiership.

That was thanks in no small measure to the contribution of controversial skipper Roy Keane, who kept possession in the opposition half with a fantastic 87.1% level of accuracy and also made more passes than any other player in enemy territory, despite missing several games through injury.

Keane's midfield colleague Paul Scholes also registered an excellent pass completion rate, finding a team-mate with 82.5% of his balls over the halfway line.

Somewhat unexpectedly, the bronze medal for offensive passes went not to a high-profile midfielder from one of the top clubs in the Premiership, but to Lee Hendrie of Aston Villa who posted an 81.7% accuracy record.

Dietmar Hamann and Craig Bellamy were the most accurate passers for Liverpool and Newcastle United respectively and were joined in the top 10 by Tugay of Blackburn Rovers who enjoyed an excellent first season in England.

Arsenal had the most representatives in the chart – five in total - with Cameroon international Lauren leading the way. He crossed the halfway line from his right-back position to complete 80.6% of his passes, a ratio superior to that of his illustrious team-mates Robert Pires and Patrick Vieira.

Fulham's player-coach John Collins epitomised his team's excellence on the ball, finding another white shirt with 78.8% of his passes in the opposition half. Following the appointment of Italian legend Franco Baresi as director of football, Fulham fans are likely to see their team adopt an even more cosmopolitan style at Loftus Road in 2002-03.

TACKLES

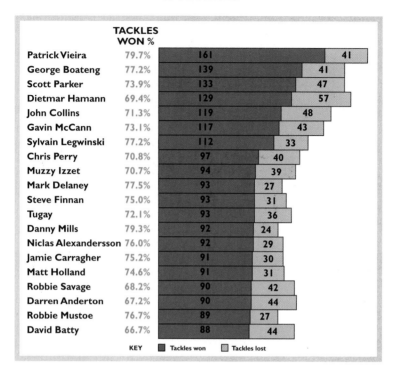

	TACKLES WON %	Tackles won	Tackles lost
Patrick Vieira	79.7%	161	41
George Boateng	77.2%	139	41
Scott Parker	73.9%	133	47
Dietmar Hamann	69.4%	129	57
John Collins	71.3%	119	48
Gavin McCann	73.1%	117	43
Sylvain Legwinski	77.2%	112	33
Chris Perry	70.8%	97	40
Muzzy Izzet	70.7%	94	39
Mark Delaney	77.5%	93	27
Steve Finnan	75.0%	93	31
Tugay	72.1%	93	36
Danny Mills	79.3%	92	24
Niclas Alexandersson	76.0%	92	29
Jamie Carragher	75.2%	91	30
Matt Holland	74.6%	91	31
Robbie Savage	68.2%	90	42
Darren Anderton	67.2%	90	44
Robbie Mustoe	76.7%	89	27
David Batty	66.7%	88	44

KEY ■ Tackles won □ Tackles lost

Anyone questioning Patrick Vieira's commitment to Arsenal need only look at the table above.

Having not even made the top 20 for tackling during 2000-01, Vieira threw himself into 16 more challenges than his closest rival, Dietmar Hamann of Liverpool. Furthermore, with his superb 79.7% success rate, the French international was successful in winning possession a full 22 more times than anyone else, making him the only player to relieve more than 150 opponents of the ball.

The news that George Boateng decided to request a move from Aston Villa at the end of the season will have hit the manager and fans hard – the combative midfielder was second only to Vieira in terms of tackles won.

Scott Parker joined Boateng on the 180 attempted tackles mark. The Charlton man clearly flourished upon being given a regular place in the starting XI and on this kind of form may be confident of playing some part in England's Euro 2004 plans, though he may have to curb his aggresive style if he is to avoid picking up as many bookings in the future.

The 2000–01 season's top tackler, Olivier Dacourt of Leeds, was absent from the list following a string of injuries throughout the campaign, with Danny Mills taking over as the Whites' main ball-winner.

Strangely, not a single Manchester United player made the top 20, while Fulham were the most-represented side in the list with three players making more than 90 successful challenges.

Sweden and Everton midfielder Niclas Alexandersson – who stunned England with his World Cup strike – was a prolific tackler in the Premiership, making 121 challenges.

As usual, the majority of ball-winning was done in the centre of the park – just five defenders made the top 20, while strikers were conspicuous by their absence.

THE DIRTIEST

DISCIPLINARY POINTS

Player	Points	Foul committed = 1pt	Yellow card = 3pts	Red card = 6pts
Patrick Vieira	123	87	10	1
Robbie Savage	110	68	14	
George Boateng	108	93	5	
Garry Flitcroft	102	81	7	
Barry Hayles	102	84	6	
Gavin McCann	99	72	9	
David Batty	99	75	8	
Muzzy Izzet	98	65	9	1
Alan Shearer	97	85	2	1
Nikos Dabizas	96	78	6	
Danny Mills	92	50	10	2
Scott Parker	92	59	9	1
Paul Ince	91	52	11	1
Paul Warhurst	91	61	8	1
Duncan Ferguson	90	66	6	1
Lucas Neill	90	63	9	
Sylvain Legwinski	86	62	8	
David Weir	83	62	5	1
Chris Marsden	82	64	4	1
James Beattie	82	73	3	

KEY   ▢ Foul committed = 1pt   ▢ Yellow card = 3pts   ▢ Red card = 6pts

Arsenal fans – and Arsène Wenger – may bemoan the treatment of Patrick Vieira at the hands of referees, but the stats are damning. The French midfielder was, for 2001–02 at least, the Premiership's most indisciplined player thanks to a combination of 87 fouls, 10 bookings and a red card, earned against Leicester in the third game of the season.

There was a player who conceded more free-kicks, however – Aston Villa's George Boateng clattered 93 opponents and picked up five yellow cards to claim second place, although, following his tally of nine bookings in the previous campaign, this did demonstrate something of an improvement for the Dutchman.

No team had more than two players in the top 20, although there were a number of sides with a pair of naughty boys with some explaining to do. Leicester City were the only club with two men in the top 10 – Robbie Savage and Muzzy Izzet did not help the Foxes' cause by conceding 133 fouls between them and Savage's total of 14 bookings was more than any other player in the Premiership.

Clearly a certain type of player is prone to conceding fouls – nine of the 20 most indisciplined players also featured in the top tacklers list and all but one of those, Danny Mills of Leeds being the exception, was a midfielder. Mills in fact made the bad boys list thanks largely to his two red cards during the campaign, while none of the other players have a pair of dismissals to their name.

One notable absentee was Blackburn Rovers defender Craig Short who was the only player to be sent off three times in the Premiership, seeing red against Manchester United, Sunderland and Fulham.

But it was possible to win the ball fairly – seven Premiership sides have no representative in the list.

85 Alan Shearer conceded more fouls

THE CLEANEST

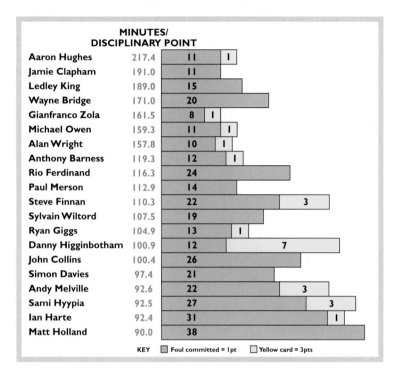

	MINUTES/ DISCIPLINARY POINT	Foul committed = 1pt	Yellow card = 3pts
Aaron Hughes	217.4	11	1
Jamie Clapham	191.0	11	
Ledley King	189.0	15	
Wayne Bridge	171.0	20	
Gianfranco Zola	161.5	8	1
Michael Owen	159.3	11	1
Alan Wright	157.8	10	1
Anthony Barness	119.3	12	1
Rio Ferdinand	116.3	24	
Paul Merson	112.9	14	
Steve Finnan	110.3	22	3
Sylvain Wiltord	107.5	19	
Ryan Giggs	104.9	13	1
Danny Higginbotham	100.9	12	7
John Collins	100.4	26	
Simon Davies	97.4	21	
Andy Melville	92.6	22	3
Sami Hyypia	92.5	27	3
Ian Harte	92.4	31	1
Matt Holland	90.0	38	

KEY ▮ Foul committed = 1pt ▯ Yellow card = 3pts

While attention was generally focussed on the 'dirtiest' players in the Premiership, there were those out there who chose to ply their trade in an angelic fashion and avoid unwanted attention from the men in black.

Newcastle United's Aaron Hughes was the league's top halo-wearer for 2001-02, with just 11 free-kicks conceded in 3,043 minutes of football. If only he could have avoided picking up a booking at Chelsea on the opening day of the season, he would have had an almost perfect record.

Another saint was Jamie Clapham of Ipswich, who committed the same number of offences and avoided a card of either colour throughout the season, but he sat below Hughes in the table by virtue of having played almost a thousand minutes less football than the Newcastle man.

Demonstrating a temperament that won the approval of Sven-Göran Eriksson among others during 2001-02, Ledley King of Tottenham took third place with just 15 fouls conceded. Such discipline may well help King play a part in England's Euro 2004 campaign.

The team with the most self-righteous fans will be Fulham – they had three representatives in the top 20 in the shape of Andy Melville, John Collins and Steve Finnan. The latter two both feature in the top tacklers table, which showed how well both performed their ball-winning duties throughout the season.

One curious entrant is Derby's Danny Higginbotham – the former Manchester United man committed just 12 fouls in 3,330 minutes on the pitch, but was prevented from finishing higher in the top 20 by being booked on seven occasions.

For the second season running, Ipswich skipper Matt Holland went the entire campaign without being booked, although he did commit 38 fouls – more than anyone else in the chart.

than any other English player

SAVES

	SAVES/SHOTS RATIO	Shots inside box saved	Shots outside box saved
David Seaman	82.6%	25	13
Jerzy Dudek	78.9%	59	38
David James	77.3%	56	53
Nigel Martyn	75.0%	56	55
Dean Kiely	74.1%	77	63
Carlo Cudicini	73.5%	46	29
Edwin van der Sar	73.4%	68	45
Brad Friedel	72.8%	70	56
Thomas Sorensen	70.9%	60	45
Mark Schwarzer	70.7%	40	25
Shay Given	70.5%	67	57
Matteo Sereni	70.4%	53	35
Neil Sullivan	70.3%	55	49
Ian Walker	69.9%	65	56
Jussi Jaaskelainen	69.8%	69	42
Peter Schmeichel	69.7%	51	34
Andy Oakes	68.9%	50	23
Steve Simonsen	67.5%	38	41
Paul Jones	67.3%	56	49
Fabien Barthez	67.2%	48	40

KEY ☐ Shots inside box saved ☐ Shots outside box saved

David Seaman had to put up with plenty of 'over-the-hill' jibes in 2001–02, but responded in the best way possible – by letting his goalkeeping do the talking on the way to winning his second Premiership and FA Cup double. The Arsenal goalkeeper held off competition for his number one jersey from the two young goalkeepers at the club by saving an unrivalled 82.6% of shots on his goal.

Thirty-eight years old and still playing for his country, Seaman was such a commanding presence between the sticks that the Arsenal defence clearly fed off his own confidence. It perhaps vindicated Arsène Wenger's decision not to buy Jerzy Dudek when he had the chance – the ex-Feyenoord goalkeeper eventually joined Liverpool, where he saved 78.9% of the shots fired at him to come second to Seaman in the list.

Seaman did sit out a large part of the season through injury of course, which meant that Dudek's tally of 97 saves beat that of the Gunners 'keeper by 59. However, not even the Polish international could match the haul of 140 saves made by his Irish counterpart Dean Kiely, of Charlton.

West Ham splashed out a significant fee on David James in summer 2001 and, despite missing the start of the season with a serious knee injury, the England man performed well for his new club. The former Watford, Liverpool and Aston Villa 'keeper saved 77.3% of the shots fired at him during the campaign.

Another man who built up a reputation for extraordinary agility was Carlo Cudicini of Chelsea. The Italian fought off the challenges to his place in the starting XI from Mark Bosnich and Ed de Goey with 75 stops in all.

It was interesting to note that the three stoppers who made the England squad all featured in the top four 'keeper rankings.

67.2% Fabien Barthez's saves-to-shots ratio was

SAVES INSIDE

	SAVES/SHOTS RATIO	SHOTS INSIDE BOX SAVED
David Seaman	80.6%	25
Jerzy Dudek	70.2%	59
Carlo Cudicini	67.6%	46
Edwin van der Sar	66.0%	68
David James	65.9%	56
Dean Kiely	65.3%	77
Andy Oakes	64.9%	50
Mark Schwarzer	63.5%	40
Brad Friedel	63.1%	70
Nigel Martyn	62.9%	56

David Seaman turned back the clock towards the end of 2001-02 and posted some excellent shot-stopping figures. Just 19.4% of the shots fired at him from inside the area ended up in the back of the net – a far more impressive ratio than any other Premiership 'keeper could maintain, in a welcome and timely return to form.

Dean Kiely saved more shots from close range than anyone else, with 77 stops to his name in total.

SAVES OUTSIDE

	SAVES/SHOTS RATIO	SHOTS OUTSIDE BOX SAVED
Jerzy Dudek	97.4%	38
David James	94.6%	53
Nigel Martyn	93.2%	55
Brad Friedel	90.3%	56
Ian Walker	90.3%	56
Dean Kiely	88.7%	63
Edwin van der Sar	88.2%	45
Thomas Sorensen	88.2%	45
Matteo Sereni	87.5%	35
Steve Simonsen	87.2%	41

Jerzy Dudek proved to be the hardest goalkeeper to beat from outside the area, letting just a single long-range effort slip through his grasp. David James had the second-finest ratio, saving 94.6% of shots fired towards his goal from distance.

But once again all were beaten to the 'most saves' award by Dean Kiely, who clearly had a busy season between the sticks for Charlton Athletic.

lower than any other regular 'keeper.

GOALS CONCEDED

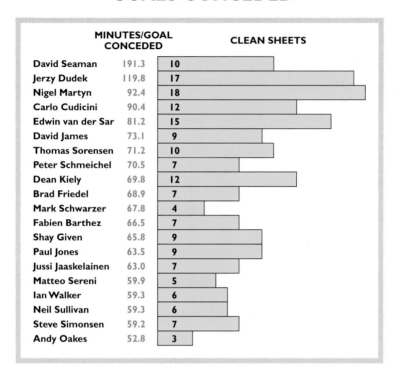

	MINUTES/GOAL CONCEDED	CLEAN SHEETS
David Seaman	191.3	10
Jerzy Dudek	119.8	17
Nigel Martyn	92.4	18
Carlo Cudicini	90.4	12
Edwin van der Sar	81.2	15
David James	73.1	9
Thomas Sorensen	71.2	10
Peter Schmeichel	70.5	7
Dean Kiely	69.8	12
Brad Friedel	68.9	7
Mark Schwarzer	67.8	4
Fabien Barthez	66.5	7
Shay Given	65.8	9
Paul Jones	63.5	9
Jussi Jaaskelainen	63.0	7
Matteo Sereni	59.9	5
Ian Walker	59.3	6
Neil Sullivan	59.3	6
Steve Simonsen	59.2	7
Andy Oakes	52.8	3

The Gunners conceded just three goals in 11 games in their extraordinary title run-in, so it was no surprise to see David Seaman as the goalkeeper with the longest stretch between goals conceded. On average it took an opposing player 191.3 minutes to beat the veteran shot-stopper, which left Seaman's record just 0.7 of a minute shy of his season-best 1998-99 count.

Seaman only played 17 league games in 2001-02, so his total haul of clean sheets was easily beaten by that miserly pair of 'keepers, Jerzy Dudek and Nigel Martyn. The Leeds man recorded the most shut-outs with 18 in all, but he let in goals more frequently than Liverpool's Dudek.

However, both remained well short of Seaman's record of minutes per goal conceded – second-placed Dudek conceded a full 71 minutes sooner on average than the Arsenal number one.

Unhappy reading for Spurs fans, was the record of goalkeeper Neil Sullivan, who kept just six clean sheets over the course of the season letting a goal past him every 59.3 minutes. Strangely, this was the exact same record as that of the man he replaced as number one at White Hart Lane, Ian Walker, who bravely attempted to save Leicester from relegation almost single-handedly.

The top goalkeeper in the previous campaign, Fabien Barthez, suffered a monumental slump in his record from a goal conceded every 157.4 minutes on average in 2000–01 to one every 66.5 minutes in 2001–02. Meanwhile, Southampton's Paul Jones' joint-high 14 clean sheets in 2000–01, was reduced by five this time around.

Andy Oakes posted the worst record of all the first-choice 'keepers and the fact that Mart Poom had a far better saves-to-shots ratio, showed how much the injured Estonian was missed.

CATCHING

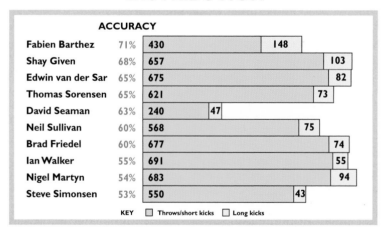

CATCH SUCCESS

Player	%	Balls caught	Balls punched
Edwin van der Sar	96%	82	27
Carlo Cudicini	95%	41	22
Matteo Sereni	95%	41	19
Jerzy Dudek	95%	58	28
Neil Sullivan	94%	49	10
Brad Friedel	94%	64	23
Dean Kiely	93%	57	28
Shay Given	93%	54	41
Ian Walker	93%	66	7
David Seaman	92%	24	3

KEY ☐ Balls caught ☐ Balls punched

With height on his side, Fulham's Edwin van der Sar was the Premiership's finest catcher of the football during 2001-02. The giant Dutchman grabbed 82 of the 112 high balls that came his way, punched another 27 of them and dropped just three.

Shay Given was by far the keenest to fist the ball away. The Newcastle 'keeper thumped 41 high balls away from the danger area – nine more than anyone else in the top flight.

DISTRIBUTION

ACCURACY

Player	%	Throws/short kicks	Long kicks
Fabien Barthez	71%	430	148
Shay Given	68%	657	103
Edwin van der Sar	65%	675	82
Thomas Sorensen	65%	621	73
David Seaman	63%	240	47
Neil Sullivan	60%	568	75
Brad Friedel	60%	677	74
Ian Walker	55%	691	55
Nigel Martyn	54%	683	94
Steve Simonsen	53%	550	43

KEY ☐ Throws/short kicks ☐ Long kicks

Occasionally known to demonstrate how it should not be done, Fabien Barthez, nonetheless, had more success with his distribution than any other goalkeeper. Just 29% of his efforts failed to find a Manchester United player.

Nigel Martyn was the busiest goalkeeper with 777 passes in all, although his success rate was a less-than-ideal 54%. Dean Kiely and Jussi Jaaskelainen also saw plenty of the ball, but were outside the top 10 for accuracy.

crosses than any other goalkeeper

OPTA PLAYER OF THE SEASON

Who was the best player in the Premiership? Who was the best player in his particular position? Who made the biggest contribution match-by-match? This section details Opta's answers.

Ruud van Nistelrooy was voted by his peers as the PFA Player of the Year, while the media opted for Arsenal winger Robert Pires as Football Writers' Footballer of the Year. The PFA Young Player of the Year was Newcastle United's Craig Bellamy.

But did these choices match up to the facts and figures? The Opta Index monitored each touch of the ball made by every player and offered a more objective viewpoint on the contribution that all players made on the pitch.

You may find the results surprising. The Index is only a guide to player performance and deals with the data in as objective a way as possible. Opta do not make subjective judgements on the quality of goals, or the importance of winning strikes, or the fact that successful dribbles by Ryan Giggs are usually more pleasing on the eye than those by David Unsworth.

Players earn points for everything they contribute on the pitch, not just the eye-catching skills, goalscoring feats or spectacular saves. There is a subjective element, though, as the points allocated for actions are calculated on the basis of the judgement of Don Howe and Opta analysts' opinions, as to the value those actions are worth.

For an in-depth explanation of the Index, see page 11.

Opta's player of the 2001-02 season was Arsenal striker Thierry Henry, who enjoyed a superb campaign, helping his club to a Premiership and FA Cup double by scoring 32 goals in all competitions.

The Frenchman hit 68 shots on target during the season, two more than any other player. His impact on the stylish Londoners was not just confined to goalscoring, as he directly set up five other goals for team-mates too.

He hit the headlines in December when he launched a ferocious tirade against referee Graham Poll, following the 3-1 home defeat to Newcastle. It turned out to be the Gunners' last setback of the campaign, but at the time it seemed like a fatal blow to the side's title ambitions.

Henry's reaction saw him eventually handed a three-match ban by the FA, but missing these games did not stop him finishing as the league's top-scorer for the first time in his career in England.

It took two goals on the last day against Everton to seal the honour though, as he sneaked past Jimmy Floyd Hasselbaink and Ruud van Nistelrooy to add yet another trophy to the Highbury cabinet and put him in confident mood for the 2002 World Cup.

For more information visit our website:

GOALKEEPERS

PLAYER NAME	TEAM	OPTA POINTS
David James	West Ham	991
David Seaman	Arsenal	821
Edwin van der Sar	Fulham	818
Jerzy Dudek	Liverpool	811
Dean Kiely	Charlton	785
Neil Sullivan	Tottenham	764
Shay Given	Newcastle	750
Thomas Sorensen	Sunderland	741
Nigel Martyn	Leeds Utd	738
Brad Friedel	Blackburn	723
Carlo Cudicini	Chelsea	707
Steve Simonsen	Everton	705
Jussi Jaaskelainen	Bolton W	673
Peter Schmeichel	Aston Villa	662
Matteo Sereni	Ipswich	660
Ian Walker	Leicester	650
Mark Schwarzer	Middlesbro	631
Andy Oakes	Derby Co	628
Fabien Barthez	Man Utd	595
Paul Jones	Southampton	547

David James suffered a freak injury in a pre-season international against Holland, just weeks after securing a move to West Ham. But he recovered brilliantly, to produce some of the best performances of his career and become Opta's highest-ranked goalkeeper in 2001-02.

When James returned to fitness in November 2001, the Hammers were in relegation trouble, but he made an average of 4.2 saves per game to help guide his side to safety and cement his place in Sven-Göran Eriksson's England plans.

David Seaman's status as England's number one had been called into question in recent years, not least by Opta statistics which ranked him as the Premiership's least effective shot-stopper in 1999–2000 and only the 17th best during the following campaign.

But the Arsenal 'keeper showed why successive national team bosses have kept faith with him, producing a string of superb displays in 2001-02 that were pivotal to the Gunners' successful double bid. Seaman saved 83% of the efforts that were fired on his goal – the best proportion in the Premiership – and kept 10 clean sheets in just 17 league games.

Fulham's Edwin van der Sar proved an excellent addition to the Premiership after his move from Juventus – the Dutch international recorded 15 clean sheets. Only two 'keepers could better that figure, Liverpool's Jerzy Dudek – who Opta rated as the division's fourth-most effective custodian – and Leeds' Nigel Martyn, who managed 17 and 18 shut-outs respectively.

Notably, Manchester United's Fabien Barthez went from being Opta's highest-ranked first-choice 'keeper in 2000–01 to 19th best in 2001-02. The Frenchman's saves-to-shots ratio dropped from a league-high 82% to a division-low 67%.

DEFENDERS

PLAYER NAME	TEAM	OPTA POINTS
Sami Hyypia	Liverpool	1,056
Rio Ferdinand	Leeds Utd	924
John Arne Riise	Liverpool	903
Ian Harte	Leeds Utd	897
Ashley Cole	Arsenal	839
Marcel Desailly	Chelsea	836
Jamie Carragher	Liverpool	835
Nikos Dabizas	Newcastle	820
John Terry	Chelsea	810
Alan Stubbs	Everton	806
David Weir	Everton	803
Mikael Silvestre	Man Utd	802
Steve Finnan	Fulham	796
Mark Fish	Charlton	795
Mark Venus	Ipswich	782
Dean Richards	Tottenham	776
Lauren	Arsenal	769
Gareth Southgate	Middlesbro	768
Ugo Ehiogu	Middlesbro	765
Sol Campbell	Arsenal	735

It is no coincidence that in the three years since Sami Hyypia joined Liverpool, the club have changed their image from a collection of 'spice boys' to being considered one of the hardest teams to beat in Europe.

The giant Finn was rated by Opta as the Premiership's most effective defender in each of his previous two campaigns in English football and achieved that title once again in 2001-02. Hyypia made 489 defensive clearances – more than any other player – and also got forward to score headers in the wins over Leicester, Ipswich and Blackburn.

Both John Arne Riise and Jamie Carragher played integral roles in helping the Reds achieve the Premiership's best defensive record in 2001-02. Norwegian Riise fired more accurate shots (26) than any player at the club except Michael Owen and was Opta's third-ranked defender,

while Carragher showed great versatility, filling in all across the back four, as well as occasionally in midfield for Gérard Houllier's team.

Leeds captain Rio Ferdinand led his side's early-season title challenge to great acclaim. Team-mate Ian Harte came in for some criticism for his defensive abilities, but still scored five times and set up four more for colleagues to finish fourth.

Arsenal's attack-minded full-back Ashley Cole also had a good season. In his first full campaign as the Gunners' first-choice left-back, Cole made more than a century of tackles and booked his place in England's World Cup squad with some outstanding individual displays.

Although Arsenal's defensive record was not as impressive as in previous years, both Lauren and Sol Campbell joined Cole in the top 20 as the new back four gradually settled.

MIDFIELDERS

PLAYER NAME	TEAM	OPTA POINTS
Roy Keane	Man Utd	1,211
Dietmar Hamann	Liverpool	844
Steven Gerrard	Liverpool	821
Patrick Vieira	Arsenal	815
Nicky Butt	Man Utd	782
Gary Speed	Newcastle	762
John Collins	Fulham	741
Frank Lampard	Chelsea	697
Tugay	Blackburn	693
Muzzy Izzet	Leicester	688
Sylvain Legwinski	Fulham	667
Per Frandsen	Bolton W	656
Matt Holland	Ipswich	647
Don Hutchison	West Ham	649
Paul Ince	Middlesbro	637
Emmanuel Petit	Chelsea	636
George Boateng	Aston Villa	602
Anders Svensson	Southampton	599
Lee Hendrie	Aston Villa	599
David Batty	Leeds United	595

Following Manchester United's Champions League semi-final exit to Bayer Leverkusen, manager Sir Alex Ferguson commented: "You just wish you had 10 Roy Keanes out there".

It was a statement that earned nods of agreement from the majority of the club's supporters, many of whom felt that if the rest of the United team had shown the same level of purpose and commitment as their captain, the club would not have finished the 2001–02 campaign without a trophy to their name.

For the fourth season in succession, Keane saw more of the ball than any other Premiership player. He rarely wasted it, finding a team-mate with an incredible 89% of his passes – the best proportion of any player in the division – to once again be Opta's highest-ranked midfielder.

Liverpool duo Dietmar Hamann and Steven Gerrard combined to form one of the most powerful midfield partnerships in Europe in 2001-02. Hamann ranked slightly higher than his colleague having made 186 challenges – more than double Gerrard's total. But there was no doubting which player came out on top when the two met in Munich in September 2001, as Gerrard nutmegged his club colleague in a fantastic display during England's famous 5-1 win over Germany.

Perhaps the most coveted midfielder in Europe, Patrick Vieira, had another influential campaign for Arsenal in 2001-02. The Frenchman was the Premiership's top tackler, making 202 challenges and showed why the likes of Real Madrid and Juventus were such great admirers.

Nicky Butt had arguably his best campaign for United, clinching a World Cup place with England, while Gary Speed's inclusion in sixth place illustrated the role he played in Newcastle's excellent season.

ATTACKING MIDFIELDERS

PLAYER NAME	TEAM	OPTA POINTS
Robert Pires	Arsenal	1,229
David Beckham	Man Utd	1,177
Paul Scholes	Man Utd	1,093
Juan Sebastian Veron	Man Utd	1,060
Ryan Giggs	Man Utd	1,006
Fredrik Ljungberg	Arsenal	983
Damien Duff	Blackburn	866
David Dunn	Blackburn	864
Laurent Robert	Newcastle	852
Steed Malbranque	Fulham	811
Nolberto Solano	Newcastle	806
Gustavo Poyet	Tottenham	803
Harry Kewell	Leeds Utd	800
Christian Ziege	Tottenham	764
Danny Murphy	Liverpool	758
Keith Gillespie	Blackburn	726
Joe Cole	West Ham	719
Darren Anderton	Tottenham	708
Trevor Sinclair	West Ham	699
Jason McAteer	Sunderland	697

While Manchester United provided four of Opta's top five attacking midfielders for 2001-02, there can be no doubt that Arsenal's Robert Pires was the outstanding creative player in the Premiership over the course of the season.

Football Writers' Footballer of the Year Pires had already set up 15 goals for team-mates by the time injury curtailed his campaign in March 2002. That total was still the highest recorded by any player in England in 2001–02 and the joint-highest figure since Opta's analysis of the Premiership began in 1996.

David Beckham was one of the players who has matched the Opta assists record. But, although the England captain only set up eight goals in 2001–02, he still had another great campaign on a personal level, scoring a career-best season-total of 11 league goals.

Paul Scholes, Juan Sebastian Veron and Ryan Giggs make up United's attacking midfield quartet. The Welshman was the Red Devils' top creative force, setting up 12 goals for colleagues in a campaign that saw him switch effortlessly between roles on the left-wing and in a central position behind Ruud van Nistelrooy.

Freddie Ljungberg's end-of-season goalscoring exploits for Arsenal helped him win the Barclaycard Player of the Year award. The Swede netted six times in five games in April, which took his final tally for the 2001–02 campaign to 12 – the highest of any midfielder in the division.

Outside Highbury and Old Trafford, Blackburn's Damien Duff and David Dunn both made great impressions upon Rovers' return to the Premiership, while Laurent Robert had an exciting first campaign in English football, following his move from Paris Saint-Germain.

ATTACKERS

PLAYER NAME	TEAM	OPTA POINTS
Thierry Henry	Arsenal	1,262
Ole Gunnar Solskjaer	Man Utd	1,118
Ruud van Nistelrooy	Man Utd	1,028
Jimmy F Hasselbaink	Chelsea	1,018
Craig Bellamy	Newcastle	1009
Sylvain Wiltord	Arsenal	989
Michael Owen	Liverpool	988
Dennis Bergkamp	Arsenal	916
Andy Cole	Blackburn	913
Alan Shearer	Newcastle	899
Paolo Di Canio	West Ham	868
Eidur Gudjohnsen	Chelsea	861
Kevin Phillips	Sunderland	859
Robbie Fowler	Leeds Utd	852
James Beattie	Southampton	833
Mark Viduka	Leeds Utd	825
Jermain Defoe	West Ham	816
Darius Vassell	Aston Villa	815
Teddy Sheringham	Tottenham	811
Marcus Stewart	Ipswich	787

During spells at Monaco and Juventus, Thierry Henry was used predominantly as a winger. However, Arsenal coach Arsène Wenger always felt that his protégée's combination of pace and skill, meant that he was best suited to a central striking role and the Gunners boss was totally vindicated in 2001–02 as Henry bagged a Premiership-high total of 24 goals.

Henry also finished the season with more shots on target (68) than any other player, highlighting why Opta rank him above PFA Player of the Year Ruud van Nistelrooy and European Footballer of the Year Michael Owen.

In fact, neither of those stars even finished second in Opta's ranking system, with Norwegian Ole Gunnar Solskjaer taking that position. Manchester United's 'baby-faced assassin' started the season on the bench, but quickly forced his way into Alex Ferguson's starting XI to form a lethal partnership with van Nistelrooy.

Solskjaer was the Premiership's deadliest finisher in 2001-02, netting with 32% of his shots. The Scandinavian also registered nine assists, which meant that he either scored or set up a goal every 79 minutes on average – the division's fastest rate.

Jimmy Floyd Hasselbaink finished one goal shy of Henry's tally, which meant that for the first time in four years, the Dutchman was not the top scorer in the league that he played in. He was the Premiership's leading marksman in 1998–99 and repeated that feat in 2000–01, while in 1999–2000 Hasselbaink was the top scorer in Spain's Primera Liga.

PFA Young Player of the Year Craig Bellamy improved dramatically after his move to Newcastle, while strike partner Alan Shearer had his most injury-free campaign in years and scored with an excellent 27% of his shots.

TEAMS OF THE SEASON

OPTA XIs

Every week, in most newspapers, there is a team of the week picked by the journalists, or their suggestion to the England manager about which players should feature in the latest squad.

And in every pub, school and office, a favourite pastime is picking a personal England team, an all-star line-up or a World XI.

This section is a definitive guide to the teams of the 2001–02 season. There is the Opta team of the season, the best and worst behaved players in the top flight and an England XI, an overseas team and an under-21 side, all based on the Opta Index.

Each team is laid out in a four-four-two formation graphic like the one shown below. Each player was selected based on being the best (or worst) in his particular position and will be shown as indicated.

For example, Ashley Cole will always feature as a left-back, Roy Keane as a central midfield player and Michael Owen as a striker.

However, there are occasions where a versatile player such as Steven Gerrard may feature in different positions for different teams in this section.

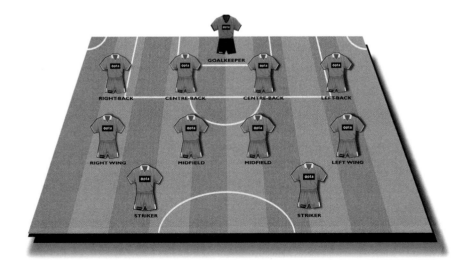

2,420 Roy Keane made more passes

TEAM OF THE SEASON

Perhaps it was a reflection of the changing nature of Premiership football that Opta's 2001–02 team of the season was the most youthful line-up in any campaign since the Index's inception, with an average age of 27.

David James was the oldest member of the team. After impressive first full campaigns for their new clubs, he and former Hammer Rio Ferdinand were the only representatives outside of the league's leading triumvirate – Arsenal, Manchester United and Liverpool.

Gunners marksman Thierry Henry took his bow in the Opta Team of the Season, top scoring with 24 Premiership goals from 134 efforts and scooping Opta's player of the season accolade in the process.

Joining Henry was colleague Robert Pires, whose tally of 15 assists equalled the record for one season, set in 1997–98 by opposite number on the right flank, David Beckham.

Pires also made the team in his debut campaign in 2000–01, while Sami Hyypia made it three appearances in his three seasons in England after another outstanding year for Liverpool – the Finn

yet again ranked as the league's top defender by Opta.

But neither player can match Beckham, who appeared in Opta's inaugural team of the season and has been an ever-present since then. Eight assists and 11 goals helped clinch his place this time around. Even his well-documented foot injury did not prevent him gaining this honour.

Roy Keane lined up in the middle following another influential campaign that saw him complete a season's-record 2,163 passes. Team-mate Paul Scholes was alongside him in the only change from the 2000–01 midfield, replacing Patrick Vieira.

Ole Gunnar Solskjaer kept Ruud van Nistelrooy out of the side after netting with a comfortably superior 32% of all attempts for his 17 strikes, while creating nine goals – a better record than his more illustrious partner.

Liverpool full-backs John Arne Riise – who smashed home seven goals in a power-packed debut season – and Jamie Carragher completed the line-up. The latter was tipped to make England's 2002 World Cup squad, but an operation saw him miss out on the finals.

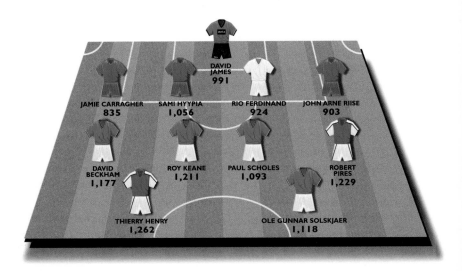

DAVID JAMES 991

JAMIE CARRAGHER 835

SAMI HYYPIA 1,056

RIO FERDINAND 924

JOHN ARNE RIISE 903

DAVID BECKHAM 1,177

ROY KEANE 1,211

PAUL SCHOLES 1,093

ROBERT PIRES 1,229

THIERRY HENRY 1,262

OLE GUNNAR SOLSKJAER 1,118

than any other Premiership player

ENGLISH XI

Sven-Göran Eriksson's policy of blooding a number of youngsters in the national side and encouraging the development of England's novices clearly had an impact on the domestic game in 2001–02.

Opta's English XI was brim full of young and upcoming talent, with Alan Shearer and 'keeper David James the only real exceptions to this.

Even James has several years to look forward to at the top of his game, though. He enjoyed a terrific first season with West Ham and stopped 77% of the 141 goal-bound shots he faced. Many questioned the wisdom of West Ham when they splashed out a considerable fee on the goalkeeper, but he has answered any critics he had in inimitable style.

The back four was made up of a youthful, but far from inexperienced, quartet. Ashley Cole and Rio Ferdinand both made England's squad for the 2002 World Cup, with Cole completing 82% of his passes – better than any other established Premiership left-back – and Ferdinand featured in a select group of only seven players to make more than 400 defensive clearances.

John Terry and Jamie Carragher missed out on the trip to the Far East through disciplinary issues and injury respectively, but the pair should have a major role to play for England in years to come.

England under-21 captain David Dunn was pivotal to Blackburn's successful campaign and specialised in long-range strikes, scoring four times from outside the area. He was joined in midfield by Manchester United duo David Beckham and Paul Scholes and Liverpool's eight-time goal provider Steven Gerrard.

Sadly, the Anfield star missed out on the World Cup through injury, although Beckham eventually made the cut after his broken metatarsal scare.

Up front, Shearer formed an Opta strike partnership with Michael Owen. The Newcastle man finished just one goal off the top of the scoring charts with 23 – four ahead of the diminutive Anfield hitman. Such was Shearer's form that sections of the media angled for his inclusion in the World Cup squad, despite the former England captain's retirement from international football.

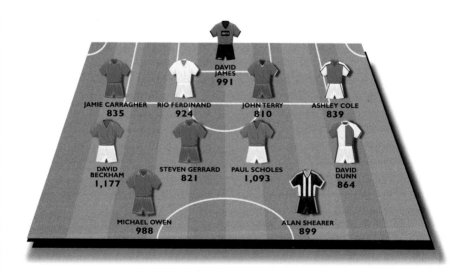

23 Alan Shearer was the highest-scoring

BRITISH ISLES XI

In recent seasons, Opta's British Isles XI has been dominated by the Republic of Ireland contingent in the Premiership – and 2001–02 was no exception.

Five of the players who made the line-up flew out with Mick McCarthy's World Cup squad, with Ireland captain Roy Keane finishing the season as the top-ranked player in Opta's British Isles XI – something he has achieved in every campaign since Opta first collated the team. He flew back without appearing in the World Cup finals after his well-publicised disagreement with McCarthy.

Instrumental as ever in Manchester United's push for honours, Keane's string-pulling saw him complete 383 more passes than his nearest challenger, David Batty, in the 2001–02 Premiership.

Dean Kiely ranked higher than Ireland number one Shay Given on the Index, conceding fewer goals, making more saves and hence recording a superior saves-to-shots ratio of 74% to Given's 70%.

Steve Finnan's purposeful bursts down Fulham's right flank resulted in 171 crosses from open play and only three Premiership stars provided more. On the opposite flank,

Ian Harte secured his third consecutive appearance in this team, scoring five goals from full-back.

Meanwhile Steve Staunton made his debut at centre-back, alongside Scottish bargain-buy David Weir, whose aerial prowess saw him make the second-highest number of headed clearances in the league. Another strong player in the air, fellow Scot Duncan Ferguson, ousted Niall Quinn in attack.

Wales' sole representative in past British XI's, Ryan Giggs, was joined in 2001–02 by Newcastle pair Gary Speed and Craig Bellamy – the latter arguably the Premiership's surprise package after his 10-goal haul in troublesome tandem with Alan Shearer. Giggs, occasionally doubling as Ruud van Nistelrooy's strike partner, scored seven times and was Manchester United's chief provider with a dozen assists.

Only Giggs and Leeds' Australian Harry Kewell burst towards goal more regularly in the league than the final team member, Blackburn's Keith Gillespie, who averaged an attacking run with the ball every nine minutes.

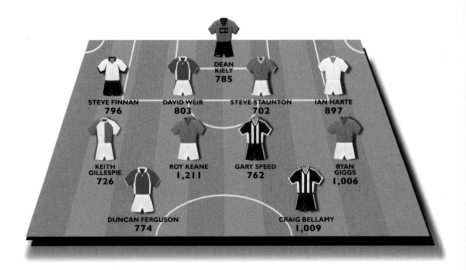

DEAN KIELY 785

STEVE FINNAN 796

DAVID WEIR 803

STEVE STAUNTON 702

IAN HARTE 897

KEITH GILLESPIE 726

ROY KEANE 1,211

GARY SPEED 762

RYAN GIGGS 1,006

DUNCAN FERGUSON 774

CRAIG BELLAMY 1,009

Englishman in the Premiership

OVERSEAS XI

In the 2000–01 campaign, 38% of all players appearing in the English Premiership came from outside of the British Isles. A year later and that proportion had risen to 41%, with English players representing just 43% of all 2001–02 Premiership protagonists.

An Englishman has yet to win Opta's player of the season award and in 2001–02 it was the turn of two Frenchmen to top the Index, with Thierry Henry closely shadowed by Robert Pires.

An incredible 50 of Arsenal's strikes saw one of the pair either scoring or setting the goal up – surprisingly they only combined for a goal three times – and that was more strikes than 13 entire teams managed in 2001–02.

Arsenal dominated the team and had two more representatives – the dependable Lauren and Freddie Ljungberg, whose dazzling run of six goals in his last six Premiership matches effectively sealed the title for Arsenal. The Swede ended the season as the highest-scoring midfielder in the league with 12 goals.

Three newcomers to England made the team – Edwin van der Sar, John Arne Riise and Juan Sebastian Veron. Van der Sar's 15 clean sheets helped him to the goalkeeper's spot, while Riise demonstrated immense ability to turn defence into attack in an instant. His goal against Manchester United at Anfield will live on in Liverpool fans' memories for years to come.

Veron may not have lived up to the hype that followed his move to Manchester United, but nonetheless he scored five times and completed more than a thousand passes in opposition territory. Colleague Ole Gunnar Solskjaer lined up ahead of the Argentine, scoring or assisting a goal once every 79 minutes on average – the league's best record.

The central defensive duo remained unchanged from 2000–01. Sami Hyypia and Marcel Desailly took up residence, with 732 clearances and nearly 200 tackles between them.

Completing the line-up was Dietmar Hamann. He anchored Liverpool's midfield to great effect, making more tackles than all Premiership players bar Patrick Vieira.

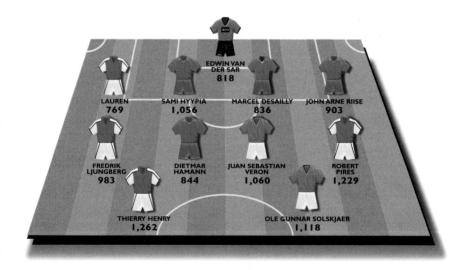

EDWIN VAN DER SAR
818

LAUREN
769

SAMI HYYPIA
1,056

MARCEL DESAILLY
836

JOHN ARNE RIISE
903

FREDRIK LJUNGBERG
983

DIETMAR HAMANN
844

JUAN SEBASTIAN VERON
1,060

ROBERT PIRES
1,229

THIERRY HENRY
1,262

OLE GUNNAR SOLSKJAER
1,118

UNDER-21

The Opta Index under-21 team of the season certainly bade well for the future of England as four of the XI were already full English internationals.

The forward line was led by Michael Owen after a season where he demolished Germany with a hat-trick in Munich and scored 19 league goals – a best-ever Premiership haul for the Liverpool striker. Alongside him was Jermain Defoe, who began to show his true potential as a top-flight goalscorer.

Defoe scored 10 times and led the West Ham attack in the absence of Paolo Di Canio or Frederic Kanoute. He was joined in Opta's under-21 side by Joe Cole, who embarked on just under 200 dribbles and earned a call-up to the World Cup squad.

On the right-hand side was Steven Gerrard who set up eight goals for his team-mates through the season and, when fit, was one of the most imposing midfielders in England. He ended the season in despair though, when a groin injury forced him to miss the World Cup finals.

David Dunn, who shone in Blackburn's first season back in the Premiership took the spot on the left wing while next to him was Scott Parker of Charlton. Parker got

stuck into 180 tackles throughout the season and only Patrick Vieira and Dietmar Hamann made more. Considerable progress from the boy who came into the limelight performing tricks on a television advert.

Stuart Taylor took his place in goal behind two centre-backs who used to play together in the same Sunday league team. Ledley King and John Terry were on the fringes of the full England side after impressive seasons for Tottenham and Chelsea respectively.

Arsenal's Stuart Taylor took the goalkeeping spot despite not playing enough Premiership football to qualify under Opta's rules. However, he made the side by virtue of being the only under-21 goalkeeper to play more than one game in the 2001-02 Premiership.

Liverpool's Norwegian left-back John Arne Riise was only one of two non-English players in the team. He hit more shots on target than any Red except Owen and recorded more crosses and dribbles than anyone else at Anfield. On the right was Scotland's Robbie Stockdale who was one of the successes of a transitional season for Middlesbrough.

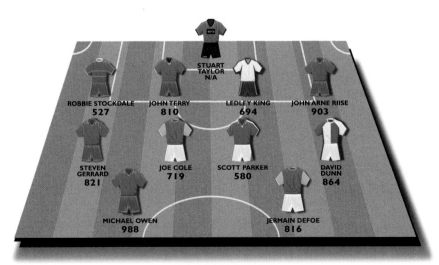

STUART TAYLOR N/A

ROBBIE STOCKDALE 527   JOHN TERRY 810   LEDLEY KING 694   JOHN ARNE RIISE 903

STEVEN GERRARD 821   JOE COLE 719   SCOTT PARKER 580   DAVID DUNN 864

MICHAEL OWEN 988   JERMAIN DEFOE 816

AGED 21 OR UNDER ON 18/8/01

DIRTY DOZEN

Opta's Dirty Dozen team was based on the average number of minutes it took a player to accumulate disciplinary points, with one point awarded per foul conceded, three per yellow card and six for each dismissal.

Away from the limelight, neighbourhood watch hero Duncan Ferguson was perceived as a family man who loved his pigeons, but the Everton talisman amassed more Opta disciplinary points on average than any other Premiership player in 2001–02.

The imposing Scotsman committed an offence almost every 18 minutes, racking up a total of 66 fouls and half-a-dozen bookings. Ferguson received his marching orders on April Fools Day after inexplicably felling Bolton's Fredi Bobic with a dig to the ribs.

Leeds United's Alan Smith made the starting XI this time around after warming the subs' bench in 2000–01. The England under-21 international committed 51 misdemeanours and was joined in the team by colleague Danny Mills, who was sent off on two occasions.

Jussi Jaaskelainen was the only top-flight custodian to be sent off twice, while

his Bolton team-mate Paul Warhurst was shown eight yellow cards and one red in just 1,872 minutes of action for the Trotters who racked up a total of seven red cards, the joint-highest total in the Premiership.

Mario Stanic was also cautioned eight times – more than any other Chelsea player – while fellow capital representative Jorge Costa bettered this tally by one. In the Midlands, Luciano Zavagno was Derby's most-booked player during his inaugural season in English football.

Only four Premiership players committed more fouls than the 81 inflicted by Blackburn skipper Garry Flitcroft, who incidentally missed the Worthington Cup final through suspension.

Stefan Schwarz started in fewer than half of Sunderland's matches, yet he averaged a booking almost every other game for the Black Cats.

Fellow strugglers Everton committed more fouls than any other side and Thomas Gravesen alone was accountable for 49. The Dane was also dismissed against Fulham, whose own bad boy, Barry Hayles, was poised in reserve.

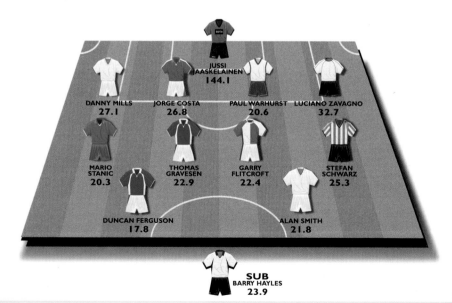

JUSSI JAASKELAINEN
144.1

DANNY MILLS
27.1

JORGE COSTA
26.8

PAUL WARHURST
20.6

LUCIANO ZAVAGNO
32.7

MARIO STANIC
20.3

THOMAS GRAVESEN
22.9

GARRY FLITCROFT
22.4

STEFAN SCHWARZ
25.3

DUNCAN FERGUSON
17.8

ALAN SMITH
21.8

SUB
BARRY HAYLES
23.9

14 Robbie Savage earned the most

CLEAN XI

The British sense of fair play comes to the fore in Opta's 2001–02 Clean XI. All but one of the players in the fair play team hailed from the United Kingdom, with only perennial good guy Gianfranco Zola representing the Premiership's overseas contingent.

The cleanest player in the 1999–2000 season, Zola was the only man to have appeared in all of Opta's Clean XI line-ups – the team based on the average number of minutes it takes a player to accumulate disciplinary points, with one point per foul conceded, three per yellow card and six for a dismissal.

Joining him in a repeat of the 1998-99 front line was Michael Owen. England's stand-in skipper conceded just 11 fouls all season, despite being illegally challenged nearly four times as often and picked up a solitary caution – one of only three accrued by the entire Clean XI in around 460 hours of football.

But Owen's record couldn't match that of the cleanest player of 2001–02, Aaron Hughes. Newcastle's versatile defender averaged a point every 217.4 minutes and made his third appearance in a row in the fair play team, despite being the only player in the line-up aside from the strikers to be cautioned in 2001–02.

Paul Merson and Ledley King appeared for the second campaign running, the pair committing just 14 and 15 fouls respectively all season, with King the Premiership's third-least frequent offender behind Hughes and Ipswich winger Jamie Clapham.

At left-back, Southampton's ever-present Wayne Bridge went without a booking in 2001–02 and has been cautioned just once in 162 hours of league football since his debut in 1998–99. The clean nature of his play helped him achieve his dream of playing for England.

Leeds United's composed defender Rio Ferdinand completed the back four, in front of Leicester's Ian Walker, who enjoyed 3,085 unblemished minutes on the pitch.

Fulham's experienced midfielder John Collins and Tottenham's Welsh youngster Simon Davies also accumulated less than a point per match to make the team – the latter's presence meaning Spurs were the only team with two representatives.

cautions in the Premiership

The 2001–02 Premiership saw the dawn of a new era for the game's officials – the age of the professional referee.

The Professional Game Match Officials Board was set up to replace the National Review Board, with the task of appointing the English league's first professional officials and then assessing their performances throughout the campaign.

The new Board released a list of 24 referees selected as the new salaried officials – the 'Select Group' – with each man earning £33,000 a year to oversee Premiership matches, plus individual match appearance fees.

With their new status inevitably came even more scrutiny for Premiership referees. Match officials attended fortnightly meetings where they were assessed by Keith Hackett and FA Premier League head of refereeing Philip Don on their performance. The Video Advisory Panel played a more significant role than ever before in disciplinary matters, reviewing incidents missed by referees, but caught on camera, while the presence of 24-hour sports channels meant that such incidents were often shown many times a day.

Not surprisingly there was a transitional period during which referees, their representatives and superiors, league managers and players became accustomed to the new disciplinary procedures in hand – and not all the changes were to people's liking.

Dermot Gallagher was one of the first officials to feel the impact of the newly created board overseeing referee performance, following an incident in Leeds United's clash with Manchester United at Old Trafford in October 2001. After failing to dismiss Leeds striker Robbie Keane following the Irishman's push on David Beckham – a red-card offence according to the letter of the law – Gallagher was appointed to less high-profile matches in the following weeks.

Later in the season, Neale Barry's comments at one of the referees' bi-weekly get-togethers about the Leeds v Aston Villa match he oversaw, were reported in the media and stirred up controversy.

"It was the most evil game I have done in five years in the Premiership," Barry stated, prompting Leeds chairman Peter Ridsdale to contact Don, FA chief executive Adam Crozier and Premier League chief Richard Scudamore to relay his discontent.

But while the meetings between officials may have left them open to some criticism, there were plenty of plusses to come from these conferences.

"One of the benefits of coming here is that we can swap information about teams and players. The referee's armoury is expanding," is how Rob Styles explained those advantages, while with meetings every couple of weeks, referees were in a good position to respond rapidly to any current issues arising in the game.

A new tougher fitness regime was also implemented and it was clear that there was a commitment to further improving the standard of refereeing. Philip Don emphasised that fact when he commented about his officials: "They've got to improve and to minimise mistakes. Eventually there will be consistency of approach and interpretation. We have to improve the standard across the board and to do that there has to be some soul-searching."

The Video Advisory Panel, made up of four ex-professional players, four ex-managers and four former referees, dealt

OVERALL RECORD

REFEREE NAME	MATCHES	FOULS	PENALTIES	YELLOW CARDS	RED CARDS	AVERAGE POINTS
M. Riley	17	579	8	74	9	51.71
P. Dowd	5	179	0	20	2	50.20
C. Foy	5	177	1	19	1	48.60
G. Barber	22	732	6	81	5	46.50
E. Wolstenholme	11	345	5	42	3	45.82
C. Wilkes	12	400	0	40	3	44.83
B. Knight	11	351	2	39	2	44.18
U. Rennie	16	520	1	42	1	40.94
J. Winter	20	638	3	51	2	40.60
A. Wiley	23	705	3	68	2	40.43
R. Styles	18.2	494	8	70	1	40.33
N. Barry	17	529	3	43	3	40.29
M. Halsey	21	612	5	64	4	40.14
P. Jones	14	427	1	40	1	39.71
A. D'Urso	23	625	3	75	9	39.70
S. Dunn	19	561	3	55	3	39.63
M. Messias	4.8	139	0	16	0	38.96
P. Durkin	21	617	5	56	3	38.95
G. Poll	24	700	6	59	5	38.54
D. Pugh	10	269	0	35	0	37.40
M. Dean	14	361	3	44	2	36.71
S. Bennett	19	496	1	55	5	36.53
D. Gallagher	16	429	1	40	2	35.25
D. Elleray	17	442	5	38	3	34.65
Totals	**380**	**11,327**	**73**	**1,166**	**71**	**40.71**

with several contentious incidents and also attracted its fair share of criticism.

Several, high-profile decisions were overturned. Indeed in 2001–02 there were no fewer than nine red cards rescinded, or no ban applied, as a result of video evidence – equating to 13% of all dismissals – with many of these reassessed by the official themselves.

Meanwhile some managers were also unhappy with the new system. Arsène Wenger highlighted his concerns over Thierry Henry's case, after the striker was handed a three-match ban for improper conduct following his confrontation with Graham Poll at the end of Arsenal's Premiership match at home to Newcastle.

"I feel TV chooses one player, he's caught on the camera on the night and is shown the whole day on TV. In my opinion it's not the FA who charged the players with what happened on the field – it's the TV who charges the players."

One of the major discussion points revolved around 'simulation', or diving as most people know it. According to the laws of the game, the offence was punishable by a yellow card, but there was even some debate about making the offence punishable by a red card in an attempt to eliminate it from the game.

Overall though, the season was notable for a reduction in the number of cards for the third successive season and a quick look at the disciplinary situation in Europe's top leagues suggested that, for all the criticism dished out by the media and some of the managers, the Premiership referees were still more lenient than their continental cousins.

On Opta's disciplinary system, each foul is awarded one point, each penalty or yellow card three points and each red card six points. The final total of disciplinary points for each referee is then divided by the number of games officiated, to produce a table showing the relative strictness of the league's men in black.

HOME TEAMS

REFEREE NAME	GAMES	FOULS	PENALTIES	YELLOW CARDS	RED CARDS	POINTS	POINTS/ GAME
M. Riley	17	269	2	32	6	407	23.94
C. Foy	5	92	0	8	0	116	23.20
P. Dowd	5	88	0	7	1	115	23.00
G. Barber	22	350	4	31	3	473	21.50
U. Rennie	16	269	0	21	0	332	20.75
E. Wolstenholme	11	171	2	12	2	225	20.45
M. Halsey	21	315	3	27	2	417	19.86
R. Styles	18.2	232	5	38	0	361	19.84
B. Knight	11	166	0	15	1	217	19.73
P. Jones	14	213	1	20	0	276	19.71
A. Wiley	23	348	2	31	1	453	19.70
J. Winter	20	321	2	19	0	384	19.20
P. Durkin	21	315	4	24	0	399	19.00
C. Wilkes	12	181	0	13	1	226	18.83
N. Barry	17	256	2	15	2	319	18.76
S. Dunn	19	273	1	24	1	354	18.63
G. Poll	24	341	2	29	2	446	18.58
A. D'Urso	23	303	2	31	4	426	18.52
M. Dean	14	184	0	16	1	238	17.00
D. Gallagher	16	208	0	15	1	259	16.19
D. Elleray	17	208	3	17	1	274	16.12
S. Bennett	19	222	0	22	3	306	16.11
M. Messias	4.8	63	0	4	0	75	15.63
D. Pugh	10	116	0	13	0	155	15.50
Total	**380**	**5504**	**35**	**484**	**32**	**7253**	**19.09**

AWAY TEAMS

REFEREE NAME	GAMES	FOULS	PENALTIES	YELLOW CARDS	RED CARDS	POINTS	POINTS/ GAME
M. Riley	17	310	6	42	3	472	27.76
P. Dowd	5	91	0	13	1	136	27.20
C. Wilkes	12	219	0	27	2	312	26.00
C. Foy	5	85	1	11	1	127	25.40
E. Wolstenholme	11	174	3	30	1	279	25.36
G. Barber	22	382	2	50	2	550	25.00
B. Knight	11	185	2	24	1	269	24.45
M. Messias	4.8	76	0	12	0	112	23.33
D. Pugh	10	153	0	22	0	219	21.90
N. Barry	17	273	1	28	1	366	21.53
J. Winter	20	317	1	32	2	428	21.40
A. D'Urso	23	322	1	44	5	487	21.17
S. Dunn	19	288	2	31	2	399	21.00
A. Wiley	23	357	1	37	1	477	20.74
R. Styles	18.2	262	3	32	1	373	20.49
S. Bennett	19	274	1	33	2	388	20.42
M. Halsey	21	297	2	37	2	426	20.29
U. Rennie	16	251	1	21	1	323	20.19
P. Jones	14	214	0	20	1	280	20.00
G. Poll	24	359	4	30	3	479	19.96
P. Durkin	21	302	1	32	3	419	19.95
M. Dean	14	177	3	28	1	276	19.71
D. Gallagher	16	221	1	25	1	305	19.06
D. Elleray	17	234	2	21	2	315	18.53
Total	**380**	**5823**	**38**	**682**	**39**	**8217**	**21.62**

7 More penalties were awarded at Stamford